Effective Management in Therapeutic Recreation Service

Third Edition

Effective Management in Therapeutic Recreation Service

Third Edition

by

Marcia Jean Carter, Re.D., CPRP, CTRS

Christen G. Smith, Ph.D., CPRP

Gerald S. O'Morrow, Ph.D., CTRS

Venture Publishing, Inc.
State College, Pennsylvania

Venture Publishing, Inc.
1999 Cato Avenue
State College, PA 16801
Phone 814-234-4561; Fax 814-234-1651

Cover by StepUp Communications, Inc.

Library of Congress Catalogue Card Number 2014947454
ISBN-10: 1-939476-05-4
ISBN-13: 978-1-939476-05-0

Table of Contents

List of Tables and Figures

Preface

Effective Management in Therapeutic Recreation Services, Third Edition provides theoretical and practical knowledge about the management of therapeutic recreation services* in health and human service organizations in North America. The text was written for upper-level undergraduate and graduate students as well as practitioners. The text was also prepared for a therapeutic recreation specialist who has responsibility for managing direct therapeutic recreation service and the assignment and direction of staff, volunteers, and interns who deliver the service.

While we realize all the information useful to a potential manager or practicing manager is not in this one volume, the intent is to present the most important portions of management information relevant to the professional who is a first-line manager. Changes are taking place on a daily basis in health and human service organizations, which in turn affect therapeutic recreation service and its management. Management of therapeutic recreation service, regardless of setting, will change dramatically in the future. Hence, we foresee that some statements may not be as appropriate as they were at the time the manuscript was prepared.

Instructor and Student Learning Tools

New features of this third edition introduced to support instructors and learners are an instructor's manual and text format with interactive pedagogical tools. The instructor's manual includes PowerPoints, test questions, and review questions. Each text chapter is introduced with learner outcomes that are then embedded in the text narrative in close proximity to the relevant learner content. Within the chapters, significant content is presented in Figures and Tables and enumerated in the chapter summary. Lastly, the text has been reduced in length so instructors may organize units according to the average number of weeks in an academic term.

New Content

Another new feature of this edition is the introduction of information relevant to therapeutic recreation management in Canada. Since publication of the second edition, academic programs in Canada are increasing; where appropriate, discussion presents information unique to Canadian learners. Likewise, throughout the text, the global interactions of health and human services are acknowledged: Students and practicing managers may engage in professional preparation, live, and practice in completely different geographic areas, so culture and diversity are integrated into topics throughout the text.

Text Organization

This third edition reflects a management perspective, as opposed to a program perspective. Therefore, in the sequence of chapters, program and consumer information follow management as quality consumer programming relies on successful execution of management functions. The third edition is organized into four parts. Section 1 considers management and leadership concepts. In Chapter 1, new to this edition, the trends and issues creating challenges to managing services are summarized and precede a brief description of the settings, populations, and responsibilities of the first-line manager. Chapter 2 outlines management functions of the first-line manager and the transitions from a practitioner to first-line manager. New to the text is consideration of organizational stress and techniques that first-line managers use to adjust to the demands of their work environment. In Chapter 3, management and leadership theories are summarized and applied to therapeutic recreation. The chapter concludes with discussion of the manager-leader's role in preparing planning statements to guide the department or agency. Organizational behavior, Chapter 4, focuses on the nature of human behavior in the department. In-depth consideration is given to change, teams, and individual factors affecting performance—topics expanded from the previous edition. Chapter 5, on decision making, problem-solving, and conflict, addresses fundamental tasks found in all management functions and in situations where people work together in a constantly changing environment. Expanded in this edition are examples of agency policies, procedures, and rules, as well as sources of conflict such as bullying.

Section 2 reviews operational aspects of management, including technology and research (Chapter 6), marketing and advocacy (Chapter 7), and financing (Chapter 8). Technology, in addition to contributing to the increasingly rapid rate of change and access to information, is also affecting how services are delivered and how professionals carry out their responsibilities. Chapter 6 introduces expanded content on health-care technology, including dashboards, electronic health records, informatics, a technology plan, and the significance of research in evidence-based practice. Health care is a business, which is most evident with the new business concepts introduced in the marketing and advocacy chapter (7). Trends like social marketing are influencing the manager's advocacy roles and concerns for assuring ethical relationships among stakeholders and the larger community that benefits from therapeutic recreation outcomes. Financing health care in the United States and Canada is the focus of Chapter 8. New to the chapter are consideration of the global fiscal challenges affecting health care, review of health-care payment shifts and legislation in Canada and the United States, coverage, and financial trends.

Human resources are the focus of Section 3 of the text. Chapters consider staffing (Chapter 9), volunteers and interns (Chapter 10), workplace communication (Chapter 11), and motivating work environments (Chapter 12). Chapter 9 covers staff planning and selection, training and development, and performance appraisal. New content includes recruitment software, e-learning, results-oriented assessments and evaluation in addition to expanded information on interviewing, orientation, staff retention, and employment regulations. Chapter 10 introduces a Canadian perspective to managing volunteers and interns. Also introduced are the changing natures of volunteer commitments and student internship needs that impact the manager's responsibility to create capacity-building experiences. Chapter 11 emphasizes that because a manager is in a high-profile position, everything a manager does communicates. An expanded emphasis is given to workplace variables, influencing communication and the manager's role as a professional advocate. The closing chapter in this section, Chapter 12, expands information on motivational theories—the manager's role in relating to the unique needs of staff in order to create a motivating environment that satisfies staff goals and department or agency goals—and shares research on intrinsic and extrinsic forms of motivation in therapeutic recreation. Also, trends like the global and generational workforce are challenging managers to introduce new intangible and tangible motivational features to the work environment.

Four chapters comprise Section 4 and focus on service delivery: They include service accountability (Chapter 13); risk, safety, security, and legal aspects (Chapter 14); quality (Chapter 15); and managing a professional future (Chapter 16). Chapter 13 introduces evidence-based staffing and enhances discussion of the manager's roles in assessment, planning, implementation, and evaluation by adding information on critical pathways. A contemporary social issue is security and personal safety in the workplace. The content of Chapter 14 expands beyond risk to address safety and security of professionals and stakeholders in health care. A number of laws, organizations, and regulations govern and provide resources in Canada and the United States to help the manager ensure safety, quality, and privacy; websites are presented, relevant terms defined, elements of safety and security plans described, and management of the therapeutic recreation process to reduce malpractice concerns is outlined. Chapter 15 presents the manager's responsibility to sustain quality in service delivery. New to this edition are reviews of quality initiatives applied to health care, evolution of quality concerns in health care, expanded definitions of quality by the Institute Of Medicine and World Health Organization, and an introduction to the American Hospital Association quality-improvement model.

Closing the text (Chapter 16) is a new chapter on managing a professional future. This chapter reiterates the trends and issues shared in the introduction and throughout the text. Also, the chapter summarizes the critical nature of ethics and ethical decision making as professional qualities and behaviors. To manage a future that advances the emerging professional's career requires continued acquisition of relevant knowledge, skills, and abilities and the flexibility to change. To accomplish these goals, a career-planning model grounded on the process of assessment, planning, implementation, and evaluation and a strategic-planning-analysis template are presented. These tools help professionals identify their assets and plan strategies to remain abreast of global and professional challenges while advancing the profession.

*The term "therapeutic recreation service" is used for ease of readership and is intended to be inclusive of the terms "recreational therapy" and "recreation therapy."

Acknowledgments

Professionals who contributed to chapters in this edition include:

M. Jean Keller, CTRS, University of North Texas, Denton, Texas (Chapter 6)

Shane Pegg, Ph.D., University of Queensland, St. Lucia Campus, Australia (Chapter 15)

Norma J. Stumbo, Ph.D., CTRS, President, Education Associates, Normal, Illinois (Chapter 15)

Health and human service professionals and organizations that generously offered materials that have contributed to this third edition include the following:

Craig Hospital, Englewood, Colorado, Kenneth R. Hosack, M.A., Director of Marketing and Public Relations

Fox Valley Special Recreation Association, Aurora, Illinois, Carolyn Nagle, MPA, CTRS, CPRP, Executive Director

Genesis Health System, Davenport, Iowa, Kelly Sigler, M.S., CTRS, Lean Specialist

Howard County, Maryland, Susan L. Potts, M.S., CTRS, Recreation Manager

National Council for Therapeutic Recreation Certification, New City, New York, Bob Riley, Ph.D., CTRS, Executive Director

Dr. Gerald S. O'Morrow conceived and was the primary author of the first edition of *Effective Management in Therapeutic Recreation Service*. With acknowledgment of continued support from his family, we are honored to have the opportunity to show our appreciation and respect for his dedication to the profession through this third edition.

Marcia Jean Carter
Christen G. Smith

SECTION 1

MANAGEMENT CONCEPTS

Chapter 1

Introducing First-Line Management: Trends Impacting Your Future

Keywords

- Care continuum
- Change
- Demographics
- Education
- Evidence-based practice
- Globalization
- Health-care business
- Holistic care
- Patient-centered care
- Research
- Technology

Learning Outcomes

After reading this introduction, students will be able to:

1. Outline trends, issues, and challenges influencing management in our profession.
2. Identify settings and populations where first-line managers are employed.
3. Outline qualities, responsibilities, and professional expectations of first-line managers.
4. Describe topics and outcomes students may expect with use of this text.

Overview

What is a first-line manager? And why are management skills critical to a new professional in recreation therapy/therapeutic recreation?

Today all practitioners are managers. While there are various levels of management (e.g., top, middle, first-line), first-line managers are responsible for delivery of therapeutic recreation service, assignment and direction of professional practitioners and volunteers, and interaction with other managers in the same organization or with others in the community who deliver similar services. There may be times, however, that the manager is responsible for providing direct service (e.g., staff on vacations or during special programs). In some large health and human-service organizations (e.g., hospitals, public or private freestanding community-based centers for persons with disabilities) and depending on the organizational structure, therapeutic recreation managers may occupy a middle-management position. In such instances, they would be responsible for implementing basic policies and plans developed by top management and for supervising and coordinating the activities of lower-level managers. The director of a rehabilitation department with a corporation like Genesis Healthcare who is responsible for several disciplines (e.g., occupational, speech-hearing, and recreation therapy) would be a middle manager, as would the manager of therapeutic recreation services in a community organization like Pathways Health Centre for Children in Ontario, Canada.

A first-line-manager position is often the first position held by a practitioner who enters management from direct services; however, there are some settings in which the first-line manager is also the sole practitioner (e.g., long-term care settings, small community-based organizations). Thus, most first-line managers have had little or no formal academic preparation in therapeutic recreation management. Their advancement is the result of competency in direct service, program knowledge, and job experience. A management position continues to be one of the options open to a practitioner to offer salary increases.

The intent of this introduction is to introduce trends, issues, and challenges impacting management in our profession; survey employment settings, responsibilities, and professional expectations of first-line managers; and outline the management topics and outcomes students may expect as a result of using this text.

Health and Human Service in the 21st Century

"Today's health-care system is continuing to undergo significant changes" (Sullivan & Decker, 2009, p. 3). Change is the norm. Change is constant and affects the organization and delivery of health and human services. As a change agent, the manager is a role model and advocate for positive outcomes that improve client programs. A climate of change presents new opportunities for professionals and our profession. Change is necessary for growth and viability of clients, organizations, and professions. A number of forces are changing health and human services. These trends and issues are briefly summarized in Table 1.1.

Change and the rapid pace of constant change is a leading force in the evolving nature of health and human service organizations and services. *Technology* is a primary contributor to the rapid pace of change. Health information technology, electronic medical records, and robotics, for example, are changing administrative responsibilities, facility operations, and client care approaches (Hoss, Powell, & Sable, 2006).

Health care is a business (Stumbo & Hoss, 2009; Sullivan & Decker, 2009). Given this, managers focus on containing *costs* even with increasingly limited resources in order to sustain services in a competitive environment. The growth rate of health-care spending continues to advance in developed countries, and paying for services is challenging for North American governments and individual clients. Accountability demands, benchmarking, and need to reduce medical errors continue to force the manager to improve *quality* and outcomes and focus on safety in the workplace. A third issue worldwide is *access* to care among various cultures, generations, and economic groups. Native Canadians, the elderly, and the financially poor experience health disparities. The recent release of Healthy People 2020 identifies one of four foundational health measures as disparities; the intent is to monitor progress in attaining the highest level of health in all people in the USA (U.S. Department of Health and Human Services, 2010).

Health care is a *global* public concern. Globalization yields common threats like natural disasters, terrorism, and pandemics, and it yields solutions like tele-a-medicine and alternative delivery models to manage escalating health spending and financing. *Demographics* worldwide like aging, income levels, and violence are adding demands to an overburdened system. The World Health Organization's International Classification of Functioning, Disability, and Health (ICF) provides a universal language and framework to describe health and disability (2002). This bio-psycho-social model integrates the medical, social, and human aspects of health. Disability is a universal human experience. As therapists, embracing this model suggests we capitalize on client strengths and include the interrelationships of our environments and human functioning as we assess and deliver interventions (Sylvester, 2011).

As the *care continuum* moves beyond the doctor's office and hospital to primary care in community centers, a broader array of health-care professionals are providing *holistic patient-centered care* (Hoss, Powell, & Sable, 2006; Sullivan & Decker, 2009). Informed citizens are participating in health-care decisions. Integrated-care networks rely on technology to share and organize client plans among professionals through community models like Medical Homes. This encourages fiscal prudence by focusing on the performance of an interdisciplinary team to produce outcomes in a timely manner (value-based performance). Concern for accessible and accommodating experiences is shifting to universal design and collaborative interventions. Similarly, while there remains a concern for management of chronic diseases like cardiovascular issues, there is an increasing acknowledgment of lifestyle behaviors that contribute to issues like obesity. This shift is prompting a focus on health-related quality of life and well-being or preventative and participation measures.

Evidence-based practice grew out of a desire to use scientific evidence to make clinical decisions (Sullivan & Decker, 2009). This effort complements challenges to improve safety, reduce costs, and validate the appropriateness of specific interventions to produce consistent client outcomes. Managers guide professionals as *research* is conducted to validate various practice models and theories in order to develop clinical guidelines and protocols. While efficacy research may be a challenge in day-to-day practice, program evaluation helps justify the effectiveness and viability of recreation therapy in holistic health. Along with *education*, research supports change and contributes to professionals' continued growth and advancement, which are essential to our careers and the vitality of our profession.

Table 1.1 Trends, Issues, and Challenges in Recreation Therapy/Therapeutic Recreation

Trend/Issue	Challenge
Change	Rapid, constant rate creates stressful environment and need to be flexible
Technology	Advancements change job functions and create information overload
Health-care business	Accountability measures, productivity levels, creative budgeting are used
Globalization	Cultural and demographic disparities are evident worldwide
Demographics	Income levels and aging societies overburden system and escalate costs
Care continuum	Practice integration, transparency, and continuous relationships are critical
Holistic care	Interdisciplinary cooperation and access to complementary care essential
Patient-centered care	Client and advocates guide intervention with professional facilitation
Evidence-based practice	Documentation and sharing of outcomes are crucial to profession
Research	Contributes to viability of profession and program effectiveness
Education	Professional advancement and growth aid in adapting to change

Learning Outcome

Outline trends, issues, and challenges influencing management in our profession.

First-Line Managers

Settings and Populations

The scope of recreation therapy/therapeutic recreation reveals a wide range of services to individuals with an equally diverse set of health and functional issues. Services are provided to individuals in residential facilities, community-based health and human service agencies and centers, rehab and outpatient services, home health agencies, hospices, and day-treatment and social programs (e.g., summer day camp, adult social clubs, and inclusion buddy aquatic programs). Populations benefiting from services vary from persons who are considered:

- old-old (85 and older) to those not yet born;
- from those with temporary dysfunction (e.g., recovering from orthopedic surgery) to those with permanent dysfunction (e.g., spinal cord injuries);
- from those with chronic lifelong disorders (e.g., autism spectrum disorder) to those with acute incidents (e.g., cardiac conditions); and
- from those with syndromes with clearly defined characteristics (e.g., intellectual disabilities) to those with non-specific definitions (e.g., persons with social and mental health needs, the abused, those with PTSD).

According to the National Council for Therapeutic Recreation Certification (NCTRC), there are 12,000 CTRSs (Certified Therapeutic Recreation Specialists) in the United States and Canada, and 70% are employed full-time with the title of therapist or therapist supervisor while 6% have administrator titles. The majority of the CTRSs practice in hospitals and skilled nursing facilities, while others are found in residential/transitional, community parks and recreation, outpatient/day treatment, and human services settings (NCTRC, 2009). Populations with whom employment is primarily found are behavioral/mental health and geriatrics (NCTRC, 2009).

"Students entering the field of therapeutic recreation need to be cognizant that there is no single definition for the delivery of therapeutic recreation services for persons with disabilities in a global society" (Genoe & Singleton, 2009, p. 39). Differing terms describe therapeutic recreation like "Diversional Therapy" in Australia and New Zealand and "Therapeutic Recreation" in Canada with "Recreation Therapy" and "Therapeutic Recreation" used in the United States. The titles used in various cultures to describe service delivery to persons with disabilities reflect social and professional constructs—government policies, social beliefs about individual abilities, and professional standards and regulations.

Research also suggests that practicing professionals differ in their perceptions of their jobs and that the scope of their responsibilities is also changing. A study of practicing professionals in North Carolina found that those persons who have been in the field and their current positions longer were more satisfied with the nature of their jobs and relationships with supervisors and coworkers (Stone, Kline, & Hammond, 2009). Professionals in another state (Pennsylvania) identified that they are increasingly performing duties beyond the traditional scope of therapeutic responsibilities as departments transition to unit-based programming and satisfy cost-containment needs (Witman & Rakos, 2008). Several tasks mentioned most frequently included ADLs (activities of daily living), safety, special events, education, and assuming various administrative responsibilities like budgeting, customer service, quality improvement, and HR (human resource) issues. Thus not only are settings and populations diverse, practicing professionals differ in their job satisfaction and are experiencing expanding job responsibilities.

Learning Outcome

Identify settings and populations where first-line managers are employed.

Managerial Qualities, Responsibilities, Professional Expectations

Even though the first-line manager holds a bottom-rung managerial position in the organization, that position is one of the most critical and valuable roles within the administration of the organization. The manager's responsibility is to turn a plan of operation into reality. The majority of objectives for any therapeutic recreation service, regardless of setting, relate to the consumer, and the first-line therapeutic recreation manager is the administrative channel through which these objectives ultimately succeed or fail. This professional must ensure that quality services for clients are delivered efficiently in an ever-changing environment of standards and regulations, consumer activism, and budget limitations. Planning for the unit, for example, is in vain if the therapeutic recreation manager cannot translate the objectives into concrete action. The first-line manager also serves as a linking agent by advocating and representing the interests of subordinates to the next managerial level and communicating, clarifying, and enforcing the directives of his or her supervisor. The first-line manager networks with those above and below to influence the status of staff and quality of services provided to clients (Whitehead, Weiss, & Tappen, 2010).

The new manager needs to have an appreciation of the organization as a functioning system. While the manager will certainly understand the dynamics of the unit as a practitioner, he or she now must develop an understanding of the interdependency of the process and events occurring in the organization, such as

- the exchange relationships and social marketing that must occur between the organization and its task environments;
- the effects of organization, structure, and climate on communication, practitioner motivation, and performance;
- the importance of occupational commitments and professional vested interests as determinants of individual and group behavior; and
- the dynamics underlying various problems like balancing cost with quality and inter-professional conflict.

Effective managers have a common affinity for understanding the nature of the larger organization within which they work. In other words, a special effort is made to understand the inner workings of the larger organization of which their unit is a part. They observe, inquire, and integrate so they feel competent in representing their employees and their organization (Whitehead, Weiss, & Tappen, 2010).

Other characteristics of a successful first-line therapeutic recreation manager would include the following: the ability to negotiate to resolve problems by using creative solutions, being able to rebound from the frustrations of today and recognize that tomorrow is another day with its own challenges and rewards, and a sense of humor—without the latter, the environment can rapidly create management burnout. The changing and challenging health and human service system requires the manager to allocate scarce resources appropriately "and to be visionary and proactive in planning for challenges yet to come" (Marquis & Huston, 2009, p. 52).

Managerial responsibilities vary with the nature of the setting, populations served, and influence of government and professional regulations and standards. Regardless, the focus in this text is on managerial job tasks and knowledge, skills, and abilities (KSAs) defined by our credentialing body and professional organizations. Table 1.2 presents a summary of the professional knowledge domains of the NCTRC job analysis organized by chapter in which the content appears (CTRA, 2006; NCTRC, 2007; West, Kinney, & Witman, 2008).

Table 1.2 Managerial Responsibilities by NCTRC Professional Knowledge Domains

Managerial Responsibilities	Chapter
Foundational Knowledge	
Legislation	8, 9
Relevant guidelines/standards	13–16
Principles of group interaction/leadership	2, 4
Practice of Therapeutic Recreation/Recreation Therapy	
Standards of practice	13–15
Codes of ethics	16
Organization of Therapeutic Recreation/Recreation Therapy Service	
Documentation procedures	13
Evaluating agency/TR/RT service program	6, 13, 15
Quality improvement	15
TR/RT service plan of operation	3
Personnel/intern/volunteer supervision	4–5, 9–10, 12
Payment system	8
Facility/equipment management	14
Budgeting/fiscal responsibility	8
Advancement of the Profession	
Accreditation standards/regulations	8–10, 13
Professionalism	2, 11, 16
TR/RT certification/recertification	9, 10, 16
Advocacy	7, 11
Legislation/regulations	6, 8, 9, 14, 15
Professional standards/ethical guidelines	16
Public relations/marketing	7
Maintaining/upgrading professional competencies	9, 13, 16
Professional associations/organizations	16
Partnership for advancement of the TR/RT profession	7
Continuing education/in-service training	16

Source: Adapted from: National Council for Therapeutic Recreation Certification (NCTRC). (2007). 2007 NCTRC job analysis report, NCTRC report on the international job analysis of Certified Therapeutic Recreation Specialists. New City, NY: Author.

Within each chapter, student learning outcomes articulate competencies of first-line managers. Each setting is unique with protocols and policies governing performance expectations. To illustrate, we introduce staffing responsibilities, realizing managers craft specific policies related to hiring, supervising, and competency assessment appropriate to their work setting. We provide example statements, documents, and web information asking you to participate in the learning experience by reviewing key words, responding to review questions, and viewing chapter PowerPoints.

Professionals are held to higher expectations due to their specialized education and training. First-line managers, therefore, not only represent their employees and the organization but also our profession to internal and external audiences. This added layer of responsibility

Learning Outcome
Outline qualities, responsibilities, and professional expectations of first-line managers.

Learning Outcome
Describe topics and outcomes students may expect with use of this text.

requires the first-line manager to model and articulate ethical behaviors and professional practices, monitor staff development, establish mentee-mentor relationships to advance their career and foster staff growth, engage in professional organizations to self-regulate the practice, contribute to the body of evidence and theories justifying our practice, and to advocate for recreation therapy/therapeutic recreation as a necessary public service and essential care team participant. The text concludes with a summary of professional expectations. Together with the trends, issues, and challenges introduced in this opening section, these professional expectations significantly influence the first-line manager's effectiveness in achieving client outcomes through unit operation. The first-line manager and our profession are judged by not only practice effectiveness but also by how fluid and competently the first-line manager represents the profession as a change agent.

References

Canadian Therapeutic Recreation Association (CTRA). (2006). *Standards of practice for recreation therapists & therapeutic recreation assistants.* Calgary, Alberta, Canada: Author.

Genoe, R., & Singleton, J. (2009). World demographics and their implications for therapeutic recreation. In N. J. Stumbo (Ed.), *Professional issues in therapeutic recreation* (pp. 31–42). Champaign, IL: Sagamore.

Hoss, M. A. K., Powell, L., & Sable, J. (2006). Healthcare trends: Implications for Therapeutic Recreation. In M. J. Carter & J. E. Folkerth (Eds.). *Therapeutic recreation education: Challenges and changes* (pp. 107–122). Ashburn, VA: NTRS/NRPA.

Marquis B. L., & Huston, C. J. (2009). *Leadership roles and management functions in nursing: Theory & application* (6th ed.). Philadelphia: Lippincott Williams & Wilkins.

National Council for Therapeutic Recreation Certification (NCTRC). (2007). *2007 NCTRC job analysis report, NCTRC report on the international job analysis of Certified Therapeutic Recreation Specialists.* New City, NY: Author.

National Council for Therapeutic Recreation Certification (NCTRC). (2009). *Recreation therapy, CTRS profile, Certified Therapeutic Recreation Specialist.* [Brochure]. New City, NY: Author.

Stone, C. F., Kline, S. M., & Hammond, A. (2009). Job satisfaction levels of therapeutic recreation specialists in North Carolina. *Annual in Therapeutic Recreation, 17,* 46–60.

Stumbo, N. J., & Hoss, M. A. K. (2009). Higher education and healthcare: Parallel issues of quality, cost, and access. In N. J. Stumbo (Ed.), *Professional issues in therapeutic recreation* (pp. 367–387). Champaign, IL: Sagamore.

Sullivan, E. J. & Decker, P. J. (2009). *Effective leadership and management in nursing* (7th ed.). Upper Saddle River, NJ: Prentice-Hall.

Sylvester, C. (2011). Therapeutic recreation, the International Classification of Functioning, Disability, and Health, and the capability approach. *Therapeutic Recreation Journal, 45*(2), 85–104.

U.S. Department of Health and Human Services. (2010). *Healthy people 2020.* Retrieved from http://www.healthypeople.gov/2020/

West, R. E., Kinney, T., & Witman, J. (Eds.). (2008). *Guidelines for competency assessment and curriculum planning for recreational therapy practice.* Hattiesburg, MS: ATRA.

Whitehead, D. K., Weiss, S. A., & Tappen, R. M. (2010). *Essentials of nursing leadership and management* (5th ed.). Philadelphia: F. A. Davis.

Witman, J. P., & Rakos, K. S. (2008). Determining the "other related duties" of therapeutic recreation and activity professionals: A pilot study. *American Journal of Recreation Therapy, 7*(2), 29–33.

World Health Organization. (WHO). (2002). *Towards a common language for functioning disability and health, ICF.* Geneva, Switzerland. Retrieved from http://www.who.int/classifications/icf/en/

Chapter 2
Becoming A First-Line Manager

Keywords

- Authority
- Burnout
- Controlling
- First-line manager
- Leader
- Leading
- Management
- Organizational Stress
- Organizing
- Planning
- Practitioner
- Responsibility

Learning Outcomes

After reading this chapter, students will be able to:

1. Diagram the hierarchy of management levels in an organization.
2. Describe the four functions of the first-line manager.
3. Identify and give an example of the four resources to be managed by the first-line manager.
4. Describe the challenges that are often experienced when a therapeutic recreation practitioner moves to a first-line manager position.
5. Explain the relationship between organizational stress and burnout.

Overview

Students may wonder why they should study management. Most are probably more concerned with finding a position in the immediate future than about envisioning management responsibilities. However, even in their first job, a young professional in therapeutic recreation may find themself in a management position. This is most likely the situation when accepting a position in a small agency, because these agencies may have only one level of management. Today's focus on healthy, active lifestyles has resulted in an increasing number of management positions that are available to therapeutic recreation professionals in the areas of health and fitness with public, private, and commercial agencies (Lussier & Kimball, 2009). The purpose of this chapter is to help students develop an understanding of a therapeutic recreation first-line manager position with a health and human service organization.

Management

Management has been defined many different ways. Perhaps the most widely accepted definition is that "*management* is the act of getting things done through other people" (Wren, 1979, p. 3). The therapeutic recreation manager is responsible for coordinating a variety of resources to effectively and efficiently accomplish the goals of an organization through delivery of high-quality, safe services that satisfy client needs.

The manager's job is similar to that of an orchestra leader. If the individual musicians played their instruments without a common score of music and without a conductor, the result would be just noise. The purpose of the conductor is to combine the sounds of the instruments played by individual musicians into pleasing music. The manager's job, like that of a conductor, is to get everyone working together to achieve the common goals of the organization. Today's managers are facilitators who teach, coach, and support the development of staff. They are motivators who offer encouragement to ensure that work units achieve success (Edginton, Hudson, Lankford, & Larsen, 2008).

Three Levels of Management

While it is expected that managers are found at the top of organizations, managers are actually found throughout an agency. Organizations have various levels of managers. Each level of management requires different management skills, and managers at each level have different responsibilities, different authority, and serve in different roles. *Responsibility* means the designated area of the organization over which a manager has charge or control. *Authority* is the right to exercise influence, give directives, or make certain decisions within the organization (Hurd, Barelona, & Meldrum, 2008). Managers who work for large organizations usually have very different job responsibilities than managers who work in smaller organizations. Likewise, managers who work with for-profit organizations may have very different responsibilities than managers who work with nonprofit or public agencies.

Learning Outcome

Diagram the hierarchy of management levels in an organization.

The three levels of management are top, middle, and first-line. Top managers are responsible for the entire organization or major parts of it. They have job titles such as chairman, chief executive officer, and president. Top managers are responsible for establishing the organization's long-range goals—five or more years. They view the organization as a whole and make decisions that will affect the entire agency. Top-level managers supervise other managers.

Middle managers have job titles such as manager, therapeutic recreation supervisor, and department head. Middle managers are responsible for implementation of top management's plans. They are responsible for setting mid- and short-term goals, one to five years, for their program unit or department. Middle managers supervise other managers.

First-line managers may have job titles such as therapeutic recreation leader, therapeutic recreation coordinator, therapeutic recreation program supervisor, and director. The first-line manager usually reports to a middle manager. First-line managers are responsible to implement the middle manager's plans. The first-line manager usually does not supervise other managers but may supervise non-manager employees. These non-manager employees are called *practitioners* because they are responsible for carrying out the day-to-day operations and services of the organization. Figure 2.1 summarizes the three levels of management.

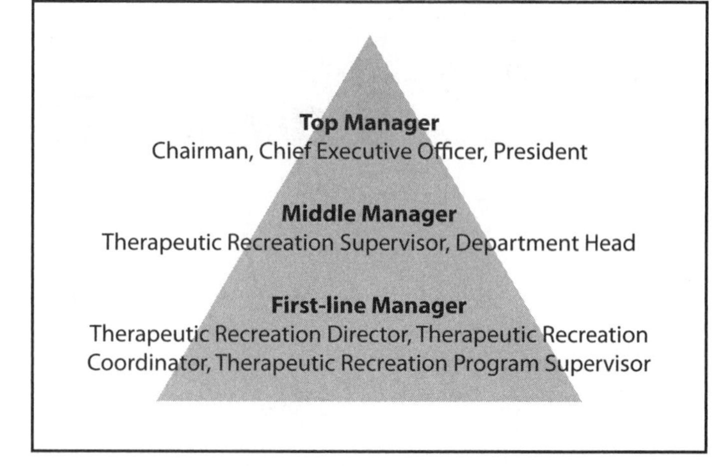

Figure 2.1 Three Levels of Management

Therapeutic Recreation First-Line Manager

Therapeutic recreation managers in health and human service organizations are considered first-line managers. First-line manager is often the first position held by a new professional who enters management from a practitioner, non-managerial position. There are some agency settings in which the first-line manager is also the sole practitioner, for example in long-term care settings or small rehab units and community-based recreation service organizations. Most first-line managers have had little or no formal academic preparation in the management of therapeutic recreation services. Their advancement is frequently the result of competency as a practitioner in direct service, program knowledge, and job experience.

First-line managers are responsible for supervising the work of non-managerial staff and volunteers. They oversee the day-to-day activities and services of the therapeutic recreation department or work unit. The focus for any therapeutic recreation service, regardless of the agency setting, is the client consumer. The first-line manager is responsible to ensure that quality services that meet the needs of consumers are delivered efficiently in an ever-changing environment of standards and regulations. They typically coordinate services with other managers in the same organization. They may also coordinate services with managers in other therapeutic recreation service agencies throughout the community.

Therapeutic recreation managers are functional managers, as opposed to general managers. Functional managers are responsible for one functional area, for example specialized therapeutic recreation services. General managers, by contrast, have broad responsibility throughout the entire organization. For example, a business manager for a hospital is a general manager. Today more therapeutic recreation managers in community-based settings like special recreation associations are assuming general managerial responsibilities because of their knowledge of the Americans with Disabilities Act (ADA).

Management Functions

This section highlights and briefly describes the diverse responsibilities of first-line managers. Every manager plans, organizes, leads, and controls. These four functions of management were first described in 1916 by Henri Fayol, an early management theorist. Fayol's description of management is still relevant today. Keep in mind that the four functions are a system; they are interrelated, overlapping, and are often performed simultaneously.

LEARNING OUTCOME

Describe the four functions of the first-line manager.

Planning

Planning is typically the starting point in the management process. It is the most fundamental of all management functions. *Planning* is the process of looking ahead and identifying a future course of action to be followed. It is a preparatory step. Planning is when the organization's management "clearly defines the path it wants to take to get from where it is to where it wants to be" (Robbins & Decenzo, 2004, p. 78).

Planning is the process of setting goals and determining in advance exactly how the goals will be achieved. The first-line manager analyzes what activities need to be done, sets priorities, and plans the best means to achieve the desired goals. Planning provides direction and a common purpose.

To succeed, therapeutic recreation organizations need planning. Although planning takes a significant amount of time, it is time well spent. Managers participate in strategic or long-range planning when they design vision, mission, and goal statements. First-line managers develop daily operational plans and contingency plans when they revise policies and procedures or set productivity levels to achieve department objectives. Performing the planning function thoroughly requires strong conceptual and decision-making skills. The challenge for the first-line manager is to convert planning into action through organizing.

Organizing

Organizing begins when planning ends. It is the action step after the plans have been formulated. *Organizing* is the process of delegating and coordinating tasks and resources, both the human resources and physical resources, required to achieve the organization's goals. The organizing function is sandwiched between planning and controlling and consists of four steps:

1. Identifying specific tasks or activities
2. Grouping the tasks or activities
3. Assigning resources and responsibilities
4. Coordinating activities

First-line managers, for example, may organize services, programs, events, staff, and volunteers. This organization may be seen in organizational charts that are pictures of assigned responsibilities. Organization occurs when the manager assigns practitioners to participate on teams or form partnerships with other entities. Successful managers put a great deal of effort into organizing. They organize by designing and developing systems, or processes, to implement plans. A significant portion of the therapeutic recreation manager's job involves organizing. Effective organizing requires both conceptual and decision-making skills.

Leading

In addition to planning and organizing, first-line therapeutic recreation managers are responsible for leading staff on a daily basis. *Leading* is the process of communicating the organization's goals to staff and influencing them to work toward achieving those goals. Leading involves inspiring, coaching, and motivating staff. Leading is a significant part of the first-line therapeutic recreation manager's responsibilities. A majority of first-line managers give 50% or more of their time to leading (Kraut, 1989; Robbins, 1997). Effective first-line managers have strong people skills and possess exceptional communication skills.

Controlling

Controlling is the evaluation function of management. It is the process of measuring performance against planned outcomes. *Controlling* is the process of establishing and implementing mechanisms, or processes, for ongoing evaluation to compare results with plans and goals. Managers establish performance standards as benchmarks, or targets, and evaluate and measure progress toward achievement. Controlling also includes identifying and implementing corrective actions that are needed to improve performance in the work unit. Examples of controlling functions for therapeutic recreation first-line managers include maintaining performance indicators, completing employee performance evaluations, monitoring the budget, complying with external regulatory program evaluations, and administering client satisfaction surveys. Controlling requires conceptual skills, decision-making skills, and communication skills.

As mentioned above, the four management functions are not linear. Managers do not plan, then organize, then lead, than evaluate. The four functions are interrelated and interdependent and happen simultaneously. Sufficient effort in each of the functions is essential for success. First-line managers focus on details in the day-to-day delivery of services and typically spend more time leading and controlling and need strong technical skills, interpersonal skills, and communication skills.

Resources to be Managed

The first-line manager in the health and human service organization is responsible for oversight and allocation of a diverse set of resources including physical resources, technological resources, financial resources, and human resources. Each of these resources will be briefly mentioned here, and subsequent chapters will provide additional discussions of these managerial responsibilities.

Learning Outcome

Identify and give an example of the four resources to be managed by the first-line manager.

Physical resources are those things that people can see and associate with the organization. Examples of physical resources include the facility, outdoor grounds or fields, and equipment. Management of physical resources includes purchasing, inventory, accessibility, cleanliness, maintenance and repair, and safety.

Technology resources support the provision of services by the health and human service organization. Technology is often a key resource that increases the organization's efficiency. Examples of technology resources include scheduling software, financial software, communication devices, and client-record management. Technology is also an essential component of enhancing the effectiveness of services. Technology is constantly changing. Larger organizations typically maintain technology staff who offer support to the entire organization. In smaller organizations, the first-line manager will likely be responsible to manage technology.

Financial resources influence many management decisions. Budget allocations, available capital, reimbursements, and service coverage and costs are examples of the financial resources that impact what the manager can do, when it can be done, and how it can be done. For example, the first-line manager must assess the available financial resources and determine programming and events to be offered throughout the year, equipment to be purchased, and the level of staffing that can be supported to achieve the expected level of service.

The first-line manager is responsible for the human resources of the organization—the people. The organization's human resources are the most important and time-consuming of the resources to be managed. The first-line manager spends a considerable amount of time and effort with training, motivating, organizing, and evaluating staff. Today volunteers are an ever-increasing human resource in many health and human service agencies. The first-line manager's responsibilities may include coordination and supervision of these volunteers, who are actively involved with delivering programs, events, and services.

First-Line Manager as a Supervisor

As supervisors, first-line managers guide, coach, and teach practitioner staff. Figure 2.2 identifies the diverse and unique skills and abilities that are required of first-line managers in their roles as supervisors in a health and human service organization.

First-Line Management as a Leader

Leadership skills are essential for first-line therapeutic recreation managers. "A *leader* is anyone who uses interpersonal skills to influence others to accomplish a

1. *Heavy reliance on technical expertise.* First-line managers are required to know the job they supervise. First-line managers spend a large portion of their time directing and overseeing the activities of practitioners. They must have expert knowledge of jobs that practitioners perform.
2. *Skills assessment.* After learning the skills required of each position, the manager must assess each practitioner's suitability for the varied positions in the department. It is up to the manager to identify areas of excellence, competence, and deficiency for every practitioner under supervision. It is important to differentiate between performance (actual level of service) and ability (capability to perform the job tasks of, for example, an entry-level CTRS position).
3. *Facilitation of work.* The therapeutic recreation manager must look for barriers within the practitioner, the staff as a group, and the organization with its various support systems. One of the manager's most important tasks is the challenge of developing positive feelings of capability and potential achievement in each practitioner. In addition, the manager attempts to manage and to facilitate change rather than regarding change as a threat. Today the external environment for all organizations is changing rapidly. The manager has an important role to lead practitioners to anticipate and embrace change. Planned change is covered in Chapter 4, on organizational behavior.
4. *Communication in two languages.* Effective communication is an essential at all levels of management. First-line managers are required to communicate in two distinct languages—that of management and that of practitioners. Differing educational backgrounds, value systems, and points of reference are just several of the potential communication barriers between the two groups.
5. *Coping with constrained authority.* Today managers must demonstrate a democratic, participatory management style. Managers must also adapt to the constraints imposed by internal and external factors, such as the employee grievance process that is included in the disciplinary procedures that most organizations provide for their workers.
6. *Reinforcing employees' good performance.* On a day-to-day basis, employee reinforcement mainly takes place verbally with compliments and praise when a job has been done well. Longer-term employee reinforcement includes regularly scheduled written performance evaluations as well as a variety of recognition rewards.
7. *Management's representative.* When practitioners think of management, their usual point of reference is their manager, the first-line manager. This places high responsibility on the first-line manager to fully communicate and reflect accurately the plans, programs, and priorities of upper-level management.

Figure 2.2 Managerial Responsibilities by NCTRC Professional Knowledge Domains

specific goal." (Sullivan, 2013, p. 41). While managers have formal authority and responsibility for the quality of work performed by their staff, leaders do not have formal authority. However, effective leaders have "the ability to cause individuals to act willingly in a desired way for the benefit of the group" (Salacuse, 2006, p. 21). For example, a first-line manager can use his or her formal authority to direct a practitioner to complete a task or a goal and the practitioner may do so willingly or unwillingly. If the practitioner completes the goal but does so unwillingly and simply complies with authority, the manager risks creating a negative attitude and an unfavorable or antagonistic work environment. On the other hand, if the first-line manager uses leadership skills to cause the practitioner to act willingly to complete the goal, the manager is more likely to elicit a positive attitude and maintain a productive work environment. Sullivan (2013) emphasizes that "all good managers are also good leaders—the two go hand in hand." Further, "both roles can be learned; skills gained enhance either role" (p. 41).

First-line managers are expected to possess a broad scope of skills. Top management has a complex set of expectations of first-line managers. Practitioner professional staff have a unique set of expectations of first-line managers. Figure 2.3 summarizes these broad and diverse expectations of first-line managers (see p. 14).

Leadership is often described in terms of the personal qualities or competencies of an individual. Leaders are skilled in empowering others, creating meaning, facilitating learning, developing knowledge, thinking reflectively, communicating, solving problems, making decisions, and working with others. Leaders generate excitement and they define their purpose and goals clearly. Leaders understand people and their needs; they recognize and appreciate differences in people, individualizing their approach as needed. "Leaders generate excitement; they clearly define their purpose and mission" (Sullivan, 2013, p. 52). They demonstrate energy and commitment, and leaders must be able to inspire others to commit to the goals of the organization.

Top Management Expectations of First-Line Managers:

- Deliver projects and programs on time and within budget
- Support senior management's goals and priorities
- Communicate agency plans, programs, and priorities to their work group; keep staff informed about the organization
- Communicate the work group's projects, accomplishments, and challenges to upper management
- Identify strategies for increased efficiency

Practitioner Professional Staff Expectations of First-Line Managers:

- Identify realistic and attainable goals and standards
- Communicate about work assignments, schedules, and other decisions that affect staff
- Involve staff in the decision-making process
- Represent the staff to upper management
- Provide rationale for decisions and direction
- Provide fair and balanced feedback for staff efforts and achievements
- Be fair—no favorites
- Listen and empathize sincerely
- Maintain a safe working environment

Figure 2.3 Expectations of First-Line Managers

Making the Transition: Practitioner to First-Line Manager

It is widely recognized that many therapeutic recreation practitioners whose professional training is in direct service move into positions with managerial responsibilities at some point in their careers. A major reason for this move is that a management position continues to be one of the few options available to a practitioner for promotion and an increased salary. Other reasons for accepting a management position include the ability to influence policies and services, to reach for power, to offer service, and to give of one's self (French & Raven, 1968).

Learning Outcome

Describe the challenges that are often experienced when a therapeutic recreation practitioner moves to a first-line manager position.

A practitioner may experience challenges in making the transition to a position as manager. To some extent these challenges are similar to those of any new job or new professional role. Several challenges in making the transition from practitioner to management role are discussed briefly.

The first-line therapeutic recreation manager may experience frustrations associated with being creative in a bureaucratic agency environment that operates under well-defined procedures. There may be very few outlets and limited time for creativity and innovation. The new role may include significant documentation demands for accountability. He or she is often expected to balance an ever-increasing workload without increases in staff and may have to deal with reductions in staff.

The move into a manager's position often affects the nature of relationships with colleagues. While still a practitioner, the new manager was likely to have participated in a social group that valued mutuality and cooperation. He or she probably enjoyed opportunities to vent frustration, to gain support, and to exchange ideas and information with other practitioners. The manager's new status makes it increasingly difficult for him or her to maintain those relationships with colleagues who have now become subordinates. The change to a supervisory role usually pushes the manager and practitioners toward more formal and neutral relationships.

One of the most troublesome situations managers encounter in their first management position is exercising authority over subordinates, especially former colleagues. The problem centers on gaining support and cooperation in moving toward the goals of the organization, motivating people to change behavior or to improve performance, and gaining cooperation with changes proposed by management. The first-line manager's direct practice knowledge and skills gained as a practitioner are usually helpful in resolving these challenges. However, if various efforts fail, the new manager is often faced with the necessity of using the authority of their position to elicit the desired behavior from former colleagues. This can be very uncomfortable for the new first-line manager.

The new manager must have an appreciation of the organization as a functioning system. While the new manager will certainly understand the dynamics of the department as a practitioner, he or she now must develop an understanding of the relationship and interdependency of the processes and events occurring throughout the organization. The effective manager must have a good knowledge and awareness of other health and human service resources in the community, especially those providing therapeutic recreation, inclusion experiences, and active lifestyle services, and must understand the referral processes for these agencies. The first-line manager must have a good understanding of the therapeutic recreation continuum and therapeutic recreation process and their application regardless of the agency setting.

The first-line manager must have an understanding of the purposes and activities of the professional membership organizations that serve therapeutic recreation professionals. This includes national professional membership organizations, state affiliation organizations, and the professional certification and licensure organizations. New first-line managers must recognize the importance of active participation in professional organizations, maintain current professional certification and licensure, and encourage certification/licensure for his or her staff. However, new managers may encounter challenges in securing the time and financial resources needed for their own professional involvement and development and the development of their staff.

Finally, the manager must understand the differences between direct service and management and recognize the unique skills and perspectives needed in each of these roles. While the new first-line manager probably has those skills related to direct service, he or she should be particularly aware that management is itself a professional activity that requires a different skill set. The new manager must commit significant time and effort into developing strong managerial skills. Figure 2.4 offers a reflection of the variables that affect the therapeutic recreation manager.

Organizational Stress Management

Many of the frustrations and pressures we experience on a daily basis cause us to feel stress. Hans Selye (1974), one of the first researchers to study the concept of stress,

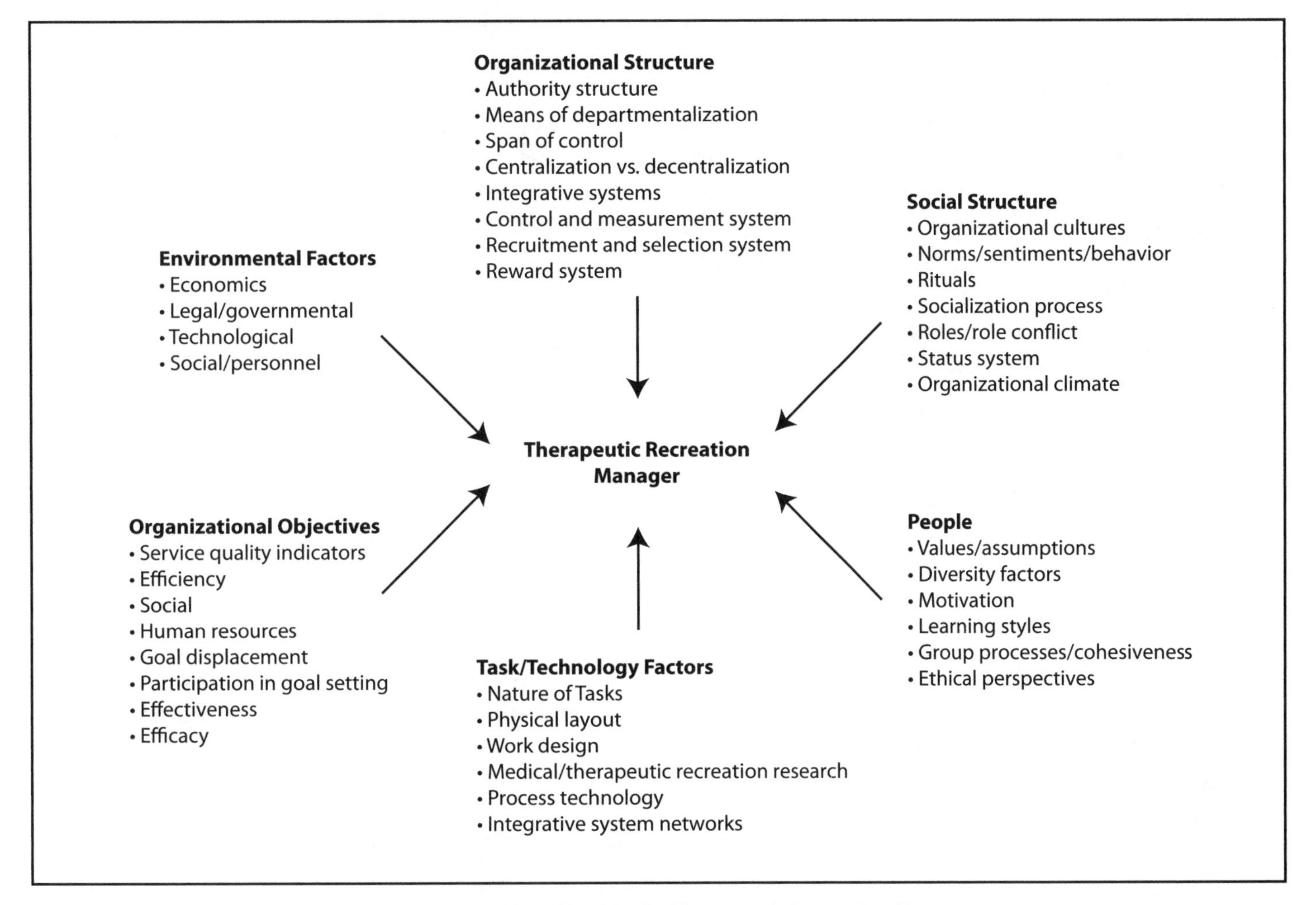

Figure 2.4 Variables Affecting the Therapeutic Recreation Manager

described stress as the nonspecific response of the body to any demand. When these demands occur in the workplace, it is referred to as *organizational stress*. According to a 2007 nationwide poll by the American Psychological Association, 75% of Americans identify work as a significant source of stress (APA, 2007). A number of sources of stress are present in a health and human service organization that affect first-line managers as well as the practitioners they supervise. One of the leading contributors to organizational stress is technology. The ability to be instantly connected through texting, e-mail, cell phones, and the Internet causes stress. While technology undoubtedly improves our lives, constant connection to work and information overload contribute to stress. Workers today are finding it increasingly difficult to keep pace with messaging demands, disengage from the workplace, and focus on their personal priorities. The results of a recent survey indicated that 62% of at-work e-mail users check work e-mail over the weekend, and 19% check it five or more times in a weekend. More than 50% said they check it on vacation, with the highest amount coming from mobile device users at 78% (Gifford, 2009). Other study results published in the *Wall Street Journal* indicate that 92% of studied respondents said they make or take work-related communications outside of the office, including during vacations. Nearly three fourths say they stay "switched on" during weekends, and 20% have interrupted a date for work reasons (Lexamark International, 2006).

Heavy workloads with unrealistic deadlines also contribute to organizational stress. Today first-line managers and practitioners in health and human service organizations are expected to do more with fewer resources. Today, as health and human service organizations are downsizing, managers have responsibility for supervision of more staff and additional functions. They are often overworked. The increased workload, including documentation and accountability demands, unrealistic expectations, and the resulting perception of loss of control over the work environment, results in stress.

The physical workspace may be stressful. Small, cramped work spaces, poorly organized workstations, or insufficient equipment are examples of workspace stressors. First-line managers may also experience stress as a result of being assigned responsibility without having the corresponding authority to complete the work. Realignment, downsizing, right-sizing, merging, and reorganization of the organization often results in ambiguity in job assignments or role definition.

Communication is a stress factor in the health and human service organization. Examples of communication stressors include administration's inability to respond quickly because of delays in internal communication. The manager may receive unclear or insufficient information regarding a work assignment. Delayed or insufficient feedback regarding performance is an often-cited source of stress in the workplace.

Finally, the legal complexities under which health and human service organizations operate are a contributing stress factor. Service providers must operate in compliance with significantly more and increasingly complex regulations. These regulations are constantly changing, some are vague or inconsistent, and documentation requirements are time consuming.

Consequences of Organizational Stress

Today's fast-paced and ever-changing environment contributes to feelings of stress. Stressed employees tend to experience a broad spectrum of physical, psychological, and behavioral symptoms. While each individual reacts differently, common symptoms of stress include headache, fatigue, sleep disorders, and an upset stomach, in combination with feelings of irritability, anger, nervousness, and lack of motivation. Increased stress can lead to the use of ineffective, unhealthy behaviors to manage stress. Examples of these behaviors include smoking, comfort eating, poor diet choices, inactivity, and use of alcohol or drugs. Figure 2.5 identifies the behavioral symptoms of prolonged stress.

Continued exposure to organizational stress may result in burnout. The term *burnout* refers to the state of physical, mental, and emotional exhaustion caused by excessive and prolonged stress (Smith, Segal, & Segal, 2012). The employee experiencing burnout typically feels exhausted, lethargic, drained of all available energy, unfulfilled, empty, and perceives that their work has no purpose. The individual experiencing burnout often does not recognize the symptoms or the seriousness of their condition (Arnold, Glover, & Beeler, 2012). Figure 2.6 illustrates key differences between stress and burnout.

Managing Organizational Stress and Burnout

The first-line manager is a resource and a role model to practitioners in how to cope with stress and manage

Physical Symptoms of Stress

- Muscle tension in the jaw
- Digestive changes such as constipation or diarrhea
- Dry throat
- Fatigue
- High blood pressure
- Grinding teeth
- Headaches
- Indigestion
- Muscle aches
- Pounding of heart
- Shortness of breath
- Upset stomach

Psychological Symptoms of Stress

- Anger
- Anxiety
- Apathy
- Cynicism
- Defensives
- Depression
- Difficulty concentrating
- Feelings of helplessness, hopelessness, or worthlessness
- Feelings of being misunderstood or unappreciated
- Hypersensitivity
- Insecurity
- Irritability
- Lack of direction
- Pessimism
- Resentment
- Sadness
- Insomnia
- Isolation or withdrawal from others
- Lessened enjoyment of activities that were once pleasurable
- Loss of sex drive
- Procrastination
- Readiness to argue

Behavioral Symptoms of Stress

- Increased smoking
- Increased use of alcohol or drugs
- Nail biting
- Neglect of responsibility
- Poor job performance
- Unusually poor hygiene

Adapted from Arnold, Glover, & Beeler (2012)

Figure 2.5 Prolonged Stress: Physical, Psychological, and Behavioral Symptoms of Stress

time. The attitude and energy level of managers directly affects staff productivity and satisfaction. Additionally, the first-line manager can identify and take action to manage some sources of organizational stress. Organizational stress-management strategies include the following:

Stress

- Feeling overly engaged or involved
- Over-reactive
- Exudes urgency and hyperactivity
- Loss of energy
- Primary damage is physical
- May kill you prematurely

Burnout

- Feeling disengaged
- Sharp and blunt responses
- Exudes helplessness and hopelessness
- Loss of motivation, ideals, and hope
- Primary damage is emotional
- May make life seem not worth living

Adapted from Arnold, Glover, & Beeler (2012)

Figure 2.6 The Differences Between Stress and Burnout

1. Training to improve job performance.
2. Cross-training and job enrichment to increase the variety of work responsibilities.
3. Matching the job responsibilities with the individual's goals.
4. Decision making, autonomy, and sense of choice.
5. Identifying and eliminating conflicting demands on practitioners.
6. Managing communication to reduce information overload.
7. Increasing organizational communication to keep practitioners informed about what is happening in the organization beyond the work unit.
8. Team building among practitioners in the work unit.
9. Emphasizing the importance and value of work breaks and vacation time.
10. Encouraging healthy active lifestyles including eating right, getting enough sleep, drinking plenty of water, and participating in regular exercise (e.g., taking a walk/run, working out, or playing sports). (Lussier & Kimball, 2009; Sullivan, 2013)

LEARNING OUTCOME

Explain the relationship between organizational stress and burnout.

How managers handle the pressure of the workday and use time is a reflection of their own attitude and influences how they expect staff to approach workday demands and use time. Effective organizational stress-management strategies improve job performance, increase worker satisfaction, and encourage healthy lifestyles.

Managing Time

Time-management skills are essential for first-line therapeutic recreation managers in health and human service organizations. When they are able to successfully implement time-management strategies to control their workload, stress declines and personal productivity increases. "Time management enables people to get more done in less time with better results" (Lussier & Kimball, 2009, p. 432). Three strategies for effective time management include analyzing time-use habits, setting objectives, and controlling interruptions.

Time Analysis

The first step to successful time management is to perform a time analysis to determine how the first-line manager is currently using time during the work day. A time log is a method of tracking daily activities. A time log, also known as an activity log, is a form upon which the first-line manager records actual activities in 30- or 60-minute time increments over a period of 5 to 10 typical working days. The purpose of keeping a time log is to help first-line managers assemble an accurate profile of how they are spending their time.

The second step in the analysis process is to review the time log and identify time-use patterns. This analysis helps the first-line manager understand their daily routine of activities. The first-line manager can review the logs to determine which activities are essential and high-priority tasks for their job and which activities are lower priority and can be delegated to others or even eliminated entirely. The purpose of the time analysis is to assist the first-line therapeutic recreation manager to identify how to manage the work day more efficiently.

Setting Objectives

Setting objectives is an essential time-management strategy. Managers who get things done set objectives. Objectives help the first-line manager to identify priorities. These highly effective individuals are able to focus on the tasks with the greatest impact to their job, their work unit, and their organization. Well-written objectives are SMART: simple, measurable, attainable, realistic, and time-specific.

The key to successful time management is scheduling activities and then protecting the planned time to complete those activities. The purpose of the schedule, or to-do list, is to allocate time and focus attention toward accomplishment of objectives. A schedule helps the first-line manager prioritize their activities. This daily schedule is typically in the form of a daily to-do list. The first-line manager must know their personal peak time of the day. This is the time when their level of energy is highest and they are most productive. When the most productive time of the day is focused on the most important tasks, the result is better quality work that is completed in the least time. Finally, the first-line manager can increase their efficiency by scheduling routine tasks to minimize the number of transitions between various types of tasks. For example, the manager can check and reply to emails at specific times and only a few times of the day or process all client reports at the same time each week.

Controlling Interruptions

An interruption occurs any time one activity is stopped prior to completion to give attention to a different activity. Many interruptions interfere with a task that is less important and less urgent than current activities. While interruptions are an inevitable part of the workplace, they can be time-wasters. Good time management includes identifying and reducing the frequency and duration of interruptions (Sullivan, 2013). First-line therapeutic recreation managers in health and human service organizations commonly experience interruptions like phone calls, email, text messages, drop-in visitors, reports and paperwork, and meetings. These interruptions, as well as strategies for managing these interruptions, are discussed below.

Phone calls: Phone calls are a frequent source of interruptions. Managing phone calls can be accomplished with several strategies. First, to better manage outgoing calls, schedule a block of time during the day to make phone calls and complete all calls during the scheduled time. Plan each call with notes for discussion items and questions. Planning results in more efficient conversations and helps ensure that all necessary information is exchanged during the phone call. Close each phone call with a summary of the discussion including key points of agreement and action steps to be taken. This summary can avoid errors, misunderstandings, and the need to review the discussion later. Minimize socializing during calls. Calls can be warm, courteous, and focused. To manage incoming calls, use voicemail to take messages and enable others to respond to recurring inquiries by providing staff with routine information. Finally, when leaving voice mail requesting a return call, suggest preferred call times and clearly state the reason for the call.

E-mail: E-mail is an ideal means of communication for the first-line therapeutic manager to use to distribute information, make requests, or respond to requests. E-mail is quick, easy, and efficient. However, e-mail can also be a distraction and time-waster. To minimize interruptions, turn off the pop-up or alarm notification for new incoming e-mail. Establish a habit of checking e-mail at specific, scheduled times in the day. For example, it may be sensible to review e-mail first thing in the morning, a second time just before lunch, and a third time an hour before the normal close of business. Finally, e-mail is most effective when the message is well planned and clearly written.

Drop in visitors: Drop-in visitors are unscheduled, impromptu meetings with practitioners, coworkers, and others in the workplace. While it is impossible to eliminate all impromptu meetings, several strategies will help to decrease the frequency and duration of these interruptions. Schedule regular meeting times with staff who need to discuss routine matters. For example, the first-line manager may wish to schedule a consistent weekly meeting time with each practitioner they supervise to exchange information. Encourage other staff and coworkers to set meeting appointments. Schedule and inform staff of time blocks that are available for drop-in discussions (Sullivan, 2013). When a drop-in visitor enters the office, stand to greet the visitor, and remain standing. This gesture is gracious, and usually results in a discussion that is brief. Arranging the furniture in the office space with the desk positioned to minimize eye contact with the doorway area also discourages drop-in visitors. If interruptions cannot be stopped due to workspace arrangement or other factors, go elsewhere to complete work tasks that require focused, uninterrupted time.

Reports and Paperwork: Writing and reading reports, memos, letters, forms and other materials is an essential part of a first-line therapeutic recreation manager's job. To manage paperwork efficiently, schedule time to review paperwork. Resist the temptation to review paperwork that arrives between scheduled review times. The goal, although not possible in reality, is to handle each piece of paper only once. An effective strategy is the FAST method. As each item is handled: **F**ile it, **A**ct on it (either do it or delegate it), **S**chedule it for a later time, or **T**oss it. Minimize the clutter of paperwork in the workspace. Clutter encourages paper shuffling, which is not an efficient use of time. For the priority paperwork items that will be completed later—for example, preparation of a specific report—use a planner to schedule a time to complete the report, place the paperwork in a follow-up file, label the file, and retrieve it at the appointed time. Schedule a block of time that will be needed to complete paperwork. Identify the task to be completed and estimate the amount of time needed to complete the task. When a task is to be delegated, an effective strategy is to write the due date and the name of the individual to whom it will be delegated on the paper and send it to the appropriate person. When receiving announcements of meetings and other appointments, enter the information on a planner (calendar) and discard the paperwork. Scheduling through use of a planner is the road map to time management.

Meeting Management: Meetings are necessary for accomplishing tasks in any organization. The key to successful meetings is to plan and manage them effectively (see Figure 2.7, p. 20). Productive, valuable, and engaging meetings require a clear goal, open communications, and a well-organized leader. Meetings are a primary communication tool used by managers.

In summary, first-line managers have many demands on their time and attention. The manager's time is a valuable and scarce resource; however, many first-line managers do not use their time resource effectively. The purpose of time-management strategies is to work smarter, not harder.

Summary

1. Management was defined as the act of getting things done through other people. Leadership was defined as influencing others to accomplish specific goals using relationships and interpersonal skills to influence.
2. While there are several levels of management, the therapeutic recreation manager in a health

1. Start on time—give warning only the first time;
2. End on time;
3. Develop an agenda and circulate it to the attendees prior to the meeting;
4. Only those people who are needed or involved in the meeting's purpose should attend a meeting;
5. Gather information prior to a meeting and summarize it during the meeting;
6. Stick to the agenda, avoiding interruptions, and squelch side trips around or away from the agenda;
7. Limit the amount of time for a particular agenda item and be sure that the intended agenda items get accomplished;
8. Arrange for a comfortable environment but not so plush that people would rather be there than somewhere else;
9. Type and distribute items that involve one-way communication by their very nature since verbal announcements in one-way communication instances usually waste time; and
10. Have a secretary take and distribute the minutes of the meeting within one week from the date of the meeting. Minutes should record the issue and the decisions. Brief reports of the points of a discussion may be included. When minutes are verbatim accounts of the meeting, the secretary wastes time and so do the readers—if in fact the minutes are read.

(Rigolosi, 2012, pp. 228–229)

Figure 2.7 Managing for Effective Meetings

and human service organization is considered a first-line manager.

3. In most settings this manager is usually classified as a functional manager because he or she provides a specialized service.
4. The four functions of management were described. The first-line manager in the health and human service organization is responsible for oversight and allocation of a diverse set of resources including physical resources, technological resources, financial resources, and human resources. Therapeutic recreation manager responsibilities and challenges were noted.
5. Consideration was given to challenges associated with making the transition from practitioner to first-line manager.
6. Stress-management and time-management strategies were discussed.

Critical Thinking Activities

1. Conduct an Internet search and identify the types of agencies in which therapeutic recreation is practiced. Identify the names or titles of therapeutic recreation services units in various types of therapeutic recreation agencies. Compare the common job titles for first-line managers within various types of therapeutic recreation agencies.
2. Interview several therapeutic recreation managers about the responsibilities of a first-line manager. Compare responsibilities in different types of organizations such as hospitals, residential facilities, community agencies, and nonprofit agencies. Describe the common responsibilities and the common challenges experienced by first-line managers.
3. Conduct an Internet search of professional organizations that serve therapeutic recreation professionals and the certification/licensure standards in therapeutic recreation. Identify the resources available to assist first-line managers.
4. Are you interested in being a first-line manager? Prepare a one-page summary of the skills that you bring to the management experience; identify skills that you will continue to develop.

References

American Psychological Association (2007). *Stress tip sheet*. Retrieved from http://www.apa.org/news/press/release/2007/10/stress-tips.aspx

Arnold, M., Glover, R., & Beeler, C. (2012). *Human resources management in recreation, sport, and leisure services*. State College, PA: Venture Publishing, Inc.

Edginton, C. R., Hudson, S. D., Lankford, S. V., & Larsen, D. (2008). *Managing recreation and leisure services: An introduction*. Champaign IL: Sagamore.

French, J. R. P., Jr., & Raven, B. (1968). The base of social power. In D. Cartwright & A. Zander (Eds.), *Group dynamics* (3rd ed, pp. 262–268). New York: Harper & Row.

Gifford, E. (2009). *It's 3am—Are you checking email again?* AOL Corporate Newsroom Statistic, 45th Annual Email Addiction Survey 2009, AOL.

Hurd, A. R., Barcelona,R. J., & Meldrum, J. T. (2008). *Leisure services management.* Champaign, IL: Human Kinetics.

Kraut, A. I. (1989). The role of the manager: What's really important in different management jobs. *Academy of Management Executive, 3*(4), 286–293.

Lexamark International study, Wall Street Journal 12/12/2006. Retrieved from http://www.keyorganization.com/time-management-statistics.php

Lussier, R., & Kimball, D. (2009). *Applied sport management skills.* Champaign, IL: Human Kinetics.

Rigolosi, E. (2012). *Management and leadership in nursing and health care: An experiential approach* (3rd ed.). New York: Springer.

Robbins, S. P. (1997). *Managing today.* Upper Saddle River, NJ: Prentice-Hall.

Robbins, S. P., & Decenzo, D. (2004). *The fundamentals of management: Essential concepts and applications* (4th ed.). Upper Saddle River, NJ: Prentice-Hall.

Salacuse, J. W. (2006). *Leading leaders.* New York: AMACOM.

Selye, H. (1974). *Stress without distress.* Philadelphia: J. B. Lippincott.

Smith M., Segal, J., & Segal, R. (2012). *Preventing burnout: Signs, symptoms, causes, and coping strategies.* Helpguide. Retrieved from http://www.helpguide.org/mental/burnout_signs_symptons.htm

Sullivan, E. (2013). *Effective leadership and management in nursing* (8th ed.). Boston: Pearson.

Wren, D. A. (1979). *The evolution of management thought* (2nd ed.). New York: John Wiley & Sons.

Chapter 3
Managing and Leading

Keywords

- Goals
- Hawthorne effect
- Leadership
- Manager
- Mission
- Objective
- Planning statements
- Power
- Vision

Learning Outcomes

After reading this chapter students will be able to:

1. Compare and contrast the roles and responsibilities of managers and leaders.
2. Identify and summarize the key ideas of four eras of management theory.
3. Define leadership in your own words.
4. Contrast the seven types of power and give an example of each type of power.
5. Create a model that shows the relationships among the organization's vision, mission, goals, and objectives.

Overview

Management and leadership are similar in many ways. Both involve working with people and influencing them to accomplish common goals. Both managers and leaders are found in organizations that provide therapeutic recreation services. However, Kotter (1990) indicated that management and leadership are clearly different in some important ways. Figure 3.1 summarizes and contrasts the functions of management and leadership (see p. 24).

Learning Outcome
Compare and contrast the roles and responsibilities of managers and leaders.

Every health and human service organization needs both managers and leaders to prosper and succeed. This chapter defines management and leadership and provides a historical overview of the study of management theory and leadership theory.

Management

A *manager* "is an individual employed by an organization who is responsible and accountable for efficiently accomplishing the goals of the organization" (Sullivan, 2013, p. 41). The manager is responsible for planning, organizing, leading, and controlling. Additionally, the manager in the health and human service organization is responsible for oversight and allocation of a diverse set of physical, technological, fiscal, and human resources. Marquis & Huston (2012) indicate that managers have an assigned position within the formal organization. They have a legitimate source of power due to the delegated authority that accompanies their position. Managers are expected to carry out specific functions, duties, and responsibilities and exercise control, decision making, and decision analysis. They are accountable to achieve results. Managers are responsible for allocating and coordinating people, the environment, money, time, and other resources to achieve organizational goals. Finally, they direct willing and unwilling subordinates.

This section of the chapter presents a historical review of management theory.

Management Theory

The study of management has been in existence for thousands of years and can be traced back to the Egyptians. The mere physical presence of the pyramids is evidence

	Management	Leadership
ROLE	• Produces order and consistency	• Produces change and movement
POWER	• Legitimate/Position power	• Personal power
PLANNING	• Setting deadlines and timelines • Allocating resources	• Visioning • Communicating • Strategizing
LEADING	• Assigning • Delegating	• Motivating • Inspiring • Energizing • Empowering
ORGANIZING	• Providing structure • Making job placements • Establishing rules and procedures	• Aligning people • Seeking commitment • Building teams and coalitions
CONTROLLING	• Solving problems • Developing incentives • Generating creative solutions • Taking corrective action	• Motivating, inspiring, and energizing • Empowering subordinates • Satisfying unmet needs

Figure 3.1 Functions of Management and Leadership

Learning Outcome
Identify and summarize the key ideas of four eras of management theory.

that there had to exist formal management systems. However, the study of management from a scientific perspective did not begin until the late 19th century. No single theory of management that explains all human behavior is universally accepted. This section includes an overview of four eras of management theory:

1. Classical management theory
2. Behavioral school theory
3. Human relations theory
4. Modern management theory

Classical Management Theory

Classical management theory emerged with the Industrial Revolution during the late 1880s and early 1900s. While several theorists have contributed to classical management theory, it was Frederick W. Taylor who played a dominant role in its early development and is considered "the father of scientific management" (Wren, 1987). Taylor's focus was on making an organization more efficient. In his book, *The Principles of Scientific Management* (1911), Taylor offered the following four principles of scientific management to maximize individual productivity:

1. Develop a "science" for every job by studying motion, standardizing the work, and improving working conditions.
2. Carefully select workers with the correct abilities for the job.
3. Carefully train these workers to do the job and offer them incentives to produce.
4. Support the workers by planning their work and by removing obstacles. (Wren, 1987)

Henry Gantt, Frank and Lillian Gilbreth, and Morris Cooke contributed to scientific management. Gantt humanized Taylor's differential piece-rate system by combining a guaranteed day rate (i.e., minimum wage) with an above-standard bonus (Kreitner, 1992; Robbins & Decenzo, 2004; Roth, 2000). Gantt is best known for creating a graphic bar chart that is commonly used by managers to monitor production costs (Roth, 2000). The Gilbreths were focused on efficiency and conducted time and motion studies of labor to develop their "least-waste" method. Their approach focused not on how long it took to complete a piece of work but rather on the best way to do it (Roth, 2000). The "one best way" was the one that required the fewest motions to accomplish (Wren, 1987). Cooke broadened the ideas of scientific management to include their application in universities and municipal organizations. He recognized that the concepts of efficiency, so valuable to the for-profit sector, could be equally valuable in nonprofit and service organizations (Robbins, 1980).

Henri Fayol was the first to focus on managing the total organization. Fayol primarily studied the upper-level management of organizations and felt that the need for managerial ability increased in relative importance as an individual advanced to upper-level management (Fayol, 1949). Fayol's work provided definitions regarding the basic functions for management: planning, organizing, commanding, coordinating, and controlling (Robbins & Decenzo, 2004). If goals are to be accomplished, these functions must be carried out (Fayol, 1949). Fayol defined management in these words:

> To manage is to forecast and plan, to organize, to command, to coordinate, and to control. To foresee and provide means examining the future and drawing up the plan of action. To organize means building up the dual structure, material and human, of the undertaking. To command means binding together, unifying and harmonizing all activity and effort. To control means seeing that everything occurs in conformity with established rule and expressed demand. (Fayol, 1949, pp. 5–6)

Fayol came to the conclusion that there was a set of management principles that could be used in all types of management situations regardless of the organization. Further, these principles should be used to implement the five functions (i.e., planning, organizing, commanding, coordinating, and controlling). Fayol (1949, pp. 19–20) identified the principles of management as follows:

1. Division of work
2. Authority
3. Discipline
4. Unity of command
5. Unity of direction
6. Subordination of individual interest to the general interest
7. Remuneration
8. Centralization
9. Scalar chain (line of authority)
10. Order
11. Equity
12. Stability or tenure of personnel
13. Initiative
14. Esprit de corps

Behavioral Management Theory

Behavioral management theory was initiated by Elton Mayo and his studies at Western Electric Company's Hawthorne Plant. Mayo (1933) conducted a series of studies intended to contribute to the concepts of scientific management theory but which ultimately demonstrated the impact of small group dynamics on production. Small groups of women and men were selected for an intensive study focusing on the impact of physical working conditions, the psychological capacity of the worker on productivity, and how monetary incentives played a role in work behavior. Mayo found that physical comfort and pay had little impact on productivity. His work revealed the tendency for people to perform better because of special attention and being singled out and made to feel important. This tendency became known as the *Hawthorne effect*. Mayo (1933) pointed out in *The Human Problems of an Industrial Civilization* that emotional factors are important in productivity. He also urged managers to provide work that stimulated personal satisfaction. He proposed that improvements be made by creating a less formal organizational structure and by permitting more employee participation in decision making. The implication of Mayo's studies relative to the therapeutic recreation manager is quite clear. Sometimes the only thing required to meet people's needs is to pay attention to them.

Mary Parker Follett is another behavioral scientist who suggested to managers that employees are a "complex conviction of emotions, beliefs, attitudes, and habits" (Kreitner, 1992, p. 52). Because she believed that managers had to recognize the individual's motivating desires to get employees to produce more, she suggested that managers persuade and inspire performance rather than demand it. By relying on expertise and knowledge to lead staff, rather than the formal authority of their positions, Follett suggested the workplace, like life, is developmental and the lines between one's workplace and life and between workers and managers should be erased (Roth, 2000).

In the development of the behavioral management theory, Chester Barnard is recognized as one of the outstanding contributors. According to Barnard (1938), the success of an organization depends on the cooperation of its employees and maintaining good relations with people and institutions outside the organization. The current interest in developing cooperative work groups, teams, and agency partnerships; making health care more socially responsive; and matching organizational strategies to opportunities in the community are the results of Barnard's ideas (Robbins & Decenzo, 2004).

In summary, the behavioral school brought together newly developed theories, methods, and techniques of the relevant social sciences on the study of interpersonal and intrapersonal phenomena in the organization. According to the advocates of the behavioral approach to management, today's technology, work rules, and standards do not guarantee good job performance. Success depends on motivated and skilled individuals who are committed to organizational objectives. The function of the manager is to obtain employee cooperation so they work toward organizational goals (Tappen, 2001). Our current understanding of employee motivation, organizational cultures, high-performance teams, performance appraisals, conflict management, and negotiation techniques are due in large part to the contributions of behavioral scientists (Robbins & Decenzo, 2004).

Human Relations Management Theory

Later theorists, including Kurt Lewin (1951), Abraham Maslow (1954), Douglas McGregor (1960), influenced a humanistic approach to management. Maslow is well-known for his theory based on a hierarchy of needs—physiological, safety, love and belonging, self-esteem, and self-actualization. Organizations and management theories, according to Maslow, ignore the human being's intrinsic nature and are detrimental to the psychic and physical health and well-being of employees. Although these needs, especially higher-level needs, may be suppressed, ignoring basic human needs would on Maslow's view contribute to lower productivity, high absenteeism, high turnover, low morale, and job dissatisfaction. Maslow's theory of the hierarchy of needs led to theories on motivation (Maslow, 1968). Figure 3.2 shows Maslow's theory of the hierarchy of needs.

McGregor continued to contribute to the human relations movement. His theme was people are basically good. To stimulate performance, managers should humanize work. McGregor believed that the organization should let people participate and take an active role in those decisions that affect them, have trust and confidence in people, and reduce external controls. He developed a set of assumptions about human behavior called Theory X and Theory Y. In McGregor's view, Theory X focused on the tasks to be done. In contrast, Theory Y focused on the employees and their job satisfaction. According to McGregor, Theory Y was a more appropriate view for managers to take (McGregor, 1960). Theory Y presents a more optimistic view of employees' nature and behavior at work. McGregor encouraged cordial team relations, responsible and stimulating jobs, and participation in decision making. Figure 3.3 summarizes McGregor's Theory X and Theory Y assumptions.

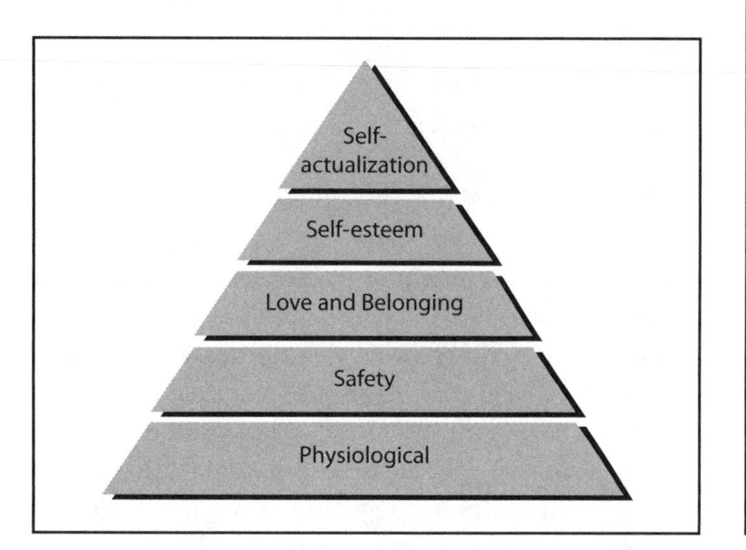

Figure 3.2 Functions of Management and Leadership

Theory X

1. An average employee intrinsically does not like work and tries to escape it whenever possible.
2. Since the employee does not want to work, he must be persuaded, compelled, or warned with punishment so as to achieve organizational goals. Close supervision is required on the part of managers.
3. Many employees rank job security as a top priority, and they have little or no aspiration/ambition.
4. Employees generally dislike responsibilities.
5. Employees resist change.

Theory Y

1. Employees can perceive their job as relaxing and normal. They want to exercise their physical and mental efforts in their jobs.
2. Employees can use self-direction and self-control to achieve the organizational objectives.
3. If the job is rewarding and satisfying, then it will result in employees' loyalty and commitment to the organization.
4. An average employee can recognize and accept responsibility.
5. The employees have skills and capabilities. Their logical capabilities should be fully utilized. The creativity, resourcefulness, and innovative potentiality of the employees can be utilized to solve organizational problems.

Figure 3.3 Theory X and Theory Y Assumptions

More recently, a Theory Z (Ouchi, 1981) has been proposed that suggests a middle ground between Theory X and Theory Y. The Theory Z model attempts to integrate common business practices from the United States and Japan. Theory Z takes a humanistic viewpoint and focuses on developing better ways to motivate people. In addition, Theory Z emphasizes collective or participative decision making, collective responsibility as opposed to personal responsibility, and recognition of mutual dependence (Ouchi, 1981). Like Maslow's theory, Theories X, Y, and Z have influenced managers as they create a motivating work environment.

In summary, according to the advocates of the behavioral approach to management, today's technology, work rules, and standards do not guarantee good job performance. Success depends on motivated and skilled individuals who are committed to organizational objectives. The function of the manager is to obtain employee cooperation so they work toward organizational goals (Whitehead, Weiss, & Tappen, 2010). Our current understanding of employee motivation, organizational cultures, high-performance teams, performance appraisals, conflict management, and negotiation techniques are due in large part to the contributions of behavioral scientists (Robbins & Decenzo, 2004).

Modern Management Theory

General Systems Theory

In the 1950s, an Austrian-born biologist named von Bertalanffy described a general systems theory that began as a biological theory and was later adapted and applied to management and organizations. According to von Bertalanffy (1972, p. 411), "in order to understand an organized whole we must know both the parts and the relations between them." The systems theory defines a system as a set of interrelated parts arranged in a unified whole to accomplish a common goal (Robbins, 1983). The organization's productivity is a result of the interactions among the interrelated parts such as the organizational structure, financial resources, technology, employees, and the clients, to name just a few. If one part of the system is removed, the nature of the system is changed as well. The key to a systems approach is the idea of stability in the organization. The more stable the organization, the more effectively the organization will respond to problems. The systems theory can be applied to any system within the organization including programs, departments, teams, as well as the organization as a whole. Systems theory has had a significant effect on management and understanding organizations.

Stumbo and Peterson's (2009) *Therapeutic Recreation Program Design: Principles and Procedures* takes a systems approach to programming. The therapeutic recreation process has characteristics of an open system: it is open, flexible, and dynamic; it is planned and goal directed; it interacts with the environment; and it emphasizes feedback. Input (i.e., data) from the consumer and practitioner is transformed by the process of analyzing, planning, and implementing, all of which occur throughout the therapeutic recreation process. The output (i.e., consumer response) is then evaluated.

Systems are either open or closed. Closed systems are usually self-contained. Open systems, on the other hand, interact with the surrounding environment for survival (see Figure 3.4). Environmental factors include political, social, and economic variables that influence system performance. By taking into account its environment, the organization's structure, process, and performance are centrally influenced by the nature of the inputs taken in from the environment and the outputs produced. Organizations such as hospitals and departments of parks and recreation are open systems because their survival depends on interaction with the surrounding environments.

The Input-Process-Output (IPO) model of Carter and Van Andel (2011) is another example of a systems approach to program design. Moreover, the IPO model

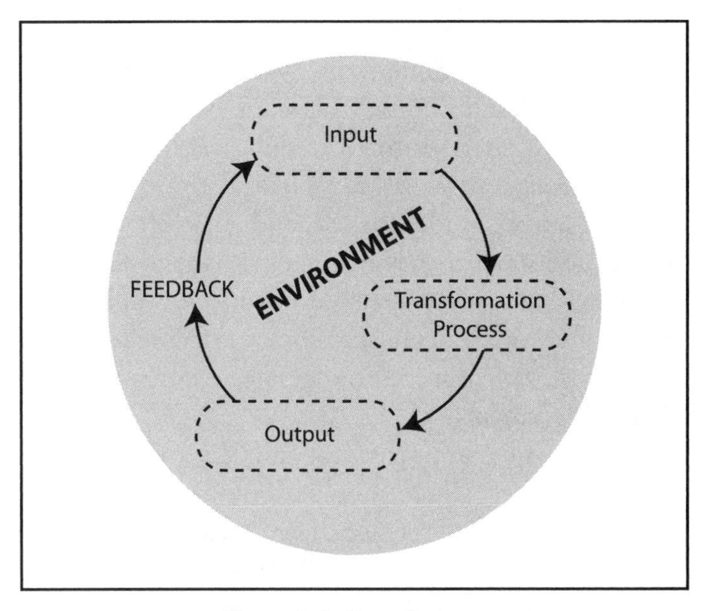

Figure 3.4 Open System

is associated with Riley's (1991) outcome-evaluation model and quality-of-care indicators.

Contingency Theory

Today, virtually all health and human service organizations must cope with an environment more complex, more changeable, and therefore more uncertain than the environments in which health care organizations have operated in the past. To meet the challenges of change, a new approach to the theory and practice of management has emerged. Contingency theory suggests that appropriate managerial behavior is contingent on a variety of elements (Kast & Rosenzweig, 1985). These elements may be the environment (e.g., consumers, third-party payers), personnel (e.g., training, shortage of staff), regulations (e.g., Americans with Disabilities Act), technology, department or organization size and goals, the administrator's power and influence, or clarity and equity of reward systems. The contingency approach is helpful to management because it emphasizes situational appropriateness. As noted by Kreitner (1992, p. 60), "People, organizations, and problems are too complex to justify rigid adherence to universal principles of organizations." According to the contingency theory, managers enhance agency performance by matching organizational structure to its environment. Therefore, the nature of therapeutic recreation services will vary with the unique features of the setting and each consumer's particular situation.

Management Theory and Therapeutic Recreation

Management is getting things done through people. Therapeutic recreation practitioners have human needs, perceptions, and aspirations. Material surroundings, wages and hours, or work cannot be considered in isolation. No therapeutic recreation practitioner should be viewed as motivated strictly by economic or rational considerations. Values, beliefs, and emotions influence each practitioner's behavior. A sensitive manager is aware of individual differences. A humanistic management atmosphere, with an emphasis on management theories to improve service, is essential for effective organizational goal achievement.

Today's environment demands diverse approaches to management. There is no best form of management for the delivery of therapeutic recreation service. The optimal management approach is contingent on the factors that confront the therapeutic recreation manager in any setting—providing the highest possible level of consumer care and service while at the same time meeting other conflicting goals, such as staying within budget and keeping staff practitioners satisfied. The contingency theory of management, complemented by the systems approach, offers a viable management approach.

Leadership

Learning Outcome
Define leadership in your own words.

There are many ways to finish the sentence, "Leadership is . . ." In fact, as Stogdill (1974) pointed out in a review of leadership research, "there are almost as many definitions of leadership as there are people who have tried to define it" (p. 7). Northouse (2010, p. 3) offers a clear, concise definition: "*Leadership* is a process whereby an individual influences a group of individuals to achieve a common goal." The four components that have been identified as central to leadership are: "(a) Leadership is a process, (b) Leadership involves influence, (c) Leadership occurs in groups, (d) Leadership involves common goals" (Northouse, 2010, p. 3).

While managers have formal authority and responsibility for the quality of work performed by their employees, leaders do not have formal authority. However, an effective leader has "the ability to cause individuals to act willingly in a desired way for the benefit of the group" (Salacuse, 2006, p. 21). When a practitioner who does not have a management role uses their interpersonal and communication skills to guide and influence coworkers to complete a goal or task, the practitioner is demonstrating leadership.

Leadership Theory

Since the beginning of humankind, some people have led and some people have followed. As people began to recognize the phenomena of leading and following, the study of leadership began. Early leadership theories identified the personal characteristics that contribute to leadership. Later theories considered the leader's actions or behaviors. A third era of leadership theory explored the situation or contingencies that explain leadership. Most recently, contemporary theories have evolved as the result of the need to humanize working environments and improve organizational performance (Sullivan, 2013).

1. Leaders need to be more intelligent than the group they lead.
2. Leaders mostly possess initiative or the ability to perceive and start courses of action not considered by others.
3. Creativity is an asset.
4. Leaders must possess emotional maturity, integrity, a sense of purpose and direction, persistence, dependability, and objectivity.
5. Communication skills are important.
6. Persuasion often is used by leaders to gain the consent of followers.
7. Leaders need to be perceptive enough to distinguish their allies from their opponents and to place subordinates in suitable positions.
8. Leaders participate in social activities. They can socialize with all kinds of people and adapt to various groups.

Hein and Nicholson (1990)

Figure 3.5 Examples of Common Leadership Traits

Trait Theories

Until the mid-1940s, the trait theory was the basis for most leadership research. According to these trait theories, individuals possessing a certain combination of physical, personal, and social traits would be effective leaders. The *Great Man Theory* is an example of an early trait theory. According to this theory, "great leaders are born, not made." By 1950, more than 100 characteristics had been identified as essential to successful leadership (Adorno, Frenkel-Brunswik, Levinson, & Sanford, 1950). While research studies have identified the importance of some traits, specific traits common to all leaders have not been identified in the research. Hein and Nicholson (1990) identified examples of common leadership traits (see Figure 3.5).

It is interesting to note that despite their limitations and contradictions, aspects of trait theories are often used as the basis for management decisions and the identification of successful leaders today (Marquis & Huston, 2012; Sullivan 2013). For example, the most physically imposing or most highly skilled therapeutic recreation practitioner in a group may be chosen as a manager on the basis of these particular leadership traits.

Behavioral Theories

During the 1930s, a second era of leadership research emerged, and it focused on the leader's behaviors and actions rather than the personal traits of the leader. This research was known as behavioral theory. According to behavioral theory, leadership was developed through training, education, and life experiences. Among the most influential and comprehensive of the behavioral research and theories are those of Lewin and Lippit (1938), Rensis Likert's (1967) Michigan studies, the Ohio State University group (Stogdill, 1974), and Blake and Mouton's (1964) managerial grid.

Autocratic

The leader solves the problem or makes the decision using information available to the leader at the time. Decisions are made alone. The focus is on accomplishment of the task rather than relationships. This style is useful in crisis situations.

Democratic

The leader shares the problem with the relevant team members as a group. Together they generate and evaluate alternatives and attempt to reach agreement (consensus) on a solution. The leader does not try to influence the group to adopt a solution and is willing to accept and implement the solution that has support of the entire group. This style creates a spirit of collaboration and joint effort that results in team members' satisfaction.

Laissez-faire

The leader takes a permissive style that assumes team members are mature, internally motivated, and self-directed. The leader provides little or no direction or facilitation. This style promotes creativity and brainstorming.

Bureaucratic

The leader relies on policy and rules to identify goals and direct work processes. Based on a lack of security and trust in themselves and the follower, this leader exercises power by applying fixed, relatively inflexible rules, and avoids decision making without formal standards. This style ensures that the same rules and policies are applied to every situation.

Figure 3.6 Behavior Styles of Leadership

The behaviorists viewed leadership as including not only the qualities of the leader but also the task, expectations, and capabilities of the group. Groups have two major functions. The first function is the performance of a task or achievement of a goal. For example, in therapeutic recreation service the goal is the delivery of quality service. The second function of a group is to strengthen the group itself. In therapeutic recreation service, examples of strengthening the group would include professional development activities and team-building activities to maintain high staff morale. According to behavior-based theorists, effective leaders acquire a pattern of learned behaviors. Figure 3.6 summarizes behavioral styles of leadership.

Theorists have come to realize that leadership tends to fall on a continuum and varies with the situation rather than fitting one behavioral style regardless of the nature

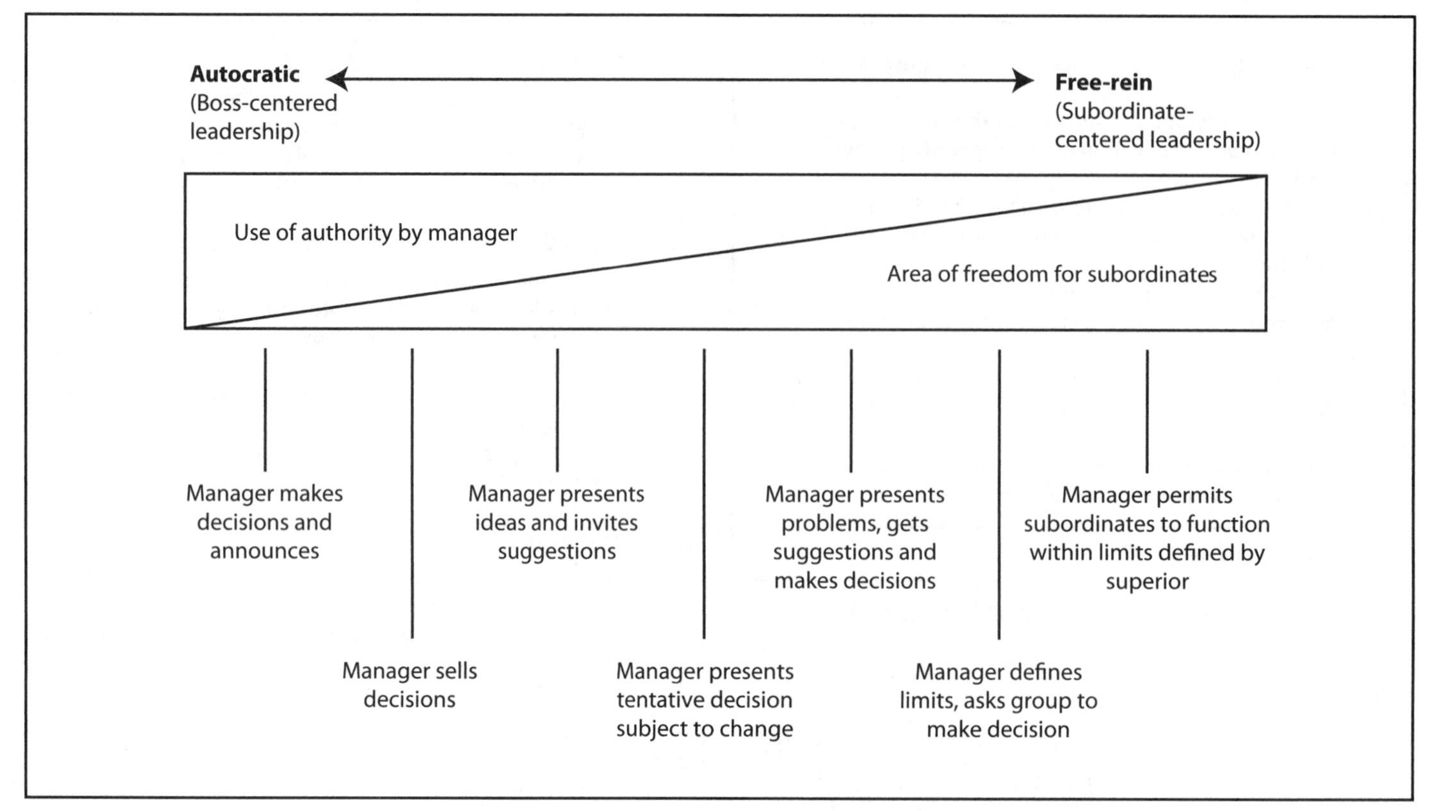

Figure 3.7 Continuum of Leadership Behavior

of the experience. Further, the behaviorists found very little success in identifying consistent relationships between patterns of leadership behavior and successful performance. The full continuum of leadership behaviors is shown in Figure 3.7. As an example, the therapeutic recreation manager using the ideal approach would focus on accomplishing the goals while at the same time maintaining open communication and an environment of mutual trust and respect among staff members.

According to Tannenbaum and Schmidt (1983), successful leaders know which behavior is the most appropriate at a particular time. The effective manager shapes their behavior after a careful analysis of self, subordinates, and organizational factors.

Contingency Theories

Contingency theories became popular during the 1950s and developed from the failure of the trait theory and behavioral theories to address the significance of the environment, the organization, the goals, and the situation on leadership. A number of contingency theories are explained in the following sections.

Fiedler's Contingency Model

One of the earliest contingency theories was Fiedler's Contingency Model of Leadership Effectiveness (Fiedler, 1967). The focus of attention in this model was on the performance of the group. Fiedler argued that effective group performance depends on the proper match between the leader's style of interacting with subordinates and the degree to which the situation gives control and influence to the leader. Fiedler identified three aspects of a situation that structure the leader's role: (a) leader-member relations, (b) task structure, and (c) leader position power. Leader-member relations involve the amount of confidence and loyalty the subordinates have in their leader. Task structure refers to the degree to which a task can be defined and measured in terms of progress toward completion. The structure is generally high if progress is easy to define and measure and low if it is difficult to define and measure. Position power relates to the leader's authority in the organization (e.g., hiring, firing, reward, punishment). Fiedler stated that the more positive the leader-member relationship, the more highly structured the task, and the greater the position power, the greater the influence. In addition, of the three situational dimensions, the most important is leader-member followed by task structure. The least important is position power. Fiedler's contingency theory model is shown in Figure 3.8. In summary, Fiedler (1967, p. 32) believed "successful leadership was an interaction of leadership styles and the situation."

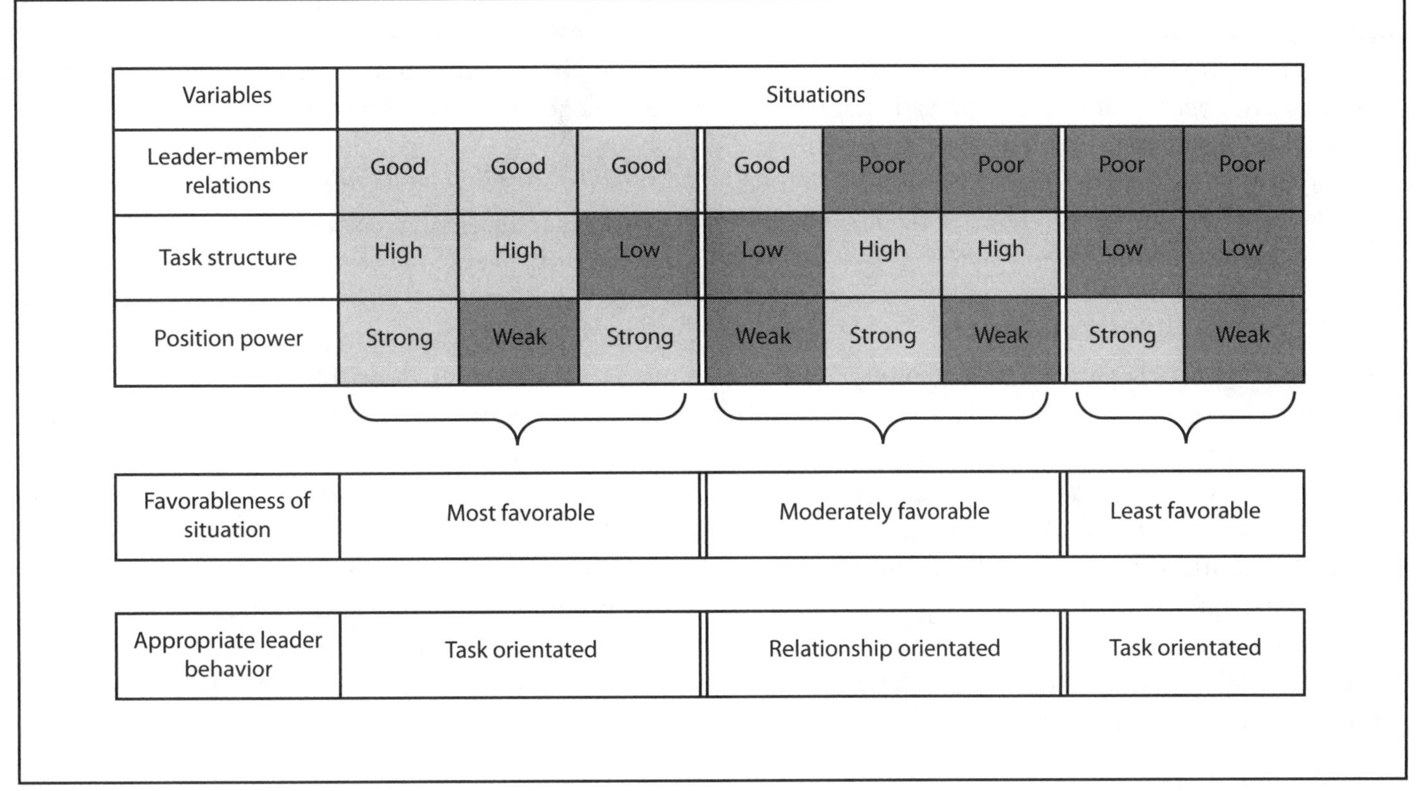

Figure 3.8 Fiedler's Contingency Theory Model

Life-Cycle Model

The life-cycle theory of Hersey and Blanchard (1982) states that the leader's behavior will vary based on the maturity of the subordinates and the situation. Job maturity is defined by the individual's technical knowledge and skill in performing a task. This is combined with the individual's feeling of self-esteem and confidence. An individual can be extremely mature, both personally and in relation to the task, in one particular situation; however, if the situation changes, the person may experience a decrease in maturity in relation to either the task itself or feelings of self-confidence. For example, an experienced psychiatric therapeutic recreation practitioner understands his or her role, has the knowledge and skills necessary to provide quality service to the patient, and is confident in the relationship with both peers and other professionals. The therapeutic recreation manager gives this practitioner a great deal of program freedom and finds ways of intellectually challenging the staff member. If this practitioner transfers to the physical rehabilitation unit within the hospital, the practitioner will have to learn new skills and develop a new set of relationships. Temporarily, the practitioner will experience feelings of insecurity. Both personal and job maturity will decrease and the practitioner will require direction from the manager in this unit. As the practitioner gains knowledge and confidence, the manager allows more freedom and supports the practitioner in making decisions and implementing service. The life-cycle model, shown in Figure 3.9 (see p. 32), therefore emphasizes the importance of the maturity level of the staff. As employees mature, "leadership style becomes less task focused and more relationship oriented" (Marquis & Huston, 2012, p. 39).

Path-Goal Model

Path-goal theory is about how leaders motivate subordinates to accomplish goals. This theory focuses on employee motivation as a means to enhance employee performance and employee satisfaction. "Employees will be motivated if they think they are capable of performing their work, if they believe their efforts will result in a certain outcome, and if they believe that the payoffs for doing their work are worthwhile" (Northouse, 2010, p. 125).

According to House and Mitchell (1974), the leader will consider the situation and the characteristics of the individual involved and determine what leadership style will increase the subordinate's motivation to perform the task or reach the goal. In brief, the leader shows the way down the "path" to reach the goal and provides rewards for the individual as an incentive. "Path-goal theory provides a set of general recommendations based on characteristics of subordinates and tasks for how leaders should act in various situations if they want to be effective. "It informs us about when to be directive, supportive, participative, or achievement-oriented" (Northouse, 2010, p. 135). Figure 3.10 illustrates the Path-goal theory of leadership.

Contemporary Theories

Managers in today's health and human service environment place increasing value on collaboration and team work. The complexity of the work environment requires coordination and cooperation among managers and staff. "Leaders must use additional skills, especially group and political leadership skills, to create collegial work environments" (Sullivan, 2013, p. 42). The more recent leadership theories emphasize mutual goals of leaders and followers focusing on the relational nature of leader-participant interactions (Russell, 2012).

Transactional Leadership

Transactional leadership refers to a group of leadership models that focus on the exchanges that occur between leaders and followers (Northouse, 2010). Leadership is viewed as a series of transactions or exchanges. "Leaders are successful to the extent that they understand and meet the needs of followers and use incentives to enhance employee loyalty and performance" (Sullivan, 2013, p. 43). Transactional leaders help staff to recognize task responsibilities, identify goals, and meet desired performance levels. Transactional leadership is aimed at maintaining the status quo by performing work according to desired standards of practice emphasizing interpersonal dependence and reward for achieving the standard.

Transformational Leadership

Transformational leaders enhance the motivation, morale, and performance of followers by connecting the follower's sense of identity and self to the mission and the collective identity of the organization. The leader serves as a role model who inspires their followers. Transformational leaders understand the needs and motives of followers and seek to help them reach their fullest potential (Northouse, 2010). The manager who has a vision and empowers staff to effect change as a result of their commitment to this ideal is transformational. Transformational leaders encourage others to exercise leadership. "The transformational leader inspires followers and uses power to instill a belief that followers also have the ability to do exceptional things" (Sullivan, 2013, p. 43).

Charismatic Leadership

In his theory of charismatic leadership, House (1976) suggested that charismatic leaders act in unique ways that have specific charismatic effects on their followers. The personality characteristics of charismatic leaders include dominance, having a strong desire to influence others, self-confidence, and a strong sense of one's own moral values. In addition, charismatic leaders demonstrate four specific behaviors. First, the charismatic leader is a strong role model for the beliefs and values they want their followers to adopt. Second, the charismatic leader appears competent to followers. Third, they articulate

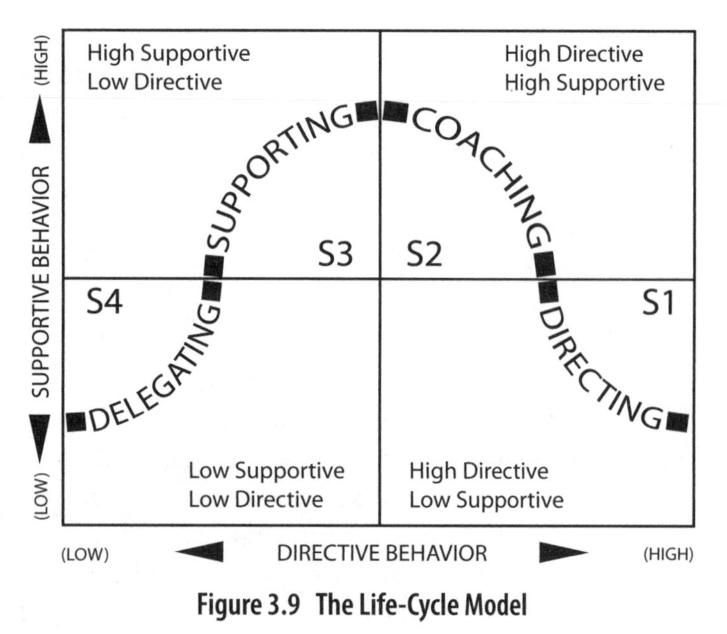

Figure 3.9 The Life-Cycle Model

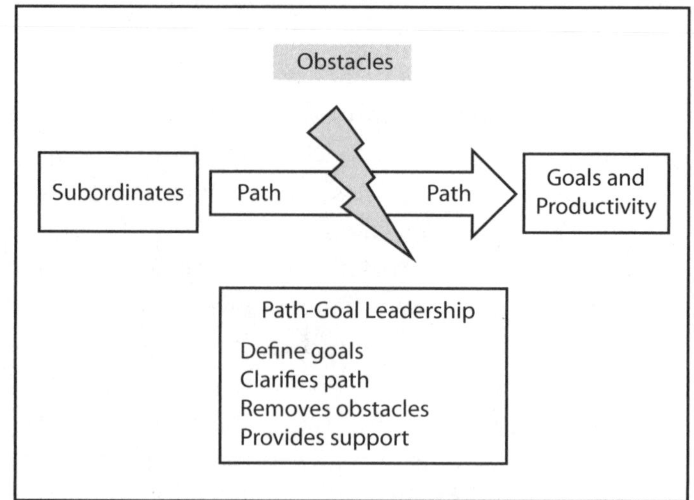

Figure 3.10 Path-Goal Theory

ideological goals and have moral overtones. Finally, charismatic leaders communicate high expectations for followers and demonstrate confidence in the followers' ability to achieve these expectations (Northouse, 2010). It is important to recognize that few leaders possess genuine charisma.

In summary, health and human service organizations require a variety of innovative leadership approaches to add to a more humanistic work environment while improving organizational performance. Today, effective therapeutic leaders have the ability to use diverse leadership styles to serve client consumers and achieve organizational goals.

Leadership and Power

Base of Power

Power is the ability to impose the will or desire of one person, or group of persons, on another individual, or group of individuals, to influence and alter behavior. Power does not exist by itself—it is always part of a relationship. How that power is used ultimately determines the effectiveness of the leader (Hersey & Blanchard, 1982). To gain power, effectively maintain it, and skillfully use it, therapeutic recreation managers must be aware of the sources and types of power. They must also understand how that power may be applied within the client-customer care-delivery process. Power is classified as either position power or personal power. Position power is based on an assigned position or job within the organization. On the other hand, personal power is the result of interpersonal skills and the ability to build trust and establish relationships.

Learning Outcome

Contrast the seven types of power and give an example of each type of power.

French and Raven (1968) are credited with identifying five types of power. They explained the sources or bases from which power emanates and called these bases legitimate, coercive, reward, expert, and referent. The therapeutic recreation manager has legitimate power and authority based on his or her position. Reward and coercive powers are present based on the right to hire, evaluate, promote, or discharge individuals. Expert power is derived from professional knowledge and demonstrated management skills. Referent power may also be present based on attractiveness and a pleasant, motivating personality. Hersey and Blanchard (1982) added information power, the ability to gain and share valuable information, and connection power, connections with influential people, for a total of seven types of power. Besides the sources of their own power, therapeutic recreation managers need to be aware of and concerned with the power of others, since the source of others' power can dilute his or her power. There is no one best type of power. Effective leaders use as many of the seven bases of power as possible. "Each of these bases of power increases a leader's capacity to influence the attitudes, values, or behaviors of others" (Northouse, 2010, p. 7). The seven types of power are considered in more detail below.

1. *Reward power* comes from the ability of the manager to give awards. The use of positive sanctions is the hallmark of a good manager. This is demonstrated through compensation, verbal praise, taking staff to lunch, and so forth. When monetary rewards are insufficient or nonexistent, then subtle forms of reward and acknowledgment assume special importance. One who can distribute rewards that others view as valuable will have power over them.
2. *Coercive power* is the opposite of reward power—a manager deliberately withholds rewards or punishes to promote compliance. Staff react to this power out of fear of the negative ramifications resulting from failing to comply. Withholding sanctions is clearly part of the system. For example, an employee whose performance is unsatisfactory does not deserve a merit increase. This type of power can be somewhat subjective.
3. *Legitimate power* relates to official position in the organizational hierarchy. In most organizations, this power is recognized. In health and human service organizations, the physicians have a unique power.
4. *Referent power*, sometimes called *charismatic power*, is the therapeutic recreation manager's ability to use influence because the staff identifies with the manager as a leader. Employees generally identify with a person who has the

resources or personal traits they believe are desirable. If a manager's leadership style is working, staff practitioners will choose to emulate some of the manager's more attractive qualities. Thus, the greater the attraction, the greater the identification, and subsequently the greater the referent power.

5. *Expert power* is the influence a manager possesses as a result of his or her expertise, special skill, or knowledge. Therapeutic recreation managers gain power through knowledge. Managerial knowledge and knowledge of the organization, including its mission, goals, objectives, and operations, will help a manager to acquire power.
6. *Information power* is the power that results from the ability of an individual to gain and share valuable information.
7. *Connection power* becomes a reality when the manager is perceived as having close contact with other influential people.

The wise therapeutic recreation manager will use all sources of power while moving between the various sources as circumstances warrant (see Figure 3.11).

Power Strategies

Preston (2005) offers managers in health and human service organizations several strategies to communicate leadership power. The therapeutic recreation manager can strengthen his or her power using the following approaches:

- First, powerful people remain calm when faced with negativity. They are rarely surprised, or at least rarely act surprised. They look unflappable, in touch with the facts, and in command of the situation.
- Information is a power source. Powerful people share information. Preston advises leaders to cultivate a powerful image by ensuring that those around them are informed and knowledgeable. Information sharing establishes the manager's credibility as being fair and trustworthy. Preston notes that powerful people have large networks of working relationships with a wide variety of people both inside and outside the organization. These networks provide access to information, help in building coalitions, and extend a manager's reputation and image well beyond the immediate environment.
- Powerful people deliberate carefully and stand by their position. They can change their minds often while considering options; however, they stick by their decision once it is made.
- Preston advises managers to learn to accept praise. Powerful people graciously accept accolades from peers, superiors, and subordinates. A simple and honest "Thank you, I'm pleased by the outcome, too" is an appropriate response to a compliment.
- The effective manager cultivates relationships with those who can help. They collect on their debts and take advantage of returned favors. They also make sure to return favors by helping others. Seeking or receiving reciprocal favors from others enables both partners to achieve their respective goals.
- Powerful people know when to remain silent. Silence allows time to think and listen and may also prevent the manager from making fast decisions, especially in discussions that involve a controversial or difficult problem. Preston further advises learning to say no. Power is often attributed to those people who can say no and stick to that decision. The "no" has to come after careful deliberation—having looked at the proposal with an open mind and the options if it is not implemented. The "no" should be accompanied by specific reasons.
- Finally, Preston advises the manager to own their power. Dress in a style that is consistent with those in power. Take credit for successes, and let others know of significant accomplishments and contributions. Preston contends that "Being powerful is a skill." Using power in the right way requires learning strategies that will enable the manager to act the part and enhance their existing abilities (Preston, 2005, pp. 222–225).

Leadership and Supervision

If "leadership is a process whereby an individual influences a group of individuals to achieve a common goal" (Northouse, 2010, p. 3), it is a key factor in supervision. The supervisor is clearly interested in influencing the practitioner's behavior; therefore, some kind of

1. Use the least amount of power you can to be effective in your interactions with others.
2. Use power appropriate to the situation.
3. Learn when not to use power.
4. Focus on the problem, not the person.
5. Make polite requests, never arrogant demands.
6. Use coercion only when other methods don't work.
7. Keep informed to retain your credibility when using expert power.
8. Understand you may owe a return favor when you use your connection power.

(Sullivan, 2013, p. 92)

Figure 3.11 Rules of Using Power

"leadership event" must take place. The process of supervision involves helping practitioners increase their effectiveness in service delivery. The supervisor provides support and encouragement, builds skills and competencies, and oversees the practitioner's work. It is important to highlight those factors that make the first-line manager perform as a supervisor, because this is a special case of leadership in which the leadership activity is focused on directing subordinates. The first-line manager functions in a situation that requires management of professionally knowledgeable practitioners—people who base their work activities on a compendium of knowledge, skills, and abilities too extensive to be translated into a routine, standardized pattern of behavior. Knowledgeable workers expect more than mere wages from their work—they expect to derive a sense of satisfaction and self-esteem from work well done. They do not require a great deal of externally based motivation. They are, in effect, practitioners who can be defined both as achievement-motivated and as possessing high task maturity. They also may be quite determined about holding to internalized goals and values that dictate how they will proceed in work.

As first-line managers, supervisors must, by definition, occupy the only level of management charged with the responsibility of directing the work of non-management personnel. As supervisors, managers are directly responsible for the daily, face-to-face, immediate, and operative activities of a group of personnel. Getting the most out of knowledgeable workers requires special managerial skills. Those who are enthusiastic and perform exceptionally well in their jobs usually feel challenged by their work itself and take responsibility for their own jobs. Managing professionals requires more than overseeing; managers serve as guides and teachers who provide information and set standards. The uniqueness of being a manager or supervisor calls for, but is not limited to, the following abilities:

1. *Heavy reliance on technical expertise.* Supervisors are required to know the job they supervise. They spend a large portion of their time directing and overseeing the activities of their subordinates. Because of the problems they face at this level—with experienced and inexperienced personnel—they must have expert knowledge of jobs that their subordinates perform.
2. *Skills assessment.* After learning the skills required of each position, the manager must assess each practitioner's suitability for the varied positions in the department. It is up to the manager to identify areas of excellence, competence, and deficiency for every practitioner under supervision. It is important to differentiate between performance and ability.
3. *Facilitation of work.* The work environment needs to be monitored to identify barriers to accomplishments. Thus, the therapeutic recreation manager must look for barriers within the practitioner, the staff as a group, and the organization with its various support systems. One of the manager's most important tasks is the challenge of developing positive feelings of capability and potential achievement in each practitioner. In addition, the manager attempts to manage and to facilitate change rather than regard change as a threat to the status quo. As has been noted previously, the external environment for any organization today is changing rapidly. The manager, therefore, should attempt to lead practitioners to embrace change as a permanent way of life.
4. *Communication in two languages.* Communication is a problem at all levels of management. First-line managers are required to communicate in two distinct languages—that of management and that of workers. Differing educational backgrounds, value systems, and points of reference are just several of the major disparities between the two groups.
5. *Coping with role conflict.* Managers are neither fish nor fowl. They are not practitioners, and although they are officially classified as managers,

they are not often accepted by other middle-level or top-level managers. A first-line manager may be assumed to be like other managers, but the individual's activities, status, and security are at times quite different. The activities are associated with non-management personnel, the status is "low person on the totem pole" when it comes to management, and security is not always solid if performance is not tops. Finally, managers promoted from within face the task of learning new behaviors when being subtly or not so subtly coerced to retain the behaviors of the past role as a practitioner.

6. *Coping with constrained authority.* Today managers must adapt to a less autocratic style than their predecessors. Managers must also adapt to the constraints imposed by internal and external factors, such as the intricate appeals systems that most organizations provide for their workers. In addition, managers are required to interact in an authority relationship with two groups: subordinates and supervisors who are their superiors.
7. *Reinforcing employees' good performance.* On a day-to-day basis this reinforcement mainly takes place verbally or via e-mail with compliments and praise when a job has been done well. For the longer term, a variety of rewards may be used to recognize good performance (e.g., material rewards).
8. *The management's representative.* Rules, policies, procedures, and other dictates are implemented at the first-line manager level, so when practitioners think of management, their usual point of reference is their manager. This obviously places high responsibility on the managers to reflect accurately the vision, mission, goals, objectives, and attitudes of the management, a task made even more difficult because they rarely have the opportunity to participate in major policy decisions that may affect the people they directly supervise.

Professional Clinical Supervision

Clinical supervision is a formal process of professional support and learning which enables practitioners to develop knowledge and competence that maintains and improves the standard of care. The ideal is to receive clinical supervision from a supervisor of the same professional discipline, but this is not always available in the practice of therapeutic recreation.

Many therapeutic recreation practitioners function independently and are supervised by managers from other disciplines. An experienced professional of any discipline may provide clinical supervision, in particular, supervision related to the specific client group served. Thus, a therapeutic recreation practitioner working in mental health may receive clinical supervision from a psychiatrist or psychologist regarding diagnosis and intervention approaches. The ideal is to have clinical supervision from an experienced therapeutic recreation professional within the agency whose focus is on the therapist's growth as a reflective practitioner, which ultimately impacts client outcomes. Often clinical supervision is sought out in other ways. To have discipline-specific supervision, practitioners seek out professional mentors and participate in professional development opportunities available through professional membership organizations. State, regional, and national conferences provide important discipline-specific learning opportunities as well the opportunity to meet and interact with experienced practitioners.

Professional clinical supervision is a developmental process, which is designed to meet the practitioner at their particular developmental level and promote their continued learning and development. Issues addressed in clinical supervision include skill competence, assessment techniques, interpersonal assessment, client conceptualization, individual differences, intervention plans and goals, and professional ethics (Shank & Coyle, 2002). Clinical supervision occurs in individual sessions, in small groups, or in peer-facilitated groups. Techniques used in clinical supervision include face-to-face dialogue, observation, journaling, prescribed learning exercises and case presentations. The ultimate goal of the clinical supervision process is "practical wisdom," which is the accumulation of lessons learned and insights gained from years of experience (Krill, 1990). Clinical supervision is a highly valued resource that promotes competent professional practice.

Vision, Mission, Goals, and Objectives

LEARNING OUTCOME
Create a model that shows the relationships among the organization's vision, mission, goals, and objectives.

This section of the chapter focuses on planning statements that reflect the organization's vision, mission, goals, and objectives. These *planning statements* identify the organization's desired future. They describe where the organization is going and how it is going to get there. They are formal, written statements of the organization's desired future and the strategy for reaching that future. Organizations must focus their scarce resources on a limited scope of services. Planning statements that are clear and succinct keep the organization focused on the primary purpose, or business, and can discourage the organization from expanding into services in which it has limited expertise or insufficient resources to fully support. The planning process is time-consuming and demanding. Put in use, however, a well-thought-out plan dramatically increases the likelihood of the organization's future success.

Planning statements are a multi-level system of plans that have a hierarchical relationship; they are interrelated and mutually supportive. Each level of planning statements is essential to the broader statements it supports. The organization's vision statement is the broadest and most long-term of the planning statements. It is supported by a mission statement, which is supported by goals statements. Finally, objectives, the most specific, short-term planning statements, provide support to achievement of the goals statements. Figure 3.12 shows the relationships between the various planning statements.

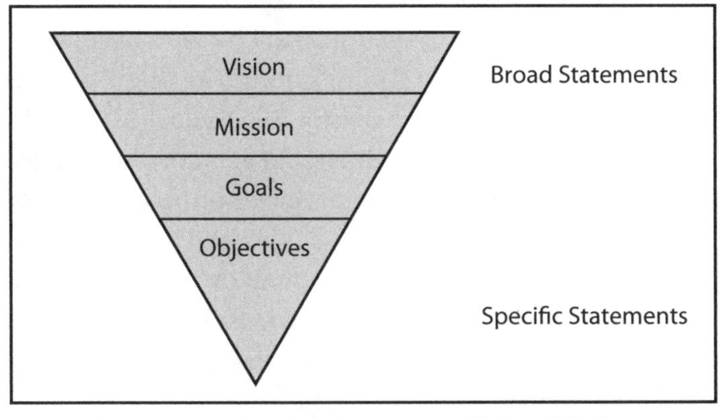

Figure 3.12 Planning Statements: Vision, Mission, Goals, and Objectives

Vision Statement

Creating the vision for the organization is the first step in the planning process. The organization's vision statement is the broadest and most long-range of all planning statements. Russoniello (1991, p. 22) defined a *vision* statement as "a description of a desired state that an organization or therapeutic recreation department commits to." According to Silvers (1994–95, p. 11) a vision statement is a "statement of what an organization stands for, what it believes in, why it exists, and what it intends to accomplish." An organization's vision statement is a word picture—a description of the future to which the organization aspires to achieve. The vision statement is an expression of shared values and beliefs and provides a focus, or a common purpose, for coordinating all of the work in an organization.

In the past, the health and human service organization's vision statement was typically developed by top management. Recognizing that employees who participate in the visioning process tend to be more committed to the organization and its vision, today most organizations include employees from all levels of the organization in the development of a vision statement. With this shift, the manager's role in the planning process has transitioned from that of a "creator" of the vision to that of a "facilitator" of the visioning process. The visioning process involves reviewing the organization's past, assessing where it is today, and creating an image of its desired future—a vision for where the organization will be in 5 to 20 years. The organization's vision statement, while it is reviewed intermittently, tends to remains consistent over time.

While the health and human service organization will have a vision statement, a therapeutic recreation department may also create a vision statement that is specific to their services. The vision is based on the shared values and beliefs of the department and its practitioners; on knowledge of the department's capabilities; on technical, regulatory, and environmental conditions; and on consumer requirements. There are several benefits to having a therapeutic recreation department vision statement. First, practitioners are likely to feel a sense of commitment to the department-level vision, which can result in increased motivation and improved job performance. Additionally, a vision statement may focus and strengthen the department-level planning and improve the work unit performance. Finally, if the organization does not have a vision, the initiation of one by the therapeutic recreation department may stimulate the organization as a whole to consider the development of a vision.

A vision statement focuses on end results but not necessarily on how to accomplish those results. The next section will describe the mission statement that supports the organization's vision.

Mission Statement

Setting the mission is the second step in the planning process. The *mission* statement identifies the organization's basic business, its reason for being, and its purpose. The mission statement is drawn from the vision statement and is a more concise and focused definition of the type of services provided by the organization. A mission statement is worded in terms of desired consumer outcomes. It describes who the customers are, what services are provided, and how the services are delivered. In this regard, Russoniello (1991, p. 25) commented that the mission statement "should reflect . . . what the consumer can expect as a result of the [therapeutic recreation] service." The mission statement gives the reason this particular therapeutic recreation department exists and the intent of its services.

Every organization, whether it is a for-profit business, a public agency, or a charitable organization with nonprofit status, needs a mission statement (Abrahams, 1995). For example, hospitals exist to provide health-care services to the community. The therapeutic recreation department in a general medical hospital exists to provide quality therapeutic recreation services to patients. In another example, local public park and recreation departments exist to provide recreation facilities and experiences to meet the needs within the community. Thus, in the therapeutic recreation division of a park and recreation department, like in the medical setting, the purpose is to provide quality therapeutic recreation services that are directed toward individuals with disabilities who live in the community.

A mission statement influences the scope of services, goals, and objectives as well as the policies and procedures of an organization. How broad or narrow a mission statement should be is a question that can be debated; there are advantages and disadvantages to both narrow and broad mission statements. A narrow statement carefully specifies the area within which the department will consider its service and can blind the department to significant threats and opportunities from other departments or service units. A broad mission statement widens the areas of service and can encourage the department to expand into services where it has limited expertise or insufficient resources to fully support.

In addition to the organization's mission statement, each department or work unit within an organization may have a mission that is supportive of, and contributes to the mission of the organization. Examples of mission statements from a community therapeutic recreation agency and a rehabilitation hospital are included in Figure 3.13.

Goals and Objectives

The health and human services organization's vision and mission are supported by goals and objectives. The goals and objectives are statements of actions for achieving the organization's vision and mission. *Goals* are short-term planning statements with a timeline for achievement ranging from less than one year to five years. Goals identify what the organization wishes to accomplish in the near-term. Goals guide the agency in its desired direction to fulfill its long-term mission and achieve its overall vision. First-line managers develop goals and objectives for their department or work unit.

Goals are used for planning throughout the organization. The organization has goals, departments have goals, individual work units have goals, and individual employees have goals. Employees at all levels are included in the goal-setting process because participation in the planning process increases employees' commitment to achieving the goals. Additionally, much research has indicated that when people set goals, they outperform those who do not set goals (Locke, 1968; Marquis & Huston, 2012).

An *objective* is the most specific of the planning statements. It describes the result to be achieved, and the actions, or strategies, to be taken to achieve a goal. Each goal statement can be expected to have multiple objectives, or action plans, that support achievement of the goal. Well-written objectives have five characteristics, as described by the SMART acronym (see Figure 3.14, p. 40): they are specific, measurable, achievable, realistic, and time-related (Drucker, 1954).

Craig Hospital

Mission Statement

"To advocate for and provide exemplary rehabilitation care to people affected by spinal cord and traumatic brain injury so that they can achieve optimal health, independence, and life quality."

Core Values

- Foster independence through education and experiences
- Encourage peer support
- Develop a family atmosphere where caring for others is shared
- Embrace a culture of safety
- Put fun into the process of rehabilitation
- Advance rehabilitation through research
- Promote life quality through advocacy and education

Our Commitment

Our exclusive dedication to patients with spinal cord injury and traumatic brain injury will remain constant, as will our commitment to value, excellence, and caring. We will continue to set the standard for quality patient outcomes and service, and as always, help patients and their families achieve their greatest possible levels of independence.

We know that when we assist patients to become independent and productive, it is in their best interest, as well as the best interest of their employer, the insurance company, taxpayers, and society as a whole. We will also be a resource to our former patients and to the professional community through publications, presentations, and consultations.

http://wwwtest1.craighospital.org/About/MissionStatement.asp

Fox Valley Special Recreation Association

OUR MISSION

The Fox Valley Special Recreation Association exists to enrich the lives of people with disabilities. Working collaboratively with member agencies and community partners, we pledge to put PEOPLE FIRST.

FVSRA VISION

The Fox Valley Special Recreation Association (FVSRA) enriches the lives of people with disabilities within the communities it serves. Formed in 1976 as an extension of the Fox Valley, Geneva, St. Charles, Batavia, Sugar Grove, Oswegoland Park Districts and the Village of South Elgin Parks and Recreation Department, we provide a diverse range of year-round recreational opportunities to enable residents with disabilities to experience active, healthy, and playful lifestyles.

Through innovative partnerships and advocacy, FVSRA seeks to be regarded as THE community resource for individuals and families of people with disabilities within our service region. Recognizing the diversity of the member agencies and populations we serve, we pledge to be "customer focused" in our approach to governance and service delivery. We further recognize that our organization's long-term stability and consistency are vitally important to those we serve.

In the years ahead we will continue to focus on sustaining and improving high user satisfaction with the services we deliver as well as those we recommend to our customers. Through education, awareness, and advocacy we will strive to remove all barriers that may inhibit people with disabilities from achieving maximum enjoyment, satisfaction, and fulfillment in their lives.

http://www.fvsra.org

Figure 3.13 Mission Statements for Therapeutic Recreation

Implications for Therapeutic Recreation

Objectives are the fundamental planning statements of therapeutic recreation because they are the end product of all therapeutic recreation activities. Objectives determine the department structure, key activities, and allocation of staff to tasks. Objectives make the work of therapeutic recreation clear and unambiguous—the results are measurable, there are deadlines to be met, and there is a specific assignment of accountability. Objectives become the basis and motivation for therapeutic recreation work and for measuring therapeutic recreation achievement regardless of setting. Objectives also give direction and make commitments that mobilize the resources and energies of therapeutic recreation for the future. They should provide for existing therapeutic recreation services and for existing consumer groups.

Well-written objectives are challenging but not impossible to reach. Objectives that are too ambitious and beyond the reasonable expectations tend to discourage managers and practitioners. On the other hand, objectives

- **S = Specific:** Objectives should clearly state what is to be accomplished. They should be detailed, focused, and concrete as to what is to be achieved.
- **M = Measurable:** Objectives should be written so that they can be assessed as to whether or not they are achieved.
- **A = Achievable:** Objectives must be achievable in the near future to maintain staff motivation to complete them. Objectives are regularly reviewed to update progress, add new objectives, and change objectives that are no longer relevant or are not achievable.
- **R = Realistic:** A well-written objective must be realistically attainable; the organization must have appropriate resources such as staff and budget.
- **T = Time-related:** In order to know if the agency is on target to achieve the goals, the objectives must be time-related, meaning there is an established time frame or deadline that indicates when the objective will be achieved.

Figure 3.14 SMART Objectives

that are offer little challenge and are too easily attained have little motivational impact and may result in under-accomplishment. Finally, objectives should be reviewed on a regular basis and updated as necessary. Refer to Chapter 13 for a discussion of APIE and service accountability.

Summary

1. The various theories of management were reviewed, including classical theory, behavioral theory, human relations theory, and modern management theory. Within these theories the contributions of various individuals, such as Taylor, Fayol, Mayo, Maslow, and McGregor, were highlighted. Systems theory and contingency theory were discussed as potential approaches to management. Consideration was given to the application of these theories to therapeutic recreation management.
2. Leadership is a process of influencing a group to set and achieve goals. There are several major theories of leadership. One of the earliest theories of leadership, the trait theory, was reviewed. This theory has been succeeded by other leadership theories, including behavioral, situational, and contemporary; however, none of these approaches has adequately defined successful leadership.
3. Power is the capacity to influence others. Effective leaders understand the sources of power and how to use it. Consideration was given to the nature of power and sources of power.
4. It was noted that planning statements, including a vision, mission, goals, and objectives, at the organization level and at the division or department level, set the stage for smooth operations. All health and human service agencies, and all therapeutic recreation managers, use planning statements.
5. The vision statement articulates what an organization and department considers important and what it hopes to achieve.
6. The mission articulates the reason for the department's existence within the organization.
7. Goals and objectives state actions for achieving the vision and mission and serve as a guide in planning work, setting priorities, and evaluating effectiveness.
8. Objectives should be SMART. This chapter concluded with the implications of objectives for therapeutic recreation.

Critical Thinking Activities

1. Identify a person, living or dead, who you consider to be a leader. Support your position based on leadership theory and descriptions in this chapter.
2. Collect and compare vision and mission statements from a therapeutic recreation department in a clinical setting, a community park and recreation setting, and a private agency. Explain the similarities and differences in statements from the various types of agencies.
3. List the personal goals you wish to achieve in the next five years. Are they verifiable? Are they attainable?
4. Interview a number of therapeutic recreation managers to identify a charismatic leader. Analyze, describe, and compare the common characteristics found in the leader(s) and characteristics of charismatic leaders.

References

Abrahams, J. (1995). *The mission statement book*. Berkeley, CA: Ten Speed.

Adorno, T. W., Frenkel-Brunswik, E., Levinson, D. J., & Sanford, R. N. (1950). *The authoritarian personality*. New York: Harper & Row.

Barnard, C. I. (1938). *The functions of the executive.* Cambridge, MA: Harvard University Press.

Blake, R. R. & Mouton, J. S. (1964). *The managerial grid.* Houston, TX: Gulf Publishing.

Carter, M. J., & Van Andel, G. E. (2011). *Therapeutic recreation: A practical approach* (4th ed.). Prospect Heights, IL: Waveland.

Craig Hospital. (2013). *Mission Statement, Values, and Our Commitment.* Retrieved from http://www.craighospital.org/Primary-Nav/About/Mission-Statement--Values-and-Our-Commitment/

Drucker, P. F. (1954). *The practice of management.* New York: Harper.

Fayol, H. (1949). *General and industrial management.* (C. Starrs, Trans.). London, England: Isaac Pitman & Sons.

Fiedler, F. E. (1967). *A theory of leadership effectiveness.* New York: McGraw-Hill.

Fox Valley Special Recreation Association. (2013). *Mission/Vision Fox Valley Special Recreation Association.* Retrieved from http://www.fvsra.org/

French, J. R. P., Jr. & Raven, B. (1968). The base of social power. In D. Cartwright & A. Zander (Eds.), *Group dynamics* (3rd ed., pp. 262–268). New York: Harper & Row.

Hein, E. C. & Nicholson, M. J. (1990). *Contemporary leadership behavior* (3rd ed.). Glenview, IL: Scott, Foresman and Company.

Hersey, P. & Blanchard, K. H. (1982). *Management of organizational behavior: Utilizing human resources* (4th ed.). Englewood Cliffs, NJ: Prentice-Hall.

House, R. J. (1976). A 1976 theory of charismatic leadership. In J. G. Hunt & L. L. Larson (Eds.), *Leadership: The cutting edge* (pp. 189–207). Carbondale, IL: Southern Illinois University Press.

House, R. J. & Mitchell, T. R. (1974, Autumn). Path-goal theory of leadership. *Journal of Contemporary Business*, 81–97.

Kast, F. E. & Rosenzweig, J. E. (1985). *Organizations and management: A systems and contingency approach* (4th ed.). New York: McGraw-Hill.

Kotter, J. P. (1990). *A force for change: How leadership differs from management.* New York: Free Press.

Kreitner, R. (1992). *Management* (5th ed.). Boston: Houghton Mifflin.

Krill, D. (1990). *Practice wisdom: A guide for helping professionals.* Newbury Park, CA: Sage.

Lewin, K. (1951). *Field theory in social science.* New York: Harper.

Lewin, K. & Lippit, R. (1938). An experimental approach to the study of autocracy and democracy: A preliminary note. *Sociometry, 1,* 292–300.

Likert, R. (1967). *The human organization.* New York: McGraw-Hill.

Locke, E. A. (1968). Toward a theory of task motivation and incentives. *Organizational Behavior and Human Performance, 3*(2), 157–189.

Marquis, B. L. & Huston, C. J. (2012). *Leadership roles and management functions in nursing* (7th ed.). Philadelphia: J. B. Lippincott Company.

Maslow, A. (1954). *Motivation and personality.* New York: Harper.

Maslow, A. (1968). *Toward a psychology of being* (2nd ed.). New York: Van Nostrand.

Mayo, E. (1933). *The human problems of an industrial civilization.* New York: Macmillan.

McGregor, D. (1960). *The human side of enterprise.* New York: McGraw-Hill.

Northouse, P. G. (2010). *Leadership: Theory and practice.* (5th ed.). Thousand Oaks, CA: Sage.

Ouchi, W. G. (1981). *Theory Z: How American business can meet the Japanese challenge.* Reading, MA: Addison-Wesley.

Preston, P. (2005). The power image: Strategies for acting and being powerful. *Journal of Healthcare Management, 50*(4): 222–225.

Riley, B. (1991). Quality assessment: The use of outcome indicators. In B. Riley (Ed.), *Quality management: Applications for therapeutic recreation* (pp. 53–67). State College, PA: Venture Publishing, Inc.

Robbins, S. P. (1980). *The administrative process.* Englewood, NJ: Prentice-Hall.

Robbins, S. P. (1983). *Organizational theory: The structure and design of organizations.* Englewood Cliffs, NJ: Prentice-Hall.

Robbins, S. & Decenzo, D. (2004). *The fundamentals of management: Essential concepts and applications* (4th ed.). Upper Saddle River, NJ: Prentice-Hall.

Roth, W. F. (2000). *The roots and future of management theory: A systems perspective.* Boca Raton, FL: St. Lucie Press.

Russell, R. V. (2012). *Leadership in recreation* (4th ed.). Champaign, IL: Sagamore.

Russoniello, C. V. (1991). "Vision statements" and "mission statements:" Macro indicators of quality performance. In B. Riley (Ed.) *Quality management: Applications for therapeutic recreation* (pp. 21–28). State College, PA: Venture Publishing, Inc.

Salacuse, J.W. (2006). *Leading leaders: How to manage smart, talented, rich, and powerful people.* New York: AMACOM.

Shank, J., & Coyle, C. (2002). *Therapeutic recreation in health promotion and rehabilitation.* State College, PA: Venture Publishing, Inc.

Silvers, D. I. (1994-95, Winter).Vision—not just for CEOs. *Management Quarterly, 35*(4), 10–14.

Stogdill, R. M. (1974). Handbook of leadership: A survey of theory and research. New York: Free Press.

Stumbo, N. J. & Peterson, C. A. (2009). *Therapeutic recreation program design: Principles and procedures* (5th ed.). San Francisco: Pearson Education.

Sullivan, E. (2013). *Effective leadership and management in nursing,* (8th ed.). Boston: Pearson.

Tannenbaum, R. & Schmidt, W. H. (1983). Effective Leadership. In E. G. C. Collins (Ed.), *Executive success: Making it in management* (pp. 151–168). New York: John Wiley & Sons.

Tappen, R. M. (2001). *Nursing leadership and management: Concepts and practice* (4th ed.). Philadelphia: F. A. Davis.

Taylor, F.W. (1911). *The principles of scientific management.* New York: Harper & Bros.

von Bertalanffy, L. (1972). The history and status of general systems theory. *The Academy of Management Journal, 15*(4) 407–426.

Whitehead, D. K., Weiss, S. A., & Tappen, R. M. (2010). *Essentials of nursing leadership and management.* (5th ed.). Philadelphia: F. A. Davis.

Wren, D. (1987). *The evolution of management theory* (3rd ed.). New York: John Wiley & Sons.

Chapter 4
MANAGING ORGANIZATIONAL BEHAVIOR

Keywords

- Cognitive dissonance theory
- Formal group
- Group development
- Group dynamics
- Informal group
- Organizational climate
- Organizational culture
- Organizational development
- Planned change
- Teams

Learning Outcomes

After reading this chapter, students will be able to:

1. Distinguish between organizational culture and organizational climate.
2. Describe the strategies a manager uses to advance change and minimize resistance to new practices.
3. Explain the factors influencing staff performance in a department.
4. Identify the elements determining group effectiveness and performance in work settings.
5. Outline the manager's responsibilities in group and team development.
6. Evaluate the benefits of team-based structures in organizations.

Overview

Therapeutic recreation managers can benefit from the study of organizational behavior because it helps them to understand and predict human behavior within individual groups, teams, and at the department level. Regardless of size, organizations have a culture and a climate that affect individual and group behavior throughout the organization. The first section explores organizational culture and climate.

Health-care organizations are undergoing continual change and are continually instituting change to remain responsive to forces like rising health-care costs, increasing technology, changing demographics, and regulatory mandates; as discussed in the second section, change is the norm (Marquis & Huston, 2009; Sullivan & Decker, 2009). In most cases, changes are planned or deliberate actions orchestrated by a change agent, the therapeutic recreation manager; the manager is responsible for dealing with human emotions and connecting and balancing all organizational aspects affected by the planned changes. Managers may alter the work environment, technology, or people (Robbins, Decenzo, & Coulter, 2011; Sullivan & Decker, 2009). The organizational culture and climate influence adjustments in any or all of these.

Numerous factors influence your performance as a professional. Likewise, group dynamics in your agency also will impact your performance as an individual and group member. Through their actions, managers develop groups and build teams to achieve organizational outcomes as they support a culture and climate responsive to personal-professional satisfaction and growth. Closing chapter sections consider factors influencing your performance, and group and team development, and the manager's roles related to each.

LEARNING OUTCOME
Distinguish between organizational culture and organizational climate.

Organizational Culture and Climate

Organizational culture is similar to societal culture in that both are pervasive and powerful forces that shape behavior. Every organization has a culture of values and behaviors. A culture consists of both the implicit and explicit contracts among individuals, including what is expected of them and the rewards or sanctions associated with compliance or noncompliance of these contracts. Further, a culture is based on a pattern of basic assumptions or behaviors that have worked in the past and are taught to new employees as the "right way" or "our way" to, for example, relate to clients and complete the APIE process. When someone speaks of "the way we do things here," or the "rules of the game," they are referring to the culture of the organization.

Organizational culture is the sum total of symbols, language, philosophies, traditions, rights, rituals, and unspoken gestures that overtly reflect the organization's norms and values. An organization's culture "is the customary way of thinking and behaving that is shared by all members of the organization and must be learned and adopted by newcomers before they can be accepted into the agency" (Tomey, 2009, p. 312). Organizational culture drives the organization shaping people's behaviors as they interact with one another.

Because people desire meaning and consistency in their work, some type of culture develops in every organization. A culture characterized by militaristic metaphorical expressions such as "we run a tight ship here" is quite different from one with family metaphors like "people care about each other here." The underlying culture of an organization can be determined by listening carefully to the metaphors and tropes.

A successful therapeutic recreation manager identifies quickly and accepts the prevailing culture before attempting to bring about change. Organizational culture is difficult to change because it operates at the level of basic beliefs, values, and perspectives. Yet to accomplish change, the manager must understand and appreciate the prevailing culture because it is the primary informal means of communication in the organization (Tomey, 2009).

Organizational climate, as opposed to the values and behaviors of organizational culture, is the emotional state shared by members of the organization. More specifically, it is a "measure of whether people's expectations about what it should be like to work in an organization are being met" (Schwartz & Davis, 1981, p. 31). The climate can be formal, relaxed, defensive, cautious, accepting, trusting, and so on. A work climate set at the top management level impacts the first-line manager, and in turn this determines the behavior of the staff in the department.

Table 4.1 Work Rules and Climate and Culture

- Create order and discipline so that the behavior of workers is goal-oriented.
- Unify the organization by channeling and limiting behaviors.
- Give members confidence that the behavior of other members will be predictable and uniform.
- Make behavior routine so managers are free to give attention to nonroutine problems.
- Prevent harm, discomfort, and annoyance to clients.
- Ensure compliance with legislation and regulations that affect the institution as a whole.

Staff members want a climate that will give them job satisfaction, high salaries, good working conditions, and opportunities for professional growth that increase self-esteem through self-actualization. Therapeutic recreation managers can establish this type of climate by emphasizing tasks that stimulate motivation and by using discipline fairly and uniformly to provide opportunity for committee assignments, to promote participation in decision making, and to reduce boredom and frustration (Conway-Rutkowski, 1984).

The organizational climate and culture is supported directly and indirectly by work rules. In addition, these rules provide assistance in motivating the employee. Liebler, Levine, and Rothman (1992, p. 222) suggested several work rules that motivate employees, refer to Table 4.1.

Learning Outcome

Describe the strategies a manager uses to advance change and minimize resistance to new practices.

Organizational Change

A theme consistent in the workplace today is change and more change (Whitehead, Weiss, & Tappen, 2010). To survive, organizations must be focused yet flexible. Systems must maximize efficiency and quality and improve care while addressing fiscal realities. Changes require modifications in technology, employees, and the work environment. Managers anticipate these modifications and become change agents who plan change within the prevailing organizational culture and climate. As change occurs, managers realize they actually may be changing an organization's culture. As a consequence, the organizational climate is impacted.

Change is inevitable in our lives and work. Any change may result in discomfort. As a consequence a manager models desired behaviors and assists staff

Table 4.2 Manager Change Agent Abilities

- Combine ideas and think realistically.
- Energize others and creatively problem-solve resistance to change.
- Articulate a vision and remain confident in the outcomes.
- Forecast the big picture yet see the details.
- Have sufficient flexibility, yet persistence enough to resist nonproductivity.
- Support and reinforce subordinates' efforts during the change process.
- Maintain a track record of integrity and successes with change experiences.
- Take risks and serve as a role model.
- View change as a challenge and opportunity for collaboration, renewal, and growth.

through constructive changes in their attitudes and values so they adopt effective behaviors to move the organization in new directions (Robbins, Decenzo, & Coulter, 2011). Employees may experience adjustments in their expectations, perceptions, attitudes, and motivation when their work environment is altered. Adjustments in the work environment may include job redesign, workload increases, and reconfigured authority relationships. The marketplace, economic variables, and technology create the need for change and are factors within the workplace that change. Technology changes work methods, processes, and equipment. Fiscal resources change as a consequence of economic swings. Marketing addresses altered target markets to compensate for prevailing financial expectations.

The manager is often the change agent or facilitates teams of individuals responsible for managing the change process (Marquis & Huston, 2009; Sullivan & Decker, 2009). As a change agent or coordinator facilitating change, the first-line manager demonstrates the abilities identified in Table 4.2.

Organizational development, or *planned change*, assumes a problem-solving approach like APIE (assessment, planning, implementation, evaluation; Sullivan & Decker, 2009; Whitehead, Weiss, & Tappen, 2010)—a process familiar to first-line managers (see Figure 4.1). During assessment, the manager conducts an organizational audit. This includes identifying what kind of change is necessary, the costs and benefits of the proposed changes, and the information or data needed to address the problem or opportunity. In the planning phase, the who, how, and when of change are identified (Sullivan & Decker, 2009). The manager considers sources of resistance and ways to overcome resistance so people are moved from their comfort zones to acceptance of change. Resources are identified to make the changes, and people are contacted who will provide feedback and evaluate progress. During implementation, the manager creates a supportive climate, provides feedback, and manages resistance to change as some discomfort is likely yet must remain within tolerable limits (Sullivan & Decker, 2009). In the final stage, evaluation, the manager weighs the costs and benefits of each change from gathered financial and qualitative information to assure a new comfort zone exists. Although change will continue at a rapid pace, managers using the APIE process create an organizational climate in which change is stabilized.

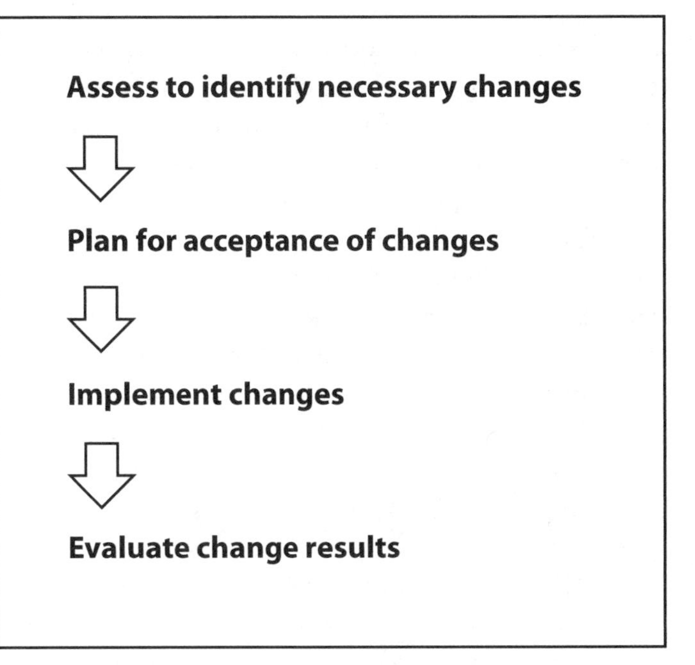

Figure 4.1 Phases of Planned Change

Response to change varies from person to person and from one situation to another. The level of resistance encountered may be less with, for example, technological changes (a practical concern) than with those affecting established norms or psychosocial needs (one's importance and power). "People tend to consider the effects of the change on their personal lives . . . more than on the welfare of the agency" (Tomey, 2009, p. 326). People go through the grieving process when they experience change because change disrupts homeostasis or balance. When people do not work through acceptance, they may disengage or withdraw, disidentify or worry and continue to do the old job, become disoriented or confused and do the wrong things, and/or become disenchanted, or angry, and negative and sabotage change efforts (Tomey, 2009). Causes of resistance to change may include inaccurate perceptions, low tolerance to change, insecurity, embarrassment, fear of the unknown, belief that change is not good for the organization, fear of losing something of value, and perceived loss of power, rewards, or relationships (Robbins, Decenzo, & Coulter 2011; Tomey, 2009).

Resistance is natural and both good and bad. The positive side of resistance requires the manager to clearly articulate why the change is needed. Resistance itself may motivate the group to do better what it is currently doing so it won't have to change. On the negative side, resistance can wear down the change agent and morale suffers (Sullivan & Decker, 2009). Gradual or planned change made in progressive stages is usually less disruptive than unpredicted change.

The manager uses a number of strategies with the APIE process to build consensus and minimize resistance during planned change (Robbins, Decenzo, & Coulter 2011; Sullivan & Decker, 2009), refer to Table 4.3.

Table 4.3 Manager's Strategies to Build Employee Consensus

- Educate and communicate with those who oppose change so they see the logic behind the change effort (identify the negative consequences of resistance while emphasizing the positive consequences of change).
- Encourage participation of resisters and those affected by the changes, presenting both the negative and positive consequences of the change.
- Maintain a climate of trust and support by helping employees deal with their fear and anxiety associated with the change effort while suggesting change may provide them new opportunities and challenges.
- Negotiate and remain open to revisions yet clear as to the desired outcome.
- Pace the change process according to the political climate (i.e., don't change too much too fast).
- Build collaboration and a coalition for support before commencing the change process by becoming familiar with the roles and functions of key staff in the department and organization.

Like people, departments and organizations grow and advance when there is planned change. Progress leads to feedback and evaluation of outcomes. This results in new opportunities and continuous quality improvement. Managers as change agents or coordinators facilitating change guide this process. Resistance to change is reduced with appropriately timed communication and adequate feedback that builds employee confidence, renewal, and collaboration (Tomey, 2009).

Learning Outcome

Explain the factors influencing staff performance in a department.

Factors Affecting Individual Performance

As evidenced during your educational experiences, people differ in their work performance. Numerous factors have been identified as affecting individual performance, including attitude, personality, motivation, perception, learning styles, diversity, and group dynamics (Baron, 1983; Robbins, Decenzo, & Coulter 2011; Tomey, 2009).

Attitude

Attitudes are mental states of readiness that exert influence on people's responses to others, situations, and objects (Tomey, 2009). They are value statements that reflect how people feel about something, their likes and dislikes. Managers are interested in job-related attitudes, in particular job satisfaction, job involvement, organizational commitment, employee passion for their work, and their attitude toward change (Robbins, Decenzo, & Coulter, 2011; Tomey, 2009). People tend to seek consistency between their attitudes and behavior. This is evident when people change what they say so their behavior is not contradictory. The *cognitive dissonance theory* suggests that the inconsistency created by differences between attitudes and behaviors is uncomfortable so people work to reduce this dissonance. When people perceive dissonance is uncontrollable, they are less likely to feel a need to change their attitude to reduce the dissonance. Likewise, when rewards like one's paycheck offset the tension created by the dissonance, individuals are less likely to feel the need to align their behavior with their responses. Positive job attitudes are generated when rewards lessen the tension created by dissonance. When employees engage in activities that appear inconsistent, like planning for discharge prior to the client's readiness to transition, the manager may reduce employee discomfort by reaffirming that length of stay (LOS) is controlled by financial contingencies over which neither the staff member nor manager has control.

Work environments are increasingly complex, temporary, and overloaded with information. Managers are concerned with employee's ability to tolerate the unknown and novelty and to adapt to change. One's attitude toward change affects the ability to process information and adapt to the unpredictability of day-to-day environments. Those who tolerate ambiguity and operate from an internal locus of control adapt better to change in the work environment. Attitudes, therefore, influence behavior and are close to the core of one's personality (Tomey, 2009).

Personality

Each person exhibits a unique combination of relatively stable behaviors and characteristics. All personalities exhibit demographic, competency, and psychological characteristics. A manager seeks to have a blend of personalities on staff, including volunteers where possible, who will be able to interact not only with one another but also with a diverse clientele. Persons of varied demographic characteristics (e.g., a 24-year-old single male graduate practitioner and a 55-year-old female practitioner aide and grandmother) present different developmental concerns, societal role expectations, and past experiences. These differences may enrich the lives of both staff members, or they may present obstacles to their working together. Encouraging acceptance and respect for the uniqueness of each person and emphasizing what each person can contribute to the organization and department is an essential role of the therapeutic recreation manager.

Just as people vary in demographic characteristics, they also have individual competency differences. The abilities, aptitudes, and skills of each staff member must match the tasks they are expected to perform. Frustration grows quickly if one's capabilities are overused or under-used. Continuing education or training activities can be practiced and/or adopted to develop or enhance job skills, but they cannot correct for the lack of a person's competence to perform the job.

Psychological characteristics also contribute to one's personality. Values, interests, and traits provide other sources of differences among individuals. Values are belief systems about what is right and important. Value systems provide the foundation for attitudes, perceptions, and personality (Tomey, 2009). They are rather stable and influence decisions and behaviors. Interests are based on likes and dislikes of different activities. Determining which activities are most relevant to the department's purpose helps the therapeutic recreation manager accurately describe the department tasks to prospective staff members. When the interests and the needs of the department's practitioners and the department's needs are congruent, work performance is enhanced. Traits are particular ways that people vary from one another; they are descriptors of the way people act or are perceived (e.g., sensitive, aggressive, self-starter).

For therapeutic recreation managers, an understanding of personality characteristics is useful in employee selection and when trying to improve individual performance and group behavior. "Personality has been established as an important determinant in vocational interests and choices" (Jin & Austin, 2000, p. 34). The Myers-Briggs Type Indicator (MBTI) is one of the more commonly used methods to identify personalities. The MBTI is a forced-choice instrument that measures four dimensions of personality to identify 16 different personality types. The dimensions include extroversion versus introversion (EI), sensing versus intuition (SN), thinking versus feeling (TF), and judging versus perceiving (JP). These dimensions influence the way people interact and solve problems (Robbins, Decenzo, & Coulter, 2011). Although results have varied, one study (Jin & Austin, 2000) identified the dominant personality types of undergraduate therapeutic recreation majors as ESFJ and ENFP. Employees must continually learn on the job. The results of evaluations like the MBTI are also useful in explaining learning styles. With this information, managers design professional development programs to match employee personality characteristics.

Motivation

We each employ certain behaviors to attain certain goals. Motivation derives from the needs and drives of a person. Needs are related to goals toward which behavior is directed. Staff with a high need for recognition will be most productive if their participation in department activities is recognized by the manager. If a staff member is asked to coordinate a staff meeting for the purpose of clarifying client goals and objectives because the manager is off that particular day, early recognition by the therapeutic recreation manager of this meeting and its contribution to the delivery of service will reinforce the practitioner's action.

Drives are directed energy. Some therapeutic recreation practitioners continually strive to be the most knowledgeable person in the department concerning the delivery of services to a particular group of clients. If this drive is identified and responded to positively by the manager, the department can benefit from the expanded

Table 4.4 Managerial Processes to Manage Perceptions

- Update information
- Use written rather than verbal methods of information giving
- Repeat information periodically
- Report information in group meetings
- Encourage asking questions for clarification
- Keep minutes of meetings
- Check the minutes for accuracy

knowledge base of this practitioner. By supporting the practitioner's quest for continued education through webinars and on-the-job training, the therapeutic recreation manager can request that the practitioner share information with the rest of the staff through an in-service training program. More about motivation is found in Chapter 12.

Perception

We tend to organize the sensory input from our environments selectively into meaningful patterns. Past experience is related to the present situation. A certain amount of selective attention allows us to fill in missing data or to simplify our response to a wide range of situations. Varied individual perceptions of a situation are evident when people are asked to describe an incident they witnessed. No two accounts of it will be exactly the same. There is also a certain amount of self-preservation in one's perception. The uniqueness with which each person perceives helps that person to create and to maintain a sense of order and constancy in a complex and changing world by filtering some of the sensory stimuli.

The therapeutic recreation manager must remain aware of the fact that perceptions vary from person to person. Several managerial strategies help to keep perceptions fairly uniform, refer to Table 4.4.

Employees react to perceptions, not to reality (Robbins, Decenzo, & Coulter, 2011). Employees organize and interpret what they see, consequently selecting cues that may cause them to misperceive another person, group, or object (Tomey, 2009). This selectivity leads to shortcuts in judgment. For example, we may assume others are like us because they possess one of our traits or we may judge one person on the basis of our perception of a group (i.e., stereotyping). In either situation, judgment is distorted and accuracy is compromised. Therapeutic recreation investigators have considered the influence of perceptions on workplace equity (Anderson & Bedini, 2002). Results suggest managers may reduce inequities by considering differences in perceptions between males and females on promotions and job satisfaction. When employees perceive inequities, they behave as if the condition actually exists. As a consequence, whether the manager's behavior is objective is less relevant than what the employee perceives (Robbins, Decenzo, & Coulter, 2011).

The more an individual disagrees with the sensory stimuli, the greater the chance for distortion of it. When a department policy is changed and announced at a staff meeting, the actual change is frequently lost. Some staff members, usually in favor of the change, may be able to articulate clearly the difference from the old and new policy requirements. However, other members, often those not in agreement with the change, may leave the meeting unable to describe the policy change and quickly forget that they are expected to change their behavior in accordance with the change in policy.

Learning Styles

Almost all complex behavior is learned, so a manager needs to understand how people learn to predict and explain practitioner responses (e.g., to policy changes). Likewise, to remain successful on the job, practitioners continue to learn. Therefore, knowledge of learning styles enables therapeutic recreation managers to design training processes so practitioners gather and process information with their dominant personality characteristics.

The MBTI indicates that professionals "gather information through sensing and intuiting and process or evaluate the information through thinking and feeling" (Tomey, 2009, p. 307). Consequently, the personality type suggests how learning occurs. To illustrate, the dominant personality types of undergraduate therapeutic recreation majors, ESFJ and ENFP (Jin & Austin, 2000), are best accommodated with structured courses having clearly stated objectives and deadlines and opportunities to discuss the gathered information.

Managers desire employees to display behavior that benefits the organization. To accomplish this, the manager "shapes" staff by guiding their learning using behavior strategies like reinforcement, reward, modeling, and if necessary, punishment (Robbins, Decenzo, & Coulter, 2011). Therapeutic recreation managers sensitive to these techniques are aware of the significance of, for example, pay increases or promotions to reward exemplary behavior. Managers expect practitioners "to read the message they

Table 4.5 Personal Differences Contributing to Diversity

- Relationship to people in authority
- Social organization, importance of the family
- Health beliefs and behaviors
- Sense of self and space
- Use of eye contact
- Expressiveness
- Time orientation and consciousness
- Communication and language
- Mental processes and learning styles
- Preferred leadership and management styles

are sending and model their behavior accordingly" (Robbins, Decenzo & Coulter 2011, p. 232).

Diversity

"Care congruent with cultural beliefs and values is essential for optimal outcomes" (Marquis & Huston, 2009, p. 400). Cultural competence is defined as the ability of healthcare providers and organizations "to understand and respond effectively to the cultural and linguistic needs brought by patients to the health-care encounter" (Stumbo & Hoss, 2007, p.99). A manager is aware that a culturally competent staff meets the needs of an increasingly diverse clientele. Cultural competence requires the manager to become more sensitive to the differences or variety each individual and group brings to the work setting (Getz, 2002; Tomey, 2009).

Cultural diversity refers to differences in patterns shared by the group. These shared patterns are learned and may lead to misunderstandings between people of different cultures. Likewise generational diversity, variances in age cohorts, brings differing perspectives to the workplace where four generations are working side by side, each operating as though their values and expectations are universal (Marquis & Huston, 2009).

One's personality is at the center of diversity (Tomey, 2009). Other personal factors are age, gender, race, education, work experience, religion, personal habits, recreational habits, and appearance. Respect for diversity comes from acknowledging the strength that comes from these differences. A number of other differences are important to managers because they impact individual and group performance, refer to Table 4.5 (Kim, King, & Park, 2009; Tomey, 2009; Whitehead, Weiss, & Tappen, 2010).

Managers sensitive to individual differences that result from these factors are likely to encourage "respect, understanding . . . and acceptance of the similarities and differences that make us human" (Whitehead, Weiss, & Tappen, 2010, p. 192). The challenge to managers is to recognize and celebrate differences while facilitating positive relationships in the workplace by addressing individual and group variances (Kim, King, & Park, 2009). Differences are descriptors of group tendencies and not predictors of individual behavior. Yet, people are born into groups each with a unique culture that affects individual and group performance.

Group Dynamics

Group dynamics significantly affect individual performance. Individuals may perceive their role is diminished as the responsibility to complete tasks is dispersed among group members. When individual members rely on group efforts, assuming their contributions are not being measured, the reduction in efficiency becomes a management concern. Individual performance is integral to the success of groups and teams; yet, the development of groups and teams is a dynamic process that impinges on the effectiveness of each of its members. The following sections discuss factors relevant to individual performance and group dynamics.

LEARNING OUTCOME

Identify the elements determining group effectiveness and performance in work settings.

Groups

People are born into a group (i.e., family) and interact with others at all stages of their lives in various groups, like peer groups or work groups. A group is an aggregate of people who interact with and influence one another over a period of time. Much of a therapeutic recreation manager's or practitioners professional life is spent in a wide variety of formal and informal groups, ranging from dyads to large professional organizations.

Groups and their performance are assuming greater importance in modern organizations. The complexity and interactions of technology and social systems (groups) are increasing. Team effort and performance have taken on greater importance in integrated health-care systems. Participatory management that empowers groups and teams of employees results in increased productivity, high- quality performance, consumer satisfaction, and increased staff morale (Glenn, 2010).

Health and human service professionals work in close proximity and depend on each other to perform their work; therefore the quality of the interaction is vital (Sullivan & Decker, 2009). Consequently, understanding the nature of groups and how groups are transformed into teams is essential to the first-line therapeutic recreation manager's effectiveness.

Teams tend to outperform individuals when tasks like designing client intervention plans require judgment, experience, and multiple skills (Robbins, Decenzo, & Coulter, 2011). Teams are more flexible and tend to respond to changing environments better than departments. "Teams function at a higher level of cooperative productivity than groups" (Tomey, 2009, p. 373) but to become proficient, teams need to go through the group-development process. Maintaining a positive group climate and building a team is a complex leadership task. Understanding group behavior and dynamics promotes a positive work climate. Formal and informal groups are found in organizations.

Formal Groups

A *formal group* is created by the formal authority of the organization to accomplish specific goals. It is part of the formal structure of the organization and usually appears on formal organizational charts. The formal group has goals specifically created to achieve organizational tasks and typically has clear-cut superior-subordinate relationships as opposed to meeting needs of group members. Committees, teams, and task forces are examples of formal groups.

Work groups enable organizations and their members to accomplish things that individuals cannot do alone. A group can pool resources, divide responsibility, represent more interest in a decision, and may provide better communication. Some of these groups are permanent (e.g., standing committees), while others are temporary (e.g., ad hoc or task forces) and usually dissolve after the group has accomplished its task (Sullivan & Decker, 2009). Permanent or standing committees are usually advisory in authority, but some may have collective authority to make and implement decisions.

While work groups have advantages, they also have disadvantages. The division of responsibility may be considered a disadvantage in many situations because there is no place to assign blame. Groups may successfully avoid action. Most group decisions are compromises; therefore, they are neither the best nor the worst decision that could be obtained. Often a group assumes no responsibility for decisions or actions. A group may engender a false sense of democracy in the organization, especially when it is dominated by a powerful chairperson. Last, groups within an organization may be in conflict. Limited resources, a difference in goals, a failure to clearly define tasks, and a false perception of the role of the group may lead directly to conflict within the group and between groups.

Informal Groups

The *informal group* evolves naturally from social interactions among coworkers as staff satisfy personal needs (Sullivan & Decker, 2009). The informal group is not created by the formal authority. In a strict sense, informal group activity constitutes those activities not officially sanctioned in any organization policy or manual. The informal group affords its members a sense of affiliation, emotional support, identification, belonging, and security. Moreover, the informal group develops its own communication network, known as the "grapevine," which is outside the formal communication channel designed by management.

The informal group can serve to complement the formal organization by generating optimal task performance and productivity and by giving social values and stability to the workplace. The informal group can also have negative and more destructive effects on the organization when it works directly in opposition to the organization's goals and objectives and creates only negative conflict that affects group task performance and productivity.

The astute therapeutic recreation manager needs to become familiar with how the informal group operates in relation to the formal organization and to one's own department. In all cases, the informal group should always complement and assist the effort of the formal group.

Learning Outcome

Outline the manager's responsibilities in group and team development.

Group Development

Groups, whether formal or informal, typically go through stages of development. "They typically form, organize, solve problems, implement solutions, and disband" (Tomey, 2009, p. 375). Like individuals, not every group achieves maturity nor does it complete the tasks of one stage prior to moving to the next stage. The model of small- group development (Tuckman, 1965; Tuckman & Jensen, 1977) identifies the stages of growth as forming, storming, norming, performing, and reforming/adjourning.

Forming

In this stage, individuals first come together and form initial impressions. They begin by determining the task of the group, although some purposes, objectives, and goals may already have been set by management. In addition, individuals try to determine role expectations of one another. Because group members are unsure of their roles, considerable attention is given to the leader in establishing the agenda (Sullivan & Decker, 2009). The stage is complete when individuals begin to perceive themselves as group members.

Storming

In the second stage, individuals begin to express themselves about goal setting, who is responsible for what, and a standard of behavior. It is not unusual for conflict among group members to arise. Members accept the existence of the group yet resist the control the group imposes on individuality. Informed leadership emerges as members compete for power and status. The manager helps the group acknowledge the conflict and resolve it in a win-win situation (Sullivan & Decker, 2009). This stage is complete when relatively clear leadership emerges and there is agreement on the group's direction (Robbins, Decenzo, & Coulter, 2011).

Norming

Teamwork begins to develop; there is a sense of group cohesiveness and openness of communications with information sharing (Sullivan & Decker, 2009). Trust and cooperation develop and goals and standards by which the group will operate are finalized. The manager interprets standards of performance and encourages consensus and relationship- building. Decisions are made about what has to be done and who will do it. If problems continue to exist or are carried over from any of the earlier stages, progress to the next stage will be slow, if at all. If the group is maturing, by the end of this stage, group members feel a sense of progress and have assimilated a common set of expectations or norms regarding member behavior (Robbins, Decenzo, & Coulter, 2011).

Performing

This is the most productive stage in group development. There is a stable pattern of personal interaction, joint problem solving, and shared leadership, including achievement of goals and objectives. The group's energy becomes task-oriented. The group has reached maturity. The manager gives feedback on work effort, and, if necessary, critiques poor work and takes steps to improve performance (Sullivan & Decker, 2009).

Re-forming/Adjourning

Some groups continue indefinitely while others have a specific time-limited purpose and are dissolved after this purpose is achieved. Those that are indefinite may be re-formed to accomplish new goals or to accommodate changes in the work environment; as a consequence, the group refocuses its activities and recycles through the previous four stages. When a group adjourns, the manager helps the group to summarize the activities that occurred over the life of the group, and assists in the evaluation of the group process and the degree to which the group achieved its purpose. When a group reforms, the manager explains the new direction and provides guidance as the group redevelops to accomplish new tasks.

Learning Outcome

Evaluate the benefits of team-based structures in organizations.

Group Dynamics

How the group functions, communicates, and interacts to achieve its goals relates to group dynamics. Effectiveness of the group is influenced by group rank, group status, group role, group size, group norms, and group cohesiveness (Robbins, Decenzo, & Coulter, 2011; Sullivan & Decker, 2009).

Group Rank

When an individual joins a group, he or she will be implicitly evaluated by the other group members. This is called *group rank*, or the position of a group member relative to the evaluation of other members of the group. The rank order can influence an individual's behavior in a group by affecting (a) the member's interactions with other group members, (b) the individual's level of aspiration, and (c) the individual's self-evaluation. All of these can combine to affect the group member's ability to perform the task assigned to him or her in the group.

Group members rank each other on a variety of characteristics, including intelligence, verbal performance, and popularity. The first-line therapeutic recreation manager as a group leader should be aware that all group members, including the group leader, will be evaluating each other throughout the life of the group and that this evaluation can affect the group member's and the group's work. It is important to note that the manager as group leader may rank a member high on a particular characteristic, but this member may not rank high on this same characteristic according to other group members. Being aware of the group rank dynamic can help the manager to avoid communication problems that affect the group's work.

Group Status

Group status is the social ranking of individuals relative to others in the group (Sullivan & Decker, 2009). A group member can bring status into the group from outside or can be assigned status as a result of behavior within the group. Status can be based on a number of characteristics, such as age, work seniority, past positions held within the organization, performance in the group, and education. Status congruence occurs when a group member's standing in each factor is consistent with the standing in other factors. When standings vary among factors, e.g. a younger, less experienced person becomes the group leader, status incongruity occurs. Status incongruity can affect individual and group performance because members that experience a range of status incongruities are not sure how to react to it. Because status is a significant motivator and has behavioral consequences, status incongruities can pose challenges to managers who want to ensure group effectiveness. The following is an example of status incongruity.

An assistant therapeutic recreation manager position is available in a large staff therapeutic recreation department in a general medical hospital. One applicant has been working in the department for only a short time in the behavioral health unit. However, the applicant had leadership positions in two previous jobs in other hospitals. In addition, the applicant has advanced education. The incongruities among these factors can pose questions in the minds of the staff as to how best to react to these inconsistencies if a new (or different) applicant is appointed to this position. Some staff may find it is difficult to work with this. It might be helpful for the manager and/or the committee choosing the assistant to arrange an interview with some staff representatives and this applicant so that the staff can discuss with the applicant some of the questions or concerns.

Group Role

A group role is the function a person assumes as a member of a group. It is often referred to as the part a person plays in a group. Role and status can be viewed as inseparable; role is the dynamic aspect of status that operationalizes the rights and duties granted by other group members. Role is often referred to as the set of expectations that group members share concerning the behavior of a person who occupies a given position in a group (Sullivan & Decker, 2009). A role acted out by a group member may or may not be useful for the task. Further, an individual in a group receives multiple role expectations and occupies multiple roles. It is important for all group members to develop role flexibility, skill, and security in a wide range of roles as well as an awareness of those roles that negatively affect the work of the group.

Broad ranges of group task roles are assumed by members who attempt to coordinate the group's efforts to remain focused and implement strategies to resolve problems (refer to Table 4.6) (Marquis & Huston, 2009, p. 457; Sullivan & Decker, 2009, p. 152–153; Tomey, 2009, p. 374).

Group maintenance roles nurture and facilitate group functioning and interpersonal needs. These positive roles focus on how group members treat each other as the task is accomplished (refer to Table 4.7) (Marquis & Huston, 2009, p. 458; Sullivan & Decker, 2009, p. 153; Tomey, 2009, p. 374).

Any positive role taken too far can have a negative impact on the group. Individuals may attempt to satisfy their own needs irrespective of the group task and maintenance roles (refer to Table 4.8) (Marquis & Huston, 2009, p. 458–459; Tomey, 2009, p. 374).

Because the group leader can assume any or all of these roles, the therapeutic recreation manager should

Table 4.6 Positive Group Task Roles

- *Initiator-Contributor:* suggests new ideas
- *Information Seeker:* clarifies suggestions
- *Opinion Seeker:* clarifies values
- *Information Giver:* offers facts or generalizations
- *Opinion Giver:* states beliefs or opinions
- *Elaborator:* extends or expands suggestions
- *Coordinator:* links ideas, suggestions
- *Orienter:* summarizes decisions, actions
- *Evaluator-Critic:* compares accomplishments to standards
- *Energizer:* prods group to accomplish goals
- *Procedural Technician:* arranges group environment
- *Recorder:* documents actions, accomplishments

Table 4.7 Positive Group Maintenance Roles

- *Encourager:* praises contributions of others
- *Harmonizer:* mediates differences between members
- *Compromiser:* yields position to maintain harmony
- *Gatekeeper:* facilitates communication and participation of all members
- *Standard Setter:* applies standards to evaluate group process
- *Group Observer:* takes notes of group process and dynamics
- *Follower:* passively accepts group decisions

Table 4.8 Roles That Inhibit Group Functioning

- *Aggressor:* disapproves, deflates status of others
- *Blocker:* is resistant and negative
- *Recognition Seeker:* calls attention to self
- *Self-Confessor:* uses group as an audience to express personal feelings
- *Playboy:* exhibits general lack of involvement, appears nonchalant
- *Dominator:* tries to control, manipulate group
- *Help Seeker:* tries to provoke sympathetic response from group members by self-depreciation
- *Special Interest Pleader:* states biases by ostensibly speaking for others

become familiar with those roles that have a more facilitating or vitalizing effect on the group's task or functioning and should strive to assume more of those positive roles. When a therapeutic recreation manager has an awareness of the roles that inhibit a group's work and are irrelevant to the group task and functioning, the manager can begin to create some sort of harmony within the group.

Group Size

Group size influences the possible relationships, communication patterns, and responsibility for participation in a group. As the number of group members increases, so does the number of possible relationships among the members. Thus, more group members mean more avenues of communication and consequently the possibility that multiple communication difficulties will arise. As groups increase in size, contributions of individual members tend to lessen (Robbins, Decenzo, & Coulter, 2011). These factors can have a negative effect on the attractiveness of the group and can contribute to greater turnover and absenteeism of its members. The larger the group, the more effort needed by the manager to coordinate and organize the collective potential of membership.

There are times, however, when a large group is advantageous. Increasing group size offers more human resources and helps accomplish the group task, especially when the task is complex. Small groups tend to foster more personal discussion and more active participation, but fewer people exist to share in the work responsibilities. Problem solving is handled more efficiently in groups of five to seven members because there is less chance for differences between the leader and members, less chance of domination by a few members, and less time required for reaching decisions (Robbins, Decenzo, & Coulter, 2011). Any size group can be well-managed and can achieve a high-task-level performance through attention to the group process and group dynamic, and with good decision-making strategies.

Group Norms

Group norms are the organized and largely shared unwritten rules or ideas that evolve in every group and determine the behavior of the group. They also function to regulate the performance of a group as an organized department. The collective will of a group determines its group norms. Norms dictate output levels, amount of socializing allowed on the job, absenteeism rates, promptness and tardiness, dress, loyalty, and levels of effort and performance (Robbins, Decenzo, & Coulter 2011). The norms adopted by the group are many and can be both positive and negative. A manager wants the group to acquire norms supportive of organizational goals.

The performance norm is especially important for the group. Members of a group with a positive performance norm give the best they can to a task or project, always striving for success. Group members with a negative performance norm may do just enough work to get by and may have an attitude of "not really caring" if they fail or if a project does not turn out well. Thus, groups with more positive norms tend to be more successful in accomplishing organizational objectives than groups with more negative norms.

Conformity to norms is strongly influenced by group cohesiveness. In a highly cohesive group there is strong conformity to group norms. Therapeutic recreation managers help groups build positive norms through their leadership (refer to Table 4.9) (Heidman & Hornstein, 1982; Homans, 1961; Napier & Gershenfeld, 1973).

Group Cohesiveness

Group cohesiveness is the end result of all the forces operating in a group that motivate members to remain or to leave the group. It is often referred to as group "we-ness" or the amount of "group-ness." "The more that members are attracted to one another and the more that a group's goals align with each individual's goals, the greater the group's cohesiveness" (Robbins, Decenzo, & Coulter, 2011, p. 248). Group cohesion can be viewed as an "organizing" force that contributes to overall group potency and vitality. This cohesive force increases the significance of membership for those who belong. When a person is attracted to a group, he or she is motivated to behave in accordance with the wishes of other group members. Groups tend to become cohesive when members not only share common goals but when they share similar values and beliefs, are motivated by the same tasks, work in close proximity to one another, and have specific needs satisfied by group involvement (Sullivan & Decker, 2009). Groups also tend to be more cohesive when group members, regardless of professional expertise, (e.g., PT, OT, or RT), receive similar compensation and perform similar tasks requiring interaction among members.

Groups with high levels of cohesiveness tend to see lower turnover and absenteeism while enforcing adherence to group norms, regardless of their effectiveness (Sullivan & Decker, 2009). A cohesive group tends to be more productive than a less cohesive group but if attitudes are unfavorable, that is, if the group's goals and those of the larger organization do not align, productivity decreases. Productivity may increase even if cohesiveness is low when the organization's goals are supported; conversely, when goals are not supported and cohesiveness is low, cohesiveness has no significant effect on productivity (Robbins, Decenzo, & Coulter, 2011).

Table 4.9 Managerial Actions Contribute to Positive Group Norms

- Emphasize positive role modeling.
- Reward desired behavior.
- Give regular feedback and performance reviews.
- Work with new group members to adopt desired behavior.
- Include desired behaviors in group-member selection criteria.
- Hold regular meetings to look specifically at task performance and member satisfaction.
- Utilize group decision making to agree on desired behaviors.

Manager's Roles in Group Performance

Groups interact to share information and make decisions to help each member perform efficiently and effectively (Robbins, Decenzo, & Coulter, 2011). Managers facilitate a positive work climate where group members feel safe discussing work-related concerns, suggesting alternative practices, and critiquing new behaviors (Sullivan & Decker, 2009).

Effective groups do not just happen—they emerge as the therapeutic recreation manager and members share common goals, communicate openly, make mutual decisions, engage in ongoing feedback, and share leadership roles congruent with situational and group needs. In effective, mature groups, each employee's talents are used and the diversity among group members is appreciated. The effective manager thinks in terms of the group as a whole while recognizing each member's performance is unique yet influenced by group participation. The astute manager is aware of the qualities of effective and ineffective groups (see Table 4.10). Productivity and worker satisfaction are influenced by group cohesiveness and alignment between the group's and organization's goals. When the manager supports and facilitates common goals, individual and mutual accountability, and complementary skills among group members, effective groups become teams.

Teams

Team-based structures tend to be more flexible and responsive to changing events than either departments or work groups (Robbins, Decenzo, & Coulter, 2011).

Table 4.10 Comparative Features of Effective and Ineffective Groups

Factors	Effective Groups	Ineffective Groups
Atmosphere	Informal, comfortable, and relaxed. It is a working atmosphere in which people demonstrate their interest and involvement.	Obviously tense. Signs of boredom may appear.
Goal setting	Goals, tasks, and objectives are clarified, understood, and modified so that members of the group can commit themselves to cooperatively structured goals.	Unclear, misunderstood, or imposed goals may be accepted by members. The goals are competitively structured.
Leadership and member participation	Shift from time to time, depending on the circumstances. Different members assume leadership at various times, because of their knowledge or experience.	Delegated and based on authority. The chairperson may dominate the group, or the members may defer unduly. Members' participation is unequal, with high-authority members dominating.
Goal emphasis	All three functions of groups are emphasized: goal and accomplishment, internal maintenance, and developmental change.	One or more functions may not be emphasized.
Communication	Open and two-way. Ideas and feelings are encouraged, both about the problem and about the group's operation.	Closed or one-way. Only the production of ideas is encouraged. Feelings are ignored or taboo. Members may be tentative or reluctant to be open and may have "hidden agendas" (personal goals at cross-purposes with group goals.)
Decision making	By consensus, although various decision-making procedures appropriate to the situation may be instituted.	By the highest authority in the group, with minimal involvement by members; or an inflexible style is imposed.
Cohesion	Facilitated through high levels of inclusion, trust, liking, and support.	Either ignored or used as a means of controlling members, thus promoting rigid conformity.
Conflict tolerance	High. The reasons for disagreements or conflicts are carefully examined, and the group seeks to resolve them. The group accepts unresolvable basic disagreements and lives with them.	Low. Attempts may be made to ignore, deny, avoid, suppress, or override controversy by premature group action.
Power	Determined by the members' abilities and the information they possess. Power is shared. The issue is how to get the job done.	Determined by position in the group. Obedience to authority is strong. The issue is who controls.
Problem solving	High. Constructive criticism is frequent, frank, relatively comfortable, and oriented toward removing an obstacle to problem solving.	Low. Criticism may be destructive, taking the form of either overt or covert personal attacks. It prevents the group from getting the job done.
Self-evaluation as a group	Frequent. All members participate in evaluation and decisions about how to improve the group's functioning.	Minimal. What little evaluation there is may be done by the highest authority in the group rather than by the membership as a whole.
Creativity	Encouraged. There is room within the group for members to become self-actualized and interpersonally effective.	Discouraged. People are afraid of appearing foolish if they put forth a creative thought.

Source: Wilson and & Kneisl, (1983). *Psychiatric nursing, 2nd edition*, ©1983. Reprinted with permission of Pearson Education Inc., Upper Saddle River, NJ.

Additionally, it is argued that individuals working as a team can bring results that surpass in quantity and quality the contributions of individuals working independently. Teams tend to be more effective when dealing with increasingly complex and chronic care needs, keeping pace with the demands of new technology, responding to payor demands, and when delivering care across settings (Bodenheimer, Chen, & Bennett, 2009; Greiner & Knebel, 2003). Work groups share information and make decisions that help each member do his/her job more effectively and efficiently (Robbins, Decenzo, & Coulter, 2011): There is no need to engage in collective work requiring joint effort. Work groups become teams when individuals "apply group process skills to achieve specific results" (Sullivan & Decker, 2009, p. 148). Work *teams* are groups whose members work on common goals "using their positive synergy, individual and mutual accountability, and complementary skills" (Robbins, Decenzo, & Coulter, 2011, p. 249). Effective work teams exchange ideas, coordinate work activities, "and develop an understanding of other team members' roles" (Sullivan & Decker, 2009, p. 148) resulting in performance levels greater than the sum of each individual's efforts. Thus, the goals and functions of work groups and teams vary (Robbins, Decenzo, & Coulter, 2011; Tomey, 2009; refer to Table 4.11). In the 21st century, the primary building block of reengineered organizations is the establishment of teams to supplant individuals as the fundamental work unit. The positive synergy of work teams helps organizations improve quality, safety, and performance, creating opportunities for increased productivity without necessarily adding costly resources.

Initially, the implementation of teams within health and human service organizations was associated with total quality management (TQM). Therapeutic recreation managers and practitioners participate as members of TQM or continuous quality improvement (CQI) teams, which focus on improving quality, safety and consumer satisfaction as well as being members of various unit treatment teams that develop comprehensive intervention plans required by accreditation organizations (Shank & Coyle, 2002). A variety of care delivery avenues and settings are emerging like managed care, community-based care, and rehabilitation centers that require teams to provide necessary coordination focused on quality evidence-based responsive client care (Greiner & Knebel, 2003). Thus, valued professional competencies of today's employees emphasize the ability to cooperate, coordinate, and to think as a team contributing to a larger system (Greiner & Knebel, 2003).

Table 4.11 Variations between Groups and Teams

Groups	Teams
Sharing of information to achieve individual goal(s)	Collective performance toward common purpose
Varied and random skills among members	Complementary and supportive skills among members
Individual performance and accountability	Individual and mutual accountability to achieve outcome (s)
Neutral energy may or may not result in performance enhancement	Positive synergy toward improved performance
Appointed or elected leadership within group and/or by management	Shared leadership among team and manager

Sources: Robbins, Decenzo, & Coulter, 2011; Tomey, 2009

Table 4.12 Qualities of Effective Teams

- A common plan and purpose with an understanding of their team goals
- Relevant technical expertise (CTRS competencies) and interpersonal skills
- Adequate resources
- Individual and joint accountability and recognition systems
- High mutual trust and collegiality among members
- Unified commitment to the team
- Open and effective communication skills, problem-solving, decision-making, and negotiation skills
- Supportive internal and external environment and relationships
- Effective leadership and efficient operating procedures

People-oriented, goal-directed, quality-driven organizational cultures are conducive to team development (Tomey, 2009). While team membership is based on specific competencies to accomplish desired tasks, members are often from different professions and may even be from different job levels. Effective teams possess several qualities, which are listed in Table 4.12 (Robbins, Decenzo, & Coulter, 2011; Tomey, 2009).

Manager's Roles in Team Performance

Effective managers can motivate teams to undertake even the most difficult responsibilities. The manager assumes the role of a coach or facilitator, guiding and supporting efforts. Additionally, the manager encourages development of teams by hiring, training, and educating team members, setting expectations, building relationships, acquiring resources, allowing processing time, protecting the team from political obstacles, promoting group member benefits, increasing interdependence, and recognizing cooperative (rather than competitive) contributions (Robbins, Decenzo, & Coulter, 2011; Sullivan & Decker, 2009; Tomey, 2009).

The manager faces a number of challenges as teams are created and used in health and human service settings. The challenge of creating team players in an individualistic culture or an established organization that rewards individual performance may be evident. Working as a team may counter views of work and life (e.g., individual rather than collective values of teamwork). Working individualistically is like a group of sprinters who display uncoordinated effort while a relay team coordinates independent efforts (Tomey, 2009). Another concern when teams operate within departments is that department managers' responsibilities are absorbed within the team. Diversity in the workplace leads to another challenge. Diversity, including that attributed to global teams, provides fresh perspectives yet may result in teams taking more time to resolve issues or solve problems (Robbins, Decenzo, & Coulter, 2011). A diverse team may spend more time discussing issues, yet the chance decreases that a weak alternative is chosen.

In general, employees that have moved into teams are better satisfied and quality is improved. It is incumbent on the manager to articulate the challenges as well as the benefits of using teams to promote quality, safety, and efficient responsiveness, and respond more efficiently to client needs. When team members' skills complement each other's expertise, complex situations are addressed through more comprehensive interventions. Efforts of one team member reinforce others, resulting in a synergy that contributes to a highly motivated and committed group of people producing high-quality work (Glenn, 2010). In the end, a positive work climate is created.

Summary

1. Organizational culture is the customary way of behaving in an organization, whereas organizational climate is the emotional state shared by members of the organization.
2. Managers guide planned change or organizational development as they respond to economic exigencies.
3. A number of factors, including attitude, personality, motivation, perception, learning styles, diversity, and work group dynamics, explain why individuals differ in their work performance.
4. Formal and informal groups are usually found in organizations. Formal groups are created by the formal authority of the organization. Informal groups are formed by people as they work together to meet their social needs.
5. Group development occurs in stages (i.e., forming, storming, norming, performing, and reforming/adjourning). The stage of maturity reached influences group functioning.
6. Several dynamics affect work- group effectiveness, including group rank, group status, group roles, group size, group norms, and group cohesiveness. Individual group members assume roles that either enhance and promote group functioning or inhibit groups from being effective.
7. The therapeutic recreation manager encourages a high level of group productivity and staff satisfaction through specific actions.
8. Groups may transition into teams. Teams are the preferred mode of operation when quality, safety, and productivity are organizational priorities.
9. Teams face challenges attributed to cultural expectations and global diversity.

Critical Thinking Activities

1. Consider your school or college. Using the change process or APIE, describe how you might create a better place for learning by making planned change(s).
2. Make observations in a therapeutic recreation setting. Answer the following questions: Is the organization going through changes? If so, what are some of them? How can a manager build consensus and minimize resistance?
3. Reflect upon an organization for which you have been employed or volunteered. Describe examples of language, traditions, work rules, symbols, etc., reflective of the organization's culture, norms, and values. Describe how the organization's culture and climate impacted factors that affected your performance, like your attitude, motivation, perceptions, etc.
4. Consider a group in which you currently participate, like a membership organization. Identify members within the organization that portray roles allowing the group to accomplish its tasks or maintain a positive approach during group projects and, label these members using the descriptors found in this chapter.

5. Conduct a self-assessment using, for example, the Myers-Briggs Type Indicator (MBTI), to determine your personality traits. Describe your assets and liabilities resulting from the assessment. Next, review the job task analysis of the CTRS assessing the level of competence you possess for each task. Review the factors that affect your performance as an employee, including personality, and describe how these factors affect your potential to perform the CTRS job tasks.

References

Anderson, D. M., & Bedini, L. A. (2002). Perceptions of workplace equity of therapeutic recreation professionals. *Therapeutic Recreation Journal, 36*(3), 260–281.

Baron, R. A. (1983). *Behavior in organizations: Understanding and managing the human side of work.* Boston, MA: Allyn & Bacon.

Bodenheimer, T., Chen, E., & Bennett, H. D. (2009). Confronting the growing burden of chronic disease: Can the U.S. health care workforce do the job? *Health Affairs, 28*(1), 64–74.

Conway-Rutkowski, B. (1984, February). Labor relations: How do you rate? *Nursing Management,* 13–16.

Getz, D. (2002). Increasing cultural competence in therapeutic recreation. In D. R. Austin, J. Dattilo, & B. P. McCormick (Eds.), *Conceptual foundations for therapeutic recreation* (pp. 151–164). State College, PA: Venture Publishing.

Glenn, D. W., (2010). How to develop and sustain high performance teams in your laboratory. *Clinical Leadership & Management Review, 24*(4), 1–5.

Greiner, A. C., & Knebel, E. (Eds.) (2003). *Health professions education: A bridge to quality.* Washington, DC: Institute of Medicine of the National Academies.

Heidman, M. E., & Hornstein, H. A. (1982). *Managing human forces in organizations.* Homewood, IL: Irwin.

Homans, G. C. (1961). *Social behavior: Its elementary forms.* New York, NY: Harcourt Brace Jovanovich.

Jin, B., & Austin, D. R. (2000). Personality types of therapeutic recreation students based on the MBTI. *Therapeutic Recreation Journal, 34*(1), 33–41.

Kim, J., King, M., & Park, J. (2009). Culturally competent recreation therapy: Individualism and collectivism. *American Journal of Recreation Therapy, 8*(2), 17–21.

Liebler, J. G., Levine, R. E., & Rothman, J. R. (1992). *Management principles for health professionals.* Gaithersburg, MD: Aspen Publishers.

Marquis, B. L., & Huston, C. J. (2009). *Leadership roles and management functions in nursing theory and application* (6th ed.). Philadelphia, PA: Wolters Kluwer/Lippincott Williams & Wilkins.

Napier, R., & Gershenfeld, M. (1973). *Groups: Theory and experience.* Boston, MA: Houghton Mifflin.

Robbins, S. P., Decenzo, D. A., & Coulter, M. (2011). *Fundamentals of management essential concepts and applications* (7th ed.). Upper Saddle River, NJ: Prentice-Hall.

Schwartz, H., & Davis, S. (1981, Summer). Matching corporate cultures and business strategy. *Organizational Dynamics,* 30–48.

Shank, J., & Coyle, C. (2002). *Therapeutic recreation in health promotion and rehabilitation.* State College, PA: Venture Publishing, Inc.

Stumbo, N. J., & Hoss, M. A. K., (2007). Racial and ethnic disparities in healthcare: Problems and potential solutions in therapeutic recreation services. *Annual in Therapeutic Recreation, 15,* 96–104.

Sullivan, E. J. & Decker, P. J. (2009). *Effective leadership and management in nursing* (7th ed.). Upper Saddle River, NJ: Pearson Prentice-Hall.

Tomey, A. M. (2009). *Guide to nursing management and leadership* (8th ed.). St Louis, MO: Mosby Elsevier.

Tuckman, B. W. (1965, May). Developmental sequence in small groups. *Psychological Bulletin,* 384–399.

Tuckman, B. W., & Jensen, M. A. (1977). Stages of small group development revisited. *Group and Organizational Studies, 2,* 419–427.

Whitehead, D. K., Weiss, S. A., & Tappen, R. M. (2010). *Essentials of nursing leadership and management* (5th ed.). Philadelphia, PA: F. A. Davis Company.

Wilson, H. S., & Kneisl, C. R. (1983). *Psychiatric nursing* (2nd ed.). Menlo Park, CA: Addison-Wesley Publishing.

Chapter 5
Decision Making, Problem Solving, and Managing Conflict

Keywords

- Bullying
- Conflict
- Creativity
- Critical thinking
- Decision making
- Nonprogrammed decisions
- Policies
- Problem solving
- Procedures
- Programmed decisions
- Rules

Learning Outcomes

After reading this chapter students will be able to:

1. Explain the importance of critical and creative thinking to decision making and problem solving.
2. Compare the APIE process to the steps found in decision making and problem solving.
3. Define each term: policy, procedure, and rule.
4. Outline group decision-making techniques and analytical tools managers use in decision making and problem solving.
5. Describe sources of conflict that may have an effect on professionals in the workplace.
6. Describe resolution strategies and outcomes of managing conflicts in the workplace.

Learning Outcome
Explain the importance of critical and creative thinking to decision making and problem solving.

Overview

In a technological environment, health and human service managers process large amounts of information to make complex decisions (Zori & Morrison, 2009). Much of the first-line manager's time is spent critically exploring issues, making decisions, and solving problems (Marquis & Huston, 2009). Managers are expected to use knowledge from various disciplines, along with their expertise, to make decisions and to resolve problems and conflicts in dynamic situations (Sullivan & Decker, 2009). Critical thinking is used daily by managers to make decisions and solve problems (Zori & Morrison, 2009). And, decision making, problem solving, and conflict resolution are criteria used to judge the expertise and success of the manager (Marquis & Huston, 2009).

Opening the chapter is a discussion of critical thinking. Critical-thinking skills are found in rational decision making and problem solving. Yet, critical thinking is broader in scope and encompasses higher- level reasoning and creative analysis (Marquis & Huston, 2009; Sullivan & Decker, 2009).

A major portion of the chapter is devoted to decision making. This chapter section considers decision types and conditions under which decisions are made; policies, procedures, and rules; a decision-making process, including the role of creativity in the process; group decision-making processes; and tools and techniques used in decision making. Therapeutic recreation managers develop skills enabling them to make effective decisions found at the core of every management task.

Next, a chapter section considers problem solving. Decision making may or may not involve a problem yet requires the selection of one choice from among several, each of which may be appropriate; problem solving requires selecting the one correct solution. Problem solving, like decision making, is analogous to the APIE (i.e., assessment, planning, implementation, evaluation) process. A gap exists between existing and desired conditions and this prevents realization of unit goals. Using this process, the manager resolves the issue, thus closing the gap and enabling achievement of desired goals.

Finally, the chapter addresses conflict. While conflict is inevitable and complete elimination is unlikely, internal and external discord result from a variety of differences and can be constructive or destructive. Conflict may be a prerequisite to change in people and organizations. Conflict is a warning to management that something is amiss and it should stimulate search for solutions through problem solving (Sullivan & Decker, 2009; Tomey, 2009). Sources and types of conflict, including workplace violence and forms of aggression (bullying), are presented, followed by strategies to resolve conflicts. "Most day-to-day conflict is resolved with negotiation" (Marquis & Huston, 2009, p. 499). Formal negotiation is evident in collective bargaining and collective agreements. First-line managers minimize stress on staff and the organization and maximize effectiveness when they manage the sources and types of conflict.

Critical Thinking

"Critical thinking is needed to excel in the information age" (Tomey, 2009, p. 50). "Critical thinking skills and the inclination to engage in critical thinking are essential for" success as an effective manager (Zori & Morrison, 2009, p. 75). Managers must be able to process large amounts of information to make complex decisions and resolve problems so that they can create a positive work environment and deliver high-quality services. *Critical thinking*, sometimes referred to as reflective thinking, is deliberate use of reasoned analysis to reach a decision about what to believe or what to do (Whitehead, Weiss, & Tappen, 2010). While decision making and problem solving seek to find one solution, critical thinking "involves considering a range of alternatives and selecting the best one for the situation" (Sullivan & Decker, 2009, p. 105).

Learning Outcome

Compare the APIE process to the steps found in decision making and problem solving.

Critical thinking is like a jigsaw puzzle where a number of skills contribute to the whole (Castle, 2010). Thus, like the APIE process, critical thinking entails assessing underlying assumptions and information (A), exploring, analyzing, and generating alternatives (P), applying knowledge and processing skills to guide decisions and behavior (I), and judging the evidence so a conclusion or course of action is justified (E). "The essence of critical thinking is a willingness to ask questions and to be open to new ideas, new ways to do things" (Whitehead, Weiss, & Tappen, 2010, p. 10). When a manager or therapist examines a problem or makes a decision, a series of questions is used to facilitate critical analysis (refer to Table 5.1) (Sullivan & Decker, 2009; Whitehead, Weiss, & Tappen, 2010).

Table 5.1 Critical Analysis Questions

- Do I have all the information I need?
- Is it accurate?
- Am I prejudging a situation?
- Is the evidence objective, relevant, and presented completely and clearly?
- What are the possible alternative perspectives of clients, staff, and other managers?
- What is the ideal course of action?
- Do all stakeholders understand the implications and consequences of the desired action?
- Is the conclusion justified by the facts?

The skills to become a critical thinker can be learned over time. As a CTRS, you will build on your knowledge base acquired in school to make the critical-thinking process a conscious part of your behavior. Results of critical thinking may or may not be welcome, as they may lead to different views and creative solutions. Critical thinkers use scientific problem-solving to explore ambiguities found in an ever-changing health and human service practice environment. Decisions are made in complex situations. Questions that have to be addressed in complex situations include: What is the best staffing mix to prevent turnover and ensure quality services? What co-treatment interventions will facilitate partnerships yet assure RT financial benefits? Which sponsorships might garner additional resources without compromising client autonomy and confidentiality?

Decision Making

Decision making is the process of selecting one course of action from among alternatives. Managers are confronted by complex, ever-changing situations that require continuous decision making (Tomey, 2009). Decision making may or may not involve a problem but always involves choosing among alternatives "each of which may be appropriate under certain circumstances" (Sullivan & Decker, 2009, p. 108). The essence of decision making is choice. The person making a decision must recognize that a decision is necessary and identify a set of feasible alternatives before selecting one.

Decision making is a major component of each of the management functions discussed in Chapter 2. Because organizational and department life is characterized by an environment of competing values, the decision-making requirements in the position of therapeutic recreation manager are complex. Although rationality is the goal of managers, many decisions are affected by such non-rational factors as emotion, attitudes, and individual preferences and needs. Decision making, like critical thinking and problem solving, is a learned skill that improves with practice; thus, the chapter includes tools and techniques helpful to the acquisition of these skills.

Types of Decisions

Therapeutic recreation managers make many different types of decisions. In general, however, most decisions fall into one of two categories: programmed and non-programmed (Robbins, Decenzo, & Coulter, 2011). *Programmed decisions* are repetitive and routine and to the extent a definite approach has been worked out for handling them so that they do not have to be treated as new or unusual each time they occur—for example, i.e., when staff arrive late, a protocol identifies coverage practices. In many situations it becomes decision making by precedent; that is, the manager simply does what the manager or others have done in the same situation (Robbins, Decenzo, & Coulter, 2011). Policies, procedures, and rules all represent examples of programmed decisions (Sullivan & Decker, 2009). Programmed decisions are more often made by first-line managers than executive-level managers (Sullivan & Decker, 2009).

Occasionally, decisions must be made concerning a relatively unstructured or different situation. No cut-and-dried solution exists because the matter has either never arisen before or it is so important that it deserves a custom-tailored approach (Robbins, Decenzo, & Coulter, 2011). *Nonprogrammed decisions* usually include the large and dramatic. Managers faced with these situations must treat them as unique by investing blocks of time, energy, and resources into exploring the situation from all perspectives. While top managers are usually involved in nonprogrammed decisions, therapeutic recreation managers may very well be involved if the situation focuses on a new facility, legal issues, programs, or budgets.

The manager has a particular responsibility when a nonprogrammed situation arises. It is his or her responsibility to make innovative decisions in these circumstances. A participatory manager uses his or her best resource people during unique situations. Resource people can include experienced staff practitioners, personnel from other departments, or practitioners from other organizations who have special expertise. The manager is also the champion of evidence- and theory- based practices. Whenever satisfactory outcomes result from innovative decision making in nonprogrammed situations, it is the responsibility of the manager to document and to share new evidence and new theories affecting service. This contributes to the growth and verification of programmed decisions and standardized practice.

Decision-Making Conditions

Just as there are different kinds of decisions, there are also different conditions in which decisions must be made. Managers sometimes have an almost perfect understanding of conditions surrounding a decision, but at other times they have few or no clues about these conditions. These conditions may change and vary dramatically (Sullivan & Decker, 2009) as conditions within the larger organization and department alter. Thus, the manager is likely to face three different circumstances as decisions are made: certainty, risk, and uncertainty (refer to Table 5.2, p. 62) (Robbins, Decenzo, & Coulter 20011; Sullivan & Decker, 2009). Certainty, risk, and uncertainty may be viewed as a conceptual continuum that helps managers to visualize and to think about the decisions that face them. Although therapeutic recreation managers face decisions every day, they are more inclined to make decisions that fall between certainty and risk.

Policies, Procedures, and Rules

Policies, procedures, and rules are plans reduced to statements that guide the organization in decision making (Marquis & Huston, 2009). While there is a decision-making process, decision making is made easier by policies, procedures, and rules as they focus on programmed decision making (Robbins, Decenzo, & Coulter, 2011). These statements, drawn from the agency's vision, mission, values, goals, and objectives,

Table 5.2 Decision Making Conditions

Certainty

The ideal situation exists when the manager knows each alternative, the conditions surrounding each, and the outcome of each alternative.

Risk

A more common decision-making condition is one of risk; the manager knows the probabilities associated with the possible outcomes of each alternative under consideration. Managers have objective data from past experiences which lets them assign probabilities to each alternative. In decision making under condition of risk, the level of risk is moderate. However, the ability to recognize and to take a calculated risk is a skill required of all managers.

Uncertainty

In a condition of uncertainty, the manager does not know all of the alternatives, the risks associated with each, or the consequences each alternative is likely to have. Uncertainty is inevitable due to the dynamic nature of health and human services (Sullivan & Decker, 2009). Successful decisions even in uncertain situations are dependent on our knowledge, experience, and judgment.

explain how the unit's goals will be met, guide the agency's service scope, and inform the manager's decision making and problem solving (Marquis & Huston, 2009).

First-line managers rarely make policies and procedures. Rather, they interpret and apply them. Department policies and procedures, when initiated, must be within the boundaries and guidelines established by organizational policies and procedures. Policies and procedures are usually found in new employee orientation and training, personnel handbooks, on the agency intranet accessed by using policy manager software, and may also be kept in the manager's office. The use of policy-management software facilitates regular policy updating and enables accreditation visitors (e.g., CARF) to easily access and affirm practices.

The manager is responsible for updating policy and procedure statements to ensure relevancy and applicability (Marquis & Huston, 2009). With the expanding use of technology, reliance on evidence-based practices, and increasing regulations, keeping policies and procedures current is a management challenge. Additionally, departments are in flux with the needs of employees constantly changing (Marquis & Huston, 2009). Thus, the first-line manager may devote considerable time to planning and revising these statements.

Learning Outcome

Define each term: policy, procedure, and rule.

Policies

Policies explain how goals will be achieved and serve as guides that define the general course and scope of activities permissible for goal accomplishments. They serve as a basis for future decisions and actions, help coordinate plans, control performance, and increase consistency of actions by increasing the probability that different managers will make similar decisions when independently facing similar situations (Tomey, 2009). Policies "direct individual behavior toward the organization's mission and define broad limits and desired outcomes of commonly recurring situations" (Marquis & Huston, 2009, p. 158) while serving as guides to those who carry out the policies. Policies establish the boundaries or limits for the decision maker. Within these boundaries, judgment must be exercised. The degree of discretion permitted varies from policy to policy. Some policies are broad in scope and permit much latitude and at the same time allow various departments to develop supplemental policies. Others are narrow and leave little room for interpretation. Figures 5.1 and 5.2 (pp. 65–66) present examples of first a broad organizational policy on Emergency Medical Management followed by a specific department policy on outings. These are designed to be compatible while creating consistency in decision making at the department level and throughout the organization.

Policies may be either implied or expressed orally or in writing (Marquis & Huston, 2009; Tomey, 2009). An example of an implied policy is the courtesy of responding to electronic messages within 24 hours of receipt. A supervisor may state that electronic responses may not occur in the presence of clients (oral policy). If there is a personnel policy on the department or organizational website that limits use of personal electronic devices to office areas and emergency uses, the policy is a written guide for management action.

Policies emerge in several ways: originated, appealed, or imposed (Tomey, 2009). As noted previously, they may be originated by top management, but they can be generated at the department level. At times, policies may be formulated simultaneously from both directions. Policies are usually prepared through team action and circulated for comments on potential effect before final approval. Thereafter they are embodied in the organization's policy documents/website.

The second way policies come about is through appeal. When a manager does not know how to solve a problem, disagrees with a previous decision, or otherwise wants a question reviewed, he or she appeals to a higher authority for a decision (Tomey, 2009). As appeals are taken up the hierarchy and decisions are made, precedents are set, which guide future managerial actions (Tomey, 2009). Appealed policies are likely to be incomplete and unclear (Tomey, 2009). Unintended precedents can be set when decisions are made for one situation without regard for effects across the department.

Finally, policies may be externally imposed. In many instances, health and human service organizations must conform to governmental laws, practice standards of professional associations (e.g., practice standards of the American Therapeutic Recreation Association [ATRA]) and accreditation standards in health-care facilities (e.g., the Joint Commission [Joint Commission Accreditation of Healthcare Organizations-JCAHO] and CARF [Commission on Accreditation of Rehabilitation Facilities]).

Policies relative to therapeutic recreation are usually associated with delivery of services, personnel, safety and security, external laws and regulations, and various relationships and partnerships. Several guidelines are recommended for presenting policies in a handbook or on the intranet (refer to Table 5.3). Collaboration in the development of policies is encouraged by JCAHO (Paige, 2003). Collaboration across departments standardizes practice and creates opportunities to determine best practices. The use of consistent policies ensures compliance with standards and uniformity in services. Collaboration in the design, implementation, and review also allows the manager to create guidelines that the staff are likely to follow. The manager's leadership role is evident, as the policy is communicated in writing and orally to those affected. A policy's perceived value is often dependent upon how it is communicated (Marquis & Huston, 2009).

Table 5.3 Policy Statement Guidelines

1. If possible, the title of every policy should use the most common terminology (for easy location).
2. A brief description of the policy should be set out at the top of the document so that the reader can rapidly tell if it contains the desired information without having to read the entire statement.
3. Objectives (i.e., purposes) for the policy should be stated. This facilitates periodic review. If the policy no longer meets the original objectives, it will be apparent.
4. A code system should be used to enable the reader to find related policy and procedural statements.
5. All policies should be authenticated by date and by either the therapeutic recreation manager or the appropriate supervisor (refer to Figures 5.1 and 5.2 for examples of these guidelines).

Procedures

Procedures are plans that establish acceptable ways of accomplishing a specific task (Marquis & Huston, 2009). Procedures are intradepartmental or interdepartmental and consequently may not affect the entire agency or organization to the extent that policy statements do (Tomey, 2009). Procedures identify steps to implement a policy and are more exacting and numerous in the lower levels of the organization because of the necessity for more careful control while reducing the need for discretion in making a decision.

A procedure document or electronic file, like a policy document or electronic file, provides a basis for orientation and staff development and is a ready reference for all personnel. The file should be well-organized, with a table of contents and an index (Tomey, 2009). Each procedure should be easily replaceable with a revised one, especially since there is a tendency to add new practices rather than review existing practices to evaluate their effectiveness. Similar to policy updating, procedure revisions are formally approved, dated, and shared with all affected by their implementation.

Involving staff in establishing procedures increases the quality of departmental procedures and the likelihood that they will be implemented as desired. "Established procedures save staff time, facilitate delegation, reduce cost, increase productivity, and provide a means of control" (Marquis & Huston, 2009, p. 160). Standardized procedures provide a means of evaluating adherence to work protocols. Figure 5.3 illustrates the procedures associated with prioritizing clients for service. The procedural steps are listed in chronological order under the heading Procedures in the policy statement (refer to Figure 5.3, p. 67).

Rules

Rules are specific statements that tell managers what ought or ought not to be done in a given situation. "Rules describe situations that allow only one choice of action" (Marquis & Huston, 2009, p. 160). Rules "are frequently used by managers who confront a structured problem because they're simple to follow and ensure consistency" (Robbins, Decenzo, & Coulter, 2011, pp. 68–69). Because rules describe only one choice of action, there should be as few rules as possible, yet they should be enforced to help keep morale from breaking down (Marquis & Huston, 2009). Rules are often embedded in policy and procedure statements, as evidenced by reviewing the Practice sections of the policies on Emergency Medical Management and Outings found in Figures 5.1 and 5.2 (pp. 65–66).

Decision-Making Process

Decision making is a process that involves selecting one course of action among alternatives. This process uses both intuition and a rational decision- making model to make wise judgments. The process is as applicable to your decision about holiday plans as it is to staff scheduling and policy revisions (Robbins, Decenzo, & Coulter, 2011). A rational or scientific approach uses a series of steps so information and life experiences come together to achieve objectives (Marquis & Huston, 2009; Sullivan & Decker, 2009). While some steps are used simultaneously, not all are used in every decision nor are they used in the same order (Sullivan & Decker, 2009). A structured approach increases critical thinking "and is the best way to learn how to make quality decisions because it eliminates trial and error . . . a professional approach involves applying a theoretical model in problem solving and decision making" (Marquis & Huston, 2009, p. 5).

Issue Identification

The decision-making process begins by identifying the issue and analyzing the situation: "Why is a decision necessary? What needs to be determined" (Sullivan & Decker, 2009, p. 111)? This is frequently expressed as a disparity between what is and what should be (Robbins, Decenzo, & Coulter, 2009).

The therapeutic recreation manager identifies the issue and purpose for making a decision by analyzing the situation completely, including the specific objectives to be accomplished by the solution. "All too frequently decisions are made and implemented before all the facts have been gathered" (Tomey, 2009, p. 64). To avoid this, the manager asks a series of questions: What is the desirable situation? What are the presenting symptoms? What are the discrepancies? "What needs to be achieved, preserved, and avoided by whatever decision is made" (Sullivan & Decker, 2009, p.111)? Who is involved? When? Where? How? With answers to these questions the therapeutic recreation manager can develop tentative solutions and test them against what he or she knows (Tomey, 2009). Once the issue, consequences of the decision, and the outcomes of the decision are identified from all available information on the situation, the manager begins to explore possible alternatives.

As a final note, the manager's analysis identifies the limits within which the solution may fall. These limits may include budget constraints; agency policy; organizational behavior; the individual characteristics of top managers; and, the decision maker's time, energy, and conditions under which he or she operates (Sullivan & Decker, 2009).

Exploring Alternatives through Creative Thinking

Once the decision situation has been identified and the objectives and boundaries of an acceptable solution have been determined, the manager must explore and identify alternative solutions (Tomey, 2009). The greater the number of alternatives, the greater the chance of having a sound final decision (Marquis & Huston, 2009). And, when various alternatives are not explored completely, the course of action is limited.

First, the manager must determine if the situation is covered by law, policy, standards, or evidence-based practices. If not, typical sources for identifying alternatives are experience, practices in other agencies, other managers, and other interested parties. Input from others who are respected in decision making and from others, including those who may be affected by the decision, may generate or identify other ways of looking at the situation and are best practices of participatory management.

Departmental Policy, Genesis Medical Center, Davenport, Iowa

Subject: **MEDICAL** Emergency Management, Off-Campus

Effective Date: 8/92

Section: Physical Medicine and Rehabilitation

Supersedes: M: 460D- 4.15460E-21.8

Primary Responsibility: PM&R Medical Director/Service Line Director

Revised: 2/11

Cross Reference: Home Evaluations Outings, Community Reintegration Program

Review Cycle: Annually

I. POLICY:

Hospital staff will utilize established procedure for management of medical emergency situations for off-campus activities.

II. PURPOSE:

To ensure that individuals receive appropriate and timely care in the event of a medical emergency during staff-supervised outings.

III. DEFINITIONS:

Minor Injury—Abrasion, bruise, small laceration with no/minimal bleeding, etc.

Medical Emergency—Fracture, dislocation, large laceration with bleeding, respiratory arrest, cardiac arrest, sudden changes in mental status or ability to speak, etc.

IV. PRACTICE [rules]:

A. Cellular phone, Medical Emergency Bag, and a portable file containing critical information about the patients will be carried by staff on all off-campus activities.

B. Medical emergency status will be determined by staff attending the off-campus activity.

V. GENERAL CONSIDERATIONS:

All staff participating in off-campus outings must be current in their Basic Cardiac Life Support training, and at least one staff member must be certified in basic first aid.

VI. RESPONSIBILITY:

A. All staff are responsible to have sufficient knowledge of first aid to respond appropriately in a medical emergency.

B. The staff person securing the phone and medical emergency bag for the outing is responsible to ensure the phone is working properly and the emergency bag is complete prior to leaving the campus.

VII. PROCEDURE:

A. Prior to an off-campus event, the therapist responsible for the outing will obtain an order from the attending physician allowing the patient to participate in the off-campus event.

B. Prior to leaving the campus, a Cerner Report Sheet and Discharge Medication Order Form for each participating patient will be obtained by the therapist. This information will be placed in a file and added to the medical emergency bag to be used as needed during an emergency. The two reports listed above provide the following information: medical conditions, emergency contact persons, primary care physician, allergies, and list of medications.

C. In the event of a minor injury, first aid will be administered as deemed appropriate.

D. In the event of a medical emergency, emergency services will be called by dialing 911 and CPR/first aid will be administered to stabilize the ill/injured patient.

E. If the individual's condition is stable, he/she will be transported back to hospital. In the event that first aid is not sufficient to stabilize the individual, staff will call for emergency medical assistance that will assume responsibility for the individual's care.

F. Outing staff will notify the nursing unit as soon as possible that illness/injury occurred and give a report regarding the individual's status and disposition.

G. Upon return to the hospital, the outing staff will ensure that the attending physician has been notified of the incident.

H. Outing staff will complete an unusual occurrence report upon return to the unit and document facts regarding the incident in the individual's medical record.

VIII. REFERENCES:

CARF The Rehabilitation Accreditation Commission (2009) Medical Rehabilitation Standards Manual. Section 1.H. Health and Safety. Pages 56, 60.

IX. ENDORSEMENTS:

Rehabilitation Inpatient Committee/Rehabilitation Performance Improvement Committee

Reviewed: 3/03; 3/04; 3/06; 3/07; 3/08; 3/09

Reviewed/Revised: 3/99; 3/00, 3/01, 3/02, 3/05, 5/07; 3/10; 2/11

Figure 5.1 Organizational Policy

Departmental Policy, Genesis Medical Center, Davenport, Iowa
Subject: **OUTINGS**, Community Reintegration Program
Effective Date: 3/05
Section: Physical Medicine and Rehabilitation
Supersedes: M: 456-D-5.5
Primary Responsibility: PM&R Medical Director/Service Line Director
Revised: 3/11
Cross Reference: MEDICAL EMERGENCY MANAGEMENT—Off-Campus
Review Cycle: Annual

I. POLICY:

A Community Reintegration Program shall be provided to appropriate patients in order to increase physical, cognitive, psychosocial, and pre-vocational skills while at the same time promoting optimal integration into the community post-discharge.

II. PURPOSE:

To provide guidelines that ensure the safety of patients and staff during their participation in the Community Reintegration Program.

III. DEFINITIONS:

None

PRACTICE [rules]:

A. Patient must have a written order from the physician to participate in the outing.
B. When any one of the Rehabilitation vehicles are being used on an outing, the person driving the vehicle must have a valid driver's license.
C. Specific therapist or team members and the referred patient(s) will determine the type of outing that will address their needs.
D. Ratio of staff to patient(s) will be directly related to the safety needs of the patient(s) as well as their specific treatment goals.
E. When a patient's medical status deems it inappropriate to be temporarily away from the hospital, the patient will not participate in a community outing.
F. A minimum of one staff member on each outing will be trained in CPR/First Aid.
G. Alcohol consumption or nonprescription drugs are not allowed on any outing unless approved by the physician.
H. All dietary restrictions will be established prior to an outing.
I. Cellular phone, Medical Emergency Bag, and a portable file containing critical information about the patients will be carried by staff on all outings.
J. Therapeutic Recreation will pay $10 towards the cost of the outing for each patient. Any additional expenses will be the patient's responsibility.
K. A patient will not participate in a Community Reintegration session if he/she poses a risk to self or other's personal safety.
L. Community Reintegration Sessions will not be held during threatening or extreme weather conditions.

IV. GENERAL CONSIDERATIONS: N/A

V. RESPONSIBILITY:

All members of the Community Reintegration team will be responsible for participating in the decision making related to the patient outing to ensure patient and staff safety.

VI. PROCEDURE:

A. When a community reintegration outing is deemed appropriate for a patient, the Certified Therapeutic Recreation Specialist will request a written order from the Physiatrist.
B. The therapist and patient/family will meet to discuss the outing prior to the session.
C. The therapist responsible for the outing will need to make transportation arrangements prior to the outing. The following forms of transportation may be used: rehabilitation car, rehabilitation van, patient's personal vehicle, caretaker's vehicle.
D. Prior to the outing, the patient and the team will identify outcomes for the activity which will be documented in the patient Portable Profile and the Community Reintegration Note.
E. A list of patient's attending the outing will be distributed to the appropriate nursing unit 1 hour prior to the outing.
F. All nursing procedures will be completed before the outing.
G. Prior to the outing, the therapist responsible for the outing will obtain the following information: medical conditions, emergency contact persons, primary care physician, allergies, and list of medications for each patient participating in the outing. A "Medication Orders" form can be printed from Cerner. This information will be placed in a file and added to the Medical Emergency Bag to be used as needed during an emergency.
H. Documentation related to goal achievement will be included in the patient Portable Profile and in the Community Reintegration Note. This note will be located in the Therapeutic Recreation section of the electronic medical record.
I. Appropriate aspects of the outing will be discussed with all the team members at the next scheduled patient- care conference, or sooner if deemed necessary.

VII. REFERENCES:

CARF The Rehabilitation Accreditation Commission (2009) Medical Rehabilitation Standards Manual. Section 1.H. Health and Safety. Pages 56, 60.

CARF The Rehabilitation Accreditation Commission (2009) Medical Rehabilitation Standards Manual. Section 2. The Rehabilitation Process for the Persons Served. Page 109.

VIII. ENDORSEMENTS:

Physical Medicine and Rehabilitation Operations / Reviewed: 3/07; 3/09 / Reviewed/Revised: 3/06; 5/07; 4/08; 3/10; 3/11

Figure 5.2 Departmental Policy Aligned with Organizational Policy

Departmental Policy, Genesis Medical Center, Davenport, Iowa
Subject: **PRIORITIZING** of Patients
Effective Date: 6/1/95
Section: Therapeutic Recreation
Primary Responsibility: Manager Therapeutic Recreation
Revised: 5/07
Review Cycle: Annual

I. POLICY:

All Physical Medicine and Rehabilitation patients with a referral for Therapeutic Recreation will be contacted by CTRS. If patient is unreceptive or unable to tolerate TR services, they will be put on hold.

II. PURPOSE:

1. To ensure that patients who will benefit most from TR interventions will be made a priority.
2. To allow the CTRS to better prioritize their patient caseload and improve efficiency.

III. DEFINITIONS:

TR—Therapeutic Recreation
CTRS—Certified Therapeutic Recreation Specialist

IV. PRACTICE: N/A

V. GENERAL CONSIDERATIONS: N/A

VI. RESPONSIBILITY:

The Therapeutic Recreation Specialist is responsible for documenting and communicating "Hold" orders with the physician and the rest of the team.

VII. PROCEDURES:

A. When a therapeutic recreation order is received, the therapist will provide therapy to the patient daily.
B. A patient will either be seen in a small group setting or individually. This will be determined by the patient's deficits and their preference.
C. When patient is unreceptive or not able to tolerate therapeutic recreation sessions, the therapist will put the patient on hold, notify the physician and continue to monitor the patient on a weekly basis.
D. The Interdisciplinary Progress Report form will be used to document those patients who are on hold. This form will be placed in the patient's chart under the "Rehab & Therapy" tab.

VIII. REFERENCES: None

IX. ENDORSEMENTS:

Reviewed: 9/03, 9/04, 5/07 / Reviewed/Revised: 9/01, 9/02, 5/05, 6/08, 5/09

Figure 5.3 Procedures within Department Policy

Table 5.4 Creative Thinking Steps

Felt Need

Creative solutions to situations are identified. Decision- making stresses the choice of a solution, while the creative process emphasizes the novelty or uniqueness of the solution (Tomey, 2009). "Creativity is a latent quality, activated when a person becomes motivated by the need for self-expression or by the stimulation of a problem" (Tomey, 2009, p. 71).

Preparation

The second phase is a work stage from which creative ideas emerge (Tomey, 2009). "Innovation partially depends on the number of options considered. By exploring relationships among potential solutions, one may identify additional solutions" (Tomey, 2009, p. 71). Libraries and the web are used to collect data. A creative person may take notes, develop them along with other ideas, review the gathered evidence, and combine the most appropriate aspects of old solutions into new alternatives (Tomey, 2009).

Incubation

"Incubation, the third phase, is a period for pondering the situation" (Tomey, 2009, p. 72). Repetition of some thoughts with no new ideas is a sign of fatigue and indicates that it is a good time to start the incubation period. "A time should be set to reexamine the situation and review the data collected during the preparation phase" (Tomey, 2009, p. 72).

Illumination

Illumination is the discovery of a solution. "It may come to mind in the middle of the night or during the performance of another task" (Tomey, 2009, p. 72). It is recommended that the idea be recorded so the details can be preserved regardless of when the illumination occurs (Tomey, 2009).

Verification

"Verification, the fifth and final phase of creative decision making, is the period of experimentation when the idea is improved through modification and refinement" (Tomey, 2009, p. 72). The advantages and disadvantages of each alternative are weighed, resources and constraints are evaluated, and potential technical and human problems are considered. By comparing the advantages and disadvantages of options, the manager is better able to choose the most desirable alternative (Tomey, 2009).

One may also generate alternatives from professional meetings, review of periodicals, continuing education, experts in the field, research, and searching the web (Tomey, 2009). Last, when examining decisions to be made through a formal process, the manager may find that the status quo is the right alternative (Marquis & Huston, 2009).

Creativity is essential to critical thinking processes (Sullivan & Decker, 2009). "Creativity is the ability to develop and implement new and better solutions" (Sullivan & Decker, 2009, p. 106). Critical thinking using creative thought processes fosters receptivity to new options. Consequently, cultivating creativity is one way to keep a department viable by adapting to the ever-changing health and human service environment. The creative process has five steps that we can learn, which are listed in Table 5.4 (see p. 67).

Evaluating Alternatives

This step is a continuation of the previous step, including the creative process. Consideration in this step needs to be given to the feasibility of the alternative, its satisfaction, and its consequences (Griffin, 1990).

The first question to ask is whether or not an alternative is feasible. Is it within the realm of probability and practicality? A manager may want to record the pros and cons for each alternative and analyze this information to make his or her decision.

When an alternative has passed the test of feasibility, it must next be examined to see how satisfactory it would be. Satisfaction refers to the extent to which the alternative will satisfy the conditions of the decision situation. For example, the therapeutic recreation manager wants to increase programming in the community by 50%. One alternative is to hire a new practitioner. If closer examination reveals that the employment of the practitioner would only expand programming by 35%, it may not be satisfactory. Depending on the circumstances, the manager may go ahead and employ a new practitioner and search for other ways to achieve the remaining 15% expansion, or the manager may simply drop the consideration until another day (Griffin, 1990).

Finally, if the alternative is both feasible and satisfactory, its probable consequences must be assessed. From a practical viewpoint however, one cannot project every possible consequence for every alternative. Still, questions need to be addressed. To what extent will a particular alternative influence or stress other parts of the agency or organization? What will the cost be to implement the alternative? Even when an alternative is both feasible and satisfactory, the consequences might be such that it must be eliminated from further consideration (Griffin, 1990).

Selecting an Alternative

The next step in the decision-making process is to select an alternative course of action. In many situations the decision is obvious from the analysis, although managers should remember that it may be possible to have two or more acceptable alternatives.

Before implementation, managers may want to test the soundness of the decision depending on the situation and solution. Several techniques may be employed. Herbert and Estes (1977) suggested that a person assume the role of "devil's advocate." Another possible method is to project the decision into detailed plans, thereby revealing any serious flaws in the prospective course of action. Another answer is to ask others in similar managerial roles to give constructive feedback concerning the potential solution (Newman, 1964). Decisions may also be tested by trying them out on a limited basis, such as pilot testing. Last, the manager may want to review and take a second look, just as a second opinion can determine the ultimate success or failure of a solution. The manager should go back to the basics and ask: Will this decision accomplish the stated objectives? Is it workable and efficient? Will it be effective over the long term? And, can the decision be implemented? When these questions and others have been answered to the manager's satisfaction, it is time to implement the solution (Griffin, 1990).

Once a decision has been made, the manager should be aware of the natural post-decision reaction called *cognitive dissonance* (Festinger, 1975). Very simply, cognitive dissonance means that once a person makes a decision, he or she is likely to develop second thoughts because of the favorable characteristics of some of the rejected alternatives. Moreover, the manager may talk to others about the positive aspects of the decision. In doing so, the manager is attempting to convince himself or herself, as well as others, of the wisdom of the decision.

In general, the more desirable the characteristics of the rejected alternatives and the faster the decision had to be made, the greater the cognitive dissonance (Brehm & Cohen, 1962). Awareness of this natural human tendency should give therapeutic recreation managers greater objectivity in testing and evaluating their choices. Moreover, it should provide the manager with a helpful perspective in discussing with staff the merits of the decisions.

Implementing the Decision

After a decision has been reached, it needs to be implemented. In some decision situations implementation is easy; in others, it will be difficult. In the change process, there are usually two types of resistance: that incurred by the nature of .the change and that incurred by misperceptions of what the change might mean. Some individuals resist change, which is usually the result of insecurity, inconvenience, and fear of the unknown. Thus, the manager needs to communicate in a manner that does not arouse antagonism (Tomey, 2009). The decision and procedures for implementation can be explained in an effort to win cooperation. A major decision requires a plan of action when "conveying the decision to those affected and getting their commitment" (Robbins, Decenzo, & Coulter, 2011, p. 61). Anticipating most questions helps the manager to explain the changes in ways that will alleviate groundless fears (Griffin, 1990).

The therapeutic recreation manager should avoid making premature and ineffective responses to resistance as it develops. These ineffective responses include self-justification, advice giving (i.e., "What I would do if I were you . . ."), premature persuasion (i.e., "Later, you'll see it my way."), censoring (i.e., meeting opposition with disapproval), and punishing behavior.

Evaluating the Decision

Evaluation, the final step, is a matter of analyzing the positive and negative aspects of a solution derived by using a scientific thought process. Depending on the solution being evaluated, suggested methods to use alone or in combination include interviews, individual observations, surveys, quality-assurance scales, audits, and various types of questionnaires. The bottom line is evaluating whether or not the alternative chosen has served its original purpose.

Evaluation examines both the objective and subjective result. Was the result the one expected, and was the result desired positive or negative? If the alternative appears not to be working, the manager can identify the second or third choice for adoption. The manager might decide to give it more time to work or begin the decision-making process all over again.

Evaluation can occur in relation to application for future situations, or it can occur in terms of the entire decision-making process incurred for this particular situation. Which steps were performed adequately or inadequately? What did the therapeutic recreation manager learn as a result of the process? The manager who evaluates his or her decision-making experiences learns from mistakes and with each new decision he or she can add to their repertoire of choices (Marquis & Huston, 2009). Thus, through continued decision making we identify more alternatives, increasing our decision-making skills.

LEARNING OUTCOME

Outline group decision-making techniques and analytical tools managers use in decision making and problem solving.

Group Decision-Making Techniques

The widespread use of participatory management in health and human services requires therapeutic recreation managers weigh the desirability of using groups rather than making individual decisions (Sullivan & Decker, 2009). Group decision making places the manager in a facilitator and consultant role. "Compared to individual decision making, groups can provide more input, often produce better decisions, and generate more commitment" (Sullivan & Decker, 2009, p. 111). Groups have a greater quantity and diversity of information, and as a result can identify more alternatives than can the manager (Robbins, Decenzo & Coulter, 2011). Additionally, "decisions made by groups may be perceived as more legitimate than decisions made by a single person" (Robbins, Decenzo & Coulter, 2011, p. 71). Lastly, group decisions tend to be more creative and accurate than do individual decisions.

One should also recognize the disadvantages to group participation in decision making. Group decisions may result from social pressures. The subordinate may be influenced by a desire to be accepted by the group or to appease the manager. Hierarchical pressures may lead subordinates to acquiescence of the manager's desires (Tomey, 2009). Another disadvantage of group participation in decision making is the amount of work time a manager devotes to coordinating and facilitating group decisions. Also, the speed with which group decision making occurs is inferior to the time a manager might devote to the same decision situation. Other challenges to group participation in decision making may include the following:

- Every problem situation is not automatically a group issue.
- Some groups are not functioning at a level where they could produce a usable solution.
- Sometimes information cannot be shared with the staff, and the manager must make an independent decision.
- In a crisis situation, there may not be time for a group to convene and produce a solution, and the manager must do so.

Groups are best used in decision making when time and deadlines allow for group processes, the decision is multifaceted, members share the department goals, and there is a need for acceptance of the decision if it is to be properly implemented (Sullivan & Decker, 2009). The right side of the brain is intuitive and conceptual and is used in creative thinking while the left side is analytical and sequential. Processes like brainstorming, think tanks, the Delphi technique, and modeling are avenues to promote the use of the right side of the brain. A number of these techniques are used by the manager to foster creative group decision making and explore solution alternatives.

Interaction Group

One of the most common and popular forms of group decision making is an interaction group (Griffin, 1990). An existing or a newly designated group is asked to make a decision about something. Existing groups might be department staff or standing committees. Newly designated groups can be ad hoc committees, task forces, or teams. Following discussion, a decision is reached without concern for organizing or facilitating a particular interaction format. While there is value in this type of group, such as sparking new ideas and promoting understanding, the disadvantage is that it is open to political pressures.

Brainstorming

Another popular form of group decision making is brainstorming. Group members meet together, possibly away from the problem site, and generate lots of ideas without consideration of their relative value. Members do not critique ideas as they are proposed but are encouraged to improve on each other's ideas. Evaluating the merit of each solution follows after all ideas have been generated (Sullivan & Decker, 2009). The environment is the key to successful brainstorming, and participants must be comfortable within the setting. These brainstorming sessions may be called *retreats* if they last for any length of time. The major disadvantage with this form is cost and arranging a time that can accommodate everyone. Brainstorming is also a technique used in total quality management (TQM) and continuous quality improvement (CQI). However, time is not spent away from the setting.

Nominal Group Technique

In some settings and depending on the situation, the nominal group technique (NGT) might be appropriate. Nominal groups are used most often to generate creative and innovative alternatives or ideas. In the NGT process, the manager presents a problem to a group and each member silently lists what he or she believes to be the best solution or alternative. After a brief period of time, each participant is asked to give his or her idea, which is recorded. This process continues without discussion, except for simple clarification, until all ideas have been recorded. Then an open forum takes place. After each idea is openly discussed, the participants privately rank the various alternatives from least acceptable to the one solution they believe to be the best. The decision idea that receives the highest overall rating is the first choice and is presented as the decision of the group. Ultimately, the manager may retain the authority to accept or reject the group's decision.

Delphi Group Method

One group participative method is the Delphi group method. The basic format is very similar to the NGT process. The major difference is that the group membership is anonymous: Participants do not meet face-to-face. Ideas are collected through a sequence of questionnaires, usually not exceeding three, interspersed with manager-prepared summaries of participant ideas from each of the previously disseminated questionnaires (Sullivan & Decker, 2009). Only the manager who has selected the participants knows the group mix. All information gathered about the problem and all of the suggested ideas and solutions proposed by the participants are given to the manager only. Personal feedback is provided by the manager to each member with regard to all suggestions. All members of the group are made aware of the other responses and reactions being generated. The selection process is handled in a similar fashion as the NGT, but communication remains confidential and identities anonymous. When a final decision is reached, it is presented as a group decision, but participants are not identified. The time factor associated with this form rules out routine, everyday decision use. However, its use with large numbers of experts who are geographically dispersed is extensive.

Electronic Meetings

Computer technology enables managers to facilitate group generation of ideas by recording individual member ideas as they are presented during brainstorming and NGT sessions. Meeting rooms with individual terminals allow group members to enter responses onto computer screens. All comments as well as aggregate votes are displayed on a projection screen (Robbins, Decenzo & Coulter, 2011). Technology increases the speed and anonymity of responses while allowing group members to be truthful. Expense and availability of the systems may be drawbacks, yet electronic meetings are faster and cheaper than traditional face-to-face meetings. A videoconference is a variation of an electronic meeting that allows professionals in different locations to link together electronically to have face-to-face meetings: Such meetings allow feedback among professionals while saving travel time.

Analytical Decision-Making Tools

A number of analytical tools are available to the manager to "provide order and direction in obtaining and using information or . . . in selecting who should be involved in making the decision" (Marquis & Huston, 2009, p. 20). These tools visualize options to help the manager evaluate each alternative (Tomey, 2009). Computers are used with a number of these tools and to simulate models and games to explore alternatives and consequences using trial and error to select the best solution. Because real-life situations can be simulated, computers are used for training in decision making (Tomey, 2009).

Decision Grids, Gantt Charts, Consequence Tables

A spreadsheet is created to examine each alternative according to set criteria. These criteria are weighted, so the final decision is based on a numerical value. When selecting a candidate for a position, this method might be helpful. A decision grid allows one to visually compare one alternative against each of the others assigning a numeric value to each criterion (Marquis & Huston, 2009) (see Figure 5.4).

The format used in decision grids is used in Gantt charts and consequence tables. A Gantt chart is a grid with rows for tasks and columns for the time frame. When the task is in progress, a line is drawn through the time frame with an X placed at task completion (Tomey, 2009). Each step in the decision-making process is plotted by time; ultimately, the manager identifies dates for decision making and evaluating outcomes of the chosen alternative. In a consequence table, the objectives for a decision or

Alternative	Financial effect	Political effect	Departmental effect	Time	Decision
#1					
#2					
#3					
#4					

Figure 5.4 A Decision Grid

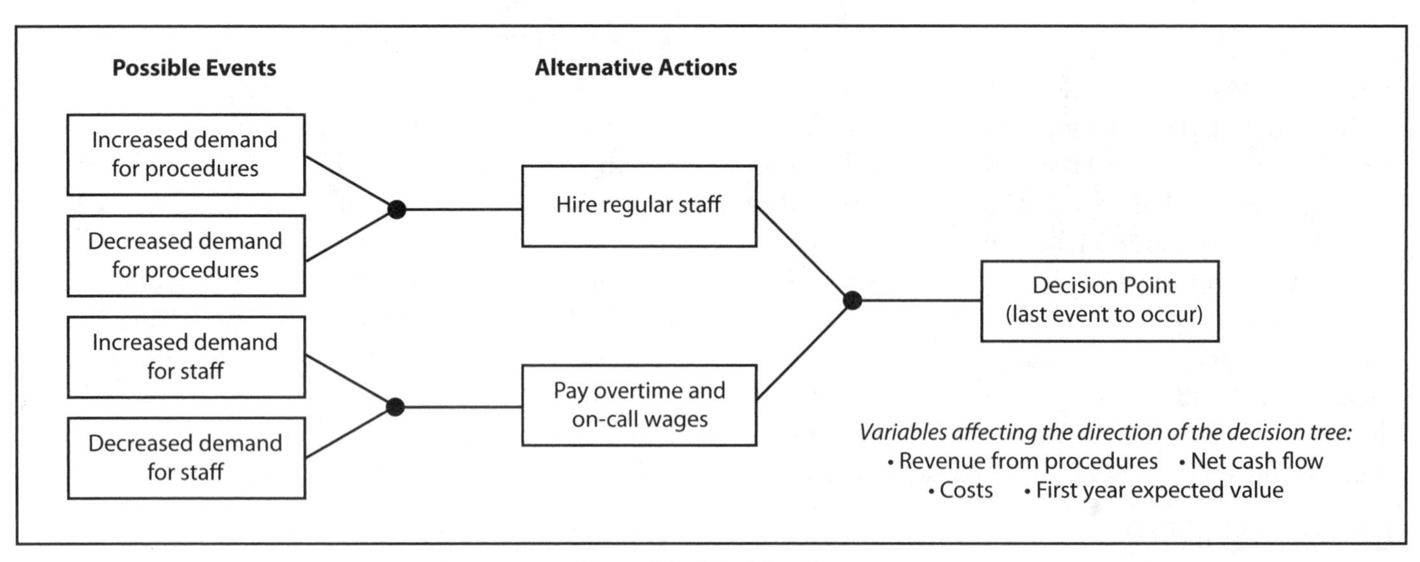

Figure 5.5 A Decision Tree

solving a problem are listed by row with each alternative placed in a separate column. Each alternative is then rated on how well it would meet each of the decision objectives; once each alternative is rated, the manager ranks the objectives selecting the most desirable choice (Marquis & Huston, 2009).

Decision Trees

A decision tree is a graphic representation that plots a decision over time as it is tied to the outcomes of other events. The tree plots the events with the alternative actions while introducing the variables affecting the direction of the decision tree. Hiring full-time versus using on-call staff illustrates managerial considerations when specific services like aquatic therapy are in demand. In Figure 5.5, variables affecting the direction of the decision tree include revenue from aquatic therapy, personnel expenses, net cash flow, and variability in demand.

Program Evaluation and Review Technique (PERT)/ Critical Path Method (CPM)

A PERT model is "a flow chart that predicts when events and activities must take place if a final event is to occur" (Marquis & Huston, 2009, p. 23). A critical path shows an activity that must occur in the sequence before management or staff may proceed. Often PERT/CPM are depicted in the same flow chart. A critical path is shown by lines that connect decision boxes according to time necessary to complete tasks. PERT charts are helpful when a group of people are working on a project and during process evaluation as the decision-making process unfolds.

Problem Solving

Management is the successful balance of two behaviors: solving problems and achieving goals. Managers usually associate problem solving with the conflict that stems from antagonistic interaction among individuals. However, problems can develop from unfinished paperwork, delays and interruptions, complaints from staff and consumers, lost or damaged supplies and equipment, excessive time spent on an activity, and absenteeism or turnover of staff. A problem is an obstruction, mental or physical, that presents itself to the individual—some undefined situation that keeps one from moving on. The manager must recognize when a problem exists and accept responsibility to find a solution.

Problem solving can be defined as a process used when a gap is perceived between an existing state and a desired state (Sullivan & Decker, 2009). Problem solving involves a series of steps similar to the decision-making process; and, one of the steps is always decision making (Marquis & Huston, 2009). The process organizes available information to come up with the best possible solution. It is a deliberate, thoughtful way to deal with an immediate situation that is creating some kind of difficulty for which there is no ready-made solution. Instead of reacting to a problem without thinking it through, problem solvers try to sort out the complexities of the situation first and then bring some thought and organization to their actions to resolve the problem (Sullivan & Decker, 2009; Whitehead, Weiss, & Tappen, 2010).

Problem solving itself does not supply answers. It is only a process by which one arrives at an answer. Its major usefulness is in providing guidelines when one is faced with a problem. Problem solving consists of steps quite similar to the therapeutic recreation process, as shown in Table 5.5. While the therapeutic recreation process refers to the use of these steps in relation to the client or group, problem solving refers to any kind of problem, whether it is related to the clients, colleagues, or department challenges.

Table 5.5 Comparison of the Problem-Solving and Therapeutic Recreation Processes

Problem Solving Steps	Therapeutic Recreation Process
Define the problem	Assessment
Gather information	
Analyze information	
Develop solutions	Planning
Make decision	
Implement	Implement
Evaluate	Evaluate

Problem-Solving Process

Define the Problem

The problem is defined in a descriptive statement that is as objective and specific as possible. The manager determines if the problem is situational, requiring only intervention with an explanation, or is complex, requiring exploration of a number of issues before the real problem emerges (Sullivan & Decker, 2009; Whitehead, Weiss, & Tappen, 2010). Defining the scope of a problem also helps the manager decide whether a lasting solution is necessary or just a stopgap measure (Sullivan & Decker, 2009). To illustrate, a manager's dissatisfaction with staff documentation might result because adherence to protocol was not in evidence (practice issue) or staff were unfamiliar with the agency's software system (stopgap, e.g., training issue). People may be vague as they are uncertain about the real problem; thus the manager must sort through feelings and facts to identify the real problem.

Gather Information

Collecting data and gathering information allows the manager to look for "clues to the scope and solution of the problem" (Sullivan & Decker, 2009, p. 115). The experiences of the manager and everyone involved are sources of information. Some data may be inaccurate, yet some will be helpful in pursuing innovative ideas. If data are unreliable or too incomplete to define the problem, more will have to be gathered before proceeding. Sometimes a manager can include gathering more data as one of the selected strategies for resolving the problem.

Sometimes it is not possible to immediately define the problem, but only to come up with several alternative solutions. If this occurs, it is necessary to gather more information on each solution before selecting one to follow through in the planning stage. Because no amount of information is ever complete, critical thinking skills are essential to analyzing evidence and potential value conflicts (Sullivan & Decker, 2009).

A manager may involve everyone in every problem-solving phase or engage different people in each, depending on the problem to be solved and input needed. Although this may not always result in objective information, misinformation is reduced as anyone involved has "an opportunity to tell what he or she thinks is wrong with a situation" (Sullivan & Decker, 2009, p. 115). When interviewing others to gain information for problem solving, open-ended questions and active listening are used. The manager needs to take care not to judge others' suggestions or to convey, verbally or nonverbally, that he or she disapproves of their ideas. If the manager does not remain open to the information he or she solicits, others will sense that their input is not really important and will stop communicating with the manager.

Analyze Information

Once a reasonably adequate amount of data has been collected, the manager begins to analyze it. Is it a problem in its own right, or is it merely a symptom of a problem that is broader in scope? It is important to look for patterns in the data as well as for clues to the underlying dynamics of the situation, remembering there are often multiple rather than single factors at work when a problem arises. A number of variables are used to analyze the collected information (refer to Table 5.6, p. 74) (Sullivan & Decker, 2009).

Table 5.6 Criteria to Review Collected Information

- Reliability
- Degree of importance
- Time sequence of events
- Cause- and- effect relationships
- Categorical factors like human (personality), technological (competencies), policy (rules, budget)
- Time frame (length) of the situation

Develop Solutions

Creativity and the critical thinking process are important as possible solutions are generated (Sullivan & Decker, 2009; Whitehead, Weiss, & Tappen, 2010). Every alternative solution or appropriate action for any given problem that one can think of should be recorded. None of these strategies should be discarded until all the possibilities have been considered. The identification of alternative solutions is needed to keep the problem solver flexible and open to the potentialities present in each situation. Some situations offer an insufficient range of feasible solutions. Thus a lack of alternatives may reflect the environmental circumstances, or it may reflect a lack of creative thought on the part of the manager. An even more complex situation is one in which there are unlimited potential alternatives. In this instance the problem solver must use categorization to select a representative but workable number of alternatives for consideration.

An uncritical attitude may discourage the use of old solutions to new problems, yet past experience may help the critical- thinking process and prepare for future problem solving (Sullivan & Decker, 2009). The manager may enter the picture and find the problem is long- standing as recognized by a comment like "We have tried this before and it didn't work." It is natural to use old solutions and to discard solutions under these circumstances. The manager uses brainstorming and creativity to foster illumination and verification of potential solution options.

Make Decision

After reviewing all of the possible actions, strategies are selected that are most feasible and satisfactory and have the fewest undesirable consequences (Sullivan & Decker, 2009). Some strategies require immediate action, as with safety and disciplinary problems, while others like technical problems, with new software programs, may require the involvement of those impacted by the change in order to minimize their resistance. Consequently, the manner in which the decision action is shared is important to ensure proper implementation.

Implement

The decision is implemented after selecting the best alternative. As a plan is put into action, the verbal or nonverbal responses to it will indicate whether to proceed or to go back and think through the process again. If the solution involves change, the manager initiates change processes so the action is implemented. Staff responds to solutions when they fit in their acceptance zone, yet a manager does not abandon a course of action because a few object (Sullivan & Decker, 2009).

Evaluate

The manager reviews the plan and compares the results and benefits with those projected with the alternative solutions. Each step is critically analyzed so revisions are made continuously. The evaluation can be subjective as well as objective, including not only the measurable results but also any feeling of accomplishment or satisfaction from having resolved the problem successfully. This evaluation should also provide clues for future action. For example, what changes have contributed to the success of the solution and will the solution continue to work? Evaluating an outcome to affirm that the solution solved the problem builds on the experience, so problem solving becomes a skill used throughout the manager's career.

While the manager can approach each step of the problem-solving process, input from a group can promote the probability of more complete data collection, creative planning, successful implementation, and evaluation indicating problem resolution. People may generate solutions early in the problem-solving process and not wait until all the facts are collected; also, people have a tendency to oversimplify or to choose a solution that has worked in the past. Individual or group approaches to problem solving are similar to decision-making techniques. Delphi and nominal group techniques, task forces, and various analytical tools are employed in individual and group problem solving. Quality circles are also used to solve problems.

Personal Elements of Making Decisions and Solving Problems

The assumption that each person who receives the same information and uses the same scientific process will come to the same decision or problem solution does not hold true (Marquis & Huston, 2009). A manager who is creative and does not mind uncertainty develops decisions and solutions differently than one who is less likely to take risks. Decision making and problem solving involve both perception and evaluation. We perceive by sensation and intuition and evaluate our perceptions by thinking and feeling. Because each person has different values and life experiences, we perceive and think differently given the same set of circumstances (Marquis & Huston, 2009).

The therapeutic recreation manager's personality can and does affect how and why certain decisions are made and certain personal and professional problems are addressed or ignored. One's culture, locus of control, self-esteem, age, developmental stage, values, personal preferences, and past experiences with illness, interventions, and decision making and problem solving may influence the process (Noone, 2002). Value judgments affect the alternatives generated and the final choice selected; for some, certain choices and solutions are not possible because of their beliefs (Marquis & Huston, 2009). Although preferred, one alternative may not be selected because it is too risky with regard to time or costs a manager perceives must be devoted to the preference. "The more mature the person and the broader his or her background, the more alternatives he or she can identify . . . Likewise, having made good or poor decisions in the past will influence a person's decision making" (Marquis & Huston, 2009, pp. 15–16). Caring, credibility, a futuristic perspective, confidence, courage, flexibility, energy, creativity, thinking outside of the box, and sensitivity tend to be qualities of successful decision makers and problem solvers (Marquis & Huston, 2009; Sullivan & Decker, 2009).

Managing Conflict

Conflict is inevitable and can be constructive or destructive. Conflict is an accepted consequence of people working together and it is often the reason for change in people and organizations (Sullivan & Decker, 2009). One estimate suggests that managers spend at least 20% of their time dealing with conflict (Sullivan & Decker, 2009). Conflict is a warning to the manager that something is amiss (Tomey, 2009). When conflict is not recognized, it tends to go underground. It then becomes less direct but more destructive and eventually becomes more difficult to confront and resolve. Thus, the therapeutic recreation manager needs to learn the sources and types of conflict and how to manage them so "subordinates' motivation and organizational productivity are not adversely affected" (Marquis & Huston, 2009, p. 487).

Conflict is the consequence of real or perceived differences in goals, attitudes, beliefs, actions, ideas, values, or feelings (a) within one individual, (b) between two or more individuals, (c) within one group, or (d) between two or more groups (Sullivan & Decker, 2009). Conflict can be a motivator to increase performance through creativity and problem solving or it can be stressful and destructive and result in workplace violence. This includes not only physical violence but also antisocial behaviors like pranks, scapegoating, or *bullying* (behavior that intends to exert power over another) that lead people to believe they have been harmed by an experience (Marquis & Huston, 2009; Sullivan & Decker, 2009). Negative consequences of conflict, besides resulting in harm, may be evident in absenteeism, turnover, and reduced service quality and productivity.

Learning Outcome

Describe sources of conflict that may have an effect on professionals in the workplace.

Sources of Conflict

When people work together in an agency there are numerous causes of conflict. Further, conflict increases with both the number of organizational levels and the number of specialties (Tomey, 2009). Conflict is greater as the degree of association increases and when some parties are dependent on others (Tomey, 2009). In addition, conflict has an effect on both the psychological health of persons involved and the efficiency of organizational performance. Unhealthy conflict relationships tend to involve feelings of low trust and low respect, which in turn are reflected in performance.

Competition for scarce resources, coupled with ambiguous jurisdictions plus the need for consensus, contributes to conflict. A manager depends on the allocation of money, personnel, supplies and equipment, and physical facilities or space to accomplish objectives. When one department, division, or unit receives fewer resources than another does, this can lead to perceptions of inequity and conflict (Sullivan & Decker, 2009; Tomey, 2009; Whitehead, Weiss, & Tappen, 2010). Because goals are the basis for allocating resources, conflict over multiple personal and organizational goals is a source of conflict (Sullivan & Decker, 2009). To illustrate, service providers desire to provide the highest level of intervention quality, while the funding source is concerned with maintaining the minimal cost to the client, that may mean reducing the length of stay or availability of alternative programs.

Individuals may have different value systems or perceptions of ethical responsibilities, which may lead to conflict. For example, top management may perceive information provided by a report from first-line managers as valuable. But the first-line manager may view the time in preparing the report and the report itself as busy work and may in the future resist completing such reports.

Different managerial or personality styles can also result in conflict. For instance, one person's style may be to discuss problems thoroughly before taking action, whereas another prefers immediate action and becomes extremely impatient with lengthy discussions. In such a situation, decision-making styles can cause conflict.

Associated with the previous example is conflict from interpersonal dynamics—in other words, the so-called personality clash when two persons distrust each other's motives, dislike one another, or for some other reason simply can't get along. Although standardized policies, rules, and procedures regulate behavior, make relationships more predictable, and decrease the number of arbitrary decisions, they impose added controls over the individual. To illustrate, men and women who value autonomy are likely to resist such controls (Tomey, 2009).

Other conflicts arise from cultural differences, beliefs, language, education, experience, skills, professional values and norms, status, pay differences, and workplace characteristics. Change may be seen as progress or as an unfortunate disruption in the present order of things. Coupled with this is change as the result of a merger or "takeover of an organization by another organization." Thus, the workplace itself generates conflict when, for example, increased workloads, multiple role demands, or economic security (layoffs) result from cost-reduction measures (Whitehead, Weiss, & Tappen, 2010). Some people perceive teamwork as a threat to their professional identity and to the territorial rights of their profession.

Off-the-job problems can bring about on-the-job conflicts. These include marital discord, alcoholism, drug use, financial problems, and mental stress. Clearly, the sources of conflict are endless, and the number of conflicts increases as the number of unresolved differences accumulates (Tomey, 2009). In summary, some conflicts result from the organizational structure and the work being done, while others evolve from personal and social relationships and communication, and, lastly, the environment or contextual factors like the work place itself or elements in a person's life are sources of issues and conflict.

Learning Outcome

Describe resolution strategies and outcomes of managing conflicts in the workplace.

Conflict Prevention and Resolution

Conflict resolution begins with preventive measures to reduce the number of conflicts within the unit, between parties from different departments, or between internal and external parties. Even before a conflict arises, a manager can take certain actions to prepare for conflict resolution.

One especially helpful prevention measure is to create a climate in which individual differences are considered natural and acceptable, with staff feeling free to speak out when difficulties do arise (Timmins, 2011). Although this does not sound difficult, there are strong pressures for conformity to counteract in establishing this climate. Encouraging open and honest communication, stressing to staff that department goals must take precedence over any individual or group goals, and having clearly defined tasks and areas of responsibility all help to reduce or avoid conflicts. A manager's effort to meet the needs of staff before a conflict arises can reduce the occurrence of conflicts.

The existence of a conflict within the department or with another department or unit within the same facility should not be interpreted as a symptom of serious malfunction but rather as a sign of a problem that needs to be resolved. It is helpful to maintain a realistically optimistic attitude that the conflict can be resolved. However, it is not unusual for those inexperienced in conflict negotiation to expect unrealistic outcomes (Sullivan & Decker, 2009).

When there are two parties or more with mutually exclusive ideas, attitudes, feelings, or goals, it is extremely difficult, without the commitment and willingness of all concerned, to arrive at an agreeable solution and to meet the needs of both parties (Sullivan & Decker, 2009).

Before managers attempt to intervene in conflict, they must be able to assess its five progressive stages (Marquis & Huston, 2009; Tomey, 2009). In the first stage, *latent conflict*, antecedent conditions like short staffing, change, budget cuts, or incompatible goals propel a situation toward conflict. Conflict may or may not result and the manager may intervene to prevent or reduce issues from escalating. If these preexisting conditions persist, a cognitive awareness of the stressful situation results; in this second stage of conflict, *perceived conflict*, one's personal perceptions can contribute to either an accurate or inaccurate assessment of the situation and affect the amount of threat or loss anticipated by the individual (Tomey, 2009). Perceived conflicts may also result when individuals have limited knowledge of the situation or when they misunderstand each other's position. At this stage conflicts may be resolved before the situation is internalized or felt. *Felt or affective conflict*, stage three, occurs when the conflict is emotionalized. Felt emotions include anger, hostility, and mistrust. Trusting may actually prevent conflict while a lack of a trusting attitude may create conflict (Tomey, 2009). Some perceive the conflict but don't feel it (i.e., person views situation as only a problem to be solved), while others feel conflict but not the problem (i.e., unable to identify cause of felt conflict). In the fourth stage, *manifest or overt conflict*, actions like debate and withdrawal are evident. People may be reluctant to address conflict due to fear of retaliation or a sense that they do not have a right to speak up (Marquis & Huston, 2009). These behaviors are learned early in life and tend to be unconsciously acquired; whereas, conflict resolution requires a conscious learning effort (Tomey, 2009). In the fifth and final stage, *conflict aftermath*, positive or negative outcomes result. Resolution is found with mutually agreed-on outcomes; a win-lose situation finds only one party truly committed to the outcome. As a consequence, conflict issues remain and may resurface to cause more conflict.

Conflict resolution begins with a decision regarding if and when to intervene. The therapeutic recreation manager should make sure the parties know when he or she is likely to intervene. Failure to intervene can allow the conflict to escalate, while early intervention may be demotivating to the parties, causing them to lose confidence in themselves and to reduce risk-taking behavior in the future. On the other hand, some conflicts are so minor, particularly if they are between two people, that intervention is not necessary and may be better handled by the two people. However, where there is potential for considerable harm to result from the conflict, the therapeutic recreation manager must intervene. Thus, once the decision to intervene is made, the manager investigates the situation, gathering information to identify the seriousness of the conflict (Timmins, 2011).

Next, the manager must make decisions as to when, where, and how the intervention should take place (Timmins, 2011). Routine problems can be handled in the manager's office, but serious conflicts should take place in a neutral location agreeable to both parties. The time and place should be one where distractions will not interfere and adequate time is available. Lastly, because conflict resolution takes time, the manager must be prepared to allow sufficient time for all parties to explain their points of view and to arrive at a mutually agreeable solution (Timmins, 2011).

Other management techniques besides personal intervention can be used to resolve conflict. Some of these include changing or clarifying goals, providing cooling-off periods, and establishing liaison persons. The latter approach is effective to reduce conflict between departments or units.

Resolution Strategies

The intent of conflict resolution is to work together more effectively (Whitehead, Weiss, & Tappen, 2010) to create a win-win situation or at the least recognition and acceptance of differences. The strategies used by the manager are influenced by the maturity of the parties, the urgency of the problem, decision to be made, and significance of the issue (Marquis & Huston, 2009; Robbins, Decenzo, & Coulter, 2011; Tomey, 2009); refer to Table 5.7 (p. 78) for review of several strategies (Marquis & Huston, 2009; Robbins, Decenzo, & Coulter, 2011; Tomey, 2009).

Resolution Outcomes

Three ways of dealing with conflict according to the outcome are: win-lose, lose-lose, or win-win (Filley, (1975). Win-lose methods include the use of competing/ forcing, negotiation, position power, mental or physical

Table 5.7 Selected Resolution Strategies

Active Listening

Too often individuals involved in an argument spend most of their time talking instead of listening. When one person is speaking, the other is busy preparing a rebuttal or thinking of additional ways to support his or her viewpoint rather than listening to what is being said. In addition, most people immediately judge the statements of others—either to agree or disagree. Frequently, the listener judges a statement from his or her point of view without consideration of the other person's perspective. True listening is not occurring—people hear what they expect or want to hear, rather than what the speaker intends to communicate. Both of these behaviors can cause disagreements to escalate into arguments. When neither person stops to listen, there is a good chance that agreement will be delayed or prevented altogether. Moreover, when emotions run high, people may say or do things they later regret. Davis, Skube, Hellervik, Gebelein, and Sheard (1992) suggested the following techniques to improve the effectiveness of active listening:

- Listen carefully to what the speaker is saying, giving full attention without thinking about how one intends to respond and without judging the speaker's statements.
- Get the speaker to clarify his or her position by asking open-ended questions starting with phrases such as the following: "Describe . . .". . . "Tell me about . . .". . . "Explain . . . . ." "How do you feel . . . . . ?"
- Periodically paraphrase what the speaker has said to ensure that one understands.
- Determine whether one's interpretations are becoming more accurate as the discussion progresses.
- Avoid interrupting the speaker.

Collaborating/Problem Solving

The slogan of this form of conflict resolution is "win-win"; both sides try to find mutually satisfying problem solutions (Tomey, 2009). Time pressures are minimal and the issue is too important for compromise. Each party sets aside their original goal to establish a supra-ordinate common goal; the focus remains on problem-solving while expressing a high concern for others' and one's own needs (Marquis & Huston, 2009; Robbins, Decenzo, & Coulter, 2011).

Avoidance

One method of dealing with conflict is to avoid it. The conflict is simply not addressed: "If we don't talk about it, the problem will go away." Avoidance does not offer a permanent way out of resolving conflict. However, if the problem is avoided for a period of time, the conflict situation may be taken to a higher authority. The technique is used in highly cohesive groups where participants do not want to do anything to interfere with good feelings each has for the other; when more information is needed, or the cost of dealing with the conflict is higher than the benefit of the solution, (Tomey, 2009). It reflects a low concern for one's own needs and needs of others—a lose-lose scenario (Tomey, 2009).

Smoothing/Accommodating

Smoothing/accommodating can be described as the process of playing down differences that exist between individuals or groups while emphasizing common interests. It is a diplomatic way of dealing with conflict by reducing the emotional component of the conflict. Differences are suppressed in smoothing, and similarities are accentuated, preserving harmony. This approach is used by managers to encourage someone to cooperate with another person. Although appropriate for minor disagreements, rarely are the conflicts actually resolved. This is a you win–I lose situation (Marquis & Huston, 2009; Tomey, 2009).

Compromise

Compromise is a middle-of-the road solution. Each party gives up something of value. While there is no clear winner, there is also no clear loser. Compromise has an advantage over restrictive and suppressive methods because conflicting persons or groups are less likely to feel hostility over the resolution of the problem. Compromise serves as a backup to resolve conflict when collaboration is ineffective. For compromise not to result in a lose-lose situation, both parties must give up something of equal value (Marquis & Huston, 2009).

Competing/Forcing

This technique considers changing the behavior of one or more of the conflicting parties. Competing occurs when one party seeks to win regardless of the cost to others. Managers may use this approach in situations involving unpopular, quick, or critical decisions (Marquis & Huston, 2009). This is a win-lose situation that also may be used when the manager is knowledgeable about the situation and able to make a sound decision (Tomey, 2009).

power, failure to respond, majority rule, and railroading a minority position (Sullivan & Decker, 2009). Win-lose outcomes often occur between groups. A potential negative consequence of this strategy is that frequent losing can lead to the loss of cohesiveness within groups and can diminish the authority of the manager. Lose-lose strategies may include compromise, smoothing/accommodating, avoidance, bribes for accomplishing disagreeable tasks, arbitration by a neutral third party, and resorting to the use of general rules instead of considering the merits of individual cases. Moreover, using a third-party arbitrator can lead to a lose-lose outcome.

Because an outsider may want to give something to each side, neither gets what is desired (Sullivan & Decker, 2009).

In win-lose and lose-lose strategies, the parties often personalize the issues by focusing on each other instead of on the problem. Intent on their personal differences, they avoid the more important matter of how to mutually solve their problem. Rather than identifying mutual needs, planning activities for resolution, and solving the problem, each party looks at the issue from his or her own point of view and strives for total victory (Sullivan & Decker, 2009).

By contrast, win-win strategies focus on goals and attempt to meet the needs of both parties; the goal is collaboration agreeable to both parties. These strategies emphasize consensus and integrative approaches to decision making (Tomey, 2009). The consensus process demands a focus on the problem (instead of on the other), on the collection of facts, on the acceptance of the useful aspects of conflict, and on the avoidance of self-oriented behavior. Integrative decision-making methods focus on the means of problem solution rather than the ends and are most often useful when the needs of the parties are polarized (Sullivan & Decker, 2009). The focus is on using the problem-solving process to guide and evaluate decision making. Both methods focus on defeating the problem, not each other.

In bringing this section and chapter to a close, it is well to note that managers need to be realistic in their conflict-resolution expectations. When two or more individuals hold mutually exclusive ideas, attitudes, feelings, or goals, it is difficult to arrive at an agreeable solution that meets the needs of everyone without the commitment and willingness of all parties involved. Negotiation skills are used in the resolution of most day-to-day conflicts and may be formalized and structured with collective bargaining (Marquis & Huston, 2009). The manager's intent is to create a win-win situation arriving at an agreeable solution among the parties involved through compromise and the resolution to accept that which may not be appropriate to change.

Summary

1. The manager's work world is greatly influenced by technology that creates a complex information environment. In this environment, a manager's competence is gauged by his or her ability to creatively and critically explore issues, make decisions, solve problems, and resolve conflicts.
2. Critical thinking is foundational to success as a manager, and like decision making, problem solving, and conflict resolution strategies, it is a process similar to APIE.
3. Decision making is the process through which choices are made. A professional approach to decision-making applies a theoretical model to reach a logical conclusion.
4. Inherent in each of the six decision-making steps (issue identification, exploring alternatives through creative thinking, evaluating alternatives, selecting an alternative, implementing a decision, evaluating a decision) is critical thinking and creativity that allow the professional to generate and examine new and better alternatives.
5. Policies explain how goals will be achieved and serve as guides that define the general course and scope of activities permissible for goal accomplishments—they set the boundaries for decision makers.
6. Procedures identify steps to implement a policy.
7. Rules are specific statements that tell managers what ought or ought not to be done in a given situation.
8. Like decision making, the problem-solving process is similar in nature to the therapeutic recreation process: define the problem, gather information, analyze the information, develop solutions, make a decision, implement and evaluate the decision. Without using critical and creative thinking, individuals try to identify the problem without gathering all the facts or try to oversimplify the problem to make it more manageable.
9. A number of techniques and tools encourage the manager and groups to incorporate critical and creative thinking into decision making and problem solving. These include interaction groups, brainstorming, NGT, Delphi methods, electronic meetings, decision grids and trees, and PERT/CPM.
10. Conflict is the consequence of real or perceived differences in goals, attitudes, beliefs, actions, ideas, values, or feelings that may be evident

within one individual, between two or more individuals, or within one group or between two or more groups.

11. Conflicts result from the organizational structure and the work being done, from personal and social relationships and communication, and are the result of contextual factors like the work place itself or elements in a person's life, like family discord or alcohol.
12. Conflict escalates through five stages. The manager may intervene to prevent or resolve conflicts. Depending on the selected resolution, the outcome of conflicts for the involved parties may be either lose-lose, win-lose, or win-win.

Critical Thinking Activities

1. What are the pros and cons of decisions made by groups (e.g., committee or task force) as compared to decisions by one person or the manager?
2. Think of an important decision you have made, such as choosing a university or choosing a major. How did you make this decision? Write out your response, supplying as much detail as possible. Did you follow a rational decision-making process or use intuition? Was it some combination of the two?
3. You are in your last semester of school with only your internship remaining to meet graduation requirements. You intend to complete an internship that will permit you to become professionally certified. As you narrow your choices you realize the financial needs of the experience may place a strain on your resources. The potential sites with the quality experiences to offer do not provide housing yet offer limited compensation like meals. Using the problem-solving process reviewed in this chapter, research and outline your alternatives, consequences, and decision describing the factors in each step of the model.

References

Brehm, J. W., & Cohen, A. R. (1962). *Exploration in cognitive dissonance*. New York, NY: John Wiley & Sons.

Castle, A. (2010). Comparing and contrasting health profiles: One dimension of critical thinking. *International Journal of Therapy and Rehabilitation, 17*(7), 345—352.

Davis, B. L., Skube, C. J., Hellervik, L. W., Gebelein, S. H., & Sheard, J. L. (1992). *Successful manager's handbook*. Minneapolis, MN: Personnel Decisions.

Festinger, L. (1975). *A theory of cognitive dissonance*. Stanford, CA: Stanford University Press.

Filley, A. C. (1975). *Interpersonal conflict resolution*. Glenview, IL: Scott, Foresman, and Company.

Griffin, R. W. (1990). *Management* (3rd ed.). Boston, MA: Houghton Mifflin.

Herbert, T. T., & Estes, R. W. (1977, October). Improving executive decisions by formalizing dissent: The corporate devil's advocate. *The Academy of Management Review, 2*(4), 662–667.

Marquis, B. L., & Huston, C. J. (2009). *Leadership roles and management functions in nursing theory and application* (6th ed.). Philadelphia, PA: Wolters Kluwer/Lippincott Williams & Wilkins.

Newman, W. H. (1964). *Administrative action*. Englewood Cliffs, NJ: Prentice-Hall.

Noone, J. (2002). Concept analysis of decision making. *Nursing Forum, 37*(3), 21–32.

Paige, J. B. (2003). Solve the policy and procedure puzzle. *Nursing Management, 34*(3), 45–48.

Robbins, S. P., Decenzo, D. A., & Coulter, M. (2011). *Fundamentals of management essential concepts and applications* (7th ed.). Upper Saddle River, NJ: Prentice-Hall.

Sullivan, E. J. & Decker, P. J. (2009). *Effective leadership and management in nursing* (7th ed.). Upper Saddle River, NJ: Pearson Prentice-Hall.

Timmins, F. (2011). Managers' duty to maintain good workplace communications skills. *Nursing Management, 18* (3), 30-–34.

Tomey, A. M. (2009). *Guide to nursing management and leadership* (8th ed.). St Louis, MO: Mosby Elsevier.

Whitehead, D. K., Weiss, S. A., & Tappen, R. M. (2010). *Essentials of nursing leadership and management* (5th ed.). Philadelphia, PA: F. A. Davis Company.

Zori, S., & Morrison, B. (2009). Critical thinking in nurse managers. *Nursing Economic$, 27*(2), 75-–80.

Section 2

MANAGING OPERATIONS

Chapter 6
Applying Technology and Implementing Research

Keywords

- Activity-contingent method
- Dashboard reports
- Electronic health record
- Evidence-based practice
- Informatics
- Interval-contingent approach
- Signal-contingent approach
- Technology plan

Learning Outcomes

After reading this chapter, students will be able to:

1. Define and explain *informatics* as it applies to the first-line therapeutic recreation manager.
2. Explain the concept of a dashboard report and identify the four characteristics of an effective dashboard report.
3. Explain the concept of an electronic health record. Outline the history and discuss the rationale for implementation of electronic health records in health and human service agencies.
4. Identify six challenges to implementing technology in health and human service agencies.
5. Define evidence-based practice. Describe the purpose and value of evidence-based practice.

Overview

Imagining the future of the therapeutic recreation profession is challenging. Can you anticipate the opportunities that innovative technology will offer? Try to envision the impacts of new research insights. While we cannot predict the future, we can be certain that technology and research will shape the future of the profession.

The development and application of new technology is changing the way health and human service agencies plan, operate, and communicate. Technology will continue to evolve in ways that will impact services. The pace and scale of change will continue to accelerate in the coming years. To take full advantage of technology's potential, first-line therapeutic recreation managers must understand the capabilities of technology systems and apply technology to achieve the organization's mission and goals. The use of technology systems enhances the management of therapeutic recreation services in a number of ways. For example, information technology systems help first-line managers make decisions about budget and finance, staffing, supplies and equipment, policies and procedures, program effectiveness, and communications. Technology can assist first-line managers in health and human service agencies to implement best practices, research, and evaluation. The purpose of this chapter is to highlight the rationale for the development of technology systems and demonstrate how these systems are effective tools for planning and managing therapeutic recreation services. This chapter also includes an overview of research applications in therapeutic recreation, with a focus on evidence-based practice.

Technology

Technology is changing the way therapeutic recreation services are designed, implemented, and evaluated. First-line therapeutic recreation managers are continuously adopting new technology that will enable increased capacity to gain higher-speed access to more resources and additional information. Technology often supports increased efficiency and reduced costs. Technology systems are being applied to maintaining client records, improving the quality of services and service delivery, supporting evidence-based and client-centered practice, and enhancing research. Information technology systems reduce the rate of errors in health and human service organizations by improving communications, making knowledge more readily accessible, assisting with calculations, performing checks in real time, assisting with monitoring, and providing decision-making support (Bates & Gawande, 2003). It is anticipated that nearly all management information will eventually be processed electronically.

Information and communication technology (ICT) is used to convey, manipulate, and store data electronically. Information and communication technology uses a variety of computing devices for e-mail, text messaging (short message service or SMS), video chat, and online social media (Perron, Taylor, Glass, & Margerum-Leys, 2010). Information and communication technology has transformed social relationships, education, health and human services, and the global community. The therapeutic recreation profession has not yet taken full advantage of the capabilities of information and communication technology for research, education, and practice. An understanding of how information and communication technology can improve all aspects of therapeutic recreation has become an essential competency for first-line therapeutic recreation managers. Competency will include the use of technology to manage employment and internships for Internet sites such as LinkedIn. Competency will also include an understanding of social media networks and how these networks can be applied to the management of health and human service organizations.

Learning Outcome

Define and explain informatics as it applies to the first-line therapeutic recreation manager.

A technology system is a set of related components (e.g., inputs, processes, and outputs) that collectively form a unified whole (Deluca & Enmark, 2002). Information technology systems are composed of people, hardware, software, data, and procedures. These systems support operational efficiency, functional effectiveness, quality service, and research in therapeutic recreation. The management of information technology is referred to as *informatics*. It is the design of systems that deliver the right information, to the right person, in the right place and time, in the right way. Health-care informatics is the study of the use of computer hardware, software, systematic languages, and data manipulation to collect and apply information in health and human services. Information technology is dramatically changing how individual client care information and provider-planning for care is entered into record, stored, and retrieved. For example, Walgreens pharmacy offers a smartphone application that enables a Walgreens customer to order a prescription refill by scanning the bar code on the medication container.

Technology Supporting Management Decisions

Effective technology plans demonstrate how an investment in technology will contribute to achieving the mission of the health and human service organization. The *technology plan* is the forward-looking strategic plan for the organization's technology needs (see Table 6.1). Technology is not an end in itself; rather it provides technological solutions that increase the organization's effectiveness. The purpose of any technology system is to incorporate the technology features and functions successfully into the daily operations of the organization to achieve specific goals and objectives (Deluca & Enmark, 2002). In developing a technology plan, the first-line manager must identify the most appropriate technology to accomplish the goals of the organization based on the availability of the resources, time, budget, and competence of the users (Hurd, Barcelona, & Meldrum, 2008). Effective technology plans are realistic and manageable relative to the agency's size and scope. The plan includes a needs assessment for telecommunication, hardware, software, and other services. The plan also includes goals and strategies for using telecommunications, information technologies, and digital applications to improve therapeutic recreation services. Staff training and development plans ensure that staff are prepared to implement the technology. Finally, ongoing evaluation of the technology plan provides for updates and revisions of the plan. Because of the rapid and constant pace of technological change, the technology plan is typically reviewed and updated every one to three years.

First-line therapeutic recreation managers must have timely, accurate, and comprehensive information to perform their responsibilities. The application of information technology systems to therapeutic recreation management is broad and varied depending on the health and human services setting. Technology systems manipulate the range of data required for planning, budgeting, decision making, monitoring, and scheduling of staff and facilities, as well as purchasing and materials management (Deluca & Enmark, 2002). Some health and human services organizations maintain internal management systems that support first-line managers in planning, implementing, scheduling, accounting, and evaluating their services. Electronic spreadsheets and databases allow for the manipulation and monitoring of data and save first-line managers time with (a) preparing budgets and billing; (b) programming and scheduling activities; (c) tracking consumer engagement in programs and activities; (d) identifying supply usage, purchasing supplies and equipment, and maintaining inventories; (e) scheduling and monitoring facilities; (f) staff and volunteer scheduling, development, and training; and (g) recordkeeping (including attendance, turnover, skills, and credentials). Gathering data, both internal and external, making a decision with data, developing decision-making criteria or standards that will be used to compare data solutions, establishing goals and objectives, deciding how to allocate resources, and developing a variety of solutions to a problem are all possible with well-designed information technology systems (Deluca & Enmark, 2002). Designing and implementing effective technology systems for therapeutic recreation services is a continuous process and managerial responsibility.

Analytics is a management function that is based on data, statistical and qualitative analysis, and explanatory and predictive modeling for decision making. Specialized software is used to combine client profiles to reveal contraindicated care, gaps in care, and opportunities for cost savings. Various business intelligence tools, such as health-care analytics, assist managers to benchmark services and outcomes (Athenahealth, 2012). More specifically, therapeutic recreation first-line managers may find having easy access to the right information will provide more options for sound decision making related to improvements in cost-effectiveness and efficiency, enable growth and expansion of services and supports, improve productivity of staff, and manage coding patterns and compliance. These software packages allow first-line managers to streamline the task of gathering data and comparing it to targets and benchmarks.

Learning Outcome

Explain the concept of a dashboard report and identify the four characteristics of an effective dashboard report.

Dashboard Reports

A *dashboard* report is an easy-to-read, often single-screen (page), real-time data report, showing a graphical presentation of the current status (snapshot) and historical trends of an organization's performance indicators. The purpose of the dashboard report is to provide information in a simple, clear format that facilitates instantaneous and informed decisions. The term "dashboard" is borrowed from the automobile dashboard. The dashboard enables the automobile driver to monitor the major functions of the car at a glance, including speed, fuel level, engine temperature, etc. Management dashboard reports provide at-a-glance views of performance indicators that are relevant to a particular goal or project. They provide managers with information about key management indicators that are on target, missing target, or wrong. Dashboards are usually used to show summaries, key trend comparisons, and exceptions. Figure 6.1 (p. 86) provides an example of a dashboard report. Effective dashboard reports incorporate simple visuals that communicate easily. Sullivan (2013) indicates that as technology advances, the use of dashboard reports to analyze data and guide decision making will become widespread.

Handheld Electronic Devices and Wireless Access

A variety of handheld electronic devices support efficient and effective management of therapeutic recreation

Table 6.1 The Technology Plan

The Technology Plan
A health and human services organization may find it helpful to engage a technology planning committee to guide the development, implementation, and evaluation of a technology plan. Plans anticipate and schedule required bidding, purchasing, installing, and training related to new technologies. The plan will include an inventory of both hardware and software—with description, name, size, number, version numbers, location, and any special notes about the equipment. A plan may address computer and network devices, telecommunications, Internet access, software, and emerging technologies. Scheduled evaluation of the technology plan is essential.

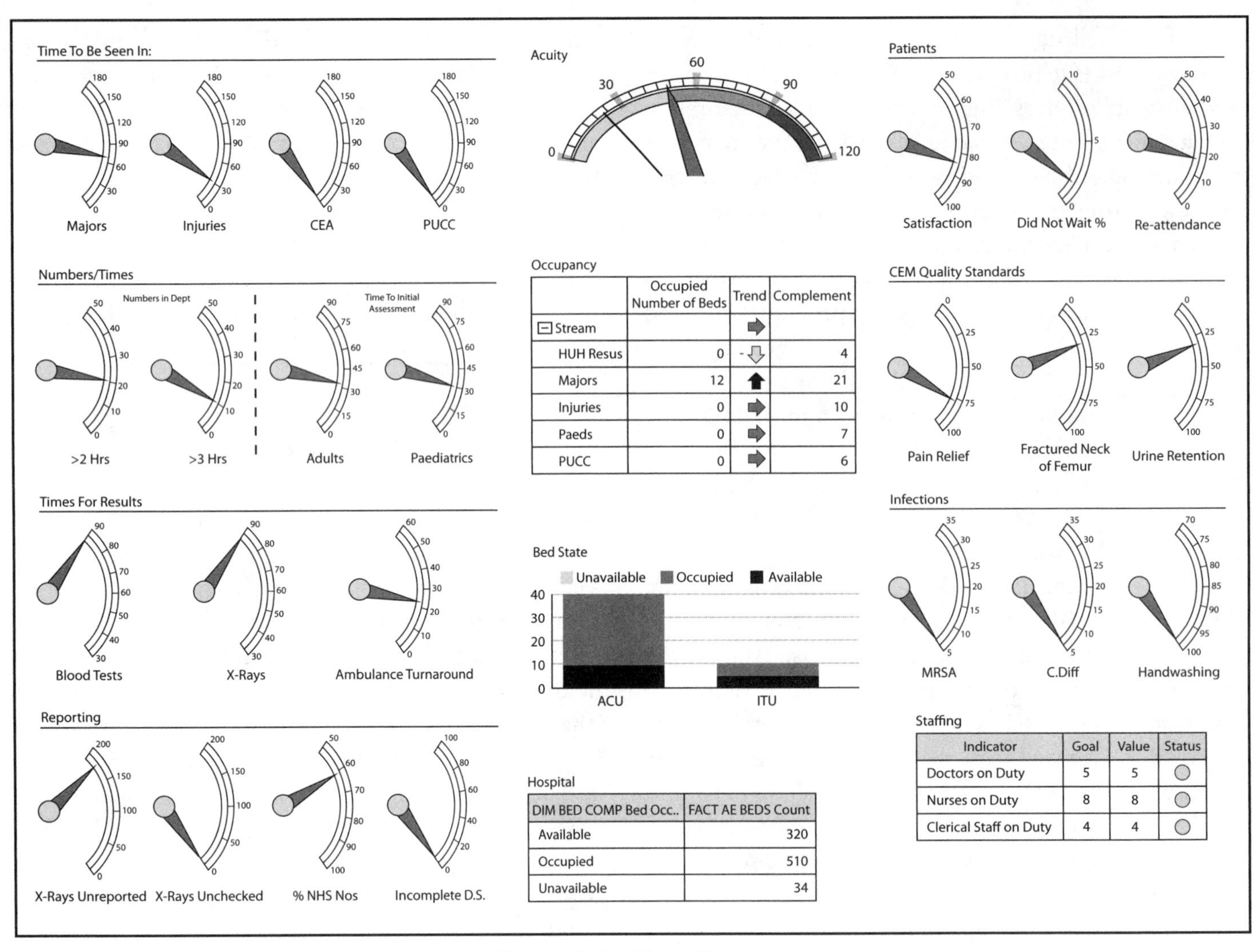

Figure 6.1 Dashboard Report

services. "Personal Digital Assistants" (PDAs) refers to a variety of handheld devices that offer a combination of computing, telephone/fax, Internet, and networking features. A typical Personal Digital Assistant can function as a cellular phone, fax sender, Web browser, and personal organizer. Personal Digital Assistants usually include handwriting recognition features and may include voice input by using voice-recognition technologies. A smartphone is a mobile phone with advanced computing capability and connectivity. The smartphone combines the functions of a Personal Digital Assistant with a mobile phone, as well as the functionality of a media player and a digital camera. A tablet computer, or simply a tablet, is a one-piece mobile computer. Tablets typically offer a touchscreen with finger gestures acting as the primary means of control, an on-screen keyboard as the principal means of data input. Tablets have functionality that is similar to Personal Digital Assistants and smartphones. Tablets typically offer a screen size greater than 7 inches, which is larger than Personal Digital Assistants and smartphones. These handheld electronic devices provide access to information resources immediately, from almost any location, when it is needed. Personal electronic devices enable care providers to manage large volumes of information more easily. In an example, a client of therapeutic recreation services with Alzheimer's disease is in an adult day care center. The client wanders from an activity area and the therapeutic recreation professional is immediately alerted over the handheld device. The same client is attending a birthday party and reaches for punch and cake. A newly hired therapeutic recreation practitioner checks the client's medical records on the handheld computer and is instantly aware the client has severe diabetes. In these illustrations, access to client data and information provided opportunities to improve the quality and safety of services.

According to the Pew Research Center's Mobile Access 2010 report, eight in ten American adults (82%) currently own a cell phone and cell owners now take advantage of various non-voice applications such as taking pictures, sending or receiving text messages, playing a game, sending or receiving e-mail, playing music, sending or receiving instant messages, and recording a video (Pew Research Center, 2010). It is estimated that six in ten American adults are now wireless Internet users and mobile data applications are growing in popularity (Pew Research Center, 2010). First-line managers will continue to be challenged as they consider new uses for mobile technology to enrich their outreach services. The use of Facebook, Twitter, and other social media outlets are available for outreach and communication with clients of therapeutic recreation services and their caregivers. For example, a therapeutic recreation practitioner organizes an electronic group of women with multiple sclerosis who encourage each other to walk daily, they compare how far they walked, how they felt after the walk, and they share tips to make exercising more comfortable. Persons who use wheelchairs enjoy listening to music in parks. With digital mapping and geographic information systems (GIS), a therapeutic recreation practitioner develops mapping and directions for ease in accessing these events.

While handheld electronics offer many benefits, similar to other technology, they also pose challenges to be managed. For example, security and privacy of client information remain both an ethical and legal challenge. Equipment loss prevention is an important responsibility. Limited knowledge of handheld electronics and financial constraints that restrict the availability of handheld electronics within the agency are additional factors limiting the wide-scale use of this technology in health and human service agencies (Marquis & Huston, 2012).

The question is what's next, and the future is unlimited. One example of a new technology is Radio Frequency Identification (RFID). Radio Frequency Identification is a wireless non-contact use of radio frequency electromagnetic fields to transfer data, for the purposes of automatically identifying and tracking tags attached to objects. The tags are slightly larger than a grain of rice and contain electronically stored information. Disney is working on a Radio Frequency Identification wristband system, Magic Bands, that will enable Disney Park guests to pay for goods, check in at rides to map their day's activities, and send data to characters in the park so Mickey can address a child personally. Therapeutic recreation services may include Radio Frequency Identification to support client services, for example individuals with autism or Alzheimer's disease who may have limited attending skills.

Internet Resources

Accessing information resources requires knowledge of information resources, the use of databases, as well as an understanding of data. First-line managers are increasingly using the Internet as both a communication tool and an information source. As a communication tool, the Internet provides access to electronic mail, file transfer protocol, and the World Wide Web (Web). As an information source, the Internet enables the first-line manager to access the latest research and evidence-based best practices information for the delivery of services. Use of the Internet as an information source for all types of information, including therapeutic recreation services, will continue to increase exponentially in the coming years.

An example of new technology using intranet resources is telehealth. Telehealth is "the use of electronic and telecommunications technologies to support long-distance clinical health care, patient and professional health-related education, public health, and health administration" (Office for the Advancement of Telehealth [OAT], n.d.; Ellis & Hartley, 2012). Examples of telehealth technologies include video-conferencing, the Internet, store-and-forward imaging, streaming media, and wireless communications.

Learning Outcome

Explain the concept of an electronic health record. Outline the history and discuss the rationale for implementation of electronic health records in health and human service agencies.

Electronic Health Records

Ellis and Hartley (2012) indicate that computerization of client data began in most health and human service agencies with management of payment and billing data. Progressive agencies began computerizing client records in the early 1980s. However, it was not until nearly 20 years later when most health and human service agencies implemented computerized health records to comply with the Health Information Portability and Accountability Act of 1996 (HIPAA). HIPAA mandated that all billing to the federal government, for Medicare and Medicaid reimbursement, use standardized documentation. In 2009, the federal government passed the Health Information Technology for Economic and Clinical Health Act (HITECH). The purpose of HITECH is to stimulate technology use in health care, including health and human service agencies (Sullivan, 2013). The goal of the legislation is to encourage meaningful use of electronic health records by health-care professionals to achieve significant improvements in client care. Accrediting bodies such as the Joint Commission on Accreditation of Healthcare Organizations (the Joint Commission), the Commission on Accreditation of Rehabilitation Facilities (CARF), and other national and local regulations, mandate the types of client information that must be charted.

Health-care records have changed dramatically as a result of technology. The *electronic health record* (EHR) is a digital record of an individual's health history that may include records from many locations and sources such as hospitals, clinics, providers, and public health agencies (Marquis & Huston, 2012). Most client recordkeeping can be managed with electronic records and the majority of health and human service organizations have uniform procedures by which client information is recorded and stored for later reference. An electronic recordkeeping system may be as simple as a listing of categories under which information is classified, or records may be comprehensive and managed with a highly sophisticated data system. In health and human service organizations, an entire therapeutic recreation treatment protocol or plan—assessment, goals and objectives, interventions, progress notes, and discharge plans—may be included in the electronic record.

Electronic records provide significant advantages for therapeutic recreation professionals and for clients. Electronic health records provide for access at the point-of-care and the electronic record information is available instantly. The use of electronic records information has helped control costs in health and human service agencies (Thompson, Velasco, Classen, & Reddemann, 2010). Continuity of care is also facilitated when client information follows the client from one setting to another. Electronic records enable constant monitoring and evaluation of a treatment plan once it is designed and implemented. Electronic records also allow for more uniformity in the monitoring of client progress across disciplines. Electronic record-keeping facilitates access to continuously updated client information. The therapeutic recreation professional is quickly made aware of changes in a client's condition that may require a different intervention plan on the basis of information from another department that is distributed to all care providers. The information that is available as a result of electronic health records facilitates more reliable client observation records and enhanced client satisfaction (Bates & Gawande, 2003). Because the electronic record system can include pre-programmed prompts for required data, the information that is recorded tends to be more accurate and complete, if it is properly formatted, when compared with written records data. Additionally, the electronic health record information is retrievable for measures of quality control (Berg & Goorman, 1999). From still another perspective, the client record contains valuable information that permits periodic reevaluation of the treatment with the client as well as providing data for therapeutic recreation research. Electronic health records can also provide pre-scheduled reminders, or notification information, to both the client and the practitioner for follow-up review (Bates & Gawande, 2003).

The process of implementation of electronic health records has not been without challenges. Financial barriers are identified as the most significant factor impacting the adoption of electronic health records in health and human service agencies. Some agencies do not have the financial resources to invest in an electronic records system. Staff training is an additional expense. Studies by allied health professions indicate a need to devote significant resources for training in order to use the electronic health record and computerized medical records systems. A large portion of time and effort of a first-line manager is training staff for the use of electronic records. Training staff for use of electronic records involves more than system navigation. Training in new roles, workflows, and methods to ensure data integrity is essential.

Securing the confidentiality of electronic health records is essential. The privacy of computerized client records is of concern as information is available to many people in various sites beyond the facility where the client is located. Safeguards are in place to protect electronic health records (see Table 6.2). All systems require password access and tracking capabilities to monitor information access. The Health Insurance Portability and Accountability Act (HIPAA) of 1996 requires that health and human service organizations using electronic records have safeguards in place to protect client privacy. Agencies that fail to meet mandated privacy requirements are subject to substantial fines for non-compliance. HIPAA has two administrative standards that address privacy and security while promoting the greater use of electronic records.

Assuring compatibility with nationwide records systems is a challenge. Resistance has been high to implementation of a standardized system. Vreeman, Taggard, Rhine, and Worrell (2006) stress the importance of managers and practitioners ensuring their terminology is adequately recognized in nationwide electronic health record initiatives to allow for appropriate exchanges of information and advancing clinical practice and research.

A critical aspect of information systems development and use is identification of necessary data elements and how they are collected, when, where, and how they are used. The design, implementation, and evaluation of electronic records are ongoing processes. Further research is needed to gain a better understanding of the effects of electronic records on the therapeutic recreation process and outcomes of services.

LEARNING OUTCOME

Identify six challenges to implementing technology in a health and human service agency.

Technology Opportunities and Barriers

First-line managers in health and human service agencies must maintain an understanding of evolving technology systems, how technology can enhance the profession, and how to apply available technology to improve practice, management, and research. Technology systems in therapeutic recreation have the potential to help managers provide high-quality and safe services, promote evidence-based and client-centered practice, access data necessary to support sound decision making, and support research initiatives. Technology supports therapeutic recreation managers in identifying the services and interventions that most effectively and efficiently meet the needs of clients. Aligning technology with the health and human service agency's mission is essential as these new opportunities are considered. De Veer, Fleuren, Bekkema, and Francke (2011) shared several recommendations for managers regarding implementation of new technology. First, involve the users as early as possible in the planning process to assess the relevance of the technology and the potential benefits for the users and the clients. Second, pilot testing new technology in daily practice in the organization is helpful in determining proper functioning as well as the benefits of the technology. Finally, engaging practitioners and clients in the introduction, training, and dissemination of new technology is an effective means of evaluating its relevance, ease of application, and overall suitability for the agency's needs.

Table 6.2 Data Security for Electronic Health Records

Data Security for Electronic Health Records

There are a number of tools that are designed to protect the security and confidentiality of data traveling over public and private networks. A brief overview of these systems follows.

- A *digital certificate* is one of several electronic means used to secure Internet-based transactions. Issued by a certificate authority, a digital certificate contains enough information to authenticate the identity of a person or organization sending or receiving data over the Internet.
- *Encryption* is another tool used to secure data being transmitted electronically. Encrypted data are converted from their original form into a form that cannot be understood except by the intended recipient of the data, who has possession of an algorithm that will unscramble the data.
- *Firewalls* are electronic programs that provide an electronic barrier between an organization's internal, private data and operations and the outside world.
- *Backing up data* and *storing data* are additional factors to be managed when working with information technology systems. Some organizations will have data repositories or warehouses for storing large data sets, particularly clinical or financial data.

Despite the substantial opportunities for improvement of therapeutic recreation practice, management, and research, the development, testing, and adoption of technology systems in therapeutic recreation remains limited. Determining which technological advances can and should be used to promote efficiency and effectiveness at each level of the health and human service organization requires considerable analysis. Technology is a high-cost investment and some agencies may not have the financial resources that are required for hardware, software, staff training, and related costs. Managers must assess the need for and provide staff with adequate training to appropriately and fully utilize the technology tools and applications that may be available. The training may be costly and training time impacts service-delivery time. Staff resistance, or slow acceptance, of new technology is a challenge. There may be a tendency for practitioners to perceive technology systems as relatively unimportant to their day-to-day practice or knowledge development. Finally, finding a balance between technological options and the need for human touch, caring, and one-on-one, face-to-face interaction with clients requires a balance between efficiency and effectiveness (Marquis & Huston, 2012). Technology may increase or decrease human interactions, as well as the sharing of information depending on how a system is designed. Some clients report feeling less satisfied with the practitioner using a computer because it "felt less personal" (Marquis & Huston, 2012). As a result of these challenges, and others, functionality, capabilities, and overall use of technology vary widely from one provider type (e.g., hospital, rehabilitation clinical facilities, geriatric care facilities) to another (Roop, 2011).

Applying Technology to Research

Evidence-Based Practice in Therapeutic Recreation

LEARNING OUTCOME

Define evidence-based practice. Describe the purpose and value of evidence-based practice.

An emerging trend in the health and human service professions is the development of evidence-based practice. The concept began in medicine and is being applied throughout health care. *Evidence-based practice* is a "problem-solving approach to the delivery of health care that integrates the best evidence from studies of [client] care data with clinician expertise and [client] preferences and values" (Ellis & Hartley, 2012, p. 571; Fineout-Overholt, Melnyk, Stillwell, & Williamson, 2010). Evidence-based practice can be described as the selection of best-available treatments for which there is some evidence of efficacy; evidence must be gathered through well-designed and meaningful research efforts with client groups and the treatment must be applicable to daily practice (Mrkic, 2011). The goal of evidence-based practice is for the therapeutic recreation professional to provide the best possible program that, on the available evidence at hand, is known to have the most desirable, intended, and meaningful outcomes (Stumbo, 2003b). Stumbo & Pegg (2010) state that the overall aim of evidence-based practice is to reduce wide and unintended variations in practice, and, instead, use the best cumulative evidence possible to inform, enlighten, and direct practice of therapeutic recreation. It has emerged as a strategy to improve quality by using the best available knowledge integrated with clinical experience and client values to provide care (Sullivan, 2013; Houser & Oman, 2010). More about evidence-based practice is found in Table 6.3.

Therapeutic recreation professionals have a responsibility to continually work to improve their base of knowledge and to identify appropriate application of that knowledge to specific client treatments. They are responsible for making decisions about treatments. Those decisions must be based on supporting evidence, rather than habit, common practice, or tradition. Law (2002) suggests that evidence-based practice is probably one of the most misunderstood concepts in health care today because of its newness and the degree to which it differs from traditional practice.

Therapeutic recreation first-line managers must continue to ask and answer the following questions:

- How do we know that what we do is effective?
- How can our practice and service be improved?

While appearing to be simple, these questions challenge the therapeutic recreation profession daily as the profession continues seeking to clearly establish and gain recognition for its unique role and function.

Documentation of the significance of client improvements (outcomes) after a therapeutic recreation intervention (treatment) is essential; it is the future of therapeutic recreation. In the absence of demonstrated effectiveness and accountability, funding for therapeutic recreation in health and human service agencies will be cut back or eliminated. Evidence-based practice provides regulators, payers, and clients increased assurance of desirable and intended outcomes. It is a means of ensuring effective client treatment that validates continued inclusion of the therapeutic recreation profession in health and human services.

This process of purposeful intervention is necessary to maintain accreditation with CARF and the Joint Commission. These procedures also allow for fiscal accountability within prospective payment systems (PPS) used in health care. The prospective payment system is designed to anticipate the costs of particular services associated with a specific health-care procedure or service. Regardless of how much an agency spends on treating a client, insurance companies reimburse the agency for services based on the pre-established rates, and as a result, the services must be facilitated in a competent yet cost-effective manner.

Evidence-Based Practice Model for Implementation

Belsey and Snell (2001) (as cited in Stumbo, 2003a) explain that evidence-based practice involves four actions by the therapeutic recreation professional: (1) production of evidence through research and scientific review, (2) production and dissemination of evidence-based clinical guidelines, (3) implementation of evidence-based, cost-effective practice through education and management of change and, (4) evaluation of compliance with agreed practice guidance and patient outcomes (p. 29). There are a number of models for implementation of evidence-based practice. While the models describe similar concepts, each uses slightly different questions and a different series of steps. The University of North Carolina (UNC, n.d.; Flemming, 1988) has offered a simple five-question rubric, "Five A's," to encourage adoption of evidence-based practice. The five-question rubric includes the following:

1. Ask: Asking appropriate questions.
2. Acquire: Review of literature for scientific evidence to answer the question.
3. Analyze: Critically analyze the evidence found for validity and the ability to generalize it.
4. Apply: Use the best available evidence, clinical expertise, the client's perspective, and knowledge of available resources to plan care.
5. Assess: Evaluate performance through a process of self-reflection, audit, or peer assessment.

Researchers are important partners in the development of evidence-based best practice and services. Using research evidence supports the therapeutic recreation first-line manager. McCormick and Lee (2001), Stumbo and Pegg (2010), and many others have emphasized the need for research to support evidence-based therapeutic recreation practice and service. First, research evidence reduces the time required to conceptualize, design, deliver, and evaluate a program. Second, it provides comparative data against which to evaluate outcomes. Finally, research provides documentation that services are developed and delivered using evidence-based best practices. Research will contribute to

Table 6.3 Categories of Evidence

Categories of Evidence
While all forms of evidence are useful for clinical decision making, a randomized control design and statistical evidence are the most rigorous. • Anecdotal—derived from experience • Testimonial—reported by an expert • Statistical—built from a scientific approach • Case Study—an in-depth analysis used to translate to other clinical situations • Non-experimental design research—gathering factors related to a clinical condition • Quasi-experimental design research—a study limited to one group of subjects • Randomized control trial—uses both experimental and control groups to determine the effectiveness of an intervention
(Sullivan, 2013; Hader, 2010)

documentation of the values of interventions and strengthen the profession. Therapeutic recreation professionals will be assured that their intervention or treatments are the best services to meet client needs. Ultimately this research will benefit clients because clients will be assured that they are receiving the most effective treatments as a result of evidence-based practice.

Challenges to Implementation of Evidence-Based Practice

Health and human service agencies are confronted with a number of barriers that limit the implementation of evidence-based practice. Ellis & Hartley (2012) identify three common barriers to evidence-based practice. First, access to information resources may be limited. Therapeutic recreation services may be offered in a variety of settings. While academic medical settings may offer easy access to many information resources, small clinical agencies or community-based programs are not likely to provide similar access to resources. A second common barrier to evidence-based practice is available time. In many health and human service settings, the typical workday does not provide time to research new practices. Time is focused on the delivery of client services and there is no time to seek information for establishing new policy or protocol for treatment or practice. Finally, a common barrier is background and training of practitioners. Many practicing therapeutic recreation professionals do not have formal training in research. Therapeutic recreation practitioners lack a background in understanding and valuing research. Without adequate academic background in research understanding, practitioners may find it challenging to develop research questions, analyze data, and effectively interpret research results and evaluate evidence for practice. Spector (2010) adds that negative attitudes toward research can also be a barrier for implementation of evidence-based practice. The more positive a therapeutic recreation professional's attitude toward research, the more likely he or she is to use research in practice.

Enhancing Research

There are many aspects of the therapeutic recreation profession that offer opportunities for study. Current research priorities include identification of where and how professionals work (i.e., scope of practice), skills needed to perform the work (i.e., education), and benefits/outcomes of the work (i.e., efficacy). Technology systems may facilitate this research. There are also a number of different research methods that can be used to explore these aspects of the profession. In the past, therapeutic recreation professionals have demonstrated an over-reliance on survey research. Case study, single-subject, daily experience, and mixed methods are additional research methods used to enhance practice and each research method is supported by data gathered and reported using information technology systems. Each method is highlighted and briefly discussed.

A case study may focus on an individual, group, event, or community. When compiled for client record-keeping and other purposes, data are used for research to understand actions in the context of a specific situation or case. Case studies also allow the collection of data over time to discern developmental patterns. Case studies allow first-line managers and researchers to explore complex sets of decisions and to recount the effects of decisions over time. Data from technology systems can be merged from various sources efficiently. The management of data over time may be expedited when computerized. Case study research, with support of technology systems, may contribute valuable information to the theoretical, practical, and technical knowledge of therapeutic recreation (McCormick, 2000).

Single-subject research designs are used to examine the effects of therapeutic recreation. Additionally, single-subject research designs complement the ability of therapeutic recreation professionals to meet the individual needs of clients. Using technology systems with well-documented intervention results to promote specific outcomes with clients is a key part of single-subject research designs. Baseline data are important in these research designs and technology systems facilitate the gathering and access to the data about clients. The documentation of repeated observations of clients' behaviors over time is another aspect of single-subject research designs supported by technology systems. Results of measurements are graphically displayed and inferences about relationships between interventions and changes in behaviors are enhanced with technology systems. This type of formative evaluation and information about interventions applied in therapeutic recreation settings allows therapeutic recreation managers to make changes quickly to increase clients' successes. This information also allows researchers and managers to ascertain best practices.

Research may be focused on gaining an understanding of daily experiences among clients. There are three common methods for measuring daily experiences: interval-contingent, signal-contingent, and event-contingent. Common to all approaches is the collection of client responses to a set of questions during or immediately after the daily activity. Information technology systems support these research methods.

In the *interval-contingent approach,* a client is given a checklist and asked at certain scheduled intervals to complete the checklist. Interval-contingent methods examine variables one time; thus, this method is used to track clients' responses to interventions or activities. This is completed online, tabulated, and entered into an information system to be used for research, decision making, and best practice.

When using the *signal-contingent approach*, clients are instructed to describe their experience whenever they are signaled. This method has the potential to be used as a tool for examining the effects of an intervention in the daily lives of clients who are involved in therapeutic recreation services. Clients are given a personal electronic device and instructed to share what they are doing and how they feel when they are doing it, when they are signaled. Clients' entries are recorded and entered into a database and then analyzed.

Using another approach, the *event-* or *activity-contingent method,* clients are instructed to complete a self-report questionnaire each time an event occurs. This is a means of learning about specific client's behaviors. Again, technology and information technology systems support data collection, analyses, and interpretation.

There are a number of important considerations when designing studies to measure daily experiences. Technology systems may simplify the data collection and analyses processes. Because the therapeutic recreation interventions are designed to promote health and well-being during daily experiences of individuals with disabilities, these methods, supported by technology systems, enhance therapeutic recreation research and practice.

Various research methods are available to enhance therapeutic recreation professional practice. Data analyses in mixed methods research include descriptive and comparative statistics along with the conversion of raw narrative data. Technology systems in therapeutic recreation settings expedite these forms of data analyses from questionnaires and interviews. Technology systems have the potential to enhance research in therapeutic recreation. The various research designs discussed here are well-suited for studying the intricacies that affect practice and knowledge in therapeutic recreation. Technology systems promote these forms of knowing and best practice by making data more accessible. They also complete the data analyses and support decision making.

There are challenges associated with defining, measuring, and improving therapeutic recreation services. One tool that holds promise in therapeutic recreation is the Agency for Healthcare Research and Quality (AHRQ), Healthcare Cost and Utilization Project (HCUP). The Healthcare Cost and Utilization Project is a group of health-care databases and related software tools and products that brings together the data collection efforts of state data organizations, hospital associations, private data organizations, and the federal government to create a national information resource of patient-level health-care data (Clancy, 2011). Analyses of the Healthcare Cost and Utilization Project data can provide first-line managers with opportunities for quality improvement. Two major conclusions, medication-related adverse events and hospital readmissions related to the same illness, came from studying the HCUP data. The Healthcare Cost and Utilization Project databases contain clinical and nonclinical information and can generate statistics including client diagnoses, procedures, discharge status, demographics, length of stay, charges for all patients' services regardless of payer (e.g., Medicare, Medicaid, private insurance, and uninsured), comorbidities, length of hospitalization, readmissions, quality of care, preventable hospital stays, type of facility, and trends since 1993 (Agency for Healthcare Research and Quality, 2011). The Agency for Healthcare Research and Quality's Healthcare Cost and Utilization Project databases and its annual quality and disparities reports are tools that researchers and therapists can use to better understand health-care efficiencies on a broad scale. These databases and reports also provide specific data which can be used to evaluate current practices compared to national and regional trends (Clancy, 2011).

Summary

1. Technology is changing the way therapeutic recreation services are provided. Effective technology systems deliver the right information, to the right person, in the right place and time, in the right way.
2. This chapter reviewed the importance of planning for technology systems. Successful technology plans demonstrate how an investment in technology will contribute to achieving the mission of the health and human service organization. The technology plan is the forward-looking strategic plan for the organization's technology needs.
3. Technology is not an end it itself; rather it provides technological solutions that increase the organization's effectiveness. Designing and implementing effective technology systems for therapeutic recreation services is a continuous process and managerial responsibility.
4. Dashboard reports were introduced. The purpose of a dashboard report is to provide information in a simple, clear format that facilitates instantaneous and informed management decisions. Dashboard reports provide at-a-glance views of performance indicators that are relevant to a particular goal or project. It is anticipated that the use of dashboard reporting to analyze data and guide decision making will become common practice in health and human service agency management.
5. Information technology is dramatically changing how individual-client care information and provider-planning for care is entered into record, stored, and retrieved. This chapter discussed electronic health records. These are a digital record of an individual's health history. Federal legislation, including the Health Information Portability and Accountability Act of 1996 (HIPAA) and the Health Information Technology for Economic and Clinical Health Act (HITECH), has contributed to implementation of electronic health records. The purposes of the legislation was to stimulate technology use in health care, including health and human service agencies, and to encourage meaningful use of electronic health records by health-care professionals to achieve significant improvements in client care.
6. Evidence-based practice was introduced and defined as the selection of best available treatments for which there is some evidence of efficacy. The focus of evidence-based practice is on problem-solving. Therapeutic recreation professionals are responsible for making decisions about treatments. These decisions must be based on supporting evidence, rather than habit, common practice, or tradition.
7. Current research priorities in therapeutic recreation include identification of where and how professionals work and the skills needed to perform the work.
8. Various research methods that can be used to explore these aspects of the profession were presented. Case-study, single-subject, daily-experience, and mixed methods are common research methods used to enhance practice. Each method was highlighted and briefly discussed.
9. Finally, the chapter reviewed the barriers and opportunities that are impacting therapeutic recreation services as a result of technological advances.

Critical Thinking Activities

1. Visit a community-based recreation service setting and a health-care facility. Compare and contrast how each uses technology systems to manage and deliver services.
2. Conduct an Internet search to identify smartphones, PDAs, other electronic devices, and software/applications available to use to improve services and to promote client-centered practices.
3. Interview a manager to observe how budget development and monitoring are supported using data generated from technology information systems.
4. Review issues of the following professional journals and in each identify research that contributes to evidence-based practices in therapeutic recreation: *Annual in Therapeutic Recreation, Therapeutic Recreation Journal,* and *American Journal of Recreation Therapy.*

References

Agency for Healthcare Research and Quality (AHRQ). (2011). HCUP databases, Agency for Healthcare Research and Quality. Retrieved from http://www.hcup_us.ahrq.gov/databases.jsp

Athenahealth, Inc. (2012). *Whitepaper: Health-care business intelligence: Turning data into decisions.* Alpharetta, GA: Anodyne Health.

Bates, D. W. & Gawande, A. A. (2003). Improving safety with information technology. *New England Journal of Medicine, 348*, 2526–2534.

Belsey, J. & Snell, T. (2001). *What is evidence-based medicine?* Edisi pertama. USA: Hayward Medical Communications.

Berg, M. & Goorman, E. (1999). The contextual nature of medical information. *International Journal of Medical Informatics, 1,* 13–23.

Clancy, C. M. (2011). Let the data be our guide: Trends and tools for research on health-care utilization. *Health Economics, 21,* 19–23.

Deluca, J. M. & Enmark, R. (2002). *The CEO's guide to health care information systems with Web-enabled technologies.* Hershey, PA: Idea Group Publishing.

De Veer, A., Fleuren, M., Bekkema, N., & Francke, A. (2011). Successful implementation of new technologies in nursing care: A questionnaire survey of nurse-users. *BMC Medical Informatics and Decision Making, 11.* Retrieved from http://www.biomedicalcentral.com/1472-6947/11/67

Ellis, J. R., & Hartley, C. L. (2012). *Nursing in today's world: Trends, issues, and management.* (10th ed.). Philadelphia: Lippincott Williams & Wilkins.

Fineout-Overholt, E., Melnyk, B. M., Stillwell, S. B., & Williamson, K. M. (2010). Evidence-based practice step by step: Critical appraisal of the evidence. *American Journal of Nursing, 110*(7), 47–52.

Flemming, K. (1988). Asking answerable questions. *Evidence Based Nursing, 1*(2), 36–37.

Hader, R. (2010). The evidence that isn't . . . interpreting research. *Nursing Management, 41*(9), 23-26.

Houser, J., & Oman, K. S. (2010). *Evidence-based practice: An implementation guide for healthcare organizations.* Sudbury, MA: Jones & Bartlett.

Hurd, A., Barcelona, R. J., & Meldrum, J. T. (2008). *Leisure services management.* Champaign IL: Human Kinetics.

Law, M. (2002). Introduction to evidence-based practice. In M. Law (Ed.), *Evidence-based rehabilitation: A guide to practice* (pp. 3–12). Thorofare, NJ: Slack.

Marquis, B. L. & Huston, C. J. (2012). *Leadership roles and management functions in nursing: Theory and application* (7th ed.). Philadelphia: Lippincott Williams & Wilkins.

McCormick, B. P. (2000). Case study research in therapeutic recreation. *Therapeutic Recreation Journal, 34*(3), 154–163.

McCormick, B. P. & Lee, Y. (2001). Research in practice: Building knowledge through empirical practice. In N. Stumbo (Ed.), *Professional issues in therapeutic recreation* (pp. 383–400). Champaign, IL: Sagamore Publishing.

Mrkic, L., (2011). *The prevalence of evidence-based practice by the Certified Therapeutic Recreation Specialist in the intervention planning process for client treatment.* (Master's thesis, Eastern Kentucky University). Retrieved from *Online Theses and Dissertations.* Paper 51. http://encompass.eku.edu/etd/51

Office for the Advancement of Telehealth [OAT], n.d. Retrieved from http://www.hrsa.gov/ruralhealth/about/telehealth

Perron, B. E., Taylor, H. O., Glass, J. E., & Margerum-Leys, J. (2010). Information and communication technologies in social work. *Advances in Social Work, 11*(1), 67–81.

Pew Research Center. (2010). *Pew Internet & American Life Project: Mobile Access 2010.* Retrieved from http://pewinternet.org/Reports/2010/Mobile-Access2010.aspx

Roop, E. S. (2011). Meaningful use: Obstacles in geriatrics. *Aging Well, 14*(1), p 20–23.

Spector, N. (2010). Evidence-based nursing regulation: A challenge for regulators. *Journal of Nursing Regulation, 1*(1), 30–36. Retrieved from https://www.ncsbn.org/EB_Regulation_article_final.pdf

Stumbo, N. J. (2003a). Outcomes, accountability, and therapeutic recreation. In N. J. Stumbo (Ed.), *Client outcomes in therapeutic recreation services* (pp. 1–24). State College, PA: Venture Publishing, Inc.

Stumbo, N. J. (2003b). The importance of evidence-based practice. In N. J. Stumbo (Ed.), *Client outcomes in therapeutic recreation services* (pp. 25–48). State College, PA: Venture Publishing, Inc.

Stumbo, N. J., & Pegg, S. (2010). Outcomes and evidence-based practice: Moving forward. *Annual in Therapeutic Recreation, 18*, 12–23.

Sullivan, E. (2013). *Effective leadership and management in nursing* (8th ed.). Boston: Pearson.

Thompson, D., Velasco, F., Classen, D., & Reddemann, R. J. (2010). Reducing clinical costs with an HER. *Healthcare Financial Management, 64*(10), 106–108,110,112, 114.

University of North Carolina (n.d.). *Evidence Based Nursing*. Retrieved from http://www.hsl.unc.edu/services/tutorials/ebn/practice.htm_

Vreeman, D. J., Taggard, S. L., Rhine, M. D., & Worrell, T. W. (2006). Evidence for electronic health record systems in physical therapy. *Physical Therapy, 86,* 434–446.

Chapter 7
Marketing and Advocacy

Keywords

- Branding
- Bundling
- Exchange relationships
- Logo
- Market development
- Market diversification
- Market penetration
- Market positioning
- Market strategy
- Marketing
- Marketing mix
- Place
- Price
- Product
- Promotion
- Service development
- Social marketing
- SWOT analysis
- Tagline
- Target marketing

Learning Outcomes

After reading this chapter, students will be able to:

1. Identify trends impacting marketing in therapeutic recreation.
2. Define fundamental marketing concepts.
3. Outline the marketing process in therapeutic recreation.
4. Explain the first-line manager's role in marketing and advocacy.
5. Interpret the ethical challenges faced as the manager markets recreation therapy in an entrepreneurial climate.

Overview

Health and human services operate in a competitive, resource-constrained, quality-controlled environment. Managers are challenged to articulate the unique strengths of therapeutic recreation and to create strategies that will ensure the service. Strategic market planning is one avenue to ensure survival of the unit. This process is similar to the therapeutic recreation process (i.e., assess, plan, implement, and evaluate, or APIE). The intent of this chapter is to consider marketing processes and relationships created by the first-line manager to advocate for the essential values therapeutic recreation brings to individuals and communities.

The opening section considers trends influencing marketing responsibilities of the manager. Among the more significant impacts on the manager's duties are technology, payment and delivery reform, changing demographics, and an enhanced awareness of the relationship between individual health-care outcomes and values and the health and well-being of communities.

The opening section is followed by a review of fundamental concepts the manager contemplates during service and relationship marketing. Included are the traditional "P's" of marketing as well as those concepts important to value-added service marketing and establishing long-term social-exchange relationships with clients and the community.

Through strategic market planning, the first-line manager designs a market plan to enable relationship building and social marketing over extended time. The third section outlines this process, similar to the APIE process used to design programs. Target markets and their behavioral needs are identified. Action plans are prepared and appropriate strategies are selected to address the respective stakeholder's needs. Implementation of the marketing plan is evaluated. Revised strategic plans are drafted to address emerging needs of new audiences.

A manager assumes key roles in marketing unit services and creating long-standing relationships among the unit's constituents through partnerships and collaboration. The manager is instrumental in garnering resources and linking the unit to the various audiences to ensure services remain available and integral to satisfying client needs and promoting community health. Closing chapter sections introduce issues and ethical considerations that occur during marketing as the manager carries out marketing and advocacy responsibilities. Marketing dilemmas arise if quality and client needs are compromised by volume or promotion of the latest intervention. Managers remain vigilant to ensuring professional practice standards and ethical codes are properly enforced and client respect is maintained as services are marketed.

Trends

A number of trends are and will continue to impact marketing in health and human services. The first-line manager is experiencing ongoing change and a dynamic work environment as a result of significant increases in the use of technology, reforms in payment and delivery methods, diversity in clientele, and recognition of the relationship between (a) individual values and health-care outcomes and (b) the health and welfare of communities.

"Health-care Web sites are the second most commonly opened sites on the Internet" (Baum & Dowling, 2011, p.38). The Internet is a medium for generating and sharing content. Health-care consumers desire relevant information on their terms and bi-directional communication ("Brand management 2.0", 2008). Web-based communication facilitates a more effective client experience. Technology creates fast, interactive access to customized services available 24 hours a day (Tomey, 2009). Consumers are educated, assertive, and busy; they desire convenience, quality, and lower costs. Health-care providers engage in dialogue and react to actual client behaviors by using digital media and marketing databases to manage personal relationships (Tomey, 2009).

Health-care reform and constrained resources are shifting responsibility and accountability to clients and caregivers. The rising cost of insurance, reduced employer support, and escalating health-care expenses result in consumers applying the same value criteria to health-care decisions—service, price, experience—as to other purchasing decisions (Winans & Kasubski, 2011). Transition to outpatient from inpatient experiences is further accentuated by clients' desires for convenient locations where services are integrated and fees are bundled. Value-based care and coordinated-care experiences foster collaborative partnerships, as consumers are less likely to rely on a single organization to control all elements of their care (Williams, 2011).

Marketing intends to bring about exchange relationships among various target markets. These target markets are comprised of individuals having a diversity of needs and representing differing age groups, cultures, and health-care perspectives and experiences. With international and global marketing, managers address varying customs, regulations, technology influences, and client expectations and demands. The advanced aging and aging evident in developed countries necessitates a different marketing mix than the health-care concerns of underdeveloped countries. To illustrate, as a target market, the Baby Boomer's desire to remain physically attractive requires health-care providers partner with insurance companies willing to support programs like "SilverSneakers," (Healthways SilverSneakers Fitness Program is part of the Medicare Advantage or Medicare Supplement and group retiree health plans offered by employers and is available through participating locations such as gyms and YMCAs) while target markets globally address behaviors like obesity that result in health-care concerns like diabetes and cardiac conditions.

Lastly, societal and social marketing have emerged as marketing principles to enhance public welfare (Kaczynski, 2008). In this period of rapid population growth and economic, social, and environmental issues, health and human service organizations consider consumer wants and needs as they interface with societal well-being (Tomey, 2009). For example, health-care marketing can address one-time and continuing behavior, and individual or group behavior: the fitness program geared to a Boomer target audience also benefits the community, as individuals are less likely to be a burden on the health-care system and more productive at work with physical activity. These forms of marketing emphasize delivering value and managing relationships that result in individual benefits as well as community well-being.

Marketing plans and strategies used to influence consumer behaviors reflect the impact of these trends.

Individualized approaches are electronically communicated 24 hours a day through interactive dialogues among service providers, clients, and caregivers to create long-lasting relationships beneficial to client and community health.

Learning Outcome
Identify trends impacting marketing in therapeutic recreation.

Marketing Concepts

What is marketing? The financial success of our programs and services relies on marketing so much so that one definition of marketing is meeting needs profitably (Kotler & Keller, 2006). *Marketing* is the performance of activities (assessment, planning, implementation, control and evaluation of services) to accomplish organizational objectives by creating voluntary exchanges of values with target markets; this is accomplished by anticipating client needs and directing the flow of need-satisfying services from the provider to the client (Perreault, Cannon, & McCarthy, 2011; Tomey, 2009). How is this concept translated to therapeutic recreation? For many individuals, therapeutic recreation services are needed. Individuals are referred for therapeutic recreation services, and we document client outcomes that support the value and benefits of those services. However, there are many other individuals that do not receive therapeutic recreation services who might also have beneficial outcomes from participation. Therefore we market therapeutic recreation services to create the need, want, and demand for selected interventions. In return for beneficial client and community outcomes, therapeutic recreation services gain value through long-term relationships and income (e.g. fees, and/or reimbursement).

Need is a basic concept underlying marketing. Human needs are essential to our well-being. A *want* is a human need shaped by our culture or personality (e.g., we need food, I want ice cream). A *demand* is created when we are able to acquire the program or service that brings the most value or satisfaction (e.g., TRSs must create demand for services valued by clients and that satisfy desired outcomes like improved health and socially accepted leisure behaviors).

Products/goods, services, ideas/information, experiences are marketed to meet client needs and wants. A good is a tangible object like adaptive equipment, while a service is intangible, like a referral that a TRS makes during leisure-education resource awareness. Ideas and information are also intangible and focus on thoughts about actions/causes (e.g., accessibility, person-first language). By coordinating the integration of several goods and services, TRSs create brand experiences (services from a known source) during, for example, adventure therapy, dining at a themed restaurant, or visiting an interactive website. Our profession tends to focus on services marketing. This approach emphasizes our ability to maintain quality through the effective interactions among professionals and clients. We identify the need a service fulfills in order to gain client satisfaction and value by exceeding their expectations. When this is achieved, client satisfaction and value build relationships.

Exchange relationships are created as the TRS delivers services valued by clients. Relationship marketing intends to establish and maintain enduring client relationships that directly or indirectly affect service success. This relationship is characterized not only by the functional benefit of the service but also by the relational benefit. Through a helping relationship, the TRS offers services, information, and experiences that improve client functioning; in return, the client maintains a long-lasting relationship with the service provider (e.g., rehabilitation moves from inpatient to outpatient services or clients register for additional programs in subsequent seasons).

With whom does the TRS establish exchange relationships? A *market* is the actual and potential clients of a program. Relationship marketing intends to create mutually satisfying relationships with key stakeholders and partners. Through *target marketing*, the manager identifies distinct, fairly homogeneous groups who benefit directly or indirectly from services. The manager then attempts to design services to satisfy the needs that best serve each selected market *segment*. Traditional markets have included *internal* (e.g., clients and employees) and *external* (e.g., caregivers and insurers) audiences. These markets have expanded in today's digital world. Concern for the health and well-being of our communities has lead to *social marketing*. Agencies deliver services of immediate value to clients and of lasting significance to society. Concern for environmental, social, and economic issues requires the manager to "deliver value to the customer in a way that maintains or improves both the consumer's and the society's well-being" (Kotler & Armstrong, 2006, p. 11).

To achieve the goals for each target market, the manager develops a *marketing mix.* This is a set of tools or controllable variables that the manager blends to produce the desired response from each target market—everything the organization can do to influence demand for its services (Kotler & Armstrong, 2006; Perreault, Cannon, & McCarthy, 2011). These variables are organized as the four "P's": product, price, place, and promotion. *Product* is a service, idea, or experience that satisfies the client's need. *Price* is what is exchanged for the service, so the manager considers not only demand and competition but also nondollar values (e.g., client time and convenience) and dollar values (e.g., third-party payers, client fees) along with all the other variables in the marketing mix. *Place* is providing the service when and where it is needed or with efficient distribution and minimal inconvenience (Tomey, 2009). Thus managers assess the location, referral mechanisms, staff expertise, and the availability and accessibility of resources. *Promotion* occurs to communicate among TRSs, clients, and other stakeholders and partners. Technology has revolutionized promotion. Through digital media and databases, professionals and clients converse almost instantaneously, expressing needs and sharing information to achieve mutually agreed-upon goals having value to both. A *market strategy* identifies a specific target market like insurance companies and the related marketing mix used to establish and maintain mutually beneficial relationships like ensuring clients remain within their reimbursement network (as opposed to changing insurance companies due to delayed, reduced, or nonpayment of client medical bills).

Change has become and will continue to be a factor in health and human services. Strategic planning is an overall direction-setting process that attempts to adapt the organization's resources to the changing environmental (e.g., social, regulatory, economic, competitive, technological) forces to maintain a fit between the organization's goals and a changing market environment (Kotler & Armstrong, 2006). This process is initiated with the definition of a mission followed by design of department marketing plans to take advantage of specific marketing opportunities. Thus, the manager prepares a marketing plan using a process similar to APIE that defines and organizes quality services to satisfy client demand and recognize organizational goals.

Learning Outcome
Define fundamental marketing concepts.

The Marketing Process: A Marketing Plan

To successfully market a therapeutic recreation service, idea, or experience, a coherent, organized plan is essential. A typical marketing plan is complex and includes information noted in Table 7.1. The design of the plan and its contents are similar to the APIE process undertaken when programs are operationalized. The plan is the instrument that directs and coordinates the manager's marketing efforts. The plan lays out the target markets and values offered while specifying marketing strategies.

Step 1: Assessment

Step 1 of the marketing process involves assessment. Initially, it is important to assess the current situation by conducting an analysis of strengths, weaknesses, opportunities, and threats (*SWOT analysis*). An environmental scan identifies the market segments and a profile of each target market. This analysis reveals market needs, trends, growth potential, and competition. The manager reviews the current services, information (technology), experience offerings to ascertain the department's capacity to satisfy needs of each market segment. With this information, the manager may develop four types of goals: 1) *market penetration*—gaining client support (rate of use or closer relationships) in existing markets with current offerings; 2) *market development*—gaining new markets with existing department offerings; 3) *service development*—taking new services, information, experiences to existing markets; and 4) *market diversification*—taking new offerings into new markets (Perreault, Cannon, & McCarthy, 2011; Tomey, 2009). Through assessment, the manager determines which opportunities come first; most managers benefit by growing where they already have client equity (expected earnings over time), for example, where there is already market penetration or service development (Perreault, Cannon, & McCarthy, 2011).

Assessment, in addition to identifying likely department marketing goals, reveals probable target markets or those whose needs should be addressed by department

Table 7.1 Marketing Plan Outline

I. Overall Goals
- a. market penetration
- b. market development
- c. service development
- d. market diversification

II. SWOT Analysis
- a. Target market identification, geographics, demographics, behavioral factors
- b. Market needs
- c. Market trends
- d. Market growth
- e. Market competition
- f. Target market goals and objectives

III. Business Profile
- a. Expense, income, break-even forecasts
- b. Budget preparation

IV. Action Plans
- a. Service, idea or information, experience
- b. Place
- c. Price
- d. Promotion
    - i. Word of mouth/personal contact
    - ii. Advertising
    - iii. Sales incentives
    - iv. Publicity
- e. Physical evidence, people, policies and procedures, public image, and political impact
- f. Market research
- g. Budget
- h. Market positioning

VII. Implementation
- a. Marketing timetable
- b. Marketing strategies and tools
- c. Evaluation and monitoring
- d. Budget revisions

VIII. Evaluation and Control
- a. Annual report (results)
- b. Profitability report
- c. Efficiency and impact expenditures
- d. Strategic plans (opportunities, markets, services, tools)

services. In therapeutic recreation, it is possible to have diverse target audiences. Figure 7.1 is a summary of possible internal and external target audiences. Data collected on each audience enables the identification of specific group needs. Data include geographic, demographic, and behavioral tendencies. For each potential target market, the manager drafts image and action goals with specific objectives. An image goal describes how a target market might perceive the department in the future while an action goal describes quality indicators or outcome measures that are intended to position the department.

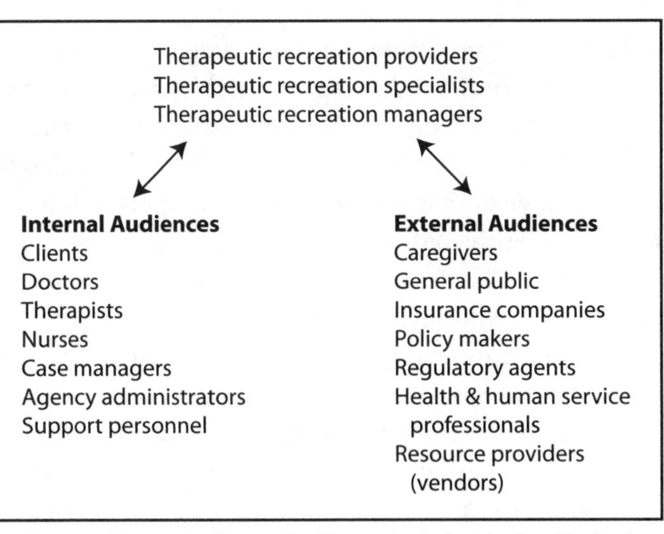

Figure 7.1 Target Audiences for Therapeutic Recreation Marketing

Target Market: Agency Administrators

1. Physicians
2. Administrators

Goals

1. Image: To become the primary access point for resource acquisition and support
2. Action: To increase the number of client referrals and financial support

Objective

1. After reviewing efficacy studies in recreation therapy, physicians and administrators will initiate a 25% increase in contacts with RT staff to plan referrals and garner resources for the department.

Figure 7.2 Marketing Goals and Objectives

Figure 7.2 illustrates the department's goals and objective for a selected target market. Once these potential audiences are identified, the manager develops marketing strategies appropriate to each group. Action plans are therefore developed during the next step of the marketing process. Throughout the marketing process, the manager considers financial resources and opportunities in order to prepare a financial plan to support department services. Initially this involves forecasting financial options.

Step 2: Planning

The second step in the marketing process is to develop an action plan. This marketing strategy or game plan outlines the marketing mix for each target market that will accomplish the target market's goals. In addition to the traditional P's of the marketing mix, the manager considers several service P's: Physical evidence, people, policies and procedures, public image, and political impact are considered, as these variables are important to establishing long-term relationships with clients (O'Sullivan, 1991). The manager selects strategies to market services that will create a meaningful difference or a competitive edge in the minds of the respective audiences. This is referred to as *market positioning* (Perreault, Cannon, & McCarthy, 2011). A position statement identifies important attributes that distinguish the department's services to particular target markets (Tomey, 2009). These main benefits are communicated to clients through unique terms, signs, and/or symbols that brand the service to differentiate it from its competitors (Kotler & Armstrong, 2006). Budgets are prepared as each service has associated revenues and expenses. And, as with APIE, the manager designs formative controls and continues to research the market to support and develop services.

A marketing mix is prepared for each target audience. This consists of blending the 4 P's and service variables to gain the response desired from each internal and external audience. Product or service line is evaluated to determine costs per client or program, client volume, payer mix, profitability, and life cycle; these considerations assist the manager as decisions are made about price. Because the client may not bear the burden of the service or the service may be prescribed or recommended by someone other than the client or family, nondollar considerations include time and convenience (e.g., minimization of nondollar costs benefit the department and client) (Tomey, 2009). Managers also consider demand and competition as the price is set. Place influences audiences' perceptions of service quality. Thus, as location is considered, also evaluated are staff expertise, referrals, accessibility, reputation, safety, welcoming appearance, attitude, and convenience. Promotion intends to inform audiences of available services and convince them to participate in order to gain certain benefits. Promotion usually occurs through advertising (paid promotion), personal contact or word of mouth, sales (short-term incentives), and publicity (unpaid promotion) (Tomey, 2009). Technology facilitates instantaneous and ongoing dialogue among managers and various audiences. Integrated messages aim to attract, retain, and motivate long-standing engagements between providers and clients.

Several additional service P's are blended with the traditional marketing-mix P's to articulate messages that garner desired client responses. Therapeutic recreation physical evidence involves the area where the intervention occurs, tokens received from participation, and documented outcomes of the exchange. Therapeutic recreation managers continually strive toward making the therapeutic recreation experience as attractive as possible. The second P, people, is critical to the provision of therapeutic recreation services. Of course, our consumers are our primary audience, but it is also essential that caregivers, family members, and other professionals be considered in the marketing process. Additionally, with group experiences, the manager considers how effective the group experience is in achieving specific client outcomes. Policies and procedures guide our marketing plans by regulating what can and cannot be done; safety and infection control, along with confidentiality, are critical aspects of delivery. The fourth P, public image, is critical to market positioning. While public image is an intangible, it can be greatly influenced by some concrete strategies, such as development of a tagline and logo to present a brand. Lastly, political impact is an increasingly important influence. Managers must learn about the political agendas of target audiences, including legislators, insurance companies, health-care organizations, and potential philanthropic groups, as these groups influence funding, agendas, and partnerships. Each audience's action plan defines marketing-mix variables intended to create a long-term relationship of value between service providers and recipients. Through ongoing marketing research,

Target Market: Clients, caregivers, family

Goal: Increase awareness of benefits/outcomes (market penetration)

Objective: Increase number of clients in leisure education services by communicating beneficial health outcomes

Service (Product): Leisure education

Price: cost recovery, fee for service, reimbursement

Promotion: personal contact, word of mouth, publicity, website

Place: outreach, inclusive setting

Physical Evidence: reintegration setting, healthy behavior checklists, nutrition logos

Policy/Procedure: transportation safety protocols, privacy statements

Public Image: department branding-Quality well-being through quality recreation therapy experiences

Political Image: partnerships with nonprofit wellness centers (Ys) and federal initiatives-Healthy People 2020

Figure 7.3 Action Plan

managers ascertain what audiences think about their services (positioning). With this information, managers continually evaluate their overall marketing goals and build budgets to create opportunities that satisfy client needs. A sample action plan is presented in Figure 7.3.

Step 3: Implementation

The third step of the marketing process involves implementation of the action plan. Implementation turns plans into actions to accomplish strategic objectives. While marketing plans present the what and the why of marketing activities, implementation is the who, where, when, and how of the plan (Kotler & Armstrong, 2006). These activities are both internal and external. Internal activities like interdepartmental collaboration and communication result in bundling and integration of services. External activities market a service having a better value, faster delivery, more convenience, and lower costs (Perreault, Cannon, & McCarthy, 2011). Social marketing implores managers to incorporate into messages the positive impacts that participation in recreation therapy has not only on the client but also on the family and community at large. Consequently, elements in the marketing mix are blended to present the benefits to internal as well as external targets. Thus, doing things right (implementation) is as important as doing the right things (strategy) (Kotler & Armstrong, 2006). Professionals connect within and outside the department/agency through digital media to exceed client expectations with value-enhanced services. A consistent approach throughout the agency creates a similar look and feel to marketing strategies. The agency develops a marketing style guide to ensure consistency and promote their unique offerings. The guide presents templates and describes who, where, when, and how tools are used to articulate desired benefits and images. An example of a comprehensive guide is the template developed by Ken-Caryl Ranch Metropolitan District. Their *Marketing Style Guide* (2004, March) includes logo elements, logo colors, logo versions, logo "don'ts", stationery, forms, envelopes, business cards, publications, staff uniforms, and name tags. Managers ensure budgets support marketing efforts and controls are in place to evaluate and take corrective actions if results suggest, for example, that different target audiences or strategies would better communicate desired outcomes. Software systems and databases enable continuous dialogue among managers, staff, and audiences while supporting and updating action plans and timetables (see Figure 7.4).

Promotion communicates between the service provider and potential audiences to influence their behaviors. It is the element in the marketing mix that presents the right service at the right place and time (Perreault, Cannon, & McCarthy, 2011). Technology has expanded relationship marketing into global social networking. TRSs use a variety of digital and traditional strategies to connect and influence behavior.

Branding

Branding is a strategy to teach clients "who" as well as what the service does and "why" the client needs the product (idea, service or experiences) (Kotler & Keller, 2006). A brand is a name, term, sign, design, symbol, or combination of these that adds dimensions to differentiate the service from other services designed to satisfy the same need (Kotler & Keller, 2006). The term "experience" implies clients are partaking in more than a service; they are benefiting from what the service will do for them (Kotler & Armstrong, 2006). Branding is the whole story about the special qualities of therapeutic recreation services.

Why is therapeutic recreation important to the client? What messages do we want to evoke in therapeutic recreation? The messages may be functional, rational, or tangible—outcomes of the experience (functional

Target Market	Strategy/Tool	Responsibility	Timeframe	Outcome
Clients	personal contact	staff	Assessment Interview	Intervention plan
Staff	webinar	manager	EOM	CEU-competency
Professionals	website	mgr/staff	ongoing	online community

Figure 7.4 Marketing Timetable

fitness), or they may be symbolic, emotional, or intangible—what therapeutic recreation represents (health and quality of life) (Kotler & Keller, 2006). Brand knowledge consists of all the beliefs, thoughts, and images clients associate with therapeutic recreation. A manager is therefore concerned that clients have the right experience and that marketing creates the desired brand knowledge of therapeutic recreation. Brands identify the source of the service and allow clients to assign responsibility to TRSs for value resulting from that service. Managers rely on the service deliverer (TRS) and the delivery (APIE process) to create brand knowledge. Thus, the quality of the interaction and selection of the right intervention (Kotler & Armstrong, 2006) create brand equity, the added value associated with therapeutic recreation. Consequently, internal marketing precedes external or interactive marketing to ensure everyone in the department and agency work as a team to provide customer satisfaction.

Product branding is evident in packaging and labeling of goods while trademarking is a legal term that identifies the words, symbols, or marks registered in a country for a particular product (Perreault, Cannon, & McCarthy, 2011). How is branding evident with therapeutic recreation services? As suggested, tools in the manager's style guide as well as the agency's external marketing strategy create brand positioning—for example, the desired place relative to competitors in the minds of target clients. Logos, taglines, bundling, and digital networking are avenues to connect with targeted clientele. Health, quality of life, and functional skills are benefits and values that can be used to help therapeutic recreation establish consistency in brand positioning.

Logo

We've all heard the expression, "A picture is worth a thousand words." That is what a *logo* is all about! Immediately when we see the "swoosh," we know that the product is Nike. The swoosh logo has helped to define the identity of that organization. Logos are pictorial representations that positively associate with the agency or service and help to define the agency's identity. Research indicates that corporate logos can be extremely effective in creating positive associations with a company and those logos, with the company name behind the symbol, increase associations with the organization through the unique, compelling, and attractive symbol (van Riel & van den Ban, 2001). As the therapeutic recreation manager looks toward developing a logo for the agency/department, he or she determines the image that should be conveyed and how this can best be symbolized through a picture that depicts, for example, outcomes like improved physical health, reduced stress, or enhanced cognitive skills.

Tagline

"Just Do It" (Nike)
"I'm Lovin' It" (McDonald's)

These are probably two of the best-known product taglines. We just need to hear the tagline, and we associate with the product. What is a tagline? A *tagline* or common slogan is a one- or two-line descriptor that comes after a product logo or agency name. Denoting excellent care, the Rehabilitation Institute of Chicago's tagline is "The best in healing and hope." A tagline reinforces unique aspects or the position of your department/agency. Table 7.2 shows the steps to follow in the development of a tagline for your department/agency.

Bundling

Why not have a cell phone for yourself and each family member, along with high-speed Internet service? Why only buy a Big Mac when for a nominal amount more you can get a value meal? These are but two examples of bundled services that are seen frequently in the business world. *Bundling* is defined as "the sale of two or more separate products in one package" (Legarreta & Miguel, 2004, p. 264). Bundling encourages us to buy more and buy services we might not consider because the added cost is less than normal so the value is better (Perreault, Cannon, & McCarthy, 2011). Packaging services assists in expanding to new target markets and selling additional services.

The concept of bundling is evident when TRSs co-treat with other therapists, as when aquatic and hippotherapy are scheduled jointly between physical and recreational therapy, or when partnerships among, for example, Y facilities, park districts, and hospitals result in outpatient or reintegration programs. Managers also bundle services when clients attend simultaneous sessions—when a visit with a physician is followed by speech and hearing and follow-up RT assessment. Bundling also occurs when clients register for programs at reduced rates as they become members at specialized centers—both

Table 7.2 Steps to Developing a Tagline

1. Get data by answering the following questions:
   - Who are your customers?
   - What benefits do you give your customers?
   - What feelings do you want to invoke in customers?
   - What action(s) are you trying to generate from customers?
   - Who is the competition and how are you different?
2. Prepare to brainstorm
   - Gather taglines from other agencies, including your competition. Look in other categories besides your own.
   - Write taglines so ideas can be mixed and matched.
   - Pay attention to the words used and how they are put together.
   - Look for a unique angle for your tagline.
3. Brainstorm with a small group
   - Generate a large number of ideas.
4. Consolidate your list
   - Pull out the words with the best potential.
5. Choose the one best tagline
   - Get opinions through a survey (possibly online) or through a focus group.

the enrollment numbers and memberships may increase as a result of the added opportunity to experience values from the programs and the facility. Concerns for the management of lifestyle issues like obesity and diabetes and rising health-care costs have resulted in health collaborations among insurers like United Healthcare and the YMCA (Harnik, 2010). Compensation is based on the number of member participants and their collective weight loss. This partnership targets a new market while capturing medical cost savings.

Digital Networking

Digital media and marketing databases are essential to interactive marketing and implementation of action plans. The Internet has shifted from an information-based resource to an electronic avenue to generate and share content (Baum & Dowling, 2011). The greatest use of digital media is projected to be in social media, considered a "buffet of digital opportunities to connect with people around the world in real time" (Yost, 2010, p. 49). Web video and secure patient portals enable seamless communication between clients and providers while improving overall efficiency of delivery (Baum & Dowling, 2011). Social media is a bridge to the department's/agency's website, which presents services clients want; it is also a tool to make the website interactive. Media and marketing databases allow the manager to attend to and react to actual client behaviors to manage personal client relationships (Tomey, 2009). Clients want relevant information on their terms; digital networking is bidirectional and creates the opportunity for managers and TRSs to talk with rather than at clients ("Brand Management 2.0", 2008). Interactive media, therefore, strengthens the relationship among clients and service providers, and in doing so makes clients feel connected and in control of the experience—the value-added dimension that distinguishes therapeutic recreation service benefits.

Marketing Benefits

The benefits movement began in the 1990s and still has strong application to the field today. The benefits approach involves a focus on the outcomes of what we do (Bright, 2000; NTRS, 2000; O'Sullivan, 1999). In therapeutic recreation, marketing benefits is critical to enhancing the perceived value of our services and conveying the importance of this service as a viable treatment modality to improve functional abilities, knowledge of leisure resources, and integration into the community (NTRS, 2000). According to NTRS (2000), "benefits-based therapeutic recreation is an approach that deliberately targets strategies that will ensure the identification and delivery of the benefits of therapeutic recreation to appropriate internal and external audiences" (p. 13). Outcomes identified with specific interventions through the helping relationship differentiate recreation therapy from competing therapies. The manager's task is to articulate these unique outcomes through evidence-based practices.

During implementation, managers select tools suited to particular internal and external audiences to convey the benefits message through interactive dialogue aimed at establishing long-term personal relationships. Technology enables continuous evaluation of effective approaches and monitoring of respective marketing costs as strategies are implemented and revisited. Adjustments in financial plans result with the use of alternative marketing strategies. Convenience, quality, and lower costs typify client expectations and, therefore, are the benchmarks used by managers to evaluate various marketing strategies and tools (Tomey, 2009).

Step 4: Evaluation and Control

The last step in the marketing process is evaluation and control. Both formative and summative evaluation are critical to determining the ongoing effectiveness of marketing strategies and plans. Control involves using evaluation results, taking corrective action to ensure objectives are met, and planning for success in the future (Kotler & Armstrong, 2006; Perreault, Cannon, & McCarthy, 2011). The manager measures performance in relationship to each marketing goal "and evaluates the causes of any differences between expected and actual performance . . . [then] takes corrective action to close the gaps between its goals and its performance" (Kotler & Armstrong, 2011, p. 55). Control is concerned with four aspects: (1) determining if planned results are being achieved, (2) examining if the department/agency is making or losing money, (3) improving efficiency and the impact of marketing expenditures, and (4) examining whether the department/agency is pursuing the best opportunities with respect to target markets, services, and marketing tools (strategic plans) (Kotler & Keller, 2006).

A marketing audit is a comprehensive, systematic, unbiased review of the department's/agency's objectives, strategies, and activities to identify problems and opportunities and to recommend a plan to improve performance (Kotler & Armstrong, 2006; Perreault, Cannon, & McCarthy, 2011). Thus, each of the P's is reconsidered. Input is gained from each client and target market. As a consequence, one target audience or service may be substituted for another, profit centers may be created or cost-recovery programs maximized; the location may be made more convenient to minimize opportunity costs; tools may be diversified to better integrate marketing strategies or address client technology preferences; and changes in staffing, policies, and the work environment may be undertaken to improve intangible qualities of therapeutic interactions. Quantitative data, such as increased number of referrals or program attendees, as well as qualitative information like anecdotal comments noting perceived satisfaction levels, are analyzed to measure attainment of planned results. Results are also reviewed in light of costs, impact, and profit of different recreation therapy services. Monies are devoted to action plans likely to be of the most benefit to the greatest number of crucial target markets. Annual allocations of marketing funds have a direct influence on which of the four goals (market penetration, market development, service development, or market diversification) the manager is able to accomplish.

Technology expedites evaluation and control, letting the manager use faster feedback to develop a competitive edge. Digital communication allows the manager to share data through the intranet and Internet almost immediately. Reports summarizing client outcomes, reimbursement rates by client type, or staffing ratios can be available whenever an online user desires access. Software programs create graphics easy to interpret. Managers may change action plans daily if desired. Likewise, clients have ready access to benchmarks denoting service quality and the advantages gained by patronizing a particular hospital or special recreation center.

Learning Outcome

Outline the marketing process in therapeutic recreation.

A wise manager makes decisions that guide the department/agency to desired outcomes, impacts, and profits. By using creative strategies and tools, we will be able not only to maintain existing services but also to expand opportunities to new client groups and different settings. We must value the time spent marketing as an opportunity to exponentially expand opportunities and to secure the placement of therapeutic recreation as a viable health and human service option in an environment of limited resources and increasing client demands.

Managerial Roles

Therapeutic recreation managers are challenged to articulate the unique benefits and to create strategies that will ensure that therapeutic recreation services remain integral to the organization's clientele. The first-line manager is the link between the department's mission, the organization, and the service quality that fosters relationships. A well conceived and designed market plan supports value-added services that aim to give the consumer more than is anticipated. A first-line manager is the central figure in designing department tools like the marketing plan, marketing goals and objectives, and a marketing timetable, to cultivate a culture in which staff deliver quality services, engage in long-term relationships, and realize the significance of intangible elements like the impact of the helping relationship on client satisfaction. Further, the manager is the link between the therapeutic recreation service, community groups, and health and human service providers. As such, primary responsibility for social marketing lies with the manager. By directly connecting with media outlets and other critical external audiences, the manager interprets the contribution of services to the health of our social fabric.

First-line managers advocate building community relations that promote access, convenience, cost containment, resource sharing, social capital, and health among various constituent groups. Through educational programs, partnerships, and volunteering, therapeutic recreation managers build networks and relationships that benefit their therapeutic recreation services while increasing their capacity to respond to consumer and social needs.

As professional advocates, managers articulate the merits of therapeutic recreation services (experiences) with referral agents, third-party reimbursers, colleagues, and political agents. Managers use evidence-based practices and the results of efficacy studies to articulate the benefits of therapeutic recreation services. Additionally, they monitor legislation and communicate with decision makers the essential benefits and values of recreation-therapy experiences. When professionals recruit students to be members of professional organizations or serve on professional committees, they are advocating for their professional future.

Learning Outcome

Explain the first-line manager's role in marketing and advocacy.

Ethics in Marketing

Conscientious managers face moral dilemmas. The best action or decision to take is not always clear (Kotler & Armstrong, 2006). When managers focus on client satisfaction, societal objectives may be compromised and vice versa—the purchase of the latest exercise equipment, while good for the economy, may not be appropriate for individual clients who need to focus on functional capacity rather than increasing muscle mass. Dilemmas result when different individuals or audiences have a stake in the outcomes and the social consequences (Perreault, Cannon, & McCarthy, 2011).

Within the department, the manager may rely on professional standards of practice and professional ethics code to guide decision-making. In addition, in the agency, the manager may be part of the team that develops organizational marketing policies to guide the development and implementation of marketing guides. Under the concept of societal marketing, a manager and team consider what is legal, allowed, and demanded by professional practice, then develop policies based on personal integrity, corporate conscience, and long-run client welfare (Kotler & Armstrong, 2006). Social conscience guides agencies and managers to apply high ethical standards and morality when making marketing decisions regardless of "what the system allows" (Kotler & Armstrong, 2006).

Professional ethics for health-care marketing, developed by the American Marketing Association, include "respecting the primacy of the client's welfare and confidentiality of the relationship with the client; providing communications to inform, not to deceive; being competitive and making fair comparisons; and being vigilant in the application of the standards" (Tomey, 2009, p. 270).

Health and human services are businesses that operate at the margin of a social market economy. Billing decisions, co-sponsored events, and committee or board composition may be influenced by factors beyond concern for client health. Clients and caregivers may lack the information or resources to compare one intervention or setting to another. Likewise, when asked to analyze the advantage of one service over another, a lack of familiarity with documented outcomes and experience values may result in the creation of imperfect images of the intent of therapeutic recreation. First-line managers, through internal and external interactions and dialogue, promote staff decisions that add value to helping relationships and quality to individual and community well-being.

Learning Outcome
Interpret the ethical challenges faced as the manager markets recreation therapy in an entrepreneurial climate.

Summary

1. The first-line manager is experiencing a constantly changing work environment as a result of significant increases in the use of technology, reforms in payment and delivery methods, diversity in clientele, and societal marketing that acknowledges the relationship between individual health-care outcomes and the welfare of communities.
2. The marketing process, like the therapeutic recreation process, involves assessment, planning, implementation, and evaluation and control.
3. Therapeutic recreation services are used by diverse audiences identified through assessment.
4. Key to planning is studying the marketing mix or the 4 P's and several service P's for each audience to present the right services to the right individuals in a timely and seamless manner.
5. During implementation each target audience's marketing plan is put into action. Strategies and tools like branding, logos, taglines, bundling, and digital networks and databases are used to highlight the benefits inherent in therapeutic experiences.
6. Evaluation and control, like each of the other steps in the marketing process, have benefited from technology. Feedback received at a faster pace results in more individualized or customized responses and interactive dialogues. These encourage stronger client and community relationships and commitments to services.
7. As a first-line manager, the therapeutic recreation manager is the link between service quality and the accomplishment of the unit's and the organization's marketing goals. The manager garners the resources and creates the culture that enables relationship building.
8. As the primary advocate, the manager articulates the benefits of evidence-based practices to community groups and health-care providers.
9. A first-line manager is challenged to respond and behave in an ethical manner as markets are penetrated, developed, and diversified. Collaboration within the department and organization facilitate adherence to professional standards and presentation of consistent messages during interactive marketing.

Critical Thinking Activities

1. List your activities for at least three hours over the weekend. How did marketing affect your decisions and behavior? How has marketing affected your college experience thus far?
2. A condo purchased by three families is home to three young adults with intellectual disabilities, each with assisted-living support from a nonprofit organization. Each condo resident uses recreation services of the local recreation agency. How are the seven service P's and the four traditional marketing P's of the local agency influenced by these residents, their families, and their caregivers? Design an action plan appropriate for this scenario.
3. Identify a recent purchase made where the purchase wasn't a single encounter but intended to be integral to a longstanding relationship. What did or could the seller do better to ensure you remain a longstanding customer of the agency?
4. What are at least two or three social benefits and service P's that might contribute to the client values of each of the following: (a) outpatient weight control/exercise program, (b) agency-sponsored sibling education and recreation group, (c) library/adapted equipment lending program, and (d) in-home assessment and reintegration evaluation?

References

Baum, N. H., & Dowling, R. A. (2011). Are you engaging with patients electronically? *Urology Times, 39*(6), 38–39.

Brand management 2.0. (2008, September). *EContent, 31*(7), 30–31.

Bright, A. D. (2000). The role of social marketing in leisure and recreation management. *Journal of Leisure Research, 32*(1), 12–17.

Harnik, P. (2010). Secrets of the private sector, how parks and recreation agencies can flex their marketing muscles. *Parks & Recreation, 45*(8), 32–35.

Kaczynski, A. T. (2008). A more tenable marketing for leisure services and studies. *Leisure Sciences, 30:* 253–272.

Ken-Caryl Ranch Metropolitan District. (2004, March). *Marketing style guide*. Littleton, CO: Author.

Kotler, P., & Armstrong, G. (2006). *Principles of marketing* (11th ed.). Upper Saddle River, NJ: Pearson Education

Kotler, P., & Keller, K. L. (2006). *Marketing management* (12th ed.). Upper Saddle River, NJ: Pearson Education.

Legarreta, J. M. B., & Miguel, C. E. (2004). Collaborative relationship bundling: A new angle on services marketing. *International Journal of Service Industry Management, 15*(3), 264–283.

National Therapeutic Recreation Society (NTRS). (2000). *The benefits of therapeutic recreation: A training and resource guide*. Arlington, VA: National Therapeutic Recreation Society.

O'Sullivan, E. (1991). Marketing experiences: It's the how, not the what. *Parks & Recreation, 26*(12), 40–42.

O'Sullivan, E. (1999). *Setting a course for change: The benefits movement in parks and recreation.* Arlington, VA: National Recreation and Park Association.

Perreault, W. D., Cannon, J. P., & McCarthy, E. J. (2011). *Basic marketing a marketing strategy planning approach* (18th ed.). New York: McGraw-Hill/Irwin.

Tomey, A. M. (2009). *Guide to nursing management and leadership* (8th ed.). St Louis, MO: Mosby Elsevier.

van Riel, C. B. M., & van den Ban, A. (2001). The added value of corporate logos: An empirical study. *European Journal of Marketing, 35*(3/4), 428–440.

Williams, J. (2011). A new road map for healthcare business success. *Healthcare Financial Management, 65*(5), 62–69.

Winans, R., & Kasubski, D. (2011). What's the attraction? Finding out why patients come to you. *PT in Motion, 3*(7), 16–22.

Yost, L. (2010). You've got tweets: Email is so yesterday. Here's how social media is driving innovative parks and recreation marketing communications. *Parks & Recreation, 45* (2), 49–53.

Chapter 8
FINANCIAL MANAGEMENT

Keywords

- Active treatment
- Appropriations
- Capital budget
- Case mix
- Cost-based pricing
- Coverage
- Fee-for-service
- Flexible or variable budget
- Health-care reform
- Incremental or line-item budget
- Managed-care organizations
- Medicaid
- Medicare
- Operating or revenue-and-expense budget
- Performance budget
- Personnel budget
- Productivity
- Program budget
- Prospective payment systems
- Retrospective reimbursement system
- Third-party reimbursement
- Value-based payment
- Zero-based budget

Learning Outcomes

After reading this chapter, students will be able to:

1. Identify the factors contributing to the global fiscal challenges in health care.
2. Outline payment shifts and legislation affecting health care in North America.
3. Compare regulations and financial practices of the Canadian and U.S. systems.
4. Define key concepts and terms in health-care financing.
5. Articulate revenue sources and expenditures in health and human services.
6. Explain the budgeting process, budget types, budget formats, and budget monitoring.
7. Describe trends and challenges in health-care financing.

Overview

"The viability of most health-care organizations today depends on their ability to use their fiscal resources wisely" (Marquis & Huston, 2009, p. 210). Complicating fiscal planning today are the dual goals of cost containment and quality client care and intervention. These foci require the manager to make changes to control costs to deliver services effectively and efficiently (McCormick, 2002). Along with vision and creativity, the manager relies on knowledge of the political, social, and economic forces shaping the health and human service environment to meet productivity and quality demands.

The first section briefly overviews milestones in health-care financing, legislation, and payment. Concepts and terms are presented. Unique features of the U.S. and Canadian systems are introduced. A second section outlines revenue sources and coverage of medical services—with a discussion of how to calculate service rates. The third section describes the budgeting process, budget types, budget formats, and the manager's role in budget monitoring. A closing section explores trends and challenges in health-care financing.

Deficits and fiscal uncertainty complicate efforts to improve quality while reducing costs. The centerpiece of this challenge is adjusting the way we use and pay for services. We open the chapter with a summary of the political, social, and economic forces influencing the delicate balance between constrained resources and managing health-care access, cost, and quality.

Health-Care Financing: Milestones and Concepts

Most of us know that health care in North America is expensive and that costs are on the rise, with few agreed-upon solutions to contain this expense. Both the USA and Canada allocate substantial public funds to health care—18.5% and 16.7%, respectively, in 2007 (Noseworthy, 2011). Costs in the USA far exceed other industrialized nations, and overall health-care performance as compared to other nations is ranked 37th by the World Health Organization (WHO) (Cors & Sagin, 2011). In this WHO report, Canadian costs are 10th with overall performance listed as 30th among the 191 participating nations (WHO, 2000). Health-care costs have been rising due to a number of political, social, and economic forces, including

- an aging population with chronic diseases (e.g., cancers, diabetes, hypertension, stroke, heart disease, asthma, and mental disorders) and care needs;
- the increased use of expensive technology, treatments, and medicine;
- rising costs of litigation;
- increasing numbers of uninsured;
- increasing administrative costs;
- a fee-for-service payment system in the USA and rising costs not covered by the Canadian Health Act, like medications;
- catastrophic and pandemic diseases and incidents;
- consumer demands;
- competitive marketing or direct-to-consumer advertising (USA); and
- redesigned systems focusing on preventive and rehabilitative services through outpatient care, home care, and other community-based service models.

A slight decrease in health-care spending was experienced during economic decline; the push for accountability by health-care providers seemed to reinforce this spending decline (Ameringer, 2012; "Boring but important," 2012; "Cutting the cost," 2010; Stephens & Ledlow, 2010; Tomey, 2009). These factors result in Canada and the USA spending more of their gross domestic product (GDP) on medical care than most other nations. The next section reviews attempts to manage health-care spending.

Learning Outcome

Identify the factors contributing to the global fiscal challenges in health care.

Milestones: United States and Canada

A review of the shifts in how we pay for health care and the legislation affecting health care helps clarify the dilemma and challenges faced by the client, health-care provider, and those who pay for health care. The shifts and landmark legislation in the USA are first summarized, followed by a similar summary of Canadian laws.

United States

During the 1920s and 1930s, most health care was paid privately by the person receiving the care. In time (by the 1950s), third-party payers like the government (e.g., Medicare and Medicaid) and insurance companies (Blue Cross and Blue Shield) assumed the responsibility for client bills and paid through a cost-based *retrospective reimbursement system* (payment followed services). In the 1970s, managed care came into being (expanding during the 1980s) in an attempt to drive down the cost of care. With costs still on the rise, legislation in the 1980s resulted in *prospective payment systems* (health-care reimbursements were based on predetermined rates regardless of the expenses incurred). By the mid-1990s, the rising costs of health care became a political concern with attempts (failed) to pass legislation providing universal coverage.

The 21st century has again experienced legislation to extend coverage to all individuals, as well as attempts to protect client information and integrate care through a continuum of services made possible, in part, by technology. Individuals are experiencing increasing out-of-pocket expenses as employers are either reducing their payment of insurance premiums or dropping coverage. Providers continue to implement initiatives to promote safety and quality while containing costs and improving productivity. A summary of the payment shifts and legislation in the USA is presented in Table 8.1.

Table 8.1 USA Payment Shifts and Legislation

- 1920s: Hospitals charged daily service and special charges for techniques (e.g., surgery). Clients paid for their health care.
- Late 1920s: All-inclusive rates were applied to specific diagnoses like tonsillectomies and maternity service.
- 1929: Blue Cross originated with a prepayment plan created for teachers by Baylor University Hospital. The teachers joined the plan and paid a fixed sum per month ($0.50).
- 1930s: Blue Cross plans grew and shifted responsibility for costs from individuals to the private sector (i.e., insurance companies) and government sources.
- 1935: Passage of the Social Security Act. The American Medical Association successfully fought inclusion of compulsory health insurance for states that voluntarily chose to participate.
- 1946: Hill Burton Act provided funding to expand and build hospitals to care for war injured.
- 1950s: Insurance plans grew. Debate flourished about the notion of health care as a basic right, as something more than a privilege for people with economic means.
- 1960s: Federal policy and legislation (e.g., Civil Rights Act of 1964, P.L. 88-352) increased citizen access to health and human services.
- 1965: Government started Medicare and Medicaid; as a result, it became the primary insurer of the elderly, poor, and certain individuals with long-term illnesses. The Social Security Act Amendments (PL 89-97) introduced a cost-based retrospective reimbursement system.
- 1972: Professional Standards Review Organizations (PSRO) created by the 1972 Social Security Amendments denied payments for Medicare and Medicaid clients if services were not deemed necessary.
- 1973: Health Maintenance Organization Act (PL 93-222) created managed care—health maintenance organizations (HMOs)—across the country as alternatives to traditional health insurance plans.
- 1974: National Health Planning and Resource Development Act (PL 93-641) attempted to curtail unnecessary expansion of facilities by requiring Certificates of Need to build new hospitals.
- 1980s: The birth of large for-profit hospital chains and the inception of marketing to consumers. Patients in hospitals came to be redefined as customers. Alternative delivery systems (e.g., substance-abuse centers, home-health services, and outpatient services) changed the direction of the industry from "medical care" toward "health care."
- 1982–1983: Tax Equity and Fiscal Responsibility Act (TEFRA; PL 97-248) and the Social Security Amendment Act (PL 98-21) created a prospective payment system based on diagnosis-related groups (DRGs) or pretreatment diagnosis billing categories for Medicare reimbursement with reimbursement based on costs related to treatment of specific DRGs.
- 1986: Consolidated Omnibus Budget Reconciliation Act (COBRA; PL 99-272) was passed and allowed terminated employees to buy group coverage for a limited time period.
- 1987: Omnibus Budget Reconciliation Act (OBRA; PL 100-203) included recreation therapy as part of the rehabilitation process for persons on Medicaid and Medicare.
- 1993: Health Security Act, legislation assuring universal access to all citizens failed.
- 1996: Health Insurance Portability and Accountability Act (PL 104-191) established national standards for electronic health-care transactions; national identifiers for providers, health plans, and employers; protected the privacy of health data; and ensured continuity of health-care coverage.
- 1997: Balanced Budget Act (BBA: PL 105-33) gave states the authority to implement managed care plans. Attempted to reduce Federal health-care dollars by calculating payment rates prior to service delivery that were based on price or historical costs.
- 1999–2000: Balanced Budget Reform Act (BBRA) and Budget Improvement and Protection Act restored cuts introduced by the 1997 BBA Act.
- 2003: The Medicare Prescription Drug, Improvement, and Modernization Act created a voluntary prescription-drug coverage program under Medicare and creation of tax-free health savings accounts.
- 2009: Health Information Technology for Economic and Clinical Health (HITECH), enacted as part of the American Recovery and Reinvestment Act, promoted adoption of health information technology (HIT) by giving incentive payments through Medicare and Medicaid to physicians and hospitals who demonstrate meaningful use of certified electronic health records (EHRs).
- 2010: Patient Protection and Affordable Care Act and the Health Care and Education Reconciliation Act (P.L. 111-148) reforms insurance and expands coverage with changes effecting payers, providers, and plan members.

Canada

Today's health-care system, a national single-payer system administered by provincial governments, is a composite of 13 provincial (10) and territorial (3) insurance systems funded by provincial and federal taxes with a federal component (Medicare) consisting of public health, regulatory, and limited service provision (doctor and hospital) functions (Noseworthy, 2011). This system evolved from the local health boards established during the mid- and late-1800s to respond to epidemics. Individuals were cared for at home, with those lacking funds cared for in hospitals operated by voluntary organizations and municipal governments. The Great Depression of the early 1900s created demands for health care that could not be financially supported by the charitable hospitals, municipal governments, and the free services of the medical profession, and the federal government passed fewer funds to the local governments. As a consequence, several provinces in the late 1940s instituted legislation to create universal coverage. In 1957 the federal government passed a piece of legislation to support provincial governments at 50% of the costs for hospital and diagnostic services. This lead to additional legislation in the 1960s to create a universal health plan through federal-provincial cost sharing (Medicare). Ultimately a 1984 act identified the criteria provinces and territories must adhere to in order to receive transfer funds from the federal government to insure persons not otherwise insured with coverage that includes hospital, physician, and dental/surgical services. Under this law, provinces and territories may be fined if physicians use extra-billing practices or hospitals charge user fees (Noseworthy, 2011).

The sustainability of the Canadian health-care system is challenged by an aging population, escalating costs of scientific advances in care and treatment, and the increasing costs borne by provincial and territorial governments and by individuals. Canadians are spending more on drugs than physicians (Chernomas, 2012). Provinces and territories are coping with health-care costs that consume one third to one half of their revenues (Noseworthy, 2011). Delays caused by limited access, prolonged waiting times, and poor service quality to Aboriginal Canadians are also system challenges (Bhatia, 2012). Consequently, political entities are reconsidering how to sustain the federal-provincial/territory funding system so coverage is adequate and accessible to all persons—a situation not unlike that faced in the USA. Table 8.2 outlines the legislative activities leading to universal health care in Canada.

Learning Outcome

Outline payment shifts and legislation affecting health care in North America.

Concepts: Regulations and Financial Practices in North America

While Canada has a national single-payer system administered by provincial governments, the USA has a mixed public/private system administered by the federal government (Barr, 2012). Thus, one difference is the role of public and private insurance. Canadians have universal access to publicly funded physician and hospital services (primarily), while in the USA the majority of the citizens rely on private insurance (employer-employee plans or private policies) to cover the cost of an array of health services. Public insurance is provided through Medicaid for the poor and through Medicare for those over 65 years of age. Thus, organization of the two systems is dissimilar due to, primarily, how the systems are financed. In Canada, hospitals and doctors are privately run but publicly funded, regulated, and not-for profit, while in the USA a number of private and for-profit

Table 8.2 Canadian Health-Care Legislation

- 1867: Constitution Act, formerly British North American Act, made provinces responsible for health-care delivery.
- 1940s: Saskatchewan (1946) and Alberta (1950) created universal coverage plans.
- 1948: Federal government introduced a series of National Health Grants to provide funds to provinces/territories for hospital construction, professional training, and public health. This increased access to hospital care but did not address the issue of how to cover operating costs.
- 1957: Hospital Insurance and Diagnostic Services Act. federal government funded 50% of these services in provinces when adopted by provincial governments.
- 1966: Medical Care Act (Medicare) adopted by all Canadian provinces, resulting in universal coverage in all provinces and territories by 1971.
- 1977: Federal-Provincial Fiscal Arrangements and Established Programs Financing Act. Rather than a 50-50 split, the federal government transferred to the provinces a lump sum based on a 3-year moving average of the Gross National Product and per capita cash payments.
- 1984: Canadian Health Act ensured there is no point-of-contact charges for medically necessary services, with provision based on need rather than willingness to pay.
- 2003: First Ministers' Accord on Health Care Renewal reaffirmed all Canadians have timely access to health services on the basis of need, regardless of where they live or move in Canada; the health-care services are of high quality, effective, patient-centered and safe; and the system is sustainable and affordable. The accord identified several priority areas, including primary health care and home care.
- 2007: The Canadian Medical Association (CMA) released a report endorsing private health care as a means to improve the universal health care system.

(http://www.canada.com/nationalpost/news/story.html?id=fe42e2be-077a-4193-a7c0-d6fc2e242269&k=12821)

companies and public government entities manage health-care services; as a consequence, multiple layers of public and private regulations exist and health-care centers and physicians operate for-profit as well as not-for-profit services. These differences create a third notable difference: In the USA, funding levels are higher in per capita spending, by percentage of the gross domestic product, and from the private sector. Further, in Canada a patchwork of payment methods (private insurance, out-of-pocket, or do without) cover non-physician and non-hospital services like long-term care, pharmaceuticals, and professional services (Noseworthy, 2011). In the States, these expenses may be partially covered and accessible through various health insurance plans. One similarity of North American health-care financing is the constraint on public funding with declining tax resources and the increasing out-of-pocket amounts and types of expenses assumed by those receiving care. Another similarity is the disparity in access to health care found among those with financial means as compared to those without, resulting in either, for example, excessive use of emergency services (USA) or doing without or delayed care (Canada). In both nations, the rising number of uninsured/underinsured is contributing to rising health-care costs and political concern to identify alternative funding sources.

Learning Outcome

Compare regulations and financial practices of the Canadian and USA systems.

Payment practices in the USA. Today's financial alternatives are influenced by past practices. Review of practices in both nations suggests the search for a solution to accessible, affordable, and accountable care is complex. We have elected to focus on past U.S. practices due to the longstanding attempt to resolve this issue, yet one ought to realize that lessons are learned by comparing the practices of both nations.

Historically individuals paid for their healthcare (1920s). Private insurance carriers began paying for care in the 1930s. These programs grew during the 1950s—largely supported by employer-paid benefit packages. During this time, *cost-based pricing* was used—insurance companies paid all the direct and indirect costs of the service plus also covered the provider's profit. Consequently, this *fee-for-service* approach resulted in the provision of more and more services, with greater billing amounts, more profits, higher health-care costs, and increasing insurance rates. During the 1960s, the government, through the Social Security Acts, attempted to control rising costs created by the fee-for-service approach by introducing Medicare and Medicaid, which were *retrospective payment systems* (reimbursement following services). During the 1970s, revisions in these acts attempted to deny payments if the services were deemed unnecessary. Also, managed care through HMOs (health maintenance organizations) attempted to drive down the cost of care by offering alternatives to traditional health insurance plans.

With costs escalating, during the 1980s revisions in the Social Security Acts created *prospective payment systems* (hospital rates with predetermined reimbursement price for services) that resulted in hospital savings and financial incentives to address specific client needs and reduce hospital length of stay. With the 1990s, political efforts resulted in legislation (BBA) that encouraged a reduction in government roles through an increase (and return) to private insurance plans available with various managed-care options.

During the 2000s, health-care reform resulted in a number of delivery systems like Accountable Care Organizations and medical homes that tie payment to quality, outcomes, and performance. Known as *value-based payment*, these pay-for-performance models encourage integrated care and coordinated management of client's needs while reducing costs and improving clinical outcomes. Employer-sponsored insurance continues to decline with individuals and the federal government making up the differences in premium costs and/or individuals remaining uninsured or underinsured. Table 8.3 (p. 116) presents a summary of payment-related programs evident since clients began to pay their hospital bills early in the 20th century.

These plans are characterized by primary-care *gatekeepers* who make referrals to specialists if necessary. Also, providers prospectively receive fixed monthly amounts, referred to as *capitation*, regardless of the amount of services rendered to clients each month. Another concept, *utilization review*, requires pre-authorization to ensure the intervention is medically necessary. Although HMOs were created as alternatives to health-insurance plans, large private insurers like Blue Cross and Blue Shield, Aetna, and Humana have created HMOs in addition to maintaining their traditional insurance plans.

Table 8.3 U.S. Payment-Related Programs

- *Third-Party Reimbursement* Third-party payment systems involve health-care providers delivering services to clients who rely on a third party or intermediary to pay the bill. The client is the *first party*, the health-care organization or doctor is the *second party*, and the agency acting on behalf of the client is the *third party*. Third-party payers include state and federal government, through, for example, Medicaid and Medicare; private organizations like Blue Cross and Blue Shield; commercial insurance companies like Prudential; managed care companies like HMOs; and, self-insured companies. Employers offer health insurance as a fringe benefit; however, increasingly, employees are paying greater portions of the premiums while employers are decreasing their portion or dropping this benefit completely.
- *Medicare and Medicaid* Introduced through the Social Security Acts, the federal government became an insurer of health care in 1965. Medicare is a federal health-insurance program for individuals over 65 and persons with catastrophic or chronic illnesses like renal failure, regardless of age. There are several parts to the government regulations: Part A is hospital insurance with regulations covering inpatient psychiatric and physical rehabilitation facilities; hospice services; inpatient, critical care, and long-term-care hospitals; skilled nursing facilities; and some home health-care services. Part B is supplementary medical insurance that pays for outpatient care, physicians, some skilled nursing, and home health. Part C or Medicare Advantage allows clients to participate in managed-care programs provided by private insurers that contract with Medicare (like Humana), which covers in- and out-patient and wellness programs. Part D is prescription drug coverage (Marquis & Huston, 2009; Passmore, 2010). Medicare is financed through Social Security payroll taxes deducted from paychecks.
- *Medicaid* is a federally assisted, state-administered program that pays for medical services of individuals with low incomes and persons who, for example, are blind or families with dependent children; these persons are not covered by Medicare. Medicaid covers physician's bills, hospital care, medications, supplies and long-term care in a nursing home or an adult care home but not assisted living.
- *Prospective Payment (PPS)* The Medicare prospective payment system was introduced in 1983 with the Social Security Acts. Health-care systems are paid a predetermined amount independent of the actual costs of delivering the service. This amount is paid based on groups of similar cases or DRGs. In 1999 the BBRA extended this form of payment to the entire American health-care system (Passmore, 2010). Payment is at a predetermined price calculated prior to service delivery. PPS pays for services in skilled nursing facilities, inpatient rehabilitation and psychiatric facilities, and hospital-based, long-term care. This cost-containment measure initially led to decreased length of stays for many clients (Marquis & Huston, 2009). Accompanying this system are regulations that ensure quality and access to medically necessary services to meet the needs of clients.
- *Managed-Care Organizations (MCO)* "MCO" is a term that describes a variety of health-care plans designed to contain the cost of delivered services to members while maintaining care quality. The 1973 Health Maintenance Organization Act set up HMOs as alternatives to traditional health-insurance plans. An HMO is a corporate body funded by insurance premiums paid by individuals and/or individuals and their employers. Physicians and other professionals practice within certain financial, geographic, and professional limits serving clients enrolled in the HMO (Marquis & Huston, 2009). Clients have low copayments and no deductibles yet are limited in providers and services to which they have access. Several plans within HMOs exist, each varying in the degree of providers available to enrollees. Point-of-service (POS) plans, at the time of service, allow the client to select providers outside of the HMO network but a higher premium and copayment or out-of-pocket amount is paid at the time of service. Exclusive provider organization (EPO) plans require the client to seek service from only the designated provider or pay all costs out of pocket. A preferred provider organization (PPO) provides services on a fee-for-service basis but provides incentives (lower costs) when the preferred provider is selected.

Health Care Reform As early as 1942 and again in 1993, universal health insurance coverage was introduced in Congress and failed. "Health-care reform" is a blanket term describing ongoing efforts by the federal government to change the way we use and pay for care (Terry, 2011). The 2010 Patient Protection and Affordable Care Act and the Health Care and Education Reconciliation Act focus on reforming insurance and expanding coverage with implementation over a period of years, 2010–2018. Ultimately, the intent is to make financially reasonable health-insurance coverage available to all individuals regardless of their health condition through reductions in payments to Medicare providers, excise taxes, increased fees on health-care suppliers and manufacturers, and increased taxes on persons with higher incomes (Wilensky, 2010). The legislation also intends to slow health-care spending and improve clinical outcomes. These goals are to be accomplished in several ways, including, for example, the creation of integrated entities like Accountable Care Organizations, which are comprised of hospitals and doctors who have teamed together to provide services and control costs. Second, these goals will be accomplished through *bundling of payments* across all providers involved in the care of a client per episode—that is, payment is based on a diagnosis and the outcome of the treatment rather than on specific sessions or interventions experienced by the client.

Learning Outcome

Define key concepts and terms in health-care financing.

Table 8.4 Fiscal Terms

- Active treatment: Services defined by CMS for Medicare and Medicaid that require an individualized plan to improve the client's condition, with periodic supervision and physician evaluation.
- Bundling: Grouping services for payment for a client for a defined time period, diagnosis or procedure.
- Capitation: Prospective payment system that pays a fixed amount for specific health services regardless of how many services are used.
- Case mix: The type of clients served by an agency.
- CMS; Centers for Medicare and Medicaid Services.
- Copayments: The out-of-pocket cost the client pays for health care.
- Coverage: The therapies paid for under contract with a third-party payer or reimbursement by an insurance company.
- Current Procedural Terminology (CPT): An AMA publication that annually identifies specific codes for procedures and treatment. These codes are used for coverage.
- Deductible: The amount of money the client must pay for health care prior to insurance coverage. Health-care insurance plans, like auto or home owner's plans, have deductible amounts like $500 or $1,000 that the owner pays before the insurance pays the remaining amount.
- Full-time equivalent (FTE): FTEs are used to calculate employee time. An FTE of 1.0 represents 40 hours worked/week for 52 weeks or 2,080 hours of pay during the fiscal year. More than one employee may equate to 1.0 FTEs, i.e., two people each working 20 hours/week per fiscal year would represent 1.0 FTE. A budget may be assigned FTEs rather than a certain number of employees or positions.
- Local coverage determinations (LCD): Policy statements about coverage of active treatment made at the local or jurisdiction level by MACs who interpret the CMS guidelines.
- Medicare Administrative Contractor (MAC): The carriers and fiscal intermediaries hired by CMS to process Medicare claims.
- National coverage determinations (NCD): Coverage determinations by CMS at the national level.
- National Provider Identifier (NPI): A 10-digit number a therapist is assigned and uses when requesting reimbursement for Medicare and Medicaid clients.
- Per diem: A specific amount per client per day.
- Productivity: A measure of the services provided by a therapist during a 15-minute period. Managers document productivity levels to achieve specific client outcomes.
- Qualified health care provider: A designation defined by each state according to credentials held by the therapist (licensure/certification) that determines who is qualified to provide therapy services.

Managers encounter a number of fiscal terms as they consider payment and health-care coverage. Found in Table 8.4 are a number of these terms and concepts (Marquis & Huston, 2009; McCormick, 2002; Passmore, 2010; Thompson, 2009).

Revenue Sources and Coverage

The first-line manager is the budgetary leader of the unit. This involves identifying revenue and expenses, determining financial needs, documenting these needs to other administrative levels and/or governing boards, and ensuring the unit's services are cost-effective and accountable to the organization's mission. A budget is the manager's written plan that documents and controls the flow of resources to ensure accountable results. Revenues and expenses comprise a major portion of the budget. In this section, primary revenue sources and coverage are summarized. Expenses are covered in the next section on budgeting.

Financing health and human services comes through a variety of sources other than insurance payments. These include appropriations from tax-based sources and legislation, contributions, grants and contracts, fees and charges, and partnering initiatives like sponsorships and cooperative programming.

Revenue Sources

Appropriations are tax-based revenues from federal, state, provincial/territory, and/or local governments that support public or government entities like municipal services, federal correctional facilities, and provincial programs for individuals who are deaf. Each public agency requests funds through either the annual or biannual budget-submission process. Governing bodies like councils and legislative bodies approve budget requests of each public agency under their jurisdiction. Funds available from governments vary because the amounts received from taxation on, for example, personal properties or sale of products fluctuates, and because political decisions and trends influence the dispersion of funding amounts among the various public agencies competing for the same fiscal resources annually or biannually.

Contributions are received through donations and fund-raising efforts conducted by development specialists or fund-raising committees. Agencies receive funds through endowments, bequests, special events, social marketing, annual campaigns, and participation in community fund drives. Unrestricted donations may be used to carry out any of the operating budget activities like purchasing supplies or paying inclusion partners. Restricted donations are earmarked for specific use like capital improvements or special events.

Grants involve obtaining funds from government agencies, foundations, corporations, and individuals. Applications for funds are usually made in accordance with guidelines provided by the funding organization. Managers interested in competing for the available funds respond to the RFPs (requests for proposal). Online applications are common, and the evaluation criteria, application deadlines, and the funding agent's priorities are outlined in the request. Companies like Microsoft and special-interest foundations like the Christopher Reeve Paralysis Foundation and Air Canada Foundation provide funds to support recreation therapy initiatives like adaptive technology and assistive devices. *Contracts* usually relate to specific experiences like contracts issued for adventure-challenge experiences or professionals to perform unique interventions like warm-water therapy. Contracts may be awarded for specific time intervals, as is found with partnerships between outdoor centers and nonprofit agencies to provide a summer camp experience with specific clientele.

Fees and charges generate revenue from persons who use agency services. Fees may be based on a sliding scale with clients paying differing amounts depending on their financial means. Fees may be charged for specific experiences or for membership with an agency.

Partnerships among agencies involve exchange of financial and physical resources, for example, an outpatient adaptive golf program may be co-sponsored by a hospital, a therapeutic division of a municipal recreation department, and a university recreation therapy program. Sponsors also support sports like Special Olympics and Paralympics. With sponsorship money, operational costs are subsidized, thereby reducing client participation costs.

Coverage

Coverage is concerned with the therapies paid for under contract with a third-party payer or reimbursement by an insurance company (Passmore, 2010). This section considers how a manager determines rates for services provided by the department or agency and the requirements to gain coverage from companies that reimburse for services provided. The manager will find coverage varies from one type of facility to another and each has policies and practices unique to managing its fiscal resources. The clientele for whom services are provided have various types of insurance coverage (or lack of coverage), so the manager's budget is impacted by this variation in coverage. The term *case mix* describes the type of clientele served by an agency. This case mix determines the amount of revenue a manager receives for services as each client's coverage varies with available revenue sources.

There are various methods used to determine rates for services provided by a unit or agency. For example, a manager operating a facility might use square footage (area in which service occurs), while an emergency room uses client visits, and an agency considers number of clients per type of service (i.e., functional interventions vs. leisure-education classes). Common methods used include costs per client or costs per program/intervention. In both methods, cost may be based on rate per hour. Hourly rates or units of service cost are based on past and present trends, nature of services provided, and client needs or acuity. Rates are calculated by determining direct costs like the therapist's salary and supplies as well as the indirect costs like electricity, administrative costs, and other overhead expenditures to offer the service. In Canada, provincial/territory governments have set fee schedules and physician rates while in the USA a complicated system of coverage codes determines rates. This system is explained in the paragraphs below.

United States

Services are commonly measured in 15-minute units per client per service. An inpatient physical rehabilitation unit may treat each client for 30 minutes while an inpatient psychiatric unit may treat each client for 45 or more minutes; the former would be reimbursed for two 15-minute time periods while the later would be reimbursed for three 15-minute time periods. The manager determines the total costs to deliver a program/intervention per hour, divides by the number of clients served, and assigns a charge to each 15-minute period per client. To illustrate, direct plus indirect costs per hour total $200.00, four (4) clients are in the group equating to $50.00/client/hour or $12.50/15-minute period.

Annually the American Medical Association (AMA) publishes the *CPT (Current Procedural Terminology)* codes manual that indicates specific codes for treatment procedures performed by health professionals. To be reimbursed these codes must be used. Aquatic therapy or therapeutic activities are examples of interventions that might be assigned CPT codes. The therapist using one of these interventions records the assigned 5-digit code, adheres to the AMA intervention description, and documents each 15-minute period the client receives the service. Additionally, CMS requires therapists to use a 10-digit number, the National Provider Identifier (NPI), when seeking reimbursement. This code is acquired by online application and is reported with documentation of client intervention by each therapist; these codes document service outcomes as revenue streams or revenue sources.

The manager also may use these 15-minute intervals to measure *productivity.* A therapist may be responsible for a certain number of productivity units each day or pay period. This term refers to the actual productive time of the therapist, time spent providing client interventions, as opposed to the unproductive time or time spent completing treatment or program plans and preparing for services. Thus, a therapist may be assigned productivity levels of 24 units per day, which represents 6 hours of direct client intervention.

Reimbursement is associated with *active treatment.* The definition of active treatment is found in the CMS regulations on Medicare and Medicaid. While Medicare insurance covers only those over 65, and Medicaid is associated with individuals with developmental disabilities (for example), private and commercial insurance agents tend to use CMS regulations to guide their coverage decisions. To meet active treatment criteria, therapies must (1) be provided under an individualized treatment plan or diagnosis, (2) have a reasonable expectation to improve the client's condition, (3) be supervised periodically, and (4) be evaluated by a physician (Thompson, 2009). Managers must ensure that the plan is maintained in medical records with progress and outcomes reported (Passmore, 2010).

Whether or not the manager receives reimbursement for recreation therapy is also influenced by local determinations and state legislators. *Local coverage determinations (LCD)* are policy statements subject to CMS guidelines. Panels of doctors serving as advisors may decide if recreation therapy interventions are necessary and expected to improve a client's condition or help in diagnosis and therefore be eligible for reimbursement. This decision is reflected in LCD statements. These statements are issued when the *National coverage determinations* from CMS do not explicitly prohibit reimbursement or no other regulations exist. CMS contracts with independent companies known as *Medicare Administrative Contractors* (MAC) to serve as carriers and fiscal intermediaries to process Medicare claims. The LCD statements guide MAC decisions to pay insurance claims.

Like Canadian policy, U.S. health-care policy is delegated to (provincial/territory) state legislatures (Thompson, 2009). As a result, each state defines who is a *qualified healthcare provider*. States tend to rely on licensure and certification to identify qualified professionals. The CTRS, if the CTRS credential is recognized for the purposes of identifying qualified health-care professionals, allows clients access to services that both the government (CMS) and commercial health insurance plans define as eligible for reimbursement. Thus, a continuing responsibility of the manager is to advocate at the local and state level for inclusion of CTRS interventions as health-related services (Passmore, 2010).

The Budgeting Process

Managing a budget is planning for a specified time in the future (the budget cycle is usually a year), monitoring how well the plan is working, then adjusting the budget accordingly for the next fiscal year (Sullivan & Decker, 2009). The budget is a visible record of the manager's capabilities and the unit's productivity (Sullivan & Decker, 2009). This section overviews the budgeting process, types of budgets, budget formats, and the manager's responsibilities to monitor the unit's or agency's budget.

The budgeting process begins with the first-line manager's review of the agency's budgeting goals, then the preparation of goals and objectives for the unit's budget based on the organizational goals. This initial step is followed by drafting the budget document or budget plan. During this second step, managers translate objectives into projected costs and revenues, write justifications for requested expenses, submit capital requests, and present the proposed budget. The proposal is presented to each level within the organization with each administrator evaluating the proposal and making adjustments. After approval by executive management, the proposal is integrated into a master budget for the organization and presented to the governing board, which might be a Council or Board of Directors for final approval. This process may take 3 to 6 months or more and is completed prior to the next 12 months or fiscal year [e.g., January 1–December 31, October 1–September 30, July 1–June 30, or April 1–March 31 in Canadian federal and provincial/territorial calendars].

Learning Outcome
Explain the budgeting process.

Once approved, the budget is an official legal document and is ready for implementation-step 3. During this step, the manager monitors and analyzes monthly and quarterly reports to avoid excess or inadequate funds at the end of the fiscal year (Marquis & Huston, 2009). Actual and budgeted expenses are compared to determine variances in predicted income and expenses with the budget adjusted or performance modified to accomplish the unit's intended objectives. The final step in the budgeting process is evaluation. Each manager is accountable for deviations and remedial action and with each successive year, variations in anticipated revenue and expenses are more accurately predicted. These four steps parallel APIE. The outcome is a plan to manage financial resources similar to the plan resulting from APIE to manage client interventions.

Types of Budgets

The manager is responsible for three types of budgets: operating, personnel, and capital.

An *operating or revenue-and-expense budget,* also known as the annual budget, identifies the day-to-day revenue and expenses for the fiscal year. This budget projects the revenue to be generated from services provided and the expenses associated with providing these services. This budget is developed during the budget process. During this process, in some settings dollar amounts are assigned by agency administrators to all units and to all categories on both income and expense sides of the budget. In some settings, by contrast, the unit manager requests funds during the budgeting process and is allocated certain amounts in the various revenue and expense categories. Regardless, the unit's past budget and future plans are used to develop the current operating budget. Revenues and expenses are separated within the budget yet the manager is responsible for balancing revenues with expenses.

The revenue is the income expected during the 12-month period. As noted earlier in the chapter, revenue sources include appropriations, contributions, grants, fees and charges, and various types of coverage (Medicare, Medicaid, private insurance, MCOs, private pay). The manager projects revenue by considering client volume, case mix, program offerings (inpatient or outpatient; functional interventions or special events), anticipated tax income, and negotiated rates *(per diem-specified reimbursement amount per client per day)* and discounts (paying less than the established rate).

Expenses the manager considers are personnel salaries, benefits, and insurance; supplies and equipment; repairs, maintenance, and depreciation; intervention and programming costs; professional and educational fees like membership fees, travel, and continuing professional development; legal fees; contractual services; and overhead expenses or indirect costs (expenses not associated with the unit's services) like utilities, IT, and mortgage payments (which may or may not be charged to the unit). Direct costs like equipment associated with specific interventions are charged directly to the expense budget of the unit. Controllable expenses are those the manager anticipates like personnel salaries while the amounts of noncontrollable expenses like entry fees are unknown. The manager projects all of these costs. Additionally, the manager anticipates inflationary expenses for items like equipment and supplies and adds this to the total expense amount requested. One approach is to take the total expense amount less personnel costs and multiple by an inflationary factor like 3–5% and add the result to the requested expense budget. As mentioned above, the manager may be given figures for all direct and indirect costs to place in the expense budget, or he or she may be given indirect cost amounts for the year and instructed to calculate only direct costs for the unit to place in the budget request.

The *personnel budget* is the largest component of the operating budget due to the labor-intensive nature of recreation therapy. This budget estimates the cost of personnel to meet the unit's objectives. The manager estimates the number of staff and the staffing mix to ensure the appropriate number of staff with proper skills are available to meet client needs. Personnel budgets are affected by several factors. Agency personnel policies like salary level per position or days allowed for educational and sick leave influence personnel amounts requested. Organizations that accredit or inspect agencies like the Joint Commission International or CARF International/CARF Canada are concerned with staffing levels that ensure client safety. Changes in technology may influence the number, skill, and time that staff spend with equipment and training to use the new devices. Daily or seasonal fluctuations in client numbers and acuity impact staffing expenses. Managers are also required to include in the personnel budget specific amounts to be deducted for Social Security, provincial/state and federal taxes, unemployment, cost of living, retirement, and health benefits (if available). Lastly, the manager plans for the expenses associated with employee turnover, recruitment, and orientation and training.

The manager's personnel budget allocation may be based on FTEs—full-time equivalents, rather than an identified number of positions. FTEs are also commonly used to calculate benefit time. FTEs are converted to number of hours worked by one person per day for so many days per week and so many weeks per year. An FTE of 1.0 represents 40 hours worked/week for 52 weeks or 2,080 hours of pay during the fiscal year. So an FTE of 1.0 on the unit payroll may be one or more persons like one full-time employee working 40 hours per week or two part-time employees, one working 30 hours or 0.75 FTEs and one working 10 hours or .25 FTEs. Thus the number of staff and staffing mix (full- and part-time) may vary to best serve the unit's clientele, as illustrated in the next paragraph.

When a full-time employee is paid but not working due to illness, vacation, jury duty, or funeral leave, and these benefit hours must be covered, the manager adjusts the FTEs upward to cover unproductive or benefit time of the full-time employee. The manager determines then totals the average number of allotted benefit days with pay and average number of sick days per employee experienced in the unit and divides by 2,080 to identify the FTE requirement to cover benefit time. Salary amounts are then added to the projected budget to reflect the unit's FTEs or proper number and mix of staff for both productive (client interaction) and nonproductive (benefit) time (Sullivan & Decker, 2009; Tomey, 2009).

Learning Outcome

Articulate expenditures in health and human services.

A *capital budget* is the third type of budget a manager may experience. Capital expenditures are related to long-term planning and include purchase of buildings or equipment, renovations or expansions, or items not used in daily operations. These items usually exceed certain dollar amounts like $1,000 or $5,000, they are usually major investments, and a long time is required to recover the costs (Marquis & Huston, 2009: Sullivan & Decker, 2009; Tomey, 2009).

In most settings, a ceiling is set on capital expenditures. Each unit manager completes specific capital equipment request forms annually or semiannually identifying by priority the capital need. Each request is then justified. This justification describes the item, identifies whether it is a new or replacement item, and presents cost estimates. When the manager maintains a unit inventory, use and replacement figures are available to help the manager project future capital purchases (Tomey, 2009).

Learning Outcome

Explain budget types.

Budget Formats

Operating budgets are designed in several formats. These formats determine the first-line manager's responsibilities as each unit's budget is part of the larger organizational budget to which the unit is accountable. Also, the format used by the organization determines how the manager responds to administrative requests during the budget development process. A first-line manager may experience incremental, zero-based, program, performance, and flexible or variable budget methods. This section briefly describes the key features of each format.

An *incremental or line-item budget* is organized with one item or category on each line. Additionally, separate columns identify amounts budgeted for the current year, amounts actually spent year-to-date, projected yearly total based on amounts actually spent, and variances or increases and/or decreases in the amounts for the new budget (Sullivan & Decker, 2009). The first-line manager may use a computer-generated spreadsheet to request funds for the next fiscal year. If so, additional columns are present as is space to justify each line item. The manager may use either the previous year's actual results or projected expenditures for the current year to calculate the next fiscal year's request. Regardless, the starting point for the next year's budget is the amount established for the current year. The manager must be familiar with the account category numbers to know how to classify salary and non-salary items, as each item like equipment or transportation is also assigned to a numbered category and the format is organized by these categories. The advantage to this format is simplicity in preparation, while the disadvantage is its lack of cost efficiency, since the astute manager learns to spend the entire budgeted amounts, knowing the next year's budget is based on the amounts in the current budget (Sullivan & Decker, 2009).

A *zero-based budget* assumes that the basis for projecting the next year's budget for the unit or an intervention in the unit is zero. Each time the budget is prepared, the manager justifies the service as if it were a first-time offering (Sullivan & Decker, 2009). Regardless of the previous year's amounts, each expenditure for the new year is justified. The manager prepares a justification describing costs with alternatives, advantages and disadvantages of the new expenditure, and its relationship to the organization's objectives. Each decision package is then prioritized with funding allocated based on the priority of the decision package (Marquis & Huston, 2009). Thus, this format requires justification for each expense so the manager is encouraged to be cost efficient; yet, this process is time consuming and may not be necessary for every item (Sullivan & Decker, 2009).

A *program budget* focuses on a specific program to meet specific objectives. Thus, the first-line manager may prepare several budgets depending on the number of services provided by the unit. Each program budget identifies the revenues and costs for an entire program over its life time. The manager ties specific program outcomes to specific goals so the cost-effectiveness of each program is clearly identified. The challenge is to present all direct costs like personnel salaries and all indirect costs like utilities to reflect the various programs that these resources support. This format also helps the manager weigh the benefits of various programs to accomplish the unit's objectives and best serve the organization.

Performance budgets focus on outcomes or results. The budget identifies the resources needed to meet productivity levels to achieve specific client or program results. To use performance budgets, the manager needs a work plan that includes costs, desired service quality levels, and outcome measures to determine the extent to which clients or programs achieve desired goals. Program and performance budgets may be integrated to make planning, budgeting, and evaluation decisions. Impact on clients or intervention impact becomes the basis for funding decisions. Thus, a disadvantage of this format is the variance in impact that may not be directly attributed to the funding but to circumstances like an unexpected acuity change in a client or group of clients. An advantage to performance budgets is the focus on outcomes and the consideration a manager gives to productivity levels to achieve desired outcomes.

The preceding descriptions are examples of fixed budgets—the amounts remain the same regardless of the volume of clients or supplies used. *Flexible or variable budgets* calculate costs based on changing volume like client census or increase in supply costs. Like a program budget, the manager identifies all direct and indirect expenses associated with a service. Then the manager compares the results to actual units of service to identify a positive or negative variance. Once these comparisons are made the manager adjusts the entire budget to compensate, if possible, for the variance. To illustrate, if the census drops and fewer resources are used, the monies in the supply account become available to compensate for other areas where the variance is negative, like transportation costs. The distinct advantage of this format is the accurate picture of the current finances and the realistic outlook for the future. Usually personnel monies cannot be shifted into other accounts nor can non-salary monies be moved into salary accounts. Consequently, flexible budgeting is best used with non-salary expenses.

Learning Outcome

Explain budget formats.

Budget Monitoring

The manager can expect to receive several types of accounting reports of the unit's financial operations on a periodic basis from the budget office or the department responsible for monitoring the cost of programs and services within the organization. Budget performance is evaluated by variance analysis. A variance is the difference between the amount that was stated in the budget for each revenue and cost and the actual revenue or cost resulting during the reporting period (Sullivan & Decker, 2009). A variance can be positive or negative. The first-line manager studies the periodic reports to determine the cause of a variance. Usually each report shows each budgeted amount for revenues and costs, the actual or current amounts, the actual year-to-date results, the year-to-date budget, and the variance from the budget (Sullivan & Decker, 2009). Organizations usually have established levels at which variance needs to be justified by the manager, this may be a dollar amount or a percentage (e.g., 5% or 10% over or under budget).

One of the manager's most important responsibilities is to manage the financial resources of the unit and respond to any variances. A variance may not be reason for changing the budget but rather a sign that alerts the manager to further explain or investigate seasonal changes or trends over time (Tomey, 2009). Keeping notes on what is learned from the variance analysis helps the manager prepare for next year's budget and remain aware of expenditures so variances are eliminated and costs are controlled.

Learning Outcome
Explain budget monitoring.

Trends and Challenges in Health-Care Financing

The manager is challenged to present quality outcome-oriented services while maintaining and/or reducing costs yet documenting high levels of productivity with fewer resources. Health-care policy is focusing on payment tied to quality and outcomes or value—the relationship of quality to payment (D'Cruz & Welter, 2010). A shift from fee-for-service to value-based reimbursement places the client's needs first rather than emphasizing profit margins. As a result, new delivery systems are evolving to address client needs and clients are experiencing changes in how they pay for their health care. A managerial challenge is to increase employee awareness of cost-containment strategies, including how employee behavior impacts the budget.

The manager plays a key role in implementing programs and incentives to make staff aware of how to prevent, reduce, and control costs (Sullivan & Decker, 2009; Tomey, 2009). Wasteful use of resources like misuse of sick time may result in negative variance. The manager is responsible for helping each staff member identify ways they help the organization meet its financial goals. For example, an in-service on personnel policies may help staff realize the negative variance that results from absenteeism. Participation on quality-improvement teams serves to inform staff of cost factors. Strategies like taking staff vacations when the census is low or during the "off-season" and creating flexible staffing patterns to adjust to census or participation fluctuations help manage costs and can be cooperatively planned by a staff committee and the manager. Cost incentives like contests for money-saving ideas and employee of the month motivate cost containment and desired behavior. Engaging staff in budgetary decisions like how to maintain economical levels of inventory while purchasing the most appropriate supplies and equipment helps monitor resources while creating employee awareness of the relationship between quality and costs.

Health care, especially in the USA, is a competitive, market-driven business (Sullivan & Decker, 2009). As such, a number of new and evolving delivery systems are emerging to meet the demands of a cost-conscious environment. Integrated health-care networks consisting of physicians and hospitals deliver a whole continuum of care through geographic coverage for the buyers of their services at fixed payments—usually the employees of particular companies. The focus of these networks is primary care and keeping clients healthy rather than providing care in more expensive hospital settings (Sullivan & Decker, 2009). Consolidation through hospital mergers and acquisitions offers greater operating efficiency (Goldstein, 2012). Large not-for-profit or established for-profit hospital companies have traditionally been involved in consolidations to gain a larger market share and leverage with commercial payers. Hospitals and health-insurance companies are affiliating to form global insurance plans, joint ventures of not-for-profit and for-profit healthcare systems are emerging, and secular and faith-based groups are merging. With these consolidations, capital becomes available for outpatient facilities and costs are reduced while quality is improved.

A third delivery-system alternative is client-centered medical homes. In this approach, a client has an ongoing relationship with a physician who guides a team that takes collective responsibility for client care (D'Cruz & Welter, 2010). Care is coordinated and focused on long-term healing relationships with measurable client improvements financially rewarded. The physician makes appropriate referrals to supportive health-care professionals like recreation therapists across the health-care system in order to meet the needs of the whole person (Hoss & Kensinger, 2010). Intervention is accessed in the least restrictive and most cost-effective environment. These systems reward evidence-based practices that improve outcomes tied to payment (value-based reimbursement). Also, we are encouraged to use the health care we need rather than rely, for example, on more visits, medicines, or opinions to solve our health-care issues.

Value-driven payment models reimburse based on the quality of care received as evidenced by client outcomes. Pay-for-performance pays providers based on the achievement of preset quality and performance measures (D'Cruz & Welter, 2010). Measures include clinical quality and effectiveness, cost management, patient satisfaction and safety, and administrative involvement. This approach complements bundled payments that reimburse based on desired outcomes balanced against cost (i.e., payment is based on the outcome of the intervention per case or episode). Bundled payments may include payments to several providers like the hospital and doctor (referred to as global payments) for a client or packaged payments that are organized around particular conditions like diabetes or episodes of treatment like cardiac surgery including, for example, the follow-up wellness program for 90 days.

Learning Outcome
Describe trends and challenges in healthcare financing.

A new form of organization prompted by health-care reform in the States, Accountable Care Organizations (ACO), integrates physician groups, hospitals, and other health-care providers, like recreation therapists, and rewards them for controlling costs and improving quality. The shared savings are distributed to the ACO participants when costs are reduced below a specified benchmark to encourage more efficient health-care delivery (Correia, 2011). With alternative delivery systems and payment options, each client makes more decisions about their health care: As a consequence, opportunities are presented to recreation therapy professionals to become actively engaged team members. Recreation therapists will advocate among physicians, clients, and health care teams to be included in client plans as a means to achieve evidence-based outcomes that are cost-effective and enhance the quality of the client's health-care experience.

Summary

1. First-line managers must be aware of their budgetary responsibilities and be cost-effective in meeting agency goals (Marquis & Huston, 2009). Today's manager is held accountable for achieving quality while maintaining or reducing costs with increasingly limited resources.
2. A budget is a plan to use an organization's resources wisely. As such, the budget reflects the manager's capability to use resources effectively and efficiently to achieve accountable results.
3. Political, social, and economic forces contribute to rising health-care costs in the USA and Canada. Examples include aging populations, new treatments and technology that are costly, chronic diseases and lifestyle behaviors that contribute to obesity and diabetes, pandemics, redesigned systems focusing on prevention, and rising litigation and administrative costs.
4. Shifts in payment and legislation in both countries have attempted to contain costs, quality, and accessible care. Initially, the person receiving care paid privately the costs or nonprofit systems provided care. More recently, third-party payers like insurance companies (USA) or the government (Canada) have paid health-care expenses.
5. Canada is a single-payer system managed at the province/territory level providing universal care for physician, hospital, and dental surgery, while the USA is a mixed-payer system comprised of government and private payments with individuals having coverage of a broad array of health-care needs.

6. Canadian legislation (Medicare) controls physician rates, sets fee schedules, and monitors hospital charges. Increases in care, therefore, result from non-regulated needs like medications. In the USA, by contrast, cost increases are due to increased costs of most aspects of care.
7. Political reform efforts desire to change the way we use and pay for health care. The intent is to contain costs, sustain the system, improve access (universal coverage for all), and relate performance to outcomes (integrate providers and financially reward them for improved health rather than number of visits). These efforts in both countries are due to escalating costs like medication (Canada) and reduced employer health benefits (USA) resulting in increased out-of-pocket expenses, increased wait times, and increasing numbers of uninsured and unserved persons.
8. Financing health and human services comes through a variety of sources including appropriations from tax-based sources and legislation, contributions, grants and contracts, fees and charges, and partnering initiatives like sponsorships and cooperative programming.
9. Coverage is concerned with the therapies paid for under contract with a third-party payer or reimbursement by an insurance company. The manager's budget is impacted by the various coverage programs like Medicare, private pay, and employer paid through employee benefits. Each entity may reimburse different amounts, require different co-pays or deductibles, and cover/not cover specific interventions. Thus, the manager's revenues vary with the agency's case mix.
10. The budgeting process may take 3 to 6 months or more and is completed prior to the next 12 months or fiscal year with the manager gaining approval and adjusting the unit budget to satisfy the goals and benchmarks found in the organizational budget.
11. The manager is responsible for three types of budgets: operating, personnel, and capital—the operating budget is the day-to-day plan that does include personnel monies while the capital budget is for large, long-term projects.
12. A first-line manager may experience incremental, zero-based, program, performance, and flexible or variable budget formats—the chosen format influences how the manager responds to each administrative level during the budget process.
13. One of the manager's most important responsibilities is to manage the financial resources of the unit and respond to any variances. The manager monitors reports to identify positive or negative variances. With each budget cycle the manager becomes more aware of how to deliver cost-conscious services that satisfy quality expectations of clients and the organization.
14. A trend is to consolidate health-care organizations to enhance integrated delivery of health-care services across the care continuum with payment following the client rather than the volume of care interventions received by the client.
15. With these models, the CTRS must become an advocate to ensure they function as part of the team to gain reimbursement for specific interventions. Many clients served by these new models "can be effectively treated by recreation therapy in the least restrictive environment" (Hoss & Kensinger, 2010).

Critical Thinking Activities

1. What are the similarities and differences found in the Canadian and USA health-care systems as related to financing, organization, and care delivery? What lessons can be learned from each system as managers attempt to contain costs yet satisfy quality expectations?
2. How do staff affect budgetary performance? Suppose a manager's budget is assigned 4.5 FTEs. This includes the manager as 1 FTE and one full-time staff member who is assigned 1 FTE. To reduce benefit costs, the manager may only hire part-time employees (25 hours or less). What are the manager's alternatives for filling the remaining 2.5 FTEs?
3. Which pieces of legislation have influenced shifts in who pays for health care and how we pay for healthcare in North America?
4. How does the manager determine variances in budget performance? What situations might cause the manager to have a positive variance and a negative variance?

5. Conduct a search of several websites to identify grants available to support health-related projects: Sites might include:

   - Foundation Center: http://www.foundationcenter.org
   - Grantsmanship Center: http://www.tgci.com
   - U.S. Government Printing Office: http://www.gpo.gov/fdsys/
   - Catalog of Federal Domestic Assistance: http://www.cfda.gov
   - Canadian Government Grants: http://www.canada-grants.com/
   - Canadian Grant Information: http://governmentgrant.com/canada-grants
   - American Therapeutic Recreation Association: http://www.atra-online.com
   - Canadian Therapeutic Recreation Association: http://www.canadian-tr.org

References

Ameringer, C. F. (2012). Chronic diseases and the high price of U.S. healthcare. *Phi Kappa Phi Forum, 92*(1), 4–6.

Barr, D. A. (2012). Bending the Medicare cost curve for physician's services: Lessons learned from Canada. *Journal of General Internal Medicine, 27*(11), 1555–1559. doi:10.1007/s11606-012-2091-8

Bhatia, S. (2012). Alternative financing for health care: A path to sustainability? *Canadian Medical Association Journal, 184*(7), E337–E338. doi:10.1503/cmaj.110672

Boring but important health-care spending curbed by recession. (May 11, 2012). *The Week*, 6.

Chernomas, R. (2012). Sustainability. *Canadian Dimension, 46*(4), 35–39.

Correia, E. W. (2011). Accountable care organizations: The proposed regulations and the prospects for success. *The American Journal of Managed Care, 17*(8), 560–568.

Cors, W. K., & Sagin, T. (2011). Overtreatment in health care: How much is too much? *Physician Executive, 37*(5), 10–16.

Cutting the cost of health care. (October 22, 2010). *The Week*, 15.

D'Cruz, M. J., & Welter, T. L. (2010). Is your organization ready for value-based payment? *Healthcare Financial Management, 64*(1), 64–70.

Goldstein, L. (2012). The new wave of hospital consolidation. *Healthcare Financial Management, 66*(4), 60–67.

Hoss, M. A. K., & Kensinger, K. (2010). Medical home: Is there a place for recreational therapy? *American Journal of Recreation Therapy, 9*(2), 13–20.

Marquis, B. L., & Huston, C. J. (2009). *Leadership roles and management functions in nursing: Theory & application* (6th ed.). Philadelphia: Lippincott Williams & Wilkins.

McCormick, B. P. (2002). Healthcare in America: An overview. In D. R. Austin, J. Dattilo, & B. P. McCormick (Eds.), *Conceptual foundations for therapeutic recreation* (pp. 185–206). State College, PA: Venture Publishing, Inc.

Noseworthy, T. (2011). Health resource allocation a made-in-Canada description. *The Journal of Legal Medicine, 32*(1), 11–16. doi:10.1080/01947648.2011.550823

Passmore T. R. J. (2010). *Coverage of recreational therapy: Rules and regulations* (2nd ed.). Hattiesburg, MS: American Therapeutic Recreation Association.

Stephens, J. H., & Ledlow, G. R. (2010). Real healthcare reform: Focus on primary care access. *Hospital Topics, 88*(4), 98–106.

Sullivan E. J., & Decker, P. J. (2009). *Effective leadership & management in nursing* (7th ed.). Upper Saddle River, NJ: Pearson/Prentice-Hall.

Terry, M. (2011). A brief guide to how current issues in healthcare reform may affect you. *Podiatry Management, 30*(5), 115–120.

Thompson, G. T. (2009). Reimbursement: Surviving prospective payment as a recreational therapy practitioner. In N. J. Stumbo (Ed.), *Professional issues in therapeutic recreation on competence and outcomes* (2nd ed., pp. 307–323). Champaign, IL: Sagamore.

Tomey, A. M. (2009). *Guide to nursing management and leadership* (8th ed.). St. Louis, MO: Mosby Elsevier.

Wilensky, G. R. (2010). Commentary healthcare reform version 1.0. *Healthcare Financial Management, 64*(5), 50–53.

World Health Organization (WHO). (2000). The World Health Report 2000—Health systems: Improving performance. Geneva, Switzerland. Retrieved from http://www.photius.com/rankings/world_health_systems.html

Section 3

MANAGING HUMAN RESOURCES

Chapter 9
STAFFING SERVICES

Keywords

- Accept error
- Benefits
- Compensation
- Cross-training
- Development
- External recruiting
- Grievance procedure
- Internal recruiting
- Interview
- Job description
- Job specifications
- Learning organizations
- Line authority
- Orientation
- Performance appraisal
- Probation
- Progressive discipline
- Recruitment
- Reject error
- Selection
- Staff authority
- Training

Learning Outcomes

After reading this chapter, students will be able to:

1. List and describe the primary steps in the human-resource planning process.
2. Differentiate between job descriptions and job specifications and explain the purposes of each.
3. Describe three common strategies for recruitment of applicants.
4. Identify two primary components of compensation.
5. Explain the purposes of new employee orientation, training, and development.
6. Describe four common methods of training and development in health and human service agencies.
7. Describe the purposes of the performance appraisal.
8. Outline the progressive discipline process.

Overview

The first-line therapeutic recreation manager in a health and human service organization is responsible for management of a broad scope of resources. "Perhaps the most essential of these activities is the management of human resources" (Arnold, Glover, & Beeler, 2012, p. xiii). Human resource management is managing the people in the organization. It is the process of anticipating and making provisions for the movement of people into, within, and out of the organization. More specifically, this includes planning for personnel needs and recruitment, selecting the right people for jobs, orienting and training, determining and managing wages and salaries, planning benefits and incentives, appraising performance, resolving disputes, and handling the process of exiting the organization. "Ultimately, human resources management is about understanding the human side of the organization. Human resources management is a process that helps to determine how both individual and organizational needs can be managed in a system that is clear, unambiguous, fair, and legal" (Hurd, Barcelona, & Meldrum, 2008, p. 224).

There are generally two broad areas of responsibilities and functions in health and human service organizations. These include positions that are directly responsible for delivering the organization's programs and services (i.e., practitioners) and positions responsible for supervision and leadership of the programs and services (i.e., managers). Managers have *line authority*: individuals in management positions have the formal authority to direct and control immediate subordinates. A second group of positions are responsible for the business-related duties that contribute to and support the programs and services. The second set of functions is formally referred to as "staff." *Staff authority* is the right to advise or counsel those with line authority. Human resource management is a staff function in the organization. They are specialists in the area of human resource management. The nature of the human resource function is advisory. Human resource specialists investigate, research, and advise the therapeutic recreation manager about managing the people in the therapeutic recreation work unit. Today, human resource management has become increasingly complex. Human resource specialists serve as expert guides and advisors who offer significant support to the first-line therapeutic recreation manager concerning personnel management.

People are the most important resource in the organization; they are also the most expensive. Up to 80% of a health and human service organization's operating budget may cover direct and indirect expenditures for personnel (Edginton, Hudson, Lankford, & Larsen, 2008). It is essential that the first-line therapeutic recreation manager be knowledgeable about human resource management practices. The purpose of this chapter is to introduce and provide a brief overview of human resource management for the first-line therapeutic recreation manager in the health and human service agency. Table 9.1 includes a listing of human resource department responsibilities.

The first section of this chapter addresses human resource planning and selection. Managers may conduct human resource inventories as they develop staffing plans to ensure that the right mix and number of personnel are in place to address present client needs and prepare to meet future agency goals. Prior to recruitment for a job vacancy—the process of locating, identifying, and attracting candidates—managers undertake a job analysis for the vacant position. Information from the job analysis is used to update or to develop a job description and specifications for the vacant position. Hiring is based on the information contained in these documents. Accurately predicting staffing needs and allocating staff resources results in efficient and effective services. Staffing decisions are fundamental to ensuring an agency hires and keeps the right personnel.

The second section of this chapter addresses staff training and development. Effective 21st-century organizations are characterized as learning organizations. Today's rapid pace of technological change demands that managers and employees continue to acquire new knowledge and learn new skills. First-line managers are expected to plan and provide training programs that are relevant and cost-effective. Staff-training needs-assessments are described in this section. Various types of training and development are also presented.

The third section of the chapter provides an overview of the performance appraisal process. Design and implementation of performance appraisal forms as well as the performance appraisal interview are considered. This section of the chapter also addresses performance problems that may result from poor employee "fit" in the organization.

The final section of this chapter includes a brief overview of employment law. First-line managers are impacted by a number of legal regulations that are

Table 9.1 Human Resource Department Responsibilities

Human Resource Department Responsibilities

Larger organizations (100 or more employees) typically have a human resource department that has responsibility for planning and managing human resource practices for the entire organization. The function of the human resource department is to advise and assist all other departments regarding staffing.

Common responsibilities include the following:

1. Establish the recruitment and selection process for all jobs to assist managers in hiring.
2. Recruit applicants for position vacancies.
3. Plan and conduct new employee orientation training and other internal training.
4. Develop a performance appraisal system for the organization.
5. Determine the compensation program guidelines; assist employees with understanding benefits.
6. Assist with personnel actions including hiring, promotion, discipline, and termination.
7. Monitor and assist with compliance with legal requirements related to employment law.
8. Maintain employment records.

designed to protect the employee and the employer and to promote fairness in the work environment.

LEARNING OUTCOME
List and describe the primary steps in the human resource planning process.

Human Resource Planning

"Human resources planning is the process of analyzing and identifying the need for [and] availability of human resources so that the organization can meet its goals and objectives" (Arnold, Glover, & Beeler, 2012, p.53; Mathis & Jackson, 2008). It is the process of anticipating human resource needs and establishing a plan for filling those needs. The human resource planning process includes a number of activities.

Position Opens

The planning process typically is initiated by an open position, or a job vacancy. The position opening may be the result of any of a number of circumstances. For example, it could be a result of a job transfer or a promotion of a practitioner. A job transfer refers to a lateral move to a position with a similar level of responsibility in the same, or a different work unit in the organization. Promotion refers to a move within the organization to a position with greater responsibilities. The vacancy may be the result of organizational changes such as reorganization or realignment, down-sizing, or other changes. The vacancy may occur as the result of a resignation to accept employment elsewhere, retirement, or the dismissal of an employee. Finally, the job opening may be the result of the addition of a new position in the organization.

Budget Review

Planning for the financial resources that are required for filling a vacant position is critical. The costs associated with the hiring process include the expenses for advertising the position vacancy, relocation and travel assistance costs, staff time and administrative support time for the hiring process, reference checks, background checks, and orientation and training costs. According to data from the U.S. Bureau of Labor Statistics (March, 2012), the average direct cost for a new employee, based on a 40-hour work week, is $63,835.20.

LEARNING OUTCOME
Differentiate between job descriptions and job specifications and explain the purposes of each.

Job Description Review and Job Analysis

All positions have job descriptions. A *job description* is a formal, written statement that defines the specific responsibilities of the position, knowledge and skills needed to perform the job, qualifications, and reporting and supervisory relationships with other positions in the organization. When a vacancy occurs, the job description for the vacant position is reviewed. First, the position may be evaluated to determine the continued need for the position in the department and the agency. Second, the existing job description is analyzed using the most current information available on knowledge, skills, equipment, training/experience, licensure/certification, working conditions, or other requirements of the position. The job tasks may be compared to the National Council for Therapeutic Recreation Certification (NCTRC) job tasks for the therapeutic recreation specialist to affirm that the competencies are common to entry-level positions. The job analysis may result in changes in the job responsibilities, qualifications, salary adjustments, job reclassification, or other revisions. Job specifications are developed from the job analysis. *Job specifications* are employee characteristics and qualifications required for satisfactory performance of the defined duties and tasks of a specific job or job function. Finally, the job description is updated based on the job analysis and job specifications.

An essential part of the job analysis is developing an accurate, realistic job description. A job description that provides the applicant with an accurate, objective understanding of the job tends to improve on-the-job performance. Employees who believe they were given accurate job descriptions are more satisfied with the organization, believe the employer stands behind them and is trustworthy, and express a lower desire to change jobs (Lussier & Kimball, 2009).

The first-line manager in smaller organizations may review and revise job descriptions. In larger agencies, the first-line therapeutic recreation manager may assist the human resource specialist in the review and revision of job descriptions. Figure 9.1 includes an example of a job description for an entry-level therapeutic recreation position with a community agency.

Howard County Government
Job Description

Functional Title: Recreation Supervisor
Class Code: 5107
Class Title: Recreation Services Coordinator II
Grade: H
Position/Location Number:
Current Incumbent:
Department: Recreation & Parks
Dept/Division: Recreational Licensed Child Care & Community Services Division
Reports To: Community Services Manager
FLSA Status: Exempt
Prepared By:
Prepared Date: January 2013
Appointing Authority: Director Recreation & Parks
Approved Date:

POSITION SUMMARY
Provides coordination and supervision of programs for youth and adults with disabilities. Provides supervision to TRIO program centers and camps. Operates within a self-sustaining and teamwork environment. Provide senior administrative support to the Manager in the Community Services Section.

CLASS DESCRIPTION
Performs professional-level recreation services work, which may include supervision, under general supervision from an administrative or technical superior. Work includes planning and directing the safe and efficient operation of activities of a recreation center, park site, playground, or seasonal recreational facility or of a County-wide, age-specific recreation program; or overseeing the marketing and participant registration for recreation programs, classes and special events; supervising assigned part-time and full-time personnel; and preparing the budget for center operations.

ESSENTIAL DUTIES AND RESPONSIBILITIES include the following. Other duties may be assigned.

Under the direction of the Community Services Manager:

- Identify current trends and develop programs for youth and adults with disabilities.
- Coordinate program instructors, locations and logistics.
- Provide exceptional customer service to participants, families, staff members and all individuals and groups impacted by the programs.
- Demonstrate financial accountability through managing program budgets including determining fee structure, tracking expense, and submitting quarterly budget reports.
- Supervise programs to ensure compliance with Department policies and completing formal site visit evaluations and inspections.
- Some evening and weekend work is required.
- Recruit, train, supervise and evaluate contingent staff.
- Provide direct leadership as needed.
- Approve leave and handle staff absences.
- Check and ensure the accuracy of time cards for staff.
- Provide outreach to community agencies and service providers to promote programming for Howard County residents with emphasis on disabilities.
- Utilize registration software to run detailed marketing and financial reports and track program enrollment.
- Input contingent staff payroll, prepare bi-weekly payroll report using web-based payroll system.
- Create and edit content for Department seasonal brochures.
- Order, purchase, and deliver program equipment and supplies.
- Responsible for identifying and applying good sustainability practices into all aspects of Department operations.

SUPERVISORY RESPONSIBILITIES
Supervises and coordinates work assignments for 5–15 contingent staff. Assist with recruiting, interviewing, training, and evaluation of staff.

MINIMUM REQUIRED EDUCATION/EXPERIENCE
Bachelor's degree and 1 year experience working with older adults or individuals with disabilities.

(CONTINUED ON NEXT PAGE)

(CONTINUED FROM PREVIOUS PAGE)

PREFERRED EDUCATION EXPERIENCE
Bachelor's degree in therapeutic recreation and 1 year experience working with older adults and individuals with disabilities.

LANGUAGE SKILLS
Ability to read, analyze, and interpret general business periodicals, professional journals, technical procedures, or governmental regulations. Ability to write reports, business correspondence, and procedure manuals. Ability to effectively present information and respond to questions from groups of managers, clients, customers, and the general public.

MATHEMATICAL SKILLS
Ability to calculate figures and amounts such as discounts, interest, commissions, proportions, percentages, area, circumference, and volume. Ability to apply concepts of basic algebra and geometry.

REASONING ABILITY
Ability to solve practical problems and deal with a variety of concrete variables in situations where only limited standardization exists. Ability to interpret a variety of instructions furnished in written, oral, diagram, or schedule form.

CERTIFICATES, LICENSES, REGISTRATIONS
Class C Maryland Driver's License
Certified Therapeutic Recreation Specialist (CTRS) or able to obtain
First Aid/CPR/AED or able to obtain
CPI (Non-violent Crisis Intervention Training) or able to obtain
Medication Technician Certification or able to obtain

PHYSICAL DEMANDS
The physical demands described here are representative of those that must be met by an employee to successfully perform the essential functions of this job. Reasonable accommodations may be made to enable individuals with disabilities to perform the essential functions.

While performing the duties of this job, the employee is regularly required to talk or hear. The employee frequently is required to sit. The employee is occasionally required to stand; walk; and use hands to finger, handle, or feel. Specific vision abilities required by this job include close vision, distance vision, and ability to adjust focus.

WORK ENVIRONMENT
The work environment characteristics described here are representative of those an employee encounters while performing the essential functions of this job. Reasonable accommodations may be made to enable individuals with disabilities to perform the essential functions. The noise level in the work environment is usually quiet.

Figure 9.1 Entry-Level Job Description

Candidate-Selection Criteria

The candidate-selection criteria is a listing of required qualifications and essential skills of the job. It is a set of criteria to be used to evaluate each candidate's "fit" for the position. The purpose of the candidate-selection criteria is to develop an objective process to evaluate each job applicant's qualifications and ability to perform the job.

The candidate selection criteria are developed from the job description and the job analysis. The job description and the job analysis provide a listing of the essential skills, education, and experience needed to perform the job. The selection criteria also identify the "required" qualifications and the "preferred" qualifications of candidates. The qualifications and skills are rank-ordered on the basis of importance; all skills and qualifications are not equally important. For example, experience with aging adults with strokes would be a higher priority than would experience with healthy, elderly adults when the manager is hiring for a rehabilitation unit. On the other hand, experience with well, aging adults would be a higher priority when the manager is hiring to fill a position in a community senior center. An applicant who possesses the Certified Therapeutic Recreation Specialist (CTRS) and Certified Park and Recreation Professional (CPRP) credentials might be given higher ratings than the applicant who has yet to be declared eligible to sit for either exam if the manager chooses to tie the job responsibilities tested by each exam to the respective job tasks of the open position.

Once the qualifications have been identified and ranked, a rating form, or a candidate selection criteria form, is developed. These ranked qualifications become the basis for the screening of candidates' application materials. It is also used by the interview committee during the interview session to rate, or to evaluate each candidate. The form provides a means of objectively assessing each candidate and assigning a ranking of the candidates on the basis of the standardized set of job qualifications. An example of a selection-criteria form is included in Figure 9.2.

Learning Outcome

Describe three common strategies for recruitment of applicants.

Recruitment Plan

Recruitment is the process of attracting the best-qualified candidates for a job opening in a timely and cost-effective manner. "The purpose of recruitment is to locate and attract enough qualified applicants to provide a pool from which the required number of individuals can be selected" (Sullivan, 2013, p. 200). The manager

SELECTION CRITERIA FORM

Position Number:	**Class Title:**
Division/District:	
Bureau/Unit:	**Date:**

List the Selection Criteria to be used for reviewing applications and interviewing applicants for the referenced position. Indicate the criteria for the position as being essential (EC) or preferred (PC). After you complete the form, sign and date the statement at the end.

Selection Criteria	EC	PC

I certify that the essential criterion listed above reflects the entry-level requirements that are listed on the current position description.

Hiring Manager's Signature	**Date:**

Figure 9.2 Selection Criteria Form

determines where to look, how to look, when to look, and how to sell the department to potential recruits (Sullivan, 2013). The type of position and level of responsibility for which applicants are being recruited influences how positions are advertised.

Internal recruiting involves filling job vacancies with current employees or personal referrals. This may include recruiting previous employees and previous applicants who can still be contacted. Many organizations have formal policies that require all job vacancies to be announced within the organization, to current employees, prior to posting vacancies externally, or outside of the organization. *External recruiting* involves notifying potential applicants outside of the organization of the agency's intent to fill a vacant position. External recruiting options are broad and varied. The most effective recruiting options are typically determined by the type and level of position for which applicants are being recruited. For example, the American Therapeutic Recreation Association (ATRA) website (http://www.atra-online.com), the therapeutic recreation directory (http://www.recreationtherapy.com), and the Canadian Therapeutic Recreation Association (http://www.canadian-tr.org/) may be the most effective sources to use when recruiting for therapeutic recreation supervisory positions. On the other hand, local career fairs, university faculty and alumni, and colleagues from professional organizations tend to be effective to advertise and recruit for entry-level positions. Figure 9.3 identifies common media for the distribution of job announcements for health and human service organizations.

E-recruitment, also referred to as Internet recruitment or online recruitment, is the use of the Internet for handling the recruitment and application process. Today many organizations use recruiting software that is designed to streamline the hiring processes. "The federal government, all 50 states, and most of the nation's large cities and counties maintain recruitment websites" (Arnold, Glover, & Beeler, 2012, p. 79; Kim & O'Connor, 2009). The federal government website, USAJobs.gov, is an example of this recruitment software students might use to locate positions with, for example, the Department of Veterans Affairs. As the number of people searching online for job announcements increases, health and human service organizations are taking advantage of recruiting software to manage the entire recruitment process. Arnold, Glover, & Beeler (2012) identify numerous advantages, as well as disadvantages of e-recruitment software. Figure 9.4 (p. 136) offers a summary of the advantages and disadvantages of recruitment software.

Common Media for Distribution of Job Announcements

- Agency website
- Internet job listing websites
- Professional associations
- Word of mouth
- University faculty
- University alumni
- Friends and associates of current employees (employee referrals)
- Employment agencies

Figure 9.3 Common Media for Distribution of Job Announcements

Job Announcement

Prior to initiating the search process for a new employee, the first-line manager, in consultation with the human resource specialist, prepares a job announcement. The job announcement describes the position, necessary qualifications to meet the job requirements, description of the agency, and instructions for how to apply for the position. The purpose of the job announcement is to notify all those who are interested and qualified about the organization's intent to fill a position; it is a recruitment tool. The job announcement is developed from the job description. The structure and content of job announcements vary with the position, the organization, and the recruitment plan. For example, some descriptions are simple and include a brief one-paragraph description of the position and the agency. On the other hand, some job announcements are designed as a website or a formal multi-colored brochure. Figure 9.5 (p. 136) includes an example of a position announcement.

Selection Process

The recruitment process results in a pool of applicants. *Selection* is the process of choosing the most qualified applicant recruited for the job. Health and human service organizations do not follow a standardized selection process, nor does each agency use the same selection process for every job. In the absence of a perfect method to select candidates, first-line therapeutic recreation managers use a variety of screening methods to identify the most appropriate candidates. The first-line manager chooses those screening methods that are most likely to predict which applicants, if hired, will be successful in the position. Screening methods must be valid and reliable. Valid methods demonstrate a relationship between the screening tool and job performance. Reliable screening tools provide consistent results. In other words, the characteristics being measured are considered to remain stable over time.

The selection process commonly includes an application form and résumé, preliminary screening (phone) interview, first interview, second interview, facility tour, assessment or testing tools, background checks, reference checks, and drug screening. The selection plan includes defining a time-line for each step in the hiring process. The timeline includes a schedule for advertising the position, the application deadline, the review of application materials, and the target dates for each step in the assessment and selection process such as interview schedules, background checks, offering the position, and finally, a start date for the new employee. The hiring plans must include a realistic time frame for candidate selection. It is important for the manager to plan an adequate amount of time to identify the ideal candidate and make the best hiring decision. However, taking too much time can lead to losing candidates to other organizations that move more quickly in making a job offer (Hurd, Barcelona, & Meldrum, 2008).

The first step in the selection process is to determine which applicants are minimally qualified to perform the duties required for a particular position. It is usually neither cost-effective nor time-effective to interview and test each applicant. The first-line manager typically uses application forms, résumés or portfolios, and other background information to establish which candidates possess minimally desired qualifications.

Application Form

The job application form is one of the most commonly used screening tools. Application forms ensure information consistency among candidates. The application form also serves important legal functions, for example notifying candidates they must have proof of citizenship or give permission for their current employers to be

Advantages of Recruitment Software

1. Reduced recruitment time.
2. Reduced recruitment-related costs.
3. Consistency in application materials.
4. Broad distribution of job announcements.
5. Legal compliance support.

Disadvantages of Recruitment Software

1. Online recruitment often results in a large pool of applicants, not all of whom are highly qualified.
2. Privacy and the security of the electronic data, similar to any electronic database, may be compromised at some time.
3. Staff training may be required to use and manage the software.
4. Technological difficulties may cause temporary interruptions in access and service.

Figure 9.4 Advantages and Disadvantages of Recruitment Software

Organization/Agency: Association of Special Recreation
Job Title: Recreation Specialist
Salary Range: $34,000–$39,500
E-mail: supervisor@asr.org
Telephone: (666)999-3333
Closing Date: Open until filled

Job Description: Association of Special Recreation is looking to hire staff who are passionate about providing quality recreational programming for individuals with disabilities. Youth/Teen Recreation Specialist, Bachelor's Degree in Therapeutic Recreation or related field. Must demonstrate the ability to develop, coordinate, lead, and evaluate a variety of recreational activities for individuals with special needs. Direct leadership of programs including; after-school programs, Jr. Special Olympics, adaptive sports, overnight trips, fitness programs, and special events. Additional responsibilities include documentation, budgeting, developing youth/teen programs for the seasonal brochures, networking, driving agency vehicles, and other duties as assigned. Prior experience in youth and teen programming is desirable. CTRS certification is strongly preferred. Ability to work and communicate with individuals with disabilities, coworkers, parents, teachers, and community personnel is essential. Lifeguard Certification, CPR & First Aid Certification, and CPI are all required within 6 months of employment. ASR is an equal opportunity employer.
Send cover letter and résumé by mail or email; no faxes accepted.

Figure 9.5 Position Announcement

contacted. Employment law restricts the type of information that can be included on an application form. Agencies often use a computer scanning process to screen application forms for minimum qualifications. Résumés and portfolios provide detailed information about applicants' qualifications. Résumés may precede, accompany, or follow application form submission. Managers may review unsolicited résumés then send application materials to those who appear qualified. Unfortunately, not all information provided by applicants is complete and accurate. The results of major studies indicate "that from one third to one half of all résumés contain overstated, misleading and/or false information, intentional omissions, and blatant errors" (Arnold, Glover, & Beeler, 2012, p. 95). Verifying the information that is included in the candidates' application materials is an essential step in the applicant screening process. References, work experience, and credentials are verified prior to on-site interviewing.

Interview

On-site screening consists primarily of individual and/or group interviews and performance simulations. "The employment interview is perhaps the most widely used selection technique" (Arnold, Glover, & Beeler, 2012, p. 99). The *interview* "is an information-seeking mechanism between an individual applying for a position and a member of an organization doing the hiring" (Sullivan, 2013, p. 205). The job interview has several purposes. First, the interview provides an opportunity to clarify information that has been gathered through the application form, résumé, references, and other application materials. A second purpose of the interview is to evaluate a candidate's communication and critical thinking skills. The interview also provides an opportunity to meet the candidate and explore their personality.

The interview process is planned. "Interviews that are well-planned and structured have higher validity" (Arnold, Glover, & Beeler, 2012, p. 99). Planning helps ensure compliance with legal requirements. Table 9.3 (p. 139) offers a summary of legal restrictions and common pre-employment interview questions. Additionally, the well-planned interview facilitates a logical sequence to the questions and a flow of conversation. The manager often develops and uses a position-specific interview guide during the interview. The interview guide is a written document with a listing of the interview questions, instructions to the manager and others involved with the interview, and the candidate selection criteria rating form. The interview guide provides for structured note-taking during the interview. The note-taking process increases the accuracy of recall for interviewers. A summary of interview preparation and planning activities is included in Table 9.2 (p. 138).

The interview is a structured conversation between the interviewers and the interviewee. The purpose of the structured conversation is to exchange information to determine if there is a mutual "fit." Interview sessions generally follow a common format or sequence of questioning. The interview typically opens with comments and introductions, which are intended to establish rapport and help the applicant relax. The interviewee is informed that interviewers will take notes, the length of the interview, and the questioning procedure (e.g., each statement or question is made by the same interviewer and in the same sequence with each applicant). A brief orientation to the agency, therapeutic recreation department services, and the position follows. Opening questions relate back to already presented background information so that the interviewee feels confident to respond to further questioning. Interviewers use probes, repetition, and paraphrasing to gain insight into how the applicant's experiences and skills relate to the job specifications. Before closing the interview, the interviewee typically has an opportunity to ask questions about the position, the organization, or the community. Additionally, the manager identifies the next step in the hiring process (e.g., when a decision will be made, how the notification will occur, what follow-up steps might be required of the candidate).

During and following the interview, observation of gestures, mannerisms, and nonverbal cues may provide valuable clues about the applicant's "fit." Documentation of verbal and nonverbal responses and behaviors establishes if the candidate is qualified and likely, if hired, to perform successfully in the position.

Background Checks

Background checks have become an increasingly common aspect of the screening and selection process. Health and human service organizations are legally liable for the character and actions of the individuals they employ. To protect the organization, the staff, as well as clients, background checks are essential prior to hiring. "Failure

Table 9.2 Preparing for the Interview

Preparing for the Interview

1. Review the job description and job specifications: The first-line manager must have a thorough understanding of the job to be filled. The manager reviews the job description and job specifications to affirm that these documents are up-to-date. If outdated or incomplete, a job analysis is conducted.
2. Plan a realistic job preview: The first-line manager is responsible to help applicants understand the job and the job responsibilities. The manager informs applicants about the job's positive and negative aspects. The first-line manager uses the job description to plan the job preview.
3. Plan the type of interview: The first-line manager plans for the structure of the interview. The interview should be conducted in a private, quiet place, without interruptions. It may be appropriate to begin in an office and then tour the facilities and work area while asking questions. Plan the tour and the questions to be asked.
4. Develop questions for all candidates: The job description and specifications are used to develop questions that relate to each of the job tasks and responsibilities. The interview should include a combination of open-ended and behavior-based questions. All questions must be job-related and non-discriminatory. Ask the questions of all candidates.
5. Develop an interview guide form: Determine the sequence of questions. One approach starts with open-ended questions and then moves to behavior-based questions, using probing questions as needed. Another approach structures the interview around the job description and specifications; the first-line manager explains each job responsibility and then asks questions relating to each responsibility.
6. Develop questions for each candidate: Review each candidate's application and résumé. It is likely that some of the information will require verification or clarification during the interview. Develop specific questions for each candidate. The individual questions must be non-discriminatory and related to the job responsibilities.

Conducting the Interview

1. Open the interview: During the first few minutes of the interview, the first-line manager's goal is to establish rapport with the candidate and to put the applicant at ease by talking about some topic not related to the job.
2. Explain the realistic job preview: Be sure the applicant understands the job requirements. Answer any questions the applicant has about the job and the organization. If the job is not what the applicant expected or wants, allow the applicant to disqualify himself or herself or close the interview at that point.
3. Ask the planned interview questions: To get the most out of the interview, the first-line manager will take notes on the applicant's responses to the interview questions. Inform each applicant that the interview will include a number of prepared questions and that their responses will be noted. During the interview, applicants should do most of the talking. Give the applicant adequate time to think and respond to each question. In addition to making sure the applicant is a good "fit" for the job requirements, the interview also provides an opportunity to observe and determine whether the applicant is a good match for the agency and its culture (Collins & Smith, 2006). If an applicant doesn't respond with a complete answer to a question, ask a probing question to gain further insight.
4. Introduce top candidates to coworkers: Introduce top applicants to people with whom they will be working to get a sense of their interpersonal skills and overall attitude. Introductions can also give the first-line manager a sense about whether the applicant is a team player.
5. Close the interview: Be honest without making a decision during the interview. Don't mislead applicants. End the interview session with a closing question such as "Is there anything else you would like to tell me about or ask me?" Thank the applicant for their time and explain the next step in the interview process, if any. Inform the applicant of when and how they will be contacted. After the interview, make notes regarding general impressions not covered by specific questions.

to do so constitutes negligent hiring if that employee harms a patient [client], visitor, or another employee" (Sullivan, 2013, p. 211). Agencies may use a third party to conduct background checks on applicants. The background check usually includes a criminal background check and Department of Motor Vehicle records, if the individual will be required to operate vehicles as part of their job responsibilities. Licensures, credentials, and references are also verified.

Selection Decision

Selection and rejection are the final steps in the employee selection process. When comparing candidates, the first-line manager considers three factors. First, the manager weighs each candidate's qualifications for the skills and knowledge that are required for the job in order of importance, placing most emphasis on the most important elements. Second, the manager weighs each candidate's qualification for desired and preferred qualities. Third, the manager considers each candidate in terms of trainability to achieve the job requirement; the amount of education and additional training each of the applicants can reasonably be expected to acquire. When several candidates offer job skill sets and qualifications that appear to be equal, the candidates' "fit" with the department, the organization, and the future

Table 9.3 Pre-Employment Questions: What is Legal

Information	Can Ask	Cannot Ask
Name	Can ask current name and whether the candidate has ever worked under a different name.	Cannot ask maiden name.
Address	Can ask current residence and length of residence.	Cannot ask whether the candidate owns or rents his or her home unless it is a BFOQ.
Age	Can ask whether candidate is within a specific age group to meet job specifications and whether he or she can offer proof of age if hired.	Cannot ask candidate's age. Cannot ask how much longer he or she plans to work before retiring.
Sex	Can ask candidate's sex only if sex is a BFOQ.	Cannot ask candidate's sex. Cannot ask questions or make comments remotely considered flirtatious or ask about sexual preferences.
Marital & Family Status	Can ask whether the candidate can meet the work schedule and whether the candidate has activities, responsibilities, or commitments that may affect attendance.	Cannot ask marital status or any questions regarding children or other family information.
National Origin, Citizenship, Race or Color	Can ask whether the candidate is legally eligible to work in the U.S. and whether this can be proven if he or she is hired.	Cannot ask candidate to identify national origin, citizenship, race, or color (or that of parents or relatives).
Language	Can ask which languages the candidate speaks or writes fluently. Can ask whether the candidate speaks or writes a specific language if it is a BFOQ.	Cannot ask the language spoken off-the-job or how the applicant learned the language.
Convictions	Can ask whether the candidate has been convicted of a felony and can ask for other information if the felony is job-related.	Cannot ask whether the candidate has ever been arrested. Cannot ask for information regarding a conviction that is not job-related.
Height & Weight	Can ask whether the candidate meets or exceeds height or weight requirements when it is a BFOQ and whether this can be proven if the candidate is hired.	Cannot ask the candidate's height or weight.
Religion	Can ask whether the candidate can meet work schedules. Can ask whether the candidate is of a specific religion when it is a BFOQ.	Cannot ask religious preferences, affiliations, or denominations.
Credit Ratings	Can ask candidate's credit rating if this is BFOQ.	Cannot ask candidate's credit rating if this is not a BFOQ.
Education & Work Experience	Can ask for education and work experience information that is job related.	Cannot ask for education and work experience information that is not job related.
References	Can ask for references and request information from references that is job related.	Cannot ask for references from a religious leader if it is not a BFOQ.
Military	Can ask for information on job-related education and experience gained in the military.	Cannot ask for dates and conditions of discharge, draft classification, or other eligibility for military service. Cannot ask about experience in non-U.S. military services.
Organizations	Can ask about membership in job-related organizations, such as unions, professional, or trade organizations.	Cannot ask about memberships in any non-job-related organization that would indicate race, religion, national origin, sex/sexual preference.
Disabilities	Can ask whether the candidate has any disabilities that would prevent him or her from performing the specific job.	Cannot ask for information that is not job related; focus on abilities, not disabilities.

human resource needs of the organization are deciding factors. The first-line manager must decide whether there is a match between the applicant's qualifications and the organization's expectations. Although the first-line manager is responsible for the hiring decision, the interview team and upper-level management typically work together to gain consensus and support for the selected candidate. This is especially true if the new employee will be working with other employees in the organization and representing the department at agency events.

There are two possible errors in the selection process. An *accept error* is the selection of a candidate who subsequently performs poorly on the job. A *reject error* is rejecting a candidate who would have been successful on the job. In either situation, the outcome is costly because direct service time is ultimately lost and recruiting and screening is time-consuming and expensive. Table 9.4 provides a listing of common selection decision mistakes. A correct decision is made when the applicant is predicted to be successful on the basis of the performance criteria used to evaluate therapeutic recreation specialists and then performs well on the job.

Job Offer

The job offer is extended to the selected candidate prior to notification of rejection to unsuccessful candidates. In the situation in which a selected candidate rejects the job offer, the manager has the opportunity to offer the position to the next most qualified candidate. A reasonable deadline is allowed for acceptance or rejection so that the manager is able to contact the next candidate without alerting the individual that they were not the first choice. Additionally, individuals who are seriously considered but not hired are possible candidates for future positions. For those applicants who are unlikely to be considered again, a personal letter explaining why their qualifications did not satisfy the job specifications is a professional courtesy.

The job offer is made in writing and the manager will request that the successful applicant confirm their acceptance of the job offer in writing. Pre-employment procedures, such as drug screening, are also clarified in writing. Finally, a *compensation* package is negotiated with the successful candidate. Compensation refers to pay and may also include benefits. Job specifications usually identify a wage or salary range commensurate with the applicant's qualifications. Additionally, employment benefits are explained to the candidate. Examples of *benefits* include health insurance, retirement plan, vacations, holidays, and professional development incentives. Compensation and benefits are also an important consideration for staff retention. Further discussion of compensation and benefits is presented later in this chapter in the section addressing staff retention. Documentation from the hiring process is retained in the event questions about hiring and rejection decisions arise in the future.

Table 9.4 Common Selection Decision Mistakes

Common Selection Decision Mistakes

- Interviewers miss important information.
- Interviewers ask illegal questions.
- Interviewers have not clearly defined selection criteria.
- Candidates are put off by the selection process.
- Interviewer's biases and stereotypes affect judgment.
- Interviewers fail to take notes or take insufficient notes.
- Interviewers misinterpret applicant information.
- Interviewers allow one characteristic to influence their judgment.
- Urgency to fill the position influences judgment.

Learning Outcome

Identify two primary components of compensation.

Probationary Period

Many health and human service organizations hire new employees on a probationary basis to assess the new hire's suitability for the position. *Probation* is a trial period during which the first-line manager will assess and evaluate the new employee to determine whether the new hire has the ability to perform the job and is likely to be successful with the organization. In addition to job skills, a first-line manager may also evaluate the new hire's ability to collaborate with coworkers, cooperate with supervisors, and interact effectively with clients. This trial period allows the first-line manager to evaluate the "fit" of the newly hired practitioner in the organization. The probationary period increases the probability of making a correct hiring decision. The length of the probationary period varies depending on the organization. Typically the probation period is 30 to 90 days. If the new employee shows promise and performs well during the probationary time, they are usually moved from probationary status to permanent status. On the other hand, the probationary period allows an organization to terminate an employee who is determined not to be performing well in their position or is otherwise deemed not suitable for a particular position.

Professional Standards

In an attempt to ensure quality consumer services, professional credentialing bodies and societies have recommended minimal and expected educational experiences and credentials for therapeutic recreation professionals. Adherence to professional guidelines facilitates the hiring of staff who are eligible to meet personnel criteria and who have the professional competencies that are essential to quality therapeutic recreation service delivery. Credentialing bodies and professional organizations set standards that affect the content that managers include in job specifications. The minimal staff requirement delineated in professional standards of practice (ATRA, 2013) for therapeutic recreation specialists is state licensure, registration, or certification, and certification with the National Council for Therapeutic Recreation Certification (NCTRC). Additionally, the written plan of operation encourages professional development activities, periodic assessment of professional competencies, and the design of individual development plans so professional competencies are maintained and enhanced for safe and effective practice. NCTRC (2012a) defines the criteria for a Bachelor's degree, with minimal credit hours in recreation, therapeutic recreation coursework, and supportive content courses. A culminating internship with a minimal number of clock hours and length of time working under the supervision of a Certified Therapeutic Recreation Specialist is the eligibility criteria for the entry-level certification exam. Upon successful completion of the exam, certification extends for 5 years with annual renewal maintenance fees. Following the 5-year period, accumulation of professional experience and continuing education in therapeutic recreation or successful reexamination ensures recertification (NCTRC, 2012b). The first-line manager may elect to include the requirement of state licensure, registration, or certification (Certified Therapeutic Recreation Specialist), or eligibility to sit for the Certified Therapeutic Recreation Specialist exam, as job specifications. If this course of action is taken, the manager must relate job knowledge, skills, and abilities to the job tasks of the Therapeutic Recreation Specialist (NCTRC, 2011).

Professional practice documents refer to therapeutic recreation specialists that maintain their competency and adhere to policies, procedures, and clinical privileges where appropriate (ATRA, 2013; CTRA, 2006). Specifically, standard-of-practice documents identify staff participation in competency opportunities that improve patient outcomes (ATRA, 2013). Regulatory bodies, for example the Joint Commission, consider competency assessment programs or the assessment, maintenance, and continual professional development of staff as quality indicators. As a consequence, first-line managers document and maintain records of staff participation in programs that offer Continuing Education Unit opportunities. Where credentials specify minimal professional expectations, privileging identifies specific agency or department practice requirements. A privileging plan sets minimal employment criteria, such as possession of the Certified Therapeutic Recreation Specialist credential, Cardiopulmonary Resuscitation, first aid, and experience in specific settings. A first-line manager may include privileging criteria in job specifications. The use of professional credentials and specific privileging or performance criteria with the demonstration of ongoing competence requires that the manager continually ensure the relevance of job specifications to therapeutic recreation practice.

Staff Training and Development

Health and human service organizations' most valuable resources are their people. The employees' skills and knowledge are the organization's future. Successful health and human service organizations are learning organizations. Their success is a result of a commitment to continuous improvement to achieve high-quality service, cost-effectiveness in operations, worker efficiency, and constant adaptation to change. *Learning organizations* are forward thinking and their culture is focused on innovation. McConnell (2002) suggested "given the pace of technological change in health care and elsewhere and social change in the world at large" the effectiveness and competitive edge of the organization depends on an ongoing investment in the training and development of its managers and employees (p. 4).

Today, employees and managers come into health and human service organizations expecting to receive training and development. They are seeking to improve their skills and gain new experiences; they expect more from their employer than a paycheck. The findings of a recent survey reported by the American Association for Training and Development indicated that 72% of employees viewed learning and development opportunities to be as important as salary when choosing their next job (Ketter, 2012). Keeping high-performing employees satisfied in their work includes planning for their future training and development needs and matching their emerging interests and abilities with new job responsibilities. "The success of both the employee and the employer lies in the appreciation for continuous learning and commitment to development" (Arnold, Glover, & Beeler, 2012, p. 165).

Learning Outcome

Explain the purposes of new employee orientation, training, and development.

Staff training and development includes all of the formal and informal activities in the organization that result in enhanced on-the-job performance. While training and development are similar in many respects, "*training* is more narrowly defined as the acquisition of knowledge and skills to aid in current job performance." *Development*, on the other hand, "focuses on an individual's life-long learning" (Arnold, Glover, & Beeler, 2012, p. 166).

There are four types of staff training that are common to nearly all organizations. First, all organizations provide training for new employees, referred to as new employee orientation. As indicated in Table 9.5, the purpose of new employee *orientation* is to inform new hires about the organization and communicate expectations of them as new employees.

Table 9.5 Purposes of New Employee Orientation

Purposes of New Employee Orientation

- Provide an overview of the organization including the mission, goals, policy, procedures, services, and organizational culture.
- Describe the department functions and services.
- Explain the new employee's job tasks and responsibilities; communicate expectations of the new hire.
- Tour the facilities.
- Introduce the new hire to coworkers.
- Accelerate the new hire's rate of assimilation into the organization and the job and reduce new-job anxiety.

A second type of common training is focused on skills that require scheduled renewal for continued certification. The renewal or updating of these skills is facilitated through regular training. Examples of certification training include cardiopulmonary resuscitation (CPR) and first aid. Third, some educational programs are mandated by federal, state or local regulations, or professional standards. For example, continuing education is a requirement for renewal of the Certified Therapeutic Recreation Specialist credential. Finally, new evidence for practice and new technologies require training, or retraining, to maintain best practices in service delivery and client care.

Training Cycle

Planning for a staff training and development program is a five-step process. The training cycle includes a needs assessment, setting objectives that identify training outcomes, planning and design of an appropriate training program, implementation of the training, and finally, evaluation of the outcomes achieved through the training.

Needs Assessment

The first step in an effective staff training and development program is a needs assessment to identify educational program needs. Today, health and human service organizations must justify how an educational activity will support and contribute to achievement of organizational goals (Sullivan, 2013). The decision to offer educational programs should be based on teaching behaviors that will result in increased effectiveness and efficiency of the department and the organization. To determine the training needs for an employee in a specific position, the most common approach to needs assessment is a job analysis or task analysis. Job descriptions, performance appraisal criteria, professional certification plans (NCTRC), and licensure requirements are resources for expected therapeutic recreation specialist job responsibilities. Task analyses prepared from review of these documents are used to compare staff performance with competencies expected of professionals in similar positions. Discrepancies become the focus of individual training plans. The training plan identifies specific performance outcomes to be achieved and demonstrated as actual on-the-job behaviors.

Objectives

After training needs have been identified, the next step in the training and development program is to establish well-defined, performance-based objectives. Training objectives, or outcomes, are specific, measurable statements that describe desired behavior with target dates for completion. Typically these objectives are included in the employee's annual goals and outcomes are evaluated through the annual performance appraisal process. In addition to identifying and establishing training objectives, the first-line manager and the practitioner create an individual development plan that focuses on the employee's long-range career development goals. Long-range employee development plans are typically multiyear plans. The employee's annual performance evaluation may include short-term annual objectives that provide a means to monitor progress toward achievement of the employee's long-range development plan.

Implementation

Implementation of staff training and development programs involves bringing together educators, learners, and the materials and methods needed for education. Training and development may be accomplished through a variety of programs, as listed in Table 9.6. Two options for training include internal training sources and external training sources. Internal training includes a broad scope of activities that occur within the organization. These activities frequently include informal coaching, mentoring, and on-the-job training. Sullivan (2013) indicates that "The most widely used educational method is on-the-job instruction" (p. 232). This type of training

Table 9.6 Types of Staff Training and Development Programs

Types of Staff Training and Development Programs
1. New employee orientation
2. On-the-job training
3. Supervisory assistance
4. Informal training
5. Job rotation or cross training
6. Apprenticeships
7. Internships
8. Coaching
9. Mentoring
10. Supervisory and management development programs
11. Leadership development programs
12. Formal education programs
13. Professional development programs

Learning Outcome

Describe four common methods of training and development in health and human service agencies..

is typically accommodated by assigning an employee to a more experienced staff member, and the learning is accomplished by observing and performing the tasks under close supervision of the experienced staff. On-the-job-training is usually the most cost-effective type of training. Internal training may also include workshops and in-service training. For example, the organization may require all managers to complete a series of supervisory skills workshops. In this example, the standardized training helps ensure that all managers have a minimal level of supervisory training. The training also provides an opportunity to communicate organizational culture and expectations of all supervisors.

Web-based training, or e-learning, is another approach to internal training that has become common in many organizations. E-learning encompasses various forms of technology-supported learning, including the Internet, videos, satellite links, and DVDs. E-learning provides agencies with staff training and development opportunities that are highly cost-effective. Advantages and disadvantages of e-learning training are summarized in Table 9.7 (p. 144).

Job rotation and *cross-training* are additional approaches to internal, on-the-job training and development. In this type of training, employees move from job-to-job at planned intervals. The purpose of the job rotation and cross-training is to broaden the employee's experiences. Job rotation and cross-training are commonly used for preparation of staff for promotion into supervisory and management positions.

Coaching is a management intervention to help employees improve their performance. Coaching is an effective strategy for the first-line manager to use when performance meets expected standards but improvement can still be attained. The purpose of coaching, similar to athletic coaching, is to eliminate problems and improve performance. Coaching an employee when a problem initially surfaces can potentially save time, prevent the development of poor morale, and avoid more serious or difficult action later, such as discipline. Positive coaching is a strategy to reinforce positive behaviors. The goal of positive coaching is to help employees become more self-aware, ensure

Table 9.7 Advantages and Disadvantages of E-Learning Training

Advantages and Disadvantages of E-Learning Training

Advantages of E-Learning:

1. The training schedule is flexible to meet individual needs.
2. E-learning can accommodate different learning styles and provide a variety of learning activities that may not be possible in traditional classroom training.
3. E-learning reduces the travel time and cost for attending classroom training programs.
4. Self-paced learning modules allow individuals to work at their own pace.
5. Participants can usually complete the training or study anywhere they have access to a computer and the Internet.
6. E-learning may be more participant-centered if it allows each individual the option to select learning materials that meet his or her level of knowledge and interest.

Disadvantages of E-learning:

1. Participants who are not highly motivated or have poor study habits may fall behind and find it difficult to keep pace with the required work.
2. Participants may feel isolated from their instructor and other participants.
3. Slow Internet connections may make it difficult or time consuming to access online course materials.
4. Material that requires hands-on lab work may be difficult to simulate in e-learning training.
5. Participants who don't have good digital file-management skills and those with emerging-level computer skills may find the complexity of downloads and other technology challenging.
6. Trainers/Instructors/Technical support may not always be available at times that are convenient for participants.

accountability, and attain professional goals. Positive coaching has been shown to help build confidence and competency and to improve the functioning of the team. Positive coaching is particularly helpful during time of transition or implementation of techniques and skills that are new to the employee.

External training includes conferences, workshops, seminars, and other organized training opportunities that are presented by organizations outside the agency. For example, training may be accomplished through attendance at state and national professional organizations, professional meetings, or courses at a college or university. Other therapeutic recreation or health and human service professionals in the community may provide training resources to help managers and practitioners remain current with best professional practices and trends. External training is typically more costly than internal training and development. Registration fees, travel expenses, and time away from the agency all contribute to the costs of external training and development.

Evaluation

The purpose of evaluation is to determine the effectiveness of staff training and development. According to Marquis and Huston (2012), a comprehensive evaluation of staff development activities measures four criteria of training and development: the employee's reactions, behavior change, organizational impact, and cost-effectiveness. Evaluation is an investigative process to determine whether the education was cost-effective, whether the objectives were achieved, and ultimately to determine if the learning was actually applied on the job. The most important criteria for measuring results are those that evaluate the employee's ability to transfer the new knowledge and skills to on-the-job performance. Transfer of new information toward improving job performance and/or agency effectiveness is one of the most critical outcomes of training and development (Sims, 1993). Information is of little value unless behavior or performance is changed. Ultimately, the evaluation process seeks to determine whether the trainee is able to apply learning to on-the-job performance. This form of evaluation occurs at defined intervals after participation in training and development. The amount of time required to incorporate new information into behavioral patterns varies with the level of difficulty of the competencies. For example, soon after staff have completed an in-service training on equipment-use procedures that require minimal behavioral change, the first-line manager might evaluate the staff by observing and questioning them to confirm the transfer of the new information and procedures into on-the-job performance. On the other hand, evaluation of newly acquired skills in delegating work, time management, or strategic planning would occur in a series of assessments over an extended period of time because of the complexity of behavioral change. The following are examples of questions to assess the transfer of information to job improvement:

- Compared to two months ago, has the supervisor delegated work assignments more effectively?
- Do recorded work activities of this month reflect improved time management as compared to the calendar kept prior to the in-service training last month?
- Have practitioners revised their individual development plans since the completion last month of the training program for the department's new mission and plan of operation?

The purpose of training and development is to increase or to improve effectiveness in the achievement of department goals. In health and human service agencies, the primary evaluation is to determine whether the training and development result in enhanced client well-being. A therapeutic recreation manager might evaluate to determine whether the service was maintained or improved through cost reductions, enhanced use of personnel or physical resources, and the application of specific interventions. Impact measurements consider quality of care, productivity, cost-benefit analyses, and follow-up information from client and caregiver surveys. Table 9.8 offers a summary of common training methods.

Training and Development Trends

Change is inherent in organizations today, including the manner in which the practice of therapeutic recreation is conducted. Changing work and social environments require that professionals continually update their knowledge and skills and respond to professional trends and the needs of clients. Health and human service organizations are a portion of the growing service industry in which "people skills" are fundamental to the quality of services delivered. Competency in communication skills, such as conflict resolution, negotiation, individual and group facilitation, public speaking, problem solving, and empathetic listening are fundamental to service-delivery approaches that emphasize participatory management and interactive leadership.

Table 9.8 Training Methods Summary

Training Methods Summary	
Training Method	**Description**
Written materials	Trainees read materials and books.
Lecture	Training materials are presented verbally. The lecture method is used when the goal is to present a great deal of material to many people.
E-learning	Training is presented through satellite links, videos, DVDs, and Internet resources.
Job rotation	Training involves moving an employee through a series of jobs so he or she gains an understanding of the tasks that are associated with various jobs in the organization. The employee learns a little about many different aspects of the organization.
Role playing, In-basket, Simulation	Likely problems and alternative solutions are presented for discussion. Experienced employees describe real-world experiences and help trainees with developing solutions to these simulations.
Internships and assistantships	Young professionals work under the supervision of an experienced professional and apply classroom learning to on-the-job situations.
Demonstration	Experienced staff or trainers show trainees how to perform the task.
Behavior modeling	Trainers demonstrate skills. Trainees observe how to perform the task correctly and then role-play the situation using the observed skills. Trainees receive feedback on how well they performed the task.
Projects	Training involves learning through completing special assignments, such as developing a new program or a service.

As the information age brings people closer together, communication with others whose culture, age, experience, and education are more unique and varied increases. Consequently, communication is an avenue to cultural awareness and sensitivity skill building. Advocacy depends on effective communication. The intent of therapeutic recreation is communicated through research, evaluation, and efficacy studies. Competence in all forms of communication is necessary and continues to be a training and development need.

Information is acquired and communicated more rapidly with today's technological resources. Each manager and therapist will continue to need knowledge and skills for processing and accessing information. Increasing amounts of information will be communicated in the practice setting to consumers, caregivers, and colleagues. As demands for accountability, quality, cost reductions, and service redistributions magnify, the time to communicate becomes less while the necessity to communicate the value of therapeutic recreation becomes greater. Consumer well-being is the central focus of intervention. The challenge is to synthesize vast amounts of information so that the intent of professional practice is properly communicated and consumer well-being is maintained and enhanced.

Training and development provide opportunities to study ethical dilemmas. To illustrate, "doing the right thing" receives mixed signals in the workplace, profession, and society. Therapists increasingly experience dilemmas in situations that involve service marketing and competition, financial reimbursement, consumer confidentiality and self-determination, teamwork, and networking. Training and development teach the facilitation skills necessary to resolve situational and professional practice dilemmas and to communicate professional and ethical standards of therapeutic recreation.

The interpersonal aspect of therapeutic recreation contributes to the need to adjust to the changing perspectives of clients, caregivers, and management. Therapeutic recreators, like other members of health and human service teams and networks, require support as the work environment becomes more people- and information-intensive. Support can be found in time and stress-management training sessions. Training and development offer avenues to adapt to changes that would otherwise contribute to "professional burnout."

Performance Appraisals

Learning Outcome
Describe the purposes of the performance appraisal.

The *performance appraisal*, also referred to as an employee evaluation, is an evaluation of an employee's on-the-job behaviors and skills. The performance appraisal is a formal, periodic evaluation of how well an individual employee has performed their job duties during a specified time period (Herringer, 2002). The purpose of the performance appraisal system is to communicate performance expectations to staff and provide feedback about how well they are meeting those expectations. The "evaluation of job performance is considered by management to be one of the most important aspects of supervising" therapeutic recreation practitioners (Arnold, Glover, & Beeler, 2012, p. 121).

Performance appraisals are important for a number of reasons. The performance evaluation is a means of determining the extent to which an individual is performing the assigned duties and responsibilities of the position. Employee evaluations provide documentation for decisions about training needs, compensation, promotions, disciplinary actions, and terminations. They provide managers with a regularly scheduled, formal opportunity to share constructive feedback with employees. Performance appraisals support and assist employees to develop to their fullest potential. Performance appraisals are also a way to provide recognition of employees' accomplishments and motivate staff toward higher achievement. Finally, employee evaluations are essential for compliance with Fair Labor Employment practices and regulations from agencies that establish professional standards, for example, the Joint Commission (Herringer, 2002).

There are two types of performance appraisals. Evaluative performance appraisals are used to determine pay raises, transfers and promotions, and demotions and terminations. Evaluative appraisals focus on the past. Developmental performance appraisals are used to improve performance, and are focused on the future. The purpose of both types of appraisals is to help employees to continuously improve their performance. When developmental and evaluative performance appraisals are conducted together, the developmental appraisal is often less effective, particularly when the employee disagrees with the evaluation. Therefore, separate appraisal processes and meetings are usually more productive for both the employee and the first-line manager.

While each health and human service agency has a unique evaluation process, there are three characteristics common to effective performance appraisal systems. First, performance appraisal systems are formal and structured. Health and human service agencies typically conduct formal evaluations of employees at the end of the probationary employment period, and most agencies conduct evaluation of employees on a scheduled annual basis. Second, performance appraisal systems are focused on job-related performance. Finally, first-line managers who supervise practitioners will evaluate the performance of those practitioners.

Performance Appraisal Systems

Each health and human service organization typically uses an agency-specific evaluation form developed by the human resource department to assess employee performance. Common measurement methods include results-oriented evaluations (objectives), critical incident reports, rubrics (behavior-anchored rating scales), ranking, and narrative. The most effective approach is typically a combination of several of these evaluation methods. Table 9.9 summarizes these five evaluation methods, and Table 9.10 (p. 148) lists potential performance-appraisal rating errors. Common criticisms of performance appraisal forms is that they include measures of non-performance-related behaviors such as initiative, creativity, willingness to take responsibility, and promotability, all of which are very difficult to measure objectively.

Results-Oriented Evaluations (Objectives)

Today there is an increasing emphasis throughout health and human service agencies on outcomes, and results-oriented assessments are becoming a common approach to employee appraisal. Results-oriented evaluations focus on setting objectives that identify specific outcomes that the employee is responsible to accomplish. The results-based performance evaluation is a two-step process. At the beginning of the evaluation period, the employee and the manager, working cooperatively, develop a set of objectives for the employee to accomplish during a specified future time frame. At

Table 9.9 Performance Appraisal Methods

Performance Appraisal Methods	
Results-Oriented Evaluations (Objectives)	Managers and employees jointly set objectives for the employee; periodically they evaluate the employee's progress in achieving those objectives and reward employees according to results.
Critical Incident Reports	Managers observe the employee and note an employee's positive and negative performance behaviors in various critical incidents throughout the performance period. This evaluation feedback is very specific. This method of evaluation relies on the manager's commitment to documentation of critical incidents throughout the evaluation period.
Rubrics (Behaviorally Anchored Rating Scale)	This method combines rating and critical incidents. It is more objective and accurate than evaluations that use either of the two methods separately. Rather than using ratings such as "excellent," "good," "average," or "poor," managers choose statements that best describe performance for that task. Well-designed rubrics make standards clear.
Ranking	Managers rank employee performance from best to worst. Managers compare employees to each other, rather than comparing each person to a standard measurement. Another similar format to ranking is the forced distribution method, which resembles grading on a curve. A predetermined percentage of employees are placed in performance categories: for example: excellent, 5%; above average, 15%; average, 60%; below average, 15%; poor, 5%.
Narrative	Managers write a statement about the employee's performance. The system varies. Managers may be allowed to write comments without structure, or they may be required to answer specific questions about performance. Narratives are often combined with other methods.

the conclusion of the evaluation period, the employee and the manager review the employee's actual performance and assess the employee's progress toward achievements of the objectives. When the objectives are well written and unambiguous, this approach to performance appraisal clearly identifies the evaluation standard. Employee involvement with setting objectives tends to result in increased motivation and commitment to accomplishment of their objectives.

Critical Incident Reports

The critical-incident-report method of performance appraisal involves identifying and describing specific situations, projects, or incidents, and a description of the employee's performance in handling the task or situation. Critical incidents occur when an employee's job performance results in noteworthy success or failure on the job. Critical-incident-reports evaluation is based on a narrative description and does not rely on the assignment of ratings or rankings. The use of critical incident reporting for performance appraisal is more demanding of supervisors. It requires that the manager write a narrative description of a situation or project when the situation occurs. The quality of the evaluation is highly dependent on the manager's written communication skills. When well prepared, the critical-incident-reports evaluation provides detailed and specific feedback for employees to improve their performance.

Rubrics (Behaviorally Anchored Rating Scale)

The Behaviorally Anchored Rating Scale (BARS) method of performance appraisal involves evaluating an individual's performance using an appraisal form with a matrix-style format that includes a listing of actual job behaviors and scale with specific narrative examples of good, moderate, and poor performance. BARS differs from "standard" rating scales in that it focuses on behaviors that are determined to be important for completing a job task or doing the job properly, rather than rating more general employee characteristics. Practitioners are graded according to their demonstration or absence of specific behavioral patterns. The BARS appraisal method is an objective approach to the performance-evaluation process. The appraisal can be developed to focus on the specific job behaviors that are most essential to the position and the organization. The major disadvantages of the BARS appraisal is that professional expertise is required to construct a BARS for a specific position. The appraisals can be very expensive and time-consuming to construct.

Ranking

The ranking method of performance appraisal requires that the manager rank-order employees. All employees in a similar group of jobs are compared with one another to determine whether their performance is better than, equal to, or less than the work of their peers. The

Table 9.10 Potential Performance-Appraisal Rating Errors

Potential Performance-Appraisal Rating Errors

Leniency error is a rater's tendency to assign higher ratings to an individual's performance than the actual performance demonstrated. Leniency is an inaccurate inflation of an individual's performance ratings. Murphy and Cleveland (1995) suggest that raters are motivated to inflate ratings in order to (a) avoid negative interpersonal relationships with subordinates, (b) make themselves as managers look better, (c) conform to organizational norms of high ratings, and (d) encourage employees to work harder to "live up to" higher ratings than their work merited.

Halo effect is a bias that happens when the supervisor evaluates the employee based on a single characteristic, such as their enthusiasm. "The halo effect operates when we draw a general impression of an individual on the basis of a single characteristic such as intelligence, sociability, or appearance" (Schneider, Gruman, & Coutts, 2012, p. 221).

Ambiguous evaluation standards are a common error with appraisal forms using rating scales. Many rating scales include words such as "outstanding," "above average," or "satisfactory." Each supervisor attaches a different meaning to the rating scale words. Although the evaluation form may provide a description of behaviors that exemplify each rating category, the individual supervisors will each interpret and assign different meanings to the words.

Recency error in performance appraisals is the result of the evaluator's reliance on the most recent occurrences of the employee's behavior as indicators of performance over the entire performance appraisal period. The recency error is typically a result of the lack of consistent documentation of the employee's performance during the appraisal period. Due to the recency error, an employee who performed highly over the course of the appraisal period may be rated low if the most recent events were negative.

primary criticism of the ranking system is the absence of objectivity in the evaluation process.

Narrative

A narrative performance evaluation requires that the appraiser document in writing the strengths, weaknesses, and characteristics of a practitioner's performance. The narrative evaluation lacks a standardized format. The appraiser is given the freedom to address incidents, attributes, behavior, or other topics that they perceive to be of greatest importance. The primary advantage of using a narrative-style performance appraisal is that evaluators have an opportunity to provide detailed descriptions of unique behaviors and accomplishments. The narrative performance appraisal has also been criticized. The supervisor's written communication skills are a significant factor in the quality of the evaluation. Further, the narrative appraisal is criticized on the basis of the subjective nature of the process.

Performance Appraisal Interview

Most organizations require formal performance appraisals of employees on an annual basis. The most important purpose or goal of the performance appraisal is to improve performance in the future. An important part of the appraisal process is a meeting between the supervisor and the employee to discuss the evaluation. This meeting is referred to as the performance appraisal interview. The performance appraisal interview should facilitate communication between the practitioner and the first-line manager. Strategies to maintain a positive approach to the performance evaluation interview include the following:

- Realize most employees believe they are meeting expectations and are surprised to hear otherwise (Feuer, 2003).
- Focus on two or three specific areas needing improvement.
- Specify a follow-up plan to assess progress in the specific areas needing improvement and set target review dates.
- Close the interview with positive comments that include praise and gratitude for work well done and express confidence in the employee's ability to improve and meet expected levels of performance.

Keep in mind that performance evaluations can be stressful for both the employee being evaluated and the supervisor completing the evaluation. It is the first-line manager's responsibility to create a relaxed yet professional atmosphere for the appraisal interview session. Specific strategies to encourage a positive, professional approach throughout the interview include the following. First, planning and preparation for the formal appraisal is critical. An agenda is prepared. Both the manager and the employee identify an uninterrupted time period sufficient in length to discuss and review the evaluation information. Holding the meeting in a private conference room, rather than the manager's office, neutralizes positional power, assures privacy, and promotes a seating arrangement that supports a collegial problem-solving process. Reiterating the significance of positive outcomes establishes an improvement-oriented climate and assures two-way communication. It is also important for the manager to reaffirm the primary objective of the review is to identify how the manager and practitioner can work together to improve performance and relate individual goals to organizational performance. At the conclusion of the appraisal discussion, the performance evaluation document is signed by the employee and manager and placed in the employee's personnel file.

Performance-Improvement Action Plan

The performance evaluation typically results in the development of a performance-improvement action plan. This plan is prepared by the manager and the employee. The format of the action plan might include a listing of objectives, target dates to review accomplishments, required resources, and progress notations. The action plan is a tool used to improve performance. The action plan identifies steps an employee will take to gain the skills and knowledge necessary to deliver services in compliance with job specifications and professional standards of practice. With this approach that includes incorporating ongoing communication into routine supervisory sessions, the anxiety created by annual performance reviews is minimized and energies are refocused toward employee improvements and success.

Learning Outcome
Outline the progressive discipline process.

Progressive Discipline

Managers have the formal authority and responsibility to discipline employees. The primary purpose of disciplinary action is to teach new skills and encourage appropriate behavior in the future. To ensure fairness, policy, regulations, and rules must be clearly communicated, a system of progressive discipline must be established, and an appeal process must be available. When staff fail to meet expected standards, the first-line manager will usually use a progressive sequence of disciplinary actions (Marquis & Huston, 2012). *Progressive discipline* is the process of administering increasingly severe warnings for repeated violations that can result in termination of employment (Sullivan, 2013). There are at least four steps in the sequence:

1. Oral (verbal) reprimand: Typically, the first step in the disciplinary process is an informal reprimand or verbal admonishment. During a meeting the manager and employee discuss the performance deficiency and ways to alter the employee's behavior to meet the standard (Marquis & Huston, 2012). The manager may place a notation in the employee's personnel file documenting the incident.
2. Written warning: A formal reprimand or written admonishment is the second step on the disciplinary process. If the same violation or behavior occurs again, the employee and the manager have a meeting. The violation or behavior is discussed and consequence of future repetition is presented in writing, along with the plan of action for the employee to follow to meet agency expectations (Marquis & Huston, 2012). Documentation of the written warning may be a memorandum or a standardized disciplinary form. Both the manager and employee sign the memorandum or disciplinary form to verify the meeting and the discussion. The employee may choose to respond in writing to the warning, after which both documents are filed in the employee's personnel file. After a definitive time period, outlined in the reprimand, the manager and employee meet again to review behavioral changes and the status of compliance with expectations.
3. Final written warning: A third step in the progressive discipline process is generally suspension from work without pay. As with the second step, a meeting is held, previous documentation of incidents along with the current infraction are reviewed, and comments are recorded and verified. The suspension is immediate yet may vary in length according to the nature of the incident—for example, excessive unexcused tardiness would result in a suspension of lesser length than threatening language toward a client.
4. Termination: Involuntary separation or dismissal is the last step in the progressive discipline process. An employee may choose to resign rather than experience termination. A termination meeting is similar to the disciplinary meetings except future improvement is not considered. The human resource department may provide procedures and documentation forms. The sequence of events during the meeting involves the following:

    a. The manager states the facts, providing concrete examples of the variance(s), and explicitly states termination as the outcome.
    b. The termination process and agency procedures are explained by the manager with each party signing agency forms.
    c. The employee is given the opportunity to explain behaviors at issue and respond to termination procedures.
    d. The manager closes with clarification of the agency's position regarding future references and assists the employee in departing immediately without undue embarrassment (Marquis & Huston, 2012; Sullivan, 2013).

Complete and accurate documentation throughout the progressive disciplinary process may allow the manager to encourage an employee to leave prior to dismissal. Also, documentation helps managers to adhere to agency disciplinary procedures.

Grievance Procedure

A grievance is any dispute or difference arising between an employee and management. Most health and human service organizations have a *grievance procedure*, which is a statement or a procedure to be followed when staff believe they have not been treated fairly by management. The grievance procedure may be used at any time, including during disciplinary proceedings, when employees believe they have not been fairly treated. As a due process procedure, complaints are put in writing. Once in writing, a sequence of procedures similar to the progressive discipline process is followed. An oral presentation to the first-line manager is followed by written submission to middle- and then top-level management. Both parties must show good faith in attempting to resolve a grievance. Negotiation, compromise, and collaboration as quickly as possible result in win-win resolution and clear, fair, two-way communication that promotes morale and productivity.

Retaining Staff

In addition to planning for staffing needs, attracting, and developing staff, successful health and human service organizations plan for staff retention. The health and human service agency must have a system in place to retain their human resources (Collins & Smith, 2006). High turnover rates reduce the productivity of the entire organization and replacing employees is expensive. Employees who perceive that their work is challenging, believe that their contributions are respected and valued, and feel that they are justly rewarded for their work tend to stay with an organization. *Compensation* is an important strategy for retaining employees. Compensation is "all the monetary rewards, both direct and indirect, provided to the employee" (Arnold, Glover, & Beeler, 2012, p.143). It includes salary or wages, other cash rewards, performance-based wages, and benefits. Compensation is important in both attracting and retaining staff (Carlson, Upton, & Seaman, 2006). There are three general compensation methods.

- Wages are paid on an hourly basis. The employee is paid an hourly rate for each hour worked.
- Salary is calculated weekly, monthly, or annually and does not take into account the number of hours worked. The employee is hired to complete the assigned responsibilities.
- Incentive pay is pay-for-performance. Incentive pay includes merit, the most productive workers get paid the most; piece rate, pay based on production; bonus, a specific reward for achievement of an objective or profit sharing in which employees get a part of the profits; and commission, pay based on sales. The purpose of an incentive pay system is to increase motivation.

Determining how much to pay each employee is a difficult decision. Some organizations use an external salary survey approach. The organization conducts salary surveys of other health and human service agencies with the same, or similar jobs, and establishes compensation based on the results of the salary survey. Another approach, an internal job evaluation, determines the worth of each job relative to other jobs in the same organization. Organizations typically group jobs into pay grades. The higher the worth or grade of the job, the higher the pay. Comparable worth is a third approach to determining pay. In comparable worth, jobs that are distinctly different but that require a similar level of ability, responsibility, skills, and working conditions are valued equally and paid equally (O'Neil, 2012). Typically these approaches are used in combination.

Benefits are a part of a compensation package that is neither direct wages nor salary. Legally required benefits in the United States include workers' compensation to cover job-related injuries, unemployment compensation, and Social Security for retirement. While benefits, in addition to those legally required, are optional, most health and human service agencies provide a benefit package to full-time professional employees. Common benefit packages include sick leave, paid holidays, vacation leave, health insurance, and retirement plans. The value, or costs of the benefits portion of the compensation package to employing agencies, has continued to increase in recent years even though reductions in specific employee benefits (e.g., health insurance) have declined. It is estimated that the average worker receives 30.8% of their compensation in benefits (U.S. Department of Labor, 2012).

Compensation and benefits are also an important consideration in the hiring process. Further discussion of compensation and benefits is presented earlier in this chapter in the section addressing the job offer.

Legal Environment

All organizations must conduct business in compliance with the law. This section of the chapter provides a brief overview of basic human resource equal opportunity employment law (see Table 9.11). Since 1935, numerous federal laws and court decisions have been implemented that affect employment practices. These laws are an attempt to correct unfair employment practices.

Employment law is complex and confusing. The laws change continuously, some laws are vague, and sometimes the laws are inconsistent (Arnold, Glover, & Beeler, 2012). Amendments to original legislation, court interpretations, and executive orders contribute to ambiguity and inconsistencies. The process for creating and enforcing the law is a three-phase process that also contributes to the complexity and confusion. First, laws are usually written in broad terms. Second, an agency under the executive branch of government is assigned the task of writing special regulations that put the new law into action. The agency assigned to this task may be a new agency created by the law or an already existing agency. Finally, the court assesses the constitutionality of laws and interprets the meaning of the law. The laws, regulations, and court decisions dictate human resource management in the health and human service agency. Noncompliance with laws exposes the agency and the manager to liability.

Equal Employment Opportunity

The goal of any health and human service organization is to achieve "equal employment opportunity". Simply stated, equal employment opportunity requires that all people are treated fairly and equally in employment decisions. The law protects against discrimination based on sexual orientation, age, disabilities, marital status, parental/pregnancy status, and military/veteran status. While the concept of equal employment seems simple, it is complex and can be very difficult to implement. Equal Employment Opportunity (EEO) is a broad concept. Equal Employment Opportunity Law is a series of laws and court decisions.

EEO law and successive court decisions have had three major impacts on selection procedures. First, organizations are more careful to use predictors and techniques that can be shown not to discriminate against protected classes. Second, organizations are reducing the use of tests, which may be difficult to defend if they screen out large number of minority applicants. Third, organizations are relying heavily on the interview process as a selection device (Sullivan, 2013, p. 212).

Canadian laws relating to human resource management practices are quite similar to those in the United States (see Table 9.12, p. 154). The Canadian Human Rights Act, a statute passed by the Parliament of Canada in 1977, provides federal legislation that prohibits discrimination on the basis of race, religion, age, marital status, sex, physical or mental disability, or national origin. This Act governs practices throughout the country. Canada's Human Resource Management environment, however, provides for decentralization of lawmaking to the provincial level.

U.S. Legislation

A number of laws impact the recruitment and selection process in health and human service organizations in the United States:

- The Equal Pay Act of 1963
- Title VII of the Civil Rights Act of 1964
- Age Discrimination Act of 1967
- Title I of the Americans with Disabilities Act of 1990 and amendments in 2009

Each of these laws is discussed briefly.

- The Equal Pay Act of 1963 (P.L. 88-38) prohibits pay discrimination on the basis of sex. The law protects men and women who perform substantially equal work in the same establishment from sex-based wage discrimination. This law and its amendments (1972 Equal Employment Opportunity Act, P.L. 92-261) cover entry-level employees or nonsupervisory staff as well as first-line managers. Differential compensation rates and employment conditions may exist if part of a seniority system or merit program, yet they must not be discriminatory. The law applies to private and government institutions.
- The Civil Rights Act, Title VII, of 1964 and its court interpretations prohibit discrimination in hiring, firing, wages, terms, conditions, and privileges of employment do not occur. The courts have determined that an applicant

Table 9.11 Major United States Federal Laws and Regulations Related to Human Resource Management

Year	Law or Regulation	Description of Provisions
1963	Equal Pay Act, as amended by Equal Opportunity Act of 1972	Prohibits pay differences based on sex for equal work. Requires employers to pay men and women similar wage rates for similar work in terms of their skill, effort, responsibility, and working conditions.
1964	Civil Rights Act, Title VII Amended 1972	Unlawful for employers to discriminate based on race, color, religion, national origin, or sex.
	Presidential Executive Orders	Prohibits private employers with federal contracts or subcontracts valued at $10,500 or more to discriminate based on:
1964	Executive Order 11141	Age
1965	Executive Order 11246	Race, color, religion, national origin
1967	Executive Order 11375	Sex
1969	Executive Order 11487	Political affiliation, marital status, and disability
1967	Age Discrimination in Employment Act Amended 1978	Prohibits discrimination in employment against individuals who are above the age of 40.
1973	Vocational Rehabilitation Act, Amended in 1974	Prohibits private employers with federal contracts or subcontracts valued over $2,500 from discriminating against qualified persons with disabilities.
1974	Privacy Act	Gives employees the legal right to examine letters of reference.
1978	Pregnancy Discrimination Act, Title VII	Prohibits employers from discriminating against women affected by pregnancy, childbirth, or related medical conditions, including abortion, and protects job security during maternity leaves.
1978	Mandatory Retirement Act	Prohibits the forced retirement of most employees before the age of 70; later amended to eliminate upper age limit.
1986	Immigration Reform and Control Act	Prohibits unlawful employment of aliens and unfair immigration-related employment practices.
1990	Americans with Disabilities Act	Prohibits employers from discriminating against and requires reasonable accommodation of essentially qualified persons with physical or mental disabilities or the chronically ill who can perform the "essential" job functions.
1991	Civil Rights Act	Reaffirms and strengthens prohibition of discrimination; permits individuals to sue for punitive damages in cases of intentional discrimination.
1993	Family and Medical Leave Act	Requires employers with 50 or more workers to allow eligible employees to take a total of 12 weeks leave during any 12-month period for one or more of the following: birth, adoption, or foster-care placement of a child; caring for a spouse, child, or parent with a serious health condition; serious health condition of the employee.

Source: U.S. Equal Employment Opportunity Commission (2013).

is to be judged based on ability. Prerequisites for a position are to be job-related (bona fide occupational qualifications). Bona fide occupational qualifications are specific qualifications that are reasonably necessary for normal operations of a business: for example, hiring a female to work in a correctional facility with female inmates. When employees are subjected to testing, it must be job-related (e.g., civil service tests administered by public agencies).

- The Age Discrimination in Employment Act of 1967 (P.L. 90-202), amended in 1978 (P.L.

Table 9.12 Summary of Canadian Employment Law

Year	Law or Regulation	Description of Provisions
1977	Human Rights Laws	Canadian Human Rights Act was passed with the express purpose of extending the law to ensure equal opportunity to individuals who may be victims of discriminatory practices based on sex, disability, or religion. It applies to federally regulated activities. Each of the provinces and territories has specific anti-discrimination laws that apply to activities that are not federally regulated.
1982	Canadian Charter of Rights and Freedoms	Prohibits employers from discrimination based on race, national or ethnic origin, color, religion, sex, age, or mental or physical disability. The law has had a major impact on the promotion and protection of human rights in Canada: · Reinforced the rights of official-language minorities. · Led to the recognition and enforcement of the rights of a number of minority and disadvantaged groups.
1986	Employment Equity Act	Organizations in Canada's federal jurisdiction are required to adopt Employment Equity Programs (EEPs) designed to increase the presence of four traditionally underrepresented groups: women, aboriginal peoples, disabled persons, and visible minorities. Applies to all employers and workers and protects workers and job seekers from unfair discrimination, and provides a framework for implementing affirmative action.
	Employment Standards	This area of employment law is governed by provincial legislation for all but a small minority of businesses that are covered by federal legislation. While the specific minimum employment standards vary by province, typically they include the following:
	Overtime	Employers are required to pay overtime for time worked over 40 or 44 hours in a week and over 8 hours in a day.
	Holidays	Most provinces recognize nine statutory holidays and require statutory holiday pay for employees who do not work the holiday. The laws also require premium rates of pay for those employees who work on holidays.
	Vacation	The majority of provinces have established 2 weeks as the basic minimum paid-vacation entitlement, and some provinces require 3 weeks for longer-serving employees.
	Leave	Most provinces require employers to provide bereavement leave and family emergency leave. This leave may be without pay. Compassionate care leave, maternity and parental leave are available. Birth mothers may be eligible for up to 52 weeks of leave.
	Minimum Termination Notice	Termination notice/pay formulas vary between provinces. The majority of provinces require approximately 1 week notification of individual termination for each year of service and up to a maximum of eight weeks' notice for longer-serving employees. Employers are generally free to implement "mass layoffs" without government regulation.
	Significant Severance Entitlements	Employers are required to provide non-union employees who are terminated without cause with "reasonable notice" of termination, or a severance payment in-lieu, unless there is a termination clause in an employment contract.
	Reasonable Notice Awards	Reasonable notice awards are set by the courts on a case-by-case basis and depend on several factors and comparison with precedents. Middle managers with 1 year of employment may receive an award of 4 to 6 months of severance. Employers can reduce and define their notice/severance obligations by implementing employment agreements with termination clauses, which the courts will enforce. Canadian employers can dramatically reduce their severance exposure by implementing employment agreements. "Bad faith" or "unduly insensitive" employer handling of termination is sanctioned by awards of additional severance. Some provinces offer "unjust dismissal" procedures that allow employees to challenge dismissals for cause, similar to a grievance.
	Labor Unions	Canadian unions are much more prevalent in the private sector. Unions represent approximately 20% of all Canadian employees.

Source: Federal Labour Standards (2013)

95-256), amended in the Lilly Ledbetter Fair Pay Act of 2009 (Pub. L. 111-2), makes it illegal to discriminate against persons 40 years of age or older in employment selection, retention, promotion, and compensation. Employers affected include both public and private agencies with 20 or more employees. The law prohibits mandatory retirement based on age.

The Americans with Disabilities Act (ADA) of 1990 (P.L. 101-336), which became effective in July 1992, addresses discriminatory practices against persons with disabilities. Title I of this act addresses employment criteria in public or private settings with 15 or more employees. Employers must make reasonable accommodations to provide access for a qualified person to a position. For example, this may include technology, physical access at the site of employment and special hearing and/or reading equipment to do the job. Also, on-site and off-site locations for training and development programs must be accessible. This law makes it illegal to discriminate against a qualified person with a disability in the private sector and in state and local governments. The act was amended (U.S. Department of Justice, 2012). The amendments have broadened the definition of a disability in several ways beneficial to employees. A number of disabilities that were not included in the original law were added. The amendments also expanded the definition of major life activities and eliminated the ameliorative effects of mitigating measures from considerations. Employers with 15 or more employees are required to make reasonable accommodations to the known disability of a qualified application if the accommodation will not impose undue hardship on the operation of the business.

Other U.S. laws and executive orders that affect recruitment, selection, and employment include the following:

- The National Labor Relations Act (Wagner Act) of 1935, the Labor Management Relations Act (Taft-Hartley Act) of 1947, Kennedy Executive Order 10988 of 1962, the 1974 amendments to the Wagner Act, and state right-to-work laws governing relationships among employers and employees who are union or nonunion members. The federal government is the arbiter of employer-employee relations through the creation of the National Labor Relations Board (NLRB) and provides for the right of workers to organize and bargain collectively with their employers.
- The Fair Labor Standards Act (FLSA), enacted by Congress in 1938 and amended numerous times, affects most private- and public-sector employment, including state, local, and federal government. It set a minimum hourly wage and established overtime pay requirements in relation to hours worked for certain employee categories. Executive, administrative, and professional employees are exempt from minimum wages and overtime pay requirements.
- Section 503 of the 1973 Rehabilitation Act (P.L. 93-112) requires affirmative action and prohibits employment discrimination by Federal government contractors and subcontractors with contracts of more than $10,000.
- Section 402 of the Vietnam Era Veterans' Readjustment Assistance Act of 1974 (P.L. 93-508) required contractors to take affirmative action to employ and advance disabled veterans and veterans of the Vietnam era.
- The Pregnancy Discrimination Act (P.L. 95-555) extended Title VII to include treatment of pregnant women; as a consequence, an employer who requires mandatory leave without regard to the employee's ability to work is in violation of the Civil Rights Act. A woman's job is protected during maternity leave.
- The Civil Rights Act of 1991 restored provisions (i.e., hiring, firing, or promotion) lost through Supreme Court decisions following the enactment of the 1964 law. Supervisors must be aware of hiring and promotion practices, known as the "glass ceiling effect" (e.g., artificial barriers) that adversely impact protected classes, seniority systems, and persons whose age might be considered an employment factor.
- The Family and Medical Leave Act of 1993 (P.L. 103-3) affects all public employers and private employers with 50 or more employees. When an employee has worked for an employer at least 12 months, the employer must provide eligible employees with up to 12 weeks of unpaid leave per 12 month period for childcare, care of an immediate family member, or an

employee's own serious health condition that precludes job performance.

- Executive Order 13145 (2000) prohibits federal departments and agencies from making employment decisions based on protected genetic information. Protected genetic information includes information about an individual's genetic tests, information about the genetic tests of an individual's family members, or information about the occurrence of a disease, medical condition, or disorder in family members of the individual.

Every first-line manager will be involved in staffing decisions, and as a result, the responsibility lies with the first-line manager to comply with the intent of laws, legislation, and executive orders. These regulations, along with professional standards, impact how the first-line manager and team of personnel specialists conduct the staffing processes and train and develop practitioners. Ultimately, retention of qualified productive staff is influenced by the manager's attention to practices outlined in human resource-related legislation and directives.

Summary

1. The first section of the chapter addressed the human resource planning process and the strategies used by first-line managers to identify and select candidates who are the best "fit" for the agency. Every first-line manager will be involved in staffing decisions. A therapeutic recreation manager, therefore, must be aware not only of the qualifications and performance expectations of therapeutic recreation specialists' positions but also of those standards and practices that have an impact on how recruiting and selection are conducted. Ultimately, first-line managers are responsible for selecting persons who are likely to perform successfully on the job.
2. The second section of the chapter introduced staff training and development programs and identified the roles and responsibilities of first-line managers in staff training and development. Successful health and human service agencies are learning organizations. They are forward-thinking and their culture is focused on innovation.
3. In today's environment of rapid and continuous change, ongoing investment in the training and development of employees and managers is essential. Today's workforce expects to have access to training and development to prepare them for their next work assignment and continued career advancement.
4. Planning for a staff training and development program is a five-step process. The training cycle includes needs assessment, setting objectives that identify training outcomes, planning and design of an appropriate training program, implementation of the training, and finally, evaluation of the outcomes achieved through the training.
5. Four types of staff training that are common to nearly all organizations include new employee orientation; scheduled renewal for continued certification; educational programs that are mandated by federal, state or local regulations, or professional standards; and finally, training for new technologies and best practices in service delivery and patient care. A variety of training methods are available to managers. E-learning is a fast-growing approach to training and development.
6. The third section of the chapter began by establishing that the performance appraisal is concerned with gathering information to determine if employees have achieved work expectations and performance goals. The most important purpose of the performance appraisal process is to improve performance in the future.
7. Various types of performance evaluation forms were presented. Strategies for planning and conducting performance evaluations and interviews were discussed. The manager's primary role is that of gathering information, giving feedback, and determining the support needed by each employee to perform as expected and to maximize his or her potential. The manager's challenge is to create a supportive environment

that focuses energy and resources on those areas of employee performance that contribute to quality, productivity, and ongoing service improvements.

8. The final section of the chapter provided a brief overview of equal opportunity employment law. Since 1935, numerous federal laws and court decisions have been implemented that affect employment practices in the United States. These laws are an attempt to correct unfair employment practices. Employment law is complex and confusing.
9. The goal of any health and human service organization is to achieve "equal employment opportunity". Simply stated, equal employment opportunity requires that all people are treated fairly and equally in employment decisions. While the concept of equal employment seems simple, it is complex and can be very difficult to implement.

Critical Thinking Activities

1. Conduct an Internet search to identify websites to recruit therapeutic recreation professionals. How do the competencies in the position announcements compare to the entry-level criteria of the CTRS credential as defined by NCTRC?
2. Conduct an Internet search on managerial coaching and mentoring. What roles are assumed by the manager? Identify corrective coaching and positive coaching examples.
3. Generate responses to the following statement: In the future, training and development in therapeutic recreation will likely focus on ______________ and will be delivered through ________________ media.
4. Conduct interviews with several first-line managers to learn about the recruitment process and the hiring process they experienced for their current position. What advice can the manager offer to you as a future professional regarding the recruitment and selection processes?

References

American Therapeutic Recreation Association (ATRA). (2013). Standards for the practice of therapeutic recreation and self-assessment guide. Hattiesburg, MS: Author.

Arnold, M., Glover, R., & Beeler, C. (2012). *Human resources management in recreation, sport, and leisure services*. State College, PA: Venture Publishing, Inc.

Canadian Therapeutic Recreation Association (CTRA). (2006). Standards of practice for recreation therapists & therapeutic recreation assistants. Calgary, Alberta, Canada: Author.

Carlson, D. S., Upton, N., & Seaman, S. (2006). The impact of human resources practices and compensation designed on performance: An analysis of family-owned SMEs. *Journal of Small Business Management, 44*, 531–543.

Collins, C. J. & Smith, K. G. (2006). Knowledge exchange and combination: The role of human resources practices in performance of high-technology firms. *Academy of Management Journal, 49*, 544–560.

Edginton, C., Hudson, S., Lankford, S., & Larsen, D. (2008). *Managing recreation and leisure services: An introduction*. Champaign, IL: Sagamore.

Federal Labour Standards. (2013). Retrieved from http://www.labor.ga.ca; http://www.hrsdc.gc.ca/eng/labour/employment_standards/federal/index.shtml.

Feuer, L. (2003). The management challenge: Making the most of your next performance appraisal. *Case Manager, 14*(5), 22–24.

Herringer, J. M. (2002). Once isn't enough when measuring staff competence. *Nursing Management, 33*(2), 22.

Hurd, A., Barcelona, R. J., & Meldrum, J. T. (2008). *Leisure services management*. Champaign, IL: Human Kinetics.

Judge, T. A., Higgins, C. A., & Cable, D. M. (2000). The employment interview: A review of recent research and recommendations for future research. *Human Resources Management Review. 10*(4), 383–406.

Kerr, K. M., & Nixon, W. B. (2008). Background screening myths. *Retail Merchandiser, 48*(4), 23–25.

Ketter, P. (2012). Strong investing in learning continues. Training Journal, 11/8/2012. Retrieved from http://www.astd.org/Publications/Magazines/TD/TD-Archive/2012/11/Editors-Note-Strong-Investment-in-Learning-Continues

Kim, S., & O'Connor, J. G. (2009). Assessing electronic recruitment implementation in state governments: Issues and challenges. *Public Personnel Management, 38*(1), 47–66.

Lussier, R. & Kimball, D. (2009). *Applied sport management skills.* Champaign, IL: Human Kinetics.

Macan, T. (2009). The employment interview: A review of current studies and direction for future research. *Human Resource Management Review, 19*, 203–218.

Marquis, B. L. & Huston, C. J. (2012). *Leadership roles and management functions in nursing: Theory and application* (7th ed.). Philadelphia: Lippincott Williams & Wilkins.

Mathis, R. & Jackson, J. (2008). *Human resources management* (12th ed.). Mason, OH: Thomson South-Western.

McConnell, C. R. (2002). The manager and continuing education. *Health Care Manager, 21*(2), 72–83.

Murphy, K., & Cleveland, J. (1995). *Understanding performance appraisal: Social, organizational, and goal-oriented perspectives.* Newbury Park, CA: Sage.

National Council for Therapeutic Recreation Certification (NCTRC). (2011). 2011 NCTRC Certification Standards: Part V—NCTRC National Job Analysis. New City, NY. Author.

National Council for Therapeutic Recreation Certification (NCTRC). (2012a). NCTRC Certification Standards: Part I—Information for New Applicants. New City, NY. Author.

National Council for Therapeutic Recreation Certification (NCTRC). (2012b). NCTRC Certification Standards: Part III—Recertification and Reentry. New City, NY. Author.

O'Neill, J. E. (2012). Comparable worth: The concise encyclopedia of economics, Retrieved from http://www.econlib.org.

Schneider, F., Gruman, J., & Coutts, L. (2012). *Applied social psychology* (2nd ed.). Los Angeles: Sage

Sims, R. R. (1993). Evaluating public sector training programs. *Public Personnel Management, 22*(4), 591–615.

Sullivan, E. (2013). *Effective leadership and management in nursing* (8th ed.). Boston: Pearson.

U.S. Bureau of Labor Statistics. (2012). Employer costs for employee compensation–December 2012. Retrieved from http://www.bls.gov/opub/ted/2013/ted_20130321.htm/

U.S. Department of Justice. (2012). Information and technical assistance on the Americans with Disabilities Act. Retrieved from http://www.ada.gov/2010_regs.htm

U.S. Equal Employment Opportunity Commission. (2000). Retrieved from http://www.eeoc.gov/policy/docs/guidance-genetic.html#I

U.S. Equal Employment Opportunity Commission. (2013). The law. Retrieved from http://www.eeoc.gov/eeoc/history/35th/thelaw/index.html

Chapter 10
Volunteer and Intern Management

Keywords

- Formative evaluation
- Interview
- Job descriptions
- Marketing plan
- Orientation
- Screening criteria
- Summative evaluation
- Supervision
- Training

Learning Outcomes

After reading this chapter, students will be able to:

1. Identify the steps in managing volunteers and interns.
2. Outline information found in volunteer and intern job descriptions.
3. Describe content found in contract/affiliation agreements.
4. Identify volunteer and intern screening criteria.
5. Give examples of interview questions managers and staff ask potential applicants.
6. Identify topics for department/agency orientation and specific volunteer/intern orientation.
7. Explain the manager's supervisory responsibilities during volunteer and intern management.
8. Summarize the information managers use to evaluate volunteer and intern experiences.
9. Describe trends and issues influencing volunteer and intern management.

**Special note: Throughout the chapter, the word "applicant" refers to both volunteers and interns. Where there might be differences between volunteer and intern management tasks, specific uniquenesses are stated; otherwise the information is similar for both volunteers and interns.*

Overview

Volunteers are a key component to the success of many health and human service organizations (Folk & Irons, 2011). In 2010 over 25% of the United States population donated more than eight billion hours of service to educational, religious, social service, and hospital settings (Corporation for National & Community Service, 2011). The latest available report from the Canadian Survey of Giving, Volunteering and Participating (CSGVP) (Statistics Canada, 2009) notes that 46% of the Canadian population over 15 years of age contributed the equivalent of 1.1 million full-time jobs in 2006 (p. 10). The spirit of volunteerism has become a basic tenet of our social fabric and a recognized means to increase an organization's capacity. Yet because professionals are operating on a shoestring and wearing multiple hats, volunteers may slide under the radar, exposing the organization to unwanted risks rather than enhancing the organization's services (Folk & Irons, 2011).

Although there is some variance in the frequency, format, and duration of clinical experiences among health and human service professions, one of the most significant experiences is the internship experience (Bloom, 2009; Hutchins, 2005/2006). "Therapeutic recreation educators consider the internship experience to be an essential component of their curricula" (Zabriskie & Ferguson, 2004, p. 33). One challenge faced by professionals is how to manage the experience to ensure placement sites offer planned transitions from knowledge acquisition to practice of essential entry-level skills (Smith, O'Dell, & Schaumleffel, 2002).

A common key to successful volunteer and intern programs is management of the relationships among stakeholders. Proper management ensures that volunteers enhance service outcomes and interns engage in deliberate rather than chance educational experiences. The process of managing volunteers and interns is similar to the manager's responsibilities with paid professionals (Bloom, 2009). This chapter addresses each phase of the management process as it relates to volunteers and interns. Chapter organization reflects the primary management steps of planning; selection and orientation; training and supervision; and evaluation, recognition and termination (refer to Table 10.1). A closing section addresses trends and issues influencing volunteer and intern management. The planning and implementation of volunteer and intern programs may be the sole responsibility of the therapeutic recreation manager or shared with those responsible for the agency-wide recruitment, placement, supervision, and evaluation of volunteers and interns. Regardless, the first-line manager is held accountable for the performance of all therapeutic recreation personnel including volunteers and interns. Therefore, information in this chapter is similar to the material covered in the previous chapter (9) on staffing professional positions.

"Students are placing a growing importance on obtaining meaningful internship experiences as a means of gaining a competitive edge for new jobs" (Beggs, Ross, & Knapp, 2006, p. 3). Today's rapidly changing and challenging world requires that higher education prepare students as problem-solvers capable of meeting complex demands (Bloom, 2009; Craig, 2011). Internships offer students opportunities to develop work-related social- and problem-solving skills while softening the transition from college to full-time employment. Organizations rely on volunteers to enhance staff services, improve the quality of life for clients, and extend agency resources. Interns and volunteers enter into exchange relationships with organizations—the department provides growth, challenges, and experience, while the volunteer and student give time, resources, and expertise. Each volunteer and intern comes to the agency to achieve specific goals. Managers plan volunteer and intern experiences to enhance services and client outcomes while ensuring volunteer and student goals are realized.

Table 10.1 Management of Agency Volunteers and Interns

Planning

1. Assess department mission and values.
2. Delineate benefits of volunteers and interns.
3. Identify regulations and standards affecting volunteers and interns.
4. Establish policies and protocols.
5. Design job descriptions and contracts/agreements.
6. Prepare staff, resources, and training processes.
7. Develop screening and selection procedures.
8. Prepare marketing plan and disseminate information on volunteer and intern opportunities.

Selection and orientation

1. Select candidates from applicant pool.
2. Interview candidates.
3. Place selected volunteers and interns.
4. Orient volunteers and interns to agency, department, and other professionals.
5. Identify training needs and expectations.
6. Review supervisory and evaluation processes and procedures.
7. Complete contracts and agreements.

Training and supervision

1. Prepare, organize, and conduct training experiences.
2. Oversee volunteer/intern/staff/client interactions.
3. Document supervisory interactions.

Evaluation, recognition, and termination

1. Complete formative evaluations.
2. Complete summative evaluations and terminations.
3. Recognize volunteers and interns.

Learning Outcome

Identify the steps in managing volunteers and interns.

Planning

Planning organizes the department to formalize relationships among volunteers, interns, and academic institutions; it also secures a pool of applicants from which volunteers and interns are selected. The manager undertakes a number of tasks (refer to Table 10.1). With the completion of these steps, policies, job descriptions, and training processes are in place; a marketing plan to recruit and retain volunteers and interns is prepared and implemented; procedures to screen and review applicants are online; and, the manager and staff are prepared to involve volunteers and interns in department operations.

Assessment

Assessment of the department's/agency's operating documents determines the roles of volunteers and interns and agency professionals. A clear mission helps the agency focus on ways volunteers and interns help the agency meet its goals (Roland & Stewart, 2008). Volunteers and interns who believe in the agency's mission become its best advocates and recruiters. Direct reference to volunteers and interns and the benefits of volunteers and interns are stated in goals and objectives found in operating documents, marketing materials, and training resources. Collectively, these statements present the intent of volunteer and intern programs and substantiate contributions of the agency to volunteerism and academic preparation.

From this assessment, the manager discerns the status of policy statements and procedures in operating protocols. A policy statement is written to include the importance of volunteers and interns to services and the accomplishment of specific department objectives. Also, benefits gained as someone volunteers or completes an internship are presented on websites and include gaining work-related skills, experiencing different points of view, improving clinical decision making, becoming aware of professional expectations, contributing to the social fabric of society, giving back to the community, developing effective interpersonal skills, and affirming or exploring career choices (Hutchins, 2005/2006; Pfahl, 2008).

Regulations and standards exist as a result of our concern for safety and risk, quality assurance, and protecting the credibility of our organizations and professionals. As part of the manager's assessment, review of existing laws and professional standards is undertaken to identify criteria and practices influencing the operation of volunteer and intern programs (Kozlowski, 2010; NCTRC, 2012; Pfahl, 2008; Pruitt, 2010). The manager considers legislation and laws like the Fair Labor Standards Act of 1938, the Health Insurance Portability and Accountability Act of 1996 (HIPAA), and the Federal Volunteer Protection Act of 1997 that outline expectations, ethical practices, and professional responsibilities. In Canada, the manager is aware of the screening implications found with legislation and statutes like the Canadian Charter of Rights and Freedoms, Canadian Human Rights Code, provincial human rights codes, Criminal Code, Privacy Act, and the Personal Information Protection and Electronic Documents Act (Volunteer Canada, 2012). Professional NCTRC criteria guide the manager as the internship is planned. Additionally, professional standards of practice suggest internships are to be highly structured, encompass existing credentialing criteria, and be part of the professional development responsibilities of recreation therapists (ATRA, 2013; CTRA, 2006; Grote & Hasl, 2003). Once familiar with these documents, the manager prepares policies and procedures to guide volunteer and intern management.

Policies and Procedures

Policies and procedures are written and published online and in operating documents like orientation and training resources; contracts and affiliation agreements; recruiting materials; supervisory and evaluation plans; and department risk, safety, and policy guidelines. Specific policies may cover legal and risk concerns and client and staff functions and interactions. For example, legal and risk documents identify specific volunteer/student roles on outings, when transporting, in emergencies, and when documenting or reporting client information. Protocols specify client-volunteer/student interactions. To illustrate, volunteers and interns may not be permitted to transfer clients without a qualified therapist present, or while in the community a volunteer or intern may not be permitted to refer to an agency by name if the reference would violate client confidentiality. Statements describe personal and professional expectations. Once general and specific policies and protocols are designed, the manager incorporates them into job descriptions, contracts, and affiliation agreements.

LEARNING OUTCOME

Outline information found in volunteer and intern job descriptions.

Job Descriptions

Managers design *job descriptions* for volunteers and interns like those prepared for professional staff (refer to Table 10.2, p. 162) (Folk & Irons, 2011; Roland & Stewart, 2008; Volunteer Canada, 2012).

Contracts and affiliation agreements detail the relationship between each volunteer/intern and the placement site. Thus, they may consist of two parts: one describing the volunteer or intern obligations and the other outlining the agency responsibilities (refer to Table 10.3, p. 162).

Sometimes groups of individuals desire to volunteer. In this situation a manager prepares a standard form to describe group responsibilities and this becomes the contract between the department and organization. For example, the letter details volunteer roles of the group for a one-time project, such as a special event on the pediatric unit or spring cleanup of the challenge course area.

The internship is a triadic relationship among students, agencies, and academic programs. These partners may enter into agreements to confirm each is able to satisfy

Table 10.2 Volunteer and Intern Job Description Information

- Position title, work sites
  - Purpose and responsibilities of position
  - Performance expectations (e.g., reference to professional credentialing expectations) and techniques to accomplish tasks
- Job requirements (e.g., duration or length, hours, days, orientation, training)
- Qualifications (e.g., job-related education, training, competence, credentials, experience, memberships, insurance, equipment, dress, medical tests, background checks, driving records, transportation, credit reports)
- Authority and supervision (e.g., limits to authority, relationships with staff, clients, other volunteers and interns, supervisor, evaluation, separation, termination, and recognition procedures)
- Miscellaneous information (e.g., in-kind benefits, unusual job-site demands, medical coverage, emergency protocols, disclaimers)
- Date of job description preparation, revision, and approval

Table 10.3 Contract/Affiliation Agreement Content

The volunteer/intern agrees to

1. become familiar and abide by department policies and procedures and professional expectations.
2. work a certain number of hours/weeks at a particular site in a particular position.
3. provide notice of nonattendance.
4. attend orientation and training and complete in-service trainings.
5. abide by laws and policies governing client interaction, risk, safety, and quality assurance.
6. accept supervisory actions and decisions (e.g., including termination) and function as a team member.

The department agrees to

1. provide training to permit volunteers/interns to work confidently and competently.
2. provide working conditions equal to paid staff.
3. conduct routine supervisory evaluations.
4. offer new assignments and/or more responsibility upon mutual agreement and with commensurate training.
5. include volunteers/interns in the APIE process and inform them of program policies and protocols.
6. adhere to the job tasks defined by the professional credentialing body.
7. provide benefits as appropriate (e.g., parking, proper identification tags, meals, access to medical library).

the other's expectations. For example, managers may wish to only accept students who have majors in therapeutic recreation and attend therapeutic recreation accredited programs. Academic institutions may desire placements with agencies where at least two CTRSs are employed and where the supervising CTRS has a certain amount of experience before taking student interns (Zabriskie & Ferguson, 2004).

Learning Outcome
Describe content found in contract/affiliation agreements.

Staff and Training Resources

The manager involves staff as volunteer and internship programs are planned to benefit from their expertise and to encourage their commitment. Training sessions devoted to volunteer and intern management prepare practitioners for transitions they will undergo as volunteers and interns assume increasing degrees of autonomy and responsibility. Training simulations and role-playing help staff (1) to visualize the significance of their roles, (2) to anticipate areas in which volunteers and students might require assistance, and (3) to gain familiarity with procedures and forms used during placements. Staff guidelines are placed with volunteer and internship documents.

Screening

The manager identifies screening and selection procedures that recognize information from regulations, policies, descriptions, and agreements. The manager identifies review processes that affirm the best match between the applicant's skills, priorities, and expectations and the department's goals and needs (Folk & Irons, 2011; Pfahl, 2008). Applications, résumés, academic records, credential verification, and background checks may be required; the manager specifies submission procedures on the agency website and through professional listservs and contacts. *Screening criteria* require applicants to submit information in several areas (refer to Table 10.4).

Internship managers may also base selection decisions on a first-come, first-served basis or may give preference to students from academic programs with pre-signed agreements. Selection may be based on the quality, timeliness, and presentation of materials. Agency-wide preset starting dates (e.g., June 1, September 1, and January 15) may be used to select students available at these rotation intervals.

After the screening criteria are determined, the manager develops a process to review applications and

Table 10.4 Volunteer and Intern Screening Criteria

- Employment and volunteer experiences with reference verifications
- Specialized training and skills in recreation therapy
- Specific coursework (e.g., clinical psychology, counseling processes)
- Reason or motive for seeking the opportunity, career goals, philosophy or value statements
- Previous experience in health care and human services with persons with illnesses or disabilities
- Source of information about the volunteer or intern opportunity
- Time parameters
- Self-assessment profile using the professional credentialing job tasks and knowledge areas
- Specific expectations of the academic program or the organization requiring the service

supportive information. This process is affected by a number of variables: size of the department, presence of an agency-wide volunteer or clinical coordinator, number of staff available to supervise, and the number of on-site placement sites (e.g., aquatic, outpatient, substance abuse). These variables also influence who is involved in actual selection. A formal rating system that collapses subjective information into quantitative terms may be used, and/or a decision to consider an applicant may be made by the manager with input from staff assigned to supervise the experience.

Learning Outcome
Identify volunteer and intern screening criteria.

Marketing Plan

The last planning step is to design a *marketing plan* to recruit and retain volunteers and interns. This includes identifying target volunteer and intern audiences, sharing information about the department's opportunities and benefits, and documenting inquiries and outcomes. Target audiences may include adults, students in recreation therapy and related health and social service professions, caregivers, youth, court-assigned volunteers, and former clients.

Adults of all ages with health-care backgrounds, and especially those between the ages of 55 and 74 who are transitioning out of full-time positions, are drawn to volunteering to shore up support during natural and man-made disasters and emergencies (Pruitt, 2010). Their knowledge, skills, and abilities are of benefit to clients and their communities. Adults gain a sense of belonging, recognition, companionship, and opportunities to remain a part of the social mainstream as they share their expertise.

Students in recreation therapy and related professions desire to receive evaluated work experience to meet degree requirements, to explore career possibilities, and to receive professional training to advance their careers and employment options. When a caregiver volunteers, focus may be on a member of his or her family or other persons with illnesses or disabilities served by the same agency (e.g., extended-care facility). Caregiver needs encompass an opportunity to advocate, to make system changes, to alleviate boredom, to compensate for losses, and to process grief.

Youth volunteers bring novelty, energy, unconditional positive regard, acceptance, and a desire to help to their experiences. Some desire to explore career options while others gain a sense of social responsibility desired by their parents or legal authorities. If volunteers are assigned by the courts, their primary objective may be to avoid institutional detainment, but authorities recognize the rehabilitative potential of volunteerism. Former clients have a vested interest and are influential recruiters (e.g., adult wheelchair athletes promote youth leagues). For this group, their needs stem from a desire to give back to those who have enhanced their well-being and to advocate for constituent group needs (e.g., accessibility). Studies (Miller, Schleien, Rider, Hall, Roche, & Worsley, 2002) document the benefits of inclusive volunteering for individuals with and without disabilities.

Person-to-person contacts and support from satisfied volunteers, interns, and faculty are the most effective recruiting tools. Volunteers and interns respond to familiar situations and those with known credibility. To illustrate, potential volunteers are more responsive to a call from the "hospital" coordinator of volunteer services than the less familiar department manager, while a potential intern is more likely to rely on past intern and alumni advice on preferred placement sites. First-line managers target student markets using the web, electronic media, and personal contact during professional meetings, advisory groups, guest presentations, and career fairs. Managers organize packets to send to academic institutions or place on the Internet that invite applicants and specify how to develop relationships between the department and academic program.

To document recruiting efforts, a spreadsheet is designed that identifies the media and contacts used with each target audience (see Table 10.5). Using a spread sheet allows the manager to record both the nature of each inquiry (e.g., Facebook, email, personal inquiry) and the source of information about the opportunity (e.g., personal referral, caregiver, and blog).

Selection and Orientation

During this phase, the manager selects from a pool of applicants those who satisfy the screening criteria. Interviews identify those qualified and perceived as the best fit to volunteer or complete their internships. Orientation introduces volunteers and interns to the working environment and to expectations. Actual placement may commence either during the orientation or at its conclusion. The orientation serves as a dress rehearsal to engage in the APIE process with clients and those on the department's team and to experience the protocols and "politics" in the unit. Literature supports the importance of orientation and training as key to being successful in starting any new position (Beggs, Ross, & Knapp, 2006; Volunteer Canada, 2012). The activities involved in selecting volunteers and interns and orienting them to the department/agency are outlined in Table 10.1, p. 160.

Selection and Interview

Selection of qualified volunteers and interns commences with a review of applicants who have satisfied the unit's screening criteria. This review verifies credential accuracy and affirms a potential match between the volunteer/intern's skills, priorities, and expectations and the department's goals and needs. During the selection process, managers may involve staff associated with placements. This enables staff and managers to consider the merits of placements from the programmatic and management perspective.

Credential reviews result in one of four actions:

1. referral to an appropriate manager or staff member for placement, or
2. referral to another volunteer or intern opportunity within the agency, or
3. recommendation to apply at later date after further training or credentials are acquired, or
4. non-selection because the applicant's skills and the department's needs are incompatible

An *interview* confirms if a match between the applicant and department is likely. With internships, managers may elect to screen prospective applicants, granting interviews to a few students. On-site interviews or alternatives like teleconferences, taped or written responses/e-mail to questions, and/or phone interviews may then follow.

Table 10.5 Marketing Plan to Recruit Volunteers and Interns

Target Audience	Benefit	Media/Contacts	Record*
Adults	Accessible health care, give back to community	RSVP, Internet, newspaper, personal contact	
Students	Work experience, career requirement	Digital media, career fairs, listservs	
Caregivers	Compensation, support	Open house, support groups	
Youth	Social responsibility, careers	Service club, Internet, high school counselor	
Court Assignment	Rehabilitation	Social workers, voluntary action center	
Former Client	Advocacy, give back	Personal contact	
Business	Corporate citizenship	Gift brochures, Chamber of Commerce, United Way	
Professional Organizations	Advocacy (February is TR month)	Annual conventions, listservs	

*Name/source of contact, type of media, and outcome of contact

Individual and/or group interviews are conducted by the manager and therapeutic recreation staff. Interviews help management and staff to determine if applicants and staff are compatible. During preliminary interviews, further screening clarifies a potential match (refer to Table 10.6).

A follow-up or on-site interview of those qualified through preliminary interviews identifies finalists and those selected. Through the interview, the manager and staff determine how the applicant's personal and professional competencies and character will enhance program and client outcomes. Therefore attributes of effective helpers like empathy, unconditional positive regard, personal boundaries, and any previous exposure to persons with disabilities are areas of investigation. Interview questions that might identify personal-professional beliefs and behaviors are key indicators of potential volunteer and intern success (refer to Table 10.7).

Managers and staff present situations or behavioral questions to determine how an applicant might respond to emergencies and to behaviors exhibited by various clients. This also helps the applicant to become aware of the types of behaviors and situations likely to be encountered (refer to Table 10.8).

Interviews are planned to allow time for the interviewee to ask questions and to observe programs. Managers may seek permission to check references, to conduct records checks, and to contact former supervisors and employers. Interviews determine the "goodness of fit." At the conclusion of the interview, the manager may elect to summarize factors that either confirm or negate a match, referral, training needs, and/or placement; and, or may indicate the time period needed to determine if the applicant will be invited to join the department team.

Acceptance letters may be accompanied by contracts or agreements that inform applicants of their placements/assignments, workdays and hours, length of commitment, client and program protocols, training, supervision, and recognition processes. Agency/department orientation materials may also be shared. Rejection letters present other options, suggest needed training, encourage application at a later date, recommend trial placements, and/or cite reasons for incompatibility. With acceptance, rejection, or referral, written notification is sent to the volunteer/intern and placed in the manager's permanent records.

Table 10.6 Preliminary Interview Content

- Program goals and client descriptors
- Agency and department mission, structure
- Volunteer/intern positions, roles, and responsibilities
- Relationships and communication among management, staff, volunteers, students, and academics
- Commitment length
- Ethics and practice protocols
- Training and supervisory requirements
- Placement, evaluation, recognition, and separation procedures

Table 10.7 Volunteer/Intern Interview Questions

- What do you anticipate will be the outcomes of this experience?
- How have you become aware of this opportunity?
- What do you perceive to be the benefit of therapeutic recreation with our clients?
- What do you believe to be essential qualities of effective helpers?
- Describe your previous roles and interactions with health-care and human-service systems and clients.
- What do you need from us to help you do your job?
- What three characteristics do you value most in people with whom you work?
- Why did you choose your major or your particular career?
- What are your personal career goals?
- Interpret your assets and liabilities as related to the particular volunteer or intern job.

Table 10.8 Volunteer/Intern Behavioral Questions

- What would you do if you and members of our staff were intervening when a client became resistive or combative?
- How would you respond if a client becomes disoriented and confused?
- How would you react to a client who uses inappropriate language to describe your character?

Learning Outcome

Give examples of interview questions managers and staff ask potential applicants.

Placement and Orientation

The goal of *orientation* is to acquaint volunteers and interns with agency/department mission, resources, and personnel and to ensure basic awareness and compliance with policies. Supervision, work schedules, assignments, evaluations, responsibilities, and expectations are clarified. Placement may occur prior to, during, or following orientation to the department/agency.

Managers use websites and manuals to familiarize trainees with the agency and department. Orientation to the agency and unit may precede orientation to specific work responsibilities (refer to Table 10.9).

Managers introduce volunteers and interns to specific work assignments and job responsibilities and support staff as they become comfortable with their supervisory responsibilities. Orientation to work assignments may occur within the particular unit and at work stations (refer to Table 10.10).

Learning Outcome

Identify topics for department/agency orientation and specific volunteer/intern orientation.

Table 10.9 Agency and Unit Orientation Topics

- Mission, vision, values, goals, and organization of department
- Roles and responsibilities of management, staff, volunteers, and interns in the department
- Financial, marketing, safety, and security protocols
- Personnel policies relating to insurance, liability, clients' rights, parking, reimbursement, emergency, quality, safety, infection controls, disaster plan, health codes, ethical conduct, dress code, personal time recording, illness, holidays
- Personal-professional "boundaries" and performance criteria
  - Professional credentials and standards
  - Digital documents and forms
  - Visits/Observations with peer colleagues and related professionals
- Location of agency-wide service units and resources
- Client programs and services, documentation, standards

Table 10.10 Work Assignment Orientation Topics

- Department staff introductions, including their roles; chain of command and communication protocols among professionals, clients, caregivers (e.g., specifically what can and cannot be stated)
- Identification of supervisory procedures, evaluation documents, promotion, separation or termination practices
- Location of professional-personal work space, what to do when reporting to work, visible identification badges
- Review of job description, recordkeeping procedures, how to perform tasks, and location of people and resources
- Client and caregiver information, intervention protocols
- Managing client/staff emergencies and unexpected work absences
- Review accreditations and regulations and professional standards of practice
- Learning outcomes and assignments
- Required in-services and available professional training options

Training, Supervision/Evaluation, Contracts

Managers expose volunteers and students to the full range of department services and assignments to acquaint them with the day-to-day expectations and potential outcomes of their experiences. Simultaneously, for interns, the academic supervisor and student review agency assignments (e.g., assessment, documentation, treatment planning) and credentialing expectations (e.g., NCTRC job analysis) to align tasks with the intern's anticipated goals. Volunteers may spend time observing other volunteers and staff to become familiar with each volunteer opportunity. Specific training needs and outcomes beneficial to the department, volunteer, and intern are identified following this review of services and required tasks.

A schedule of training and learning assignments outlines competencies to be acquired and expectations. For interns these are often organized in weekly increments (see Table 10.11). With volunteers, the responsibilities are defined in their job descriptions or assignments (see Table 10.12, p. 168). Both are required over time to gradually transition from dependence to autonomy in the performance of TR roles with increasing effectiveness (Bloom, 2009). Training opportunities are arranged at convenient times to ensure that volunteers and interns gain competencies expected to perform their tasks and satisfy the outcomes identified by the department's goals.

Managers, volunteers, interns, and academic partners review criteria and forms to be used during supervisory contacts and performance reviews. Supervision and use of these documents is influenced by a number of variables. Staff assignments determine whether or not the manager devotes time to volunteer and student supervision or the manager assigns staff to supervise. If the manager is the only department staff person, formal reviews at scheduled times might be supplemented by casual observations of volunteers and interns during routine service provision. Size and location of the service influences how frequently managers and staff are able to complete casual observations and make informal contacts; to illustrate, with outreach or community-based services that cover extended geographic areas, fewer contacts are likely as compared to the number of interactions possible when services are located in one facility/area.

As the manager reviews performance criteria with volunteers and interns, they establish a mutually beneficial communication process. Success of intern and volunteer

Table 10.11 Weekly Assignment Checklist

Weeks 1–2: Orientation/Observation/Policies and Procedures	Date Completed
☐ Attend new employee orientation	
☐ Complete all necessary paperwork	
☐ Review employee handbook	
☐ Tour facility	
☐ Review Agency's Mission/Vision Statement, Policies and Procedures and Plan of Operation	
Weeks 3–6: Presentation Skills/Disability Awareness/Program Planning	
☐ Review screening and assessment procedures	
☐ Review procedures for documentation of treatment plan, evaluation, re-evaluation, and discharge planning	
☐ Shadow agency's therapeutic recreation staff and observe treatment/programs, assessments, and evaluations	
☐ Study agency's approved list of abbreviations and documentation protocols	
☐ Demonstrate and practice procedures for escorting, transporting, and transferring patient/client	
Weeks 7–10: Assessment/Program Leadership	
☐ Maintain caseload of five patients/clients	
☐ Colead two to three group sessions per day	
☐ Complete midterm evaluation	
☐ Report reevaluation information at staffing	
☐ Submit all assignments on time	
Weeks 11–14: Program Planning	
☐ Lead all group sessions	
☐ Develop and implement one new program	
☐ Observe multidisciplinary staff treatments	
☐ Complete Special Project	
☐ Complete five assessments with appropriate interventions	
Weeks 15–16: Completion/Evaluation/Termination	
☐ Complete and present Special Project	
☐ Accomplish closure with patients/clients and staff	
☐ Complete final evaluation with site supervisor	
☐ Turn in all required projects, papers, evaluations	
☐ Turn in all agency issued supplies, equipment	

management is somewhat dependent on how effective the manager is in motivating, interpreting, and clarifying. Managers have the arduous task of helping volunteers and students assimilate the impact of the "self" on therapeutic outcomes and connecting knowledge of TR to real-time applications. Each must feel comfortable in approaching the other, giving and receiving constructive criticism, resolving interpersonal and professional conflicts, and respecting the other's competence and professional integrity.

Throughout the orientation process, managers, volunteers, students, and academic supervisors work together to clarify and delineate tasks and learning experiences. Once finalized, they are organized in an agreement or contract and kept in permanent personnel records. This document contains goals and objectives, dates, learning activities, and performance expectations. By establishing open lines of communication and outlining outcomes during the orientation process and in agreements, the manager reduces any differences in

Table 10.12 Volunteer Assignment

Job Title: Therapeutic Recreation Program Assistant—Aquatic, Adult, Youth and Wheelchair Sports.

Goals: To assist Therapeutic Recreation Staff in a variety of youth and adult programs for persons with disabilities.

Duties: Assist Staff in planning and implementing activities, demonstrating specific skills, and supervision of program participants.

Qualifications: Must be age 16 or older and have documented experience with individuals with disabilities.

Training Required: Specific training mandatory prior to programs:
- One hour of orientation to TR programs.
- Onsite orientation by unit staff.
- Forty (40) hours of training offered for summer programs.

Time Commitment:
- Afternoon and evening hours, primarily M–F and occasional weekends.
- Summer programs, 4-week sessions.
- Duration of 8–12 weeks during fall and winter/spring.

Benefit/Value:
- Career experience
- Experience with individuals with disabilities
- Safety training
- Community service

expectations that may exist, which helps to create a more satisfying experience for the student and agency (Beggs et al., 2006).

When orientations are completed, qualified volunteers and interns have had opportunities to develop "teamwork" behaviors with the manager and staff, and they are aware of others' roles. They have experienced a sampling of tasks and placements. Specific responsibilities are assigned. Communication avenues are clear, and dates for assignments and performance assessments are defined. Documentation ensures that everyone is aware of their respective tasks and expectations and how the outcomes of volunteering and the internship assist the manager in reaching the department's goals.

Training and Supervision

Training and supervision are intended to: (1) develop job-related skills; (2) expand practice knowledge; (3) facilitate partnerships among staff, volunteers, and interns; and, (4) provide opportunities leading to career advancements. Training and supervision ensure responsibilities of volunteers and interns are not left to chance (Pfahl, 2008; Roland & Stewart, 2008). Further training and supervision are important elements in risk and safety management and are known to foster retention and recruitment (Folk & Irons, 2011; Volunteer Canada, 2012).

Training

Training begins with orientation and continues throughout the trainee's commitment to ensure staff, volunteers, and interns remain updated and competently perform assigned duties. Training also permits the volunteer/intern to share expertise brought to the placement. Motivation and commitment are linked to learning about the organization, the job, and oneself (Serafino, 2001). Managers prepare and organize in-services and resources like manuals, webinars, reading files (libraries), and case studies using volunteer and intern job descriptions and the department's goals to focus training and supervisory activities.

In addition to written and digital material, a manager organizes staff and resource people, including caregivers, to present in-services on topics such as communicating with a recently traumatized patient or lifestyle monitoring in cardiac rehabilitation or providing knowledge about inclusive practices in the community. In-services are scheduled to coincide with natural program breaks and client routines. Volunteer- and intern-led in-services bring new ideas and resources to department staff. Visits to other departments and interviews with colleagues in the agency and community create awareness of professional expectations, issues, and the roles and contributions our profession makes to health and human services. Through satellite or telecommunications, managers bring educational and professional development activities offered by professional associations into the department.

Supervision

Ongoing support of volunteers/interns is a crucial element of management, whether the experience is a short-term or long-term commitment (Serafino, 2001; Volunteer Canada, 2012). Important to this support is *supervision* and communication on performance. When successful, supervision enables volunteers/interns to perform skillfully with enthusiasm and motivation. Volunteer retention, in particular, diminishes with inadequate supervision and limited personal contact. Managers guide volunteers/interns, create good working climates, encourage interest, and maximize effectiveness through communication and support that helps volunteers/interns transfer and apply how they use their knowledge and skills to benefit clients. The manager may take time away from required duties to help volunteers/interns acquire acceptable levels of competence—this requires the manager to balance pushing for achievement with backing off until the skills are perfected (Bloom, 2009).

Feedback is immediate, ongoing, positive, corrective, and supportive (Bloom, 2009). Routine one-on-one conferences are supplemented with e-mail, phone contact, observation, informal discussion, and brief, written thank-yous. With interns a dedicated time period to discuss and review the preceding week's events helps track progress and alerts the manager to the intern's perception of how well knowledge is being applied to practice. The manager also communicates with the intern's academic supervisor as the student is supervised. Constructive criticism promotes understanding (e.g., identifying a subtle client cue such as a change in body temperature that signals a need for professional staff attention). Feedback focuses on how to apply or perform rather than why perform in a certain manner—hands-on-experience with explanation is more effective than verbal instruction (Bloom, 2009).

Managers help interns process their daily experiences. They direct students to subtle cues and clinical manifestations that corroborate clinical decisions. Internship supervision may involve: (1) reviewing academic assignments and agency projects to provide informal feedback; (2) using periodic formal evaluations like the midterm and final reviews to present written critiques; (3) reviewing interns' actual documentation on services as they cosign reports; and, (4) retaining personnel files on each intern in which they document performances similar to those kept with personnel performance plans. The information accumulated from these sources helps the manager to judge intern progress and take corrective actions. For instance, managers may require additional training, recommend alternative placements, or encourage adjustment in time spent in the department or on assigned tasks.

Volunteers may outgrow their assignments, develop new interests, feel unneeded, feel burnout, experience change in their time commitments, develop improper attitudes, and/or become dissatisfied. Managers note behaviors to determine if volunteers have reached plateaus and would benefit from promotion or reassignment (Sarfit & Merrill, 2002). For example, a promotion occurs when a volunteer assists with another client or in another program area, and/or leads while staff provide support. Such an experience might lead to retention as the volunteer perceives his or her talents are better utilized.

Managers oversee volunteer/intern/staff/client interactions. Staff members vary in their training and supervisory experience. As a consequence, managers encourage communication and the proper balance between authority and delegation of responsibility. With staff, managers instill respect for volunteer/intern roles so that these individuals are not taken for granted. Managers help staff guide volunteers/interns to ensure they do not overstep boundaries by assuming professional roles for which they are not qualified.

Supervisory documentation records volunteer and intern performance. Information is used in planning, budgeting, quality improvement, risk management, promotion, termination, and recognition. Data on the number of volunteer/intern hours and equivalent dollar value of volunteer/intern hours to the agency/department are kept. Volunteer/intern responses in incident and accident reports are used in risk management. During routine supervisory sessions, the manager notes volunteer/intern compliance with job assignments while recording skill-development needs or quality of performance during informal observations. These performance reviews may result in promotion, termination, or recognition. Supervisory data are also used to evaluate volunteer/intern program operation, recognize staff contributions, and prepare references or recommendations.

Learning Outcome

Explain the manager's supervisory responsibilities during volunteer and intern management.

Evaluation, Termination, and Recognition

As managers formally and informally guide volunteers/interns during supervisory interactions, the evaluation process begins. Formative evaluations occur during the volunteer and internship experience, while summative evaluations take place at the conclusion or termination of each experience. The nature (e.g., direct service vs. supportive assignments) and length of the volunteer position (e.g., one time vs. extended time period) and academic requirements influence evaluation protocols. Managers may either prepare their own forms and/or use standardized forms prepared by the human resource department or academic institution. The manager uses information from several sources to add objectivity to decisions. This triangulated evaluation approach has each partner assessing the performance and outcomes of each of the other partners (e.g., volunteer/student, manager/staff, academic supervisor, and client). Evaluation outcomes guide the manager's recognition and separation decisions and volunteers and interns in their careers and professional development. Further, evaluation and research are considered best practices and essential to evidence-based practice (ATRA, 2013; CTRA, 2006).

Formative Evaluation

Formative evaluation is done as volunteers complete their assigned tasks. Analysis of formative data leads to immediate adjustments, such as the following:

- additional in-services on ethics in the workplace or a recreation therapist's contributions to client health and well-being
- reassignment to another unit or a different client
- referral to supportive or administrative services
- recommendation of a promotion to another job

Several types of information on volunteers are helpful to justify manager and staff time and to document quality of program enhancement through volunteerism. These measures include length of service, turnover rate, total amounts of individual and group volunteer time, number of volunteers with demographic variables, dollar-value equivalents of hours contributed, costs per client or per program, expenditure per volunteer, and staff time per volunteer. Use of qualitative data collection techniques, such as focus groups or individual in-depth interviews, help the manager understand the meaning of the experience to the volunteers and provide managers with ideas on ways to motivate and retain volunteers. Volunteers often "see things with new eyes," bringing refreshing perspectives to the unit.

During formative supervisory meetings with interns, the manager reviews reports, monitors performance, and submits comments to the academic supervisor. Assessment considers how well the student performs as a team member and is able to apply knowledge to practice. The intern's ability to work with other staff and to follow operating practices is monitored. When skill deficits are noted, the manager incorporates strategies immediately to ensure that the student exhibits tasks required by the credentialing job analysis.

Formative evaluation tools are intern reports, midterm written evaluations, and contacts between the manager and academic supervisor. If the internship is planned around a sequence of increasingly more difficult and autonomous responsibilities, evaluation focuses on the student's competence and willingness to assume these tasks and obligations and perform effectively. Managers document performance adequacy and recommend training needs. If there is impairment in the intern's performance other than what can be corrected by training, the manager, intern, and academic supervisor agree on appropriate alternatives, which could include reassignment or immediate withdrawal from the placement.

Summative Evaluation and Termination

Summative data allows the manager to make decisions to improve future services. *Summative evaluations* occur at or near the completion of one's volunteer or intern placement. With summative information, the manager may revise the training program by adding to the orientation and training schedule (e.g., more hands-on experiences with clients), modifying the supervisory process (e.g., additional manager-trainee contacts), or altering contracts to better clarify responsibilities. Managers may discontinue or terminate trainees for contract violations and unmet job expectations. Noncompliance with client protocols, staff directives, ethical and professional standards, and operational policies result in dismissal. This action is appropriate regardless of the length of the intended commitment (e.g., after an outing or one event a volunteer/intern is released if his or her actions placed the client in an at-risk position). The manager follows department/agency protocols properly documenting actions that validate managerial decisions.

Fundamental concerns the manager asks about the volunteer program include:

- Did the volunteer's support improve client services, program offerings, or department capacity?
- Did the volunteer's skills successfully support staff functions and create an effective team?
- Did the volunteer maintain a professional presence and have a positive experience?

To document increased agency capacity resulting from the use of volunteers, cost-effectiveness figures are kept by the manager. Figures kept show output per dollar spent on each volunteer and are similar to productivity measures. Managers use statistics to show costs per volunteer, per client, per program, and per volunteer service hour. The intent of presenting this information in annual and monthly reports is to show the value of added service that contributes to reduced health-care costs and increased client and staff effectiveness. Managers use 2,080 hours, or one worker year, and the salary ranges of equivalent professional positions to generate dollar-value amounts contributed through volunteer service hours. Financial reports are shared with current supporters and prospective external funding sources to promote the department and to solicit future resources. The figures presented at the beginning of the chapter by the Corporation for National and Community Service and Volunteer Canada represent the type of information shared with administrators and boards to explain the advantage of using volunteers to enhance department capacity. Summative data also reports benefits to clients, caregivers, professionals, and volunteers. The manager uses these outcomes to retain and recruit prospective volunteers and interns.

Triangulation occurs as the manager, student, and academic supervisor complete summative internship evaluations. Managers complete forms that critique the student's personal and professional competence, academic preparedness and supervision of the student, and interactions with the academic supervisor. Students assess the adequacy of their preparation and the department/agency to support the internship and their interactions and compatibility with the professional and academic supervisors. Academic supervisors consider adequacy of the manager's supervision and the department's support; compatibility of the intern experience with academic preparation; and, the student's ability to synthesize theory and practice.

At the completion of an internship, the student has had the opportunity to demonstrate entry-level practice skills, as outlined in SOP documents and the credentialing body NCTRC. Standards of these organizations are used to measure the intern's potential to perform successfully as an entry-level practitioner. The NCTRC National Job Analysis (January, 2011) verifies the experience has incorporated all of the entry-level areas described by the CTRS credential. A standardized, professionally developed tool like the Therapeutic Recreation Intern Evaluation (Cincinnati-Dayton Area Recreation Therapy Association, 1997) is useful for both midterm and final evaluations and contains categories compatible with existing credentialing and professional standards. Further, Zabriskie and Ferguson (2004) report their study respondents prefer a standardized tool that evaluates all aspects of academic/personal/professional experiences and transitions.

Comparison of midterm with final ratings reveals whether corrective action and training have resulted in progress and behavior change. Summative evaluation considers changes and growth in the intern's personal functioning. The internship is the first opportunity to ascertain how well personal attributes, values, and attitudes intertwine with professional roles. Managers observe these qualities by considering, for example, how well the student responded to supervision and multiple tasks and supervisors, the intern's comfort level with clients of diverse backgrounds, how the intern responded to unexpected client behaviors, and, the mannerisms or behaviors displayed that contributed to team engagement.

The internship is also the first opportunity to apply theory to practice. Application of theories and values to practice is fostered when the manager discusses how personal beliefs and behaviors impact professional performance. If the student has a portfolio, this is an ideal time to update documentation of experiential components with digital media of programs delivered or interventions practiced. This documentation "assists the student in projecting to employers the value of" the internship (Anderson, Schroeder, & Anderson, 2001, p. 110).

Evaluations help the academic and department supervisor prepare for future interns. Managers aware of intern's perceptions about department acceptance, degree of assistance, quality of learning opportunities, and accomplishment of internship goals are able to make adjustments before the next interns arrive. More importantly, if the intern reports feelings of token acceptance or difficulty in approaching personnel or accessing resources, managers and staff consider how to remove these barriers. The internship experience may be the first opportunity to compare personal management styles. An internship devoid of conflict would be unusual. The manager's task is to help the intern learn to disagree without resentment. The manager and academic supervisor each have expectations. Issues arise when they are not compatible or vary in their level of expectancy. Managers and academic supervisors help the intern gauge the degree of autonomy achieved during an internship and their readiness to undertake future professional challenges.

Learning Outcome
Summarize the information managers use to evaluate volunteer and intern experiences.

Recognition

Recognition energizes the work environment by supporting and motivating staff, volunteers, and interns. Because volunteers/interns value peer recognition and acknowledgment of their competence, a thank-you, handshake, e-mail, or sticky note can heighten motivation. Informal meetings and supervisory sessions among volunteers/interns, staff, and management facilitate recognition and feedback. The opportunity to perform a more complicated task independently rewards quality and motivates retention.

With volunteer programs, managers use documented work hours, projects completed, funds raised, number of newly recruited volunteers, innovative programming ideas, and suggestions resulting in time-saving service improvements as achievement indicators to reward staff and volunteers. The recipient must perceive the chosen form of recognition as valuable. For example, a senior citizen who works on the pediatric unit would enjoy a luncheon, while a service club might appreciate recognition through a digital media outlet. The nature of the contribution being recognized influences the nature of the tangible reward. Thus, if documented service hours are the chosen criterion, the value of the reward increases as the hours escalate (e.g., pins are given for 500 hours; plaques are presented for 1,000 hours).

Managers recognize staff for their support of volunteers and interns. Staff train and supervise volunteers and interns. Managers incorporate recognition of such contributions into job performance standards, documentation of supervisory experiences, released time for special training on supervision, letters of commendation in personnel files, and public acknowledgment before agency administrators, volunteers/interns, clients, and caregivers. Informal acknowledgment occurs through e-mail and personal notes. Joint staff and volunteer/intern social and appreciation events serve to recognize the value of contributions while building social connections desired by today's volunteers and interns.

Trends and Issues

A number of trends are affecting the way managers engage volunteers and interns. Volunteers are making shorter rather than longer-term commitments, desire meaningful placements, and enjoy group and virtual volunteering (Volunteer Canada, 2012). Likewise, today's intern is questioning the need to "go the extra mile" to fulfill their agency supervisor's perception of being an intern, especially without pay (Beggs et al., 2006). Volunteerism and internships are aspects of service learning that have evidenced tremendous growth as avenues to extend the boundaries of traditional educational practice (Craig, 2011). With health care focusing on quality control, accountability, cost containment, prevention, and community intervention, managers are challenged to expand their services while devoting time to properly train and supervise staff, volunteers, and interns.

A number of issues arise from these economic, demographic, and health-care trends. Youth under age 18 seek out volunteer opportunities as alternatives to inaccessible paying positions and as service learning projects. Identification of placements appropriate to the youth and clients may be a challenge. For example, youth unaware of secondary outcomes of a disability like head injuries or strokes become uncomfortable with inappropriate client behaviors or statements, yet they are bored if assigned supportive tasks. However, using a young person with a disability as a volunteer facilitates peer education that enhances community service delivery (Phoenix, Miller, & Schleien, 2002).

Quality control and cost containment evident in the health-care industry, along with social inclusion, necessitate intensive training and higher levels of volunteer and intern competence. Staff train volunteers/interns as advocates, companions, and aides. This is time-consuming, because the process is ongoing and individualized to each client's needs. Managers, therefore, institute staff-development programs to train entry-level staff as trainers so they "coach" volunteers and interns to monitor individual client progress. The importance of devoting time to training is complicated, because staff have a reduced amount of client contact time to carry out the APIE process. Also the reduction in length of time volunteers bring to agencies causes the manager to ask: "How much time to devote to training at the expense of client contact time?"

The use of clients as volunteers presents several issues. Clients perceive that through volunteering they may secure a permanent position yet may not have the physical or emotional tolerance to work full-time. Problems arise when former clients perceive that they are capable of helping recently traumatized patients when they are still adapting to their own changed lifestyles.

Managers and staff balance their workloads with the time available to devote to particular volunteer groups and interns. In particular, if interns are questioning the need to assume duties that might extend their 40-hour work week, supervisors question how much of their workload should be compromised to provide constructive criticism that may or may not result in the student applying knowledge to practice (Bloom, 2009). Likewise, when managers are wearing multiple hats and working with limited resources, volunteers are appreciated yet may be forgotten in terms of potential risks that might be minimized with time devoted to training and supervision (Folk & Irons, 2011).

Learning Outcome
Describe trends and issues influencing volunteer and intern management.

Supervision has become more complicated due to the increasing number of standards, regulations, laws, and work demands. As the volunteer or intern experience comes to a natural conclusion, the manager helps staff return to their routine workload expectations while volunteers and interns are guided to maintain client and department confidentiality. Terminating a volunteer/intern and holding staff accountable for volunteer/intern-client interactions require time and attention to employment regulations, ethics, and standards of practice. Volunteer/intern management is becoming increasingly professional (Kerka, 1998) and at times can be challenging (Bloom, 2009). Therefore managers need to ensure that the supervisors are kept abreast of new supervision strategies, regulations, best practices, and the changing needs and expectations of volunteers and student interns.

Summary

1. Volunteering and internship experiences are crucial to enhancing department capacity and the capacity of individuals to contribute to their communities and profession.
2. Volunteer-management tasks are organized into four major steps: planning; selection and orientation; training and supervision; and evaluation, recognition, and termination.
3. A major portion of the manager's time occurs during initial planning tasks as the paperwork and staff are prepared to manage volunteers and interns. Technology helps the manager present department needs to interested volunteers and interns.
4. During the selection process, the manager matches the talents and skills of volunteers with the needs of clients and department outcomes.
5. By the end of the orientation phase, managers place volunteers and interns to best use their expertise and support staff in achieving client objectives and department productivity measures.
6. During training and supervision, volunteers and interns grow in their capacity to function independently as managers oversee staff, volunteer/intern, and client interactions.
7. Through supervision, managers affirm volunteer and intern progress in applying the APIE process effectively and within the boundaries of their roles and staff expectations.

8. Evaluation documents compliance with contractual expectations and contributions to department capacity and outcomes.
9. Managers recognize and terminate volunteers and interns as well as crediting staff support of trainees.
10. Standardized forms confirm entry-level competence of interns and volunteer cost-effectiveness and civic engagement.
11. Managers use evaluation information to promote their programs, while volunteers and interns rely on this information to advance their careers and/or reaffirm their expertise and commitment to particular advocacy roles.
12. The continuing pace of change, concern for quality and accountability, demographic interests, and finite resources create issues in volunteer and intern management.
13. Managers wear multiple "hats" as they attempt to create purposeful engagements through volunteer and intern management beneficial to department clientele and trainees.

Critical Thinking Activities

1. Conduct an Internet search to locate volunteer training and education resources. Resources may be found at sites like:

   - CADIP Canada—Volunteer Programs in Canada and Abroad—http://www.cadip.org/volunteer-in-canada.htm
   - Corporation for National and Community Service—http://www.cns.gov
   - National Retiree Volunteer Coalition—http://www.nrvc.org
   - Association for Research on Nonprofit Organizations and Voluntary Action—http://www.arnova.org
   - National Civic League—http://www.ncl.org
   - Independent Sector—http://www.independentsector.org
   - Volunteer Canada—The National Voice of Volunteerism in Canada—http://volunteer.ca
   - Volunteers Correctional Services Canada—http://www.csc-scc.gc.ca/text/benevols/index-eng.shtml

2. Conduct an Internet search of possible intern sites to discover requirements, forms used, and agency expectations. In particular, review the following sites:

   - Fox Valley Special Recreation Association—http://fvsra.org/
   - Genesis Health Care, Davenport, Iowa—http://www.genesishcc.com/
   - Cunningham Children's Home, Urbana, IL—http://www.cunninghamhome.org

   These three sites represent three types of internship opportunities: community, clinical, and residential. Another site with multiple listings is http://www.recreationtherapy.com/, which lists job opportunities as well. Professional organizations like ATRA, http://www.atra-online.com, and CTRA, http://canadian-tr.org, are also points of referral to internship opportunities.

3. Review the standards of practice of ATRA (http://www.atra-online.com/displaycommon.cfm?an=1&subarticlenbr=42), the NCTRC Job Analysis (http://www.nctrc.org/standardsandpublications.htm), and the CTRA standards of practice, (http://canadian-tr.org/File/View/320c6149-f0e3-4ba7-b3fc-06c50439d999), to identify entry-level competencies to incorporate into an internship experience.

References

American Therapeutic Recreation Association (ATRA). (2000). Standards for the practice of therapeutic recreation and self-assessment guide. Alexandria, VA: Author.

Anderson, L. S., Schroeder, T., & Anderson, D. A. (2001). The use of portfolio advising with recreation and leisure services majors. *Schole: A Journal of Leisure Studies and Recreation Education, 16*, 107–123. Ashburn, VA: National Recreation and Park Association.

Beggs, B. A., Ross, C. M., & Knapp, J. S. (2006). Internships in leisure services: An analysis of student and practitioner perceptions and expectations. *Schole: A Journal of Leisure Studies and Recreation*

Education, 21, 1–19. Asburn, VA: National Recreation and Park Association.

Bloom, C. W. (2009). Perspective: Facilitating the transition from student to professional through internship. In N. J. Stumbo (Ed.), *Professional issues in therapeutic recreation on competence and outcomes* (2nd ed., pp. 389–399). Champaign, IL: Sagamore.

Canadian Therapeutic Recreation Association (CTRA). (2006). Standards of practice for recreation therapists & therapeutic recreation assistants. Calgary, Alberta: Author.

Cincinnati-Dayton Area Recreation Therapy Association. (1997). *Therapeutic recreation intern evaluation (TRIE)*. Hattiesburg, MS: American Therapeutic Recreation Association.

Corporation for National & Community Service. (2011). *U.S. profile—volunteering in America*. Retrieved from http://www.volunteeringinamerica.gov/

Craig, P. J. (2011). The impact of service-learning on college students in allied health professions. *Annual in Therapeutic Recreation, 19*, 84–104. Hattiesburg, MS: American Therapeutic Recreation Association.

Folk, T., & Irons, M. (2011). Volunteers: A great asset until they cost you. *Healthcare Risk Management, 33*(2), 18–20.

Grote, K., & Hasl, M. (2003). *Guidelines for internships in therapeutic recreation* (2nd ed.). Hattiesburg, MS. American Therapeutic Recreation Association.

Hutchins, D. A. (2005/2006). Competencies required for effective clinical supervision during the therapeutic recreation internship. *Annual in Therapeutic Recreation, 14*, 114–130. Alexandria, VA: American Therapeutic Recreation Association.

Kerka, S. (1998). *Volunteer management trends and issues alert.* Columbus, OH: ERIC clearinghouse on adult, career, and vocational education. (ERIC Document Reproduction Service No. ED414430).

Kozlowski, J. C. (2010). Unpaid student interns under the Fair Labor Standards Act. *Parks & Recreation, 45*(5), 27–32.

Miller, K., Schleien, S., Rider, C., Hall, C., Roche, M., & Worsley, J. (2002). Inclusive volunteering: Benefits to participants and community. *Therapeutic Recreation Journal, 36*(3), 247–259.

National Council for Therapeutic Recreation Certification (NCTRC). (2011, January). *Certification standards part V: NCTRC National Job Analysis.* Retrieved from http://www.nctrc.org/documents/5JobAnalysis.pdf

National Council for Therapeutic Recreation Certification (NCTRC). (2012, January). *Certification standards part 1: Introduction for new applicants.* Retrieved from http://www.nctrc.org/documents/1NewAp.pdf

Pfahl, D. M. (2008). Voluntary appreciation, *Parks & Recreation, 43*(1), 58–61.

Phoenix, T., Miller, K., & Schleien, S. (2002). Better to give than to receive. *Parks & Recreation, 37*(10), 26–33.

Pruitt, B. (2010). Volunteerism and legal considerations. *Journal of Legal Nurse Consulting, 21*(4), 16–19.

Roland, C., & Stewart, W. (2008). Research update: Vying for volunteers. *Parks & Recreation, 43*(10), 28–29.

Sarfit, R. D., & Merrill, M. (2002). Management implications of contemporary trends in volunteerism in the U.S. and Canada. *Journal of Volunteer Administration, 20*(2), 12–23.

Serafino, A. (2001). Linking motivation and commitment through learning activities in the volunteer sector. *Journal of Volunteer Administration, 19*(4), 15–20.

Smith, D. A., O'Dell, I., & Schaumleffel, N. A. (2002). Building a learning community for fieldwork students: A case study example. *Schole: A Journal of Leisure Studies and Recreation Education, 17*, 21–36. Asburn, VA: National Recreation and Park Association.

Statistics Canada. (2009). *Caring Canadians involved Canadians.* Ottawa, Ontario, Canada: Department of Ministry. Retrieved from http://www.givingandvolunteering.ca/files/giving/en/csgvp_highlights_2007.pdf

Volunteer Canada. (2012). *The Canadian code for volunteer involvement, values, guiding principles and standards of practice.* Ottawa, Ontario, Canada: Author. Retrieved from http://www.volunteer.ca/content/canadian-code-volunteer-involvement-2012-edition

Zabriskie, R. B., & Ferguson, D. D. (2004). A national study of therapeutic recreation field work and internships. *Annual in Therapeutic Recreation, 13*, 24–37). Alexandria, VA: American Therapeutic Recreation Association.

Chapter 11
Communicating Effectively in the Workplace

Keywords

- Active listening
- Collaboration
- Communication
- Delegation
- Feedback
- Filtering
- Formal communication
- Informal communication
- Meetings
- Negotiation
- Semantics

Learning Outcomes

After reading this chapter, students will be able to:

1. Explain formal and informal communication modes.
2. Identify the role of technology in workplace communication.
3. Summarize workplace variables influencing communication.
4. Describe principles of effective feedback and active listening.
5. Outline the variables affecting organizational communication.
6. Identify managerial strategies that improve organizational communication.
7. Explain the manager's communication tasks during meetings, delegation, negotiation, collaboration, and with criticism, complaints, and confrontation.
8. Describe the advocacy role of the manager during professional communication.

Overview

"Everything a manager does involves communicating" (Robbins, Decenzo, & Coulter, 2011, p. 320). Communication impacts all management activities and is the core of the helping relationship (Marquis & Huston, 2009). "Most managerial time is spent speaking and listening . . . one must have excellent interpersonal communication skills" (Marquis & Huston, 2009, p. 441). Organizational communication is more complex than interpersonal communication since there are more communication modes, individuals, and information to transmit. The intent of the chapter is to review fundamentals of interpersonal communication then explore communication from the perspective of the manager within the organization and the profession.

The first section of the chapter explores interpersonal communication skills, the impact of technology and variables impacting communication, and principles of effective communication. Managerial/organizational communication is the focus of the second section. A number of factors influence the manager's communication within the organization. In this section, the manager's tasks and skills related to meetings, delegation, negotiation, collaboration, criticism, complaints, and confrontation are also considered. The closing section describes the significant role of the manager as a professional communicator and suggests strategies for effective professional communication.

Communication is critical to effective management. Because managers get things done through others, competencies in communication are prerequisites to managerial effectiveness. "Management functions in communication ensure productivity . . . through appropriate sharing of information" (Marquis & Huston, 2009, p. 461). " The best idea . . . or the finest plan cannot take form without communication" (Robbins, Decenzo, & Coulter, 2011, p. 320).

Interpersonal Communication in the Workplace

Communication is the process of transferring thoughts and meaning from one person to another. To have communication, a purpose or message is needed that passes between the sender and the receiver. The message is encoded or converted to symbolic form and passed through a channel to the receiver, who then retranslates or decodes the message of the sender (Robbins, Decenzo, & Coulter, 2011). A concluding step in the communication process is feedback, as the sender checks to see if the message is transferred accurately by the receiver (Tomey, 2009). This communication process begins the minute two or more people become aware of each other's presence (Marquis & Huston, 2009) and occurs within the context of each participant's emotional state and background (internal climate) and the climate in the workplace or organization where the message is shared (external climate). Thus, for example, the manager's and staff members' values and stress levels (internal climate) influence the flow of communication, as does the manager-subordinate relationship in the employing agency (external climate) (Marquis & Huston, 2009).

Prior to sending a message, the manager must determine the message's purpose and how best to deliver the message. Additionally, Guffey (2004) suggested there are five factors a manager needs to consider prior to delivering a message: "the importance of the message, the amount and speed of feedback required, the necessity of a permanent record, the cost of the channel, and the degree of formality desired" (pp. 32–33). After determining the purpose of a message and reviewing these five factors, the manager selects the most appropriate mode. Table 11.1 outlines different modes and their appropriate use. Which mode to use depends on the importance or delicate nature of the message (Sullivan & Decker, 2009).More intimate modes like face-to-face or telephone are used with difficult issues or conflict, while less sensitive information is shared by voice mail or e-mail (Sullivan & Decker, 2009). With the appropriate mode selected, the manager then composes the message.

Managers and therapists use formal and informal modes of communication to share their messages. In *formal communication* each party is aware of the modes

Table 11.1 Choosing Communication Modes

Mode	Appropriate Use
Face-to-face	When you want to be persuasive, deliver bad news, or share a personal message.
Telephone call	When you need to deliver or gather information quickly, when nonverbal cues are unimportant, and when you cannot meet in person.
Voice mail message	When you wish to leave important or routine information that the receiver can respond to when convenient.
Fax	When your message must cross time zones or international boundaries, when a written record is significant, or when speed is important.
E-mail	When you need feedback but not immediately. Insecurity makes it problematic for personal, emotional, or private messages. Effective for communicating with a large, dispersed audience.
Face-to-face group meeting	When group decisions and consensus are important. Inefficient for merely distributing information.
Video or teleconference	When group consensus and interaction are important but members are geographically dispersed.
Memo	When you want a written record to explain policies clearly, discuss procedures, or collect information within an organization.
Letter	When you need a written record of correspondence with customers, the government, suppliers, or others outside an organization.
Report or proposal	When you are delivering considerable data internally or externally.
Source: Guffey, 2004	

used, whereas in *informal communication* one or the other party is unaware of the modes being used or that a message even exists. This latter form of communication is referred to as the grapevine, the political context, or the unofficial way that communication takes place in an organization.

Formal Communication Modes

The primary communication modes used by the manager are oral and written communication (Marquis & Huston, 2009). Yet any time managers are seen, nonverbal communication occurs, and because nonverbal communication reveals the emotional element of the message, "it is generally considered more reliable than verbal communication" (Marquis & Huston, 2009, p. 450).

Verbal Communication

Verbal communication is perceived as a quick way to transmit information and as a way to build trust and support. The spoken word conveys a personal caring. Day-to-day managerial interactions rely heavily on the spoken word. Emotions are expressed orally. Tone; word choice; use of silence, accents, and intonation; speed of delivery; clarity; and articulation are verbal exchange factors.

Word meanings vary with the setting in which they are used. For example, boardroom and hallway conversations have different connotations. Content is also affected by the positions held by the receiver and sender. Familiarity with each other, the setting, and content information influence how well messages are understood. Modes used to transmit and receive information influence the meaning and understanding of messages. Talking on the phone or via teleconference is distant and not necessarily as revealing as face-to-face exchanges. Listening in a crowded hallway versus a private office introduces different distortions. Moreover, one's ability to listen and attend is influenced by communication modes. Listening to a message transmitted by phone demands less attention than listening during face-to-face interactions.

Nonverbal Communication

Nonverbal communication accompanies oral communication and is present in body language, posture, space, eye contact, appearance, the environment, timing, and vocal expression (Marquis & Huston, 2009; Robbins, Decenzo, & Coulter, 2011). Interaction is initiated through nonverbal avenues, such as eye contact or gestures, then continued through oral exchanges. Phone conversations are dependent on oral exchanges; however, silence and intonation convey unspoken thoughts. Talking at an intimate distance (18 inches or less) is less formal, usually, than discussion at public distances (12 or more feet). Folded arms and legs crossed away from the speaker suggest non-receptivity, whereas open posture toward the speaker implies acceptance. Likewise, eye contact and hand gestures connote degrees of attending and active listening. A soft-spoken voice creates a different meaning from a loud voice. Because oral communication carries a nonverbal message, the greatest impact on the meaning and understanding of transactions comes from nonverbal communication—how something is said is as significant as what is said.

Appearance

Appearance is another nonverbal communication form. Unwritten and written rules govern professional attire. Written rules specify colors for specific therapies or days when staff shirts are to be worn, location and type of professional identification, and appropriateness of accessories or apparel regarding safety issues or organizational protocols. For example, if practitioners were to wear sandals or jewelry, client interactions might be affected, and if the manager were to wear casual rather than formal attire on board meeting day, the impression left might be less than the desired professional image. Impressions are created by attire and personal identification—the impact of a briefcase, business card, and lapel name pin. These impressions reflect feelings or beliefs about the unit and therapeutic recreation as a profession. Social norms and work culture determine dress protocols and standards. To illustrate, if Fridays are viewed as "casual attire" days, how are clients and staff distinguished during Friday night socials? Therapists promoted to managers consider the unwritten dress codes that influence how other professionals respond to the authority of the new position. As a result, "meeting room" rather than "functional activity" attire is more frequently worn.

Written Communication

Many types of written communication are used in organizations including memos, letters, e-mails, job descriptions, performance reviews, periodicals, or any device that transmits written words or symbols. Written documentation can be as simple as a memo and as sophisticated as an annual report. The message may be as personal or informal as "enjoy your birthday off" or as formal as the action plan following a performance review. Writing commits thoughts and feelings to record; a "hard copy" trail is created that later can become "permanent binding statements" to which a manager is legally committed. Although writing tends to reduce ambiguities, the reader may have a different understanding of the written material from the writer. An e-mail message and a message through social media are examples of communication in which what is not written may be as significant to the message as what is written. Understanding written communication is affected by factors such as the type and quality of handwriting or printed word, word choice, composition level and complexity, volume, organization, and presentation of the material. Any "written communication issued by the manager reflects greatly on both the manager and the organization . . . the manager must be able to write clearly and professionally and to use understandable language" (Marquis & Huston, 2009, p. 450).

Informal Communication Mode

Informal communication occurs through informal networks or the grapevine by word of mouth and through electronic means (Robbins, Decenzo, & Coulter, 2011). This communication is usually rapid, haphazard, prone to distortion, and the sender usually has little accountability for the accuracy of the message (Marquis & Huston, 2009; Sullivan & Decker, 2009). Rumors and gossip begin for a number of reasons: words have different meanings or are interpreted differently, time lapses occur between senders and receivers, mediums are distorted, messages are incomplete, and anxiety creates ambiguity. Less time is available on a daily basis to communicate increasing amounts of information and as a result, we use e-mail and social media to communicate our thoughts and emotions.

We each react differently to informal networks and grapevines, and these personal reactions affect how we respond personally and professionally to messages circulated in this manner. The grapevine does, however, act as a feedback loop to help judge accuracy and appropriateness of messages. To illustrate, if rumors or gossip report staffing cuts and realignments, the manager can clarify why and who will be affected and when the changes will occur.

Learning Outcome

Explain formal and informal communication modes.

Technology's Impact on Workplace Communication

Technologies such as email, social media, teleconferences, wireless communication, and telehealth are increasing communication and information access and efficiency within the organization and to distant geographical sites. Information technology has improved the manager's ability to supervise individual and team performance, employees are able to have more complete information to make faster decisions, and managers and employees have more opportunities to collaborate and share information (Robbins, Decenzo, & Coulter, 2011).Additionally, everyone in the organization, regardless of their location, is accessible 24 hours a day, 7 days a week.

As a communication tool, the manager may share one message simultaneously with a number of individuals. With the World Wide Web, the manager accesses the latest research and best-practice information so evidence-based practices are available to support quality services. Introduction of electronic health records (EHR) facilitates integrative interventions by streamlining workflow and access to client records. Technology helps the manager and staff balance the constraints placed on organizational resources as it enables quicker access and improved sharing of knowledge within the "busy" workday (Marquis & Huston, 2009).

Learning Outcome

Identify the role of technology in workplace communication.

Workplace Variables Impacting Communication

A number of variables in the workplace impact effective organizational communication. These interferences can originate with the sender, receiver, methods of communication, and the message itself. These range from physical, emotional, and semantic differences to variations in roles, gender, generations, culture, and the organizational culture. Technology, while enhancing communication opportunities and the access to information, also contributes to information overload—a factor that may cause communication challenges. Several variables that affect organizational communication are summarized.

Physical

Physical barriers may be internal, such as a speech or hearing difficulty, or external, such as a noisy or busy environment or physical separation of the manager and employees. In organizations with a large number of employees, the manager is challenged to communicate personally with each employee.

Emotional

Fear and anxiety are examples of internal barriers, while social values and judgments represent external barriers. Openness and honesty are compromised by extreme emotions, such as frustration and anger or excitement and happiness. Time, place, and people in the environment influence our emotional responses and how messages are received and sent.

Assumptions, attitudes, past experiences, expectations, educational and philosophical orientations, and family and caregiver values influence how one interprets and responds. Thus, senders and receivers view a situation from their unique perspective. To illustrate, consider the differing viewpoints held by the public and those in health and human services toward disabilities that are visually apparent and those that are "hidden" (e.g., amputation and hearing impairment).

Semantics

There is a tendency to believe that the words and terms used to send messages have the same meaning for the receiver. *Semantics* refers to the meaning of words. For a person with English as a second language, the literal interpretation of a word or phrase like "the child has a bug in their belly" would not mean the child had an upset stomach but rather a bug was in the child's stomach.

Role

We engage in behaviors that typify our roles (e.g., child, mother, father, employee, manager). Roles have certain expectations—for example, mothers nurture, children respect parents, employees and the manager are loyal to the organization. These role expectations create differentials and a frame of reference from which communication is interpreted. Those in professional roles use technical terms or jargon—for example "APIE process," a term not necessarily understood by other professionals. At any given time, one assumes multiple roles that may interfere with another. For instance, the manager who is supervising an intern may discover their maternal or paternal obligations prevent observation of the intern's best-practice research project required by the academic institution.

Gender

Gender is a significant factor in organizational communication, since men and women communicate and use language differently (Marquis & Huston, 2009; Sullivan & Decker, 2009). Men tend to be more direct and succinct, while women tend to be tactful and elaborative; men also tend to speak from the context of their roles while women use a personal style focusing on equality (Tomey, 2009). Men see the world as black and white while women see the world as gray (Marquis & Huston, 2009). Men managers tend to be more aggressive and competitive while women managers tend to be more supportive and nurturing (Marquis & Huston, 2009; Sullivan & Decker, 2009). Using gender-neutral communication (i.e., men don't yell and women don't cry) helps close the gap between gender differences (Sullivan & Decker, 2009).

Generational

Within organizations, the presence of four generations of staff is likely—Traditionals, Baby Boomers, Generation Xers, and Millennials. Communication styles vary. Traditionals tend to be more formal, Baby Boomers question more, Generation Xers want decisions without discussion, and Millennials or Generation Yers desire feedback to their messages (Sullivan & Decker, 2009).

Culture

As our world "becomes smaller" our organizations become a microcosm of diverse cultures. Each culture's attitudes, beliefs, behaviors, and values affect communication; body language, word usage, gestures, tone, and spatial orientation are culturally defined (Sullivan & Decker, 2009). To illustrate, in some cultures eye-contact and saying no are disrespectful while in others eye-contact indicates trustworthiness (Tomey, 2009). A managerial competency is understanding cultural heritage and learning to interpret cultural messages of staff and clients (Sullivan & Decker, 2009).

Organizational Culture

As discussed in Chapter 4, organizational culture drives the organization shaping people's behaviors as they interact with one another. Organizational culture is the sum total of symbols, language, philosophies, traditions, rites and rituals, and unspoken gestures that overtly reflect the organization's norms and values. The modes of communication used in the organization reflect the culture, as does who has access and who shares information. *Filtering* or the manipulation of information so the receiver views it more favorably is a function of organizational culture. The use of email as a communication mode reduces filtering as the information is more directed without intermediaries. Likewise, the more collaborative and team-oriented the unit, the less information filtering is present (Robbins, Decenzo, & Coulter, 2011).

Information Overload

Individuals have a finite capacity for processing information. When information exceeds our processing capacity, the result is information overload (Robbins, Decenzo, & Coulter, 2011). When managers have more information than can be sorted or used, the tendency is to ignore, pass over, or forget. In some instances, managers quit processing until the overload dissipates. The demand of keeping up with e-mail, faxes, phone calls, text messages, and social media contributes to information overload and results in the loss of information and less effective communication.

Table 11.2 Effective Communication Principles

1. Consider your relationship with the message receiver.
2. Consider the setting and timing of your message.
3. Identify the purpose of the communication and the receiver's goals and build trust.
4. Use direct and exact language.
5. Acknowledge the contributions of others.
6. Use active listening skills, listening for information (content) and emotions (feelings).
7. Clarify the message by asking for or observing verbal and nonverbal feedback.
8. Since actions speak louder than words, the message is best received when the sender acts congruously with the verbal intent of the message.
9. Conclude when both the sender's and receiver's messages are understood.

LEARNING OUTCOME

Summarize workplace variables influencing communication.

Principles of Effective Communication

As noted, communication challenges arise within the workplace influencing employee productivity and organizational effectiveness. "Communication skills can be learned" (Sullivan & Decker, 2009, p. 131). Thus, there are several ways managers and employees may overcome the variables impacting their interpersonal and professional communication. Table 11.2 summarizes ways to become more effective communicators (Robbins, Decenzo, & Coulter, 2011; Sullivan & Decker, 2009; Whitehead, Weiss, & Tappen, 2010).

Effective communication results when the sender and receiver interpret the intended meaning of the message similarly and respond accordingly. Although some communication variables, such as semantics and gender, are less pliable, techniques like feedback and active listening are improved with practice. Qualities such as genuineness, empathy, caring, humor, congruence, respect, and trust enhance communication processes. Effective helpers and communicators display compatibility between what is known, how it is expressed, and the actions taken. They are true to their own feelings

Table 11.3 Effective Feedback Techniques

- Ask questions about the message to see if it was received and understood.
- Ask the receiver to restate the question.
- General comments can give a manager a sense of the receiver's reaction.
- Feedback takes many forms; use of nonverbal messages like an e-mail may suggest the initial message is being clarified.
  - Give both positive and negative feedback as most people want to do their work well.
  - Give specific feedback as soon as possible so issues are resolved rather than escalate.
  - Give negative feedback in private to avoid embarrassment and focus on behavior that the receiver can control.
  - Base feedback on observable behavior (i.e., keep feedback impersonal).
  - Objective feedback is goal-oriented and based on job expectations and outcomes of behavior rather than subjective feelings.
  - When suggestions or solutions are offered, feedback helps us become aware of our problem or inappropriate behavior.

and accept the feelings of others; thus, information is shared openly. Respect and a mutual commitment are evident, and the significance, uniqueness, and contributions of each are affirmed.

LEARNING OUTCOME
Describe principles of effective feedback.

Feedback

Misunderstandings occur without feedback. Feedback is a way of giving help. Without feedback, one is unaware of how one's communication, verbal or nonverbal, affects others or how one's behavior appears to others. Feedback is confirming or correcting. With either, one may choose or not choose to change or improve oneself. Several techniques improve the effectiveness of feedback (refer to Table 11.3) (Robbins, Decenzo, & Coulter 2011; Whitehead, Weiss, & Tappen, 2010).

LEARNING OUTCOME
Describe principles of effective active listening.

Active Listening

Active listeners receive and understand the whole message without making premature judgments or interpretations. Several factors cause people not to be active listeners. These include judging or speculating on the speaker's motive, planning responses while the other is speaking, interrupting the speaker with information that finishes the thought, and sensory overload. Physical health or a medical condition may also discourage active listening.

The active listener understands the communication from the speaker's point of view. To understand the full meaning and the speaker's attitude and feelings requires concentration and is enhanced by developing empathy or putting yourself in the shoes of the speaker (Robbins, Decenzo, & Coulter, 2011). Concentration permits the active listener to place each new piece of information into the context of preceding information. Empathetic listeners step into the shoes of the speaker suspending personal thoughts and feelings. Active listeners withhold judgment on the content until the speaker finishes. The manager who uses active-listening skills enhances interpersonal and professional communication (refer to Table 11.4) (Robbins, Decenzo, & Coulter, 2011).

Communication is necessary and fundamental to functioning in the workplace (Tomey, 2009). More managers are fired due to poor interpersonal communication skills than poor technical skills (Robbins, Decenzo, & Coulter, 2011). In today's relationship-oriented work setting, interpersonal skills are essential to empower others to do their best work and to support them when problems inevitably arise (Sullivan & Decker, 2009). The skills highlighted in this section can be acquired. Effective helpers and managers exhibit active-listening skills and ensure that feedback affirms the whole meaning of messages. Communication is effective when information is accurate and understood by all in the workplace.

The Manager and Organizational Communication

The typical workday of a first-line therapeutic recreation manager consists of numerous meetings, informal interactions, one-on-one supervisory conversations, personal contacts with clients and caregivers, and colleague contact via phone, fax, the web, e-mail, and social media. Instead of following a detailed schedule, supervisors find they spend the day reacting to people and situations. The manager spends the majority of time on a particular workday communicating (Marquis & Huston, 2009).

Organizational communication patterns have become more complex in health and human services. Factors like professional specialization, decentralization of services, use of teams, corporate mergers, and downsizing of organizations that has left managers with increasing spans of control present challenges to the transmission of messages in a timely manner to appropriate personnel. Additional communication barriers

Table 11.4 Active Listening Skills

1. Make eye contact.
2. Use affirmative nods while avoiding distracting gestures.
3. Silent pauses encourage speakers to continue.
4. Asking questions, summarizing, or paraphrasing clarify meanings.
5. Listening rather than speaking allows the manager to concentrate on what is said rather than what is going to be said in return.

result from hectic, noisy, distracting work environments. As a result, achieving the organizational goals is challenging (Marquis & Huston, 2009). The manager achieves organizational goals through formal and informal meetings and by empowering the staff through delegation, negotiation, and collaboration. Also, the manager models for staff responses to criticism, complaints, and confrontation that result from daily interactions with colleagues, clients, and caregivers.

Learning Outcome
Outline the variables affecting organizational communication.

Variables Affecting Organizational Communication

A number of factors associated with groups of people working together day-to-day in a structured environment influence organizational communication. Several of the specific influences are presented in Table 11.5.

Learning Outcome
Identify managerial strategies that improve organizational communication.

Organizational Communication Strategies

The first-line manager is central to communication that flows upward to organizational administrators from direct services and downward from organizational administrators to direct service personnel. Consequently, the manager takes several actions to ensure that organizational networks link unit staff with managerial staff. Initially the manager assesses organizational communication to identify modes of communication, timeliness of communiqués, the formal and informal communication patterns, and concerns about communication (Marquis & Huston, 2009). Following this assessment the manager is aware of both the formal and informal networks of communication and to whom to say what to ensure accuracy and understanding. The manager uses additional strategies to improve organizational communication (refer to Table 11.6).

Table 11.5 Organizational Communication Variables

- *Semantics.* Jargon or technical terms used by recreation therapy, like "APIE," may be unfamiliar to upper-level administrators or colleagues from other health and human service professions.
- *Role differentials.* Real and perceived differences in rank, title, and physical location of units inhibit exchanges and interactions.
- *Organization size and structure.* As the number of employees increases, the quantity of communication increases. With teams and participatory management, the diversity of responsibilities assumed by managers and staff contribute to increasing numbers of employees becoming part of communication networks.
- *Physical factors.* Support factors such as space, availability of technology and computers, skill and resources of available support personnel, work schedules, location of direct services in relation to management, and time permitted for desk work like electronic entry of client or program notes affect the nature of face-to-face interactions, written communication, and feedback.
- *Organizational culture.* Rapid client turnaround or dramatic increases in the number of clients with diverse, multiple needs and severe deficits creates staff frustration that inhibits communication. When the intensity of the work varies with seasonal changes or client turnover, communication becomes labored and distorted as a result of staff stress and pressure.

Table 11.6 Organizational Communication Strategies

- The manager gains the confidence of others by remaining impartial and consistent, responding promptly to requests, and representing the interests of unit employees to other management levels and throughout the organization.
- Accurate information is transmitted between levels. If communication bypasses levels or goes through informal networks, it is acknowledged.
- The manager recognizes individual efforts and the work of the unit publicly and before upper-management levels.
- The manager impresses on the staff that ineffective communication can mean wasted time and resources and lowered productivity.
- Staff also is made aware that communication is subject to organizational controls, as are other organizational functions (e.g., fundraising, marketing). This helps employees understand why compliance with protocols and proper use of communication tools enhance the image of the unit.
- The manager uses multiple communication methods through which messages are transmitted, so that the meanings benefit from the impact of repetition and everyone who needs to hear the message will.

Organizational communication is also enhanced by careful planning and analysis of formal and informal exchanges. When forms are used properly and reports completed in a timely manner, others view the unit positively. All persons associated with a situation are informed of the outcomes (e.g., minutes of staff meetings sent to upper-level management garner support and awareness). The appearance of official documents leaves an impression that influences responsiveness. Committing agendas and problem alternatives to writing, for example, allows others to prepare for exchanges. The first-line manager solicits input on the relevancy of communication methods to determine their appropriateness to various audiences. For example, e-mail may elicit more input than text messages.

Verbal exchanges are also planned. Location of verbal exchanges is contemplated. Confidential material is discussed in private, as is any topic that might arouse emotional responses. Discussion between staff and management regarding resource allocations occurs on neutral territory. Verbal exchanges are planned to occur after all facts are carefully analyzed for accuracy. Positions of communicators in the conversation are planned (e.g., space between speakers or height of speaker and respondents is arranged). Discussion is focused by controls such as time and Robert's Rules of Order. The intent of conversations is stated at the outset, and summarization brings closure at the conclusion. Formally acknowledging hallway communications also helps informal communications to become barometers for needed formal communiqués.

LEARNING OUTCOME
Explain the manager's communication tasks during meetings.

Effective Meeting Strategies

Meetings matter because that's where an organization's culture perpetuates itself. The manager spends a considerable amount of work time in meetings (Tomey, 2009). Meetings are used for participatory problem solving, decision making, coordination, information sharing, and enhancing working relationships (Sullivan & Decker, 2009; Tomey, 2009). Running effective meetings is an important managerial task. Effective meeting management encourages professionals to attend and demonstrates the manager's effectiveness.

There are specific strategies a manager may use to plan and run effective meetings. Any meeting worth holding is worth planning. As Benjamin Franklin once said, "By failing to prepare, you are preparing to fail." Productive meetings are likely when the manager employs several strategies outlined in Table 11.7, p. 186.

LEARNING OUTCOME
Explain managerial tasks in the delegation of responsibilities to staff.

Delegation

Managers are increasingly leading by empowering their employees through participation in decisions that direct, coordinate, and control their work (Robbins, Decenzo, & Coulter, 2011). Delegation is the primary means a supervisor has to empower employees. Delegation is driven by the need to make quick decisions and to relieve the demands of increased load caused by the larger span of control managers experience. "*Delegation* is the process by which responsibility and authority for performing a task . . . or a decision is transferred to another person who accepts that authority and responsibility" (Sullivan & Decker, 2009, p. 135). While the manager transfers the responsibility and authority to a staff person, accountability for the outcomes or results remains with the manager. Accountability is shared as the staff person is accountable to the manager for the responsibilities assumed. Delegation benefits staff, the manager, and the organization. Employees learn by doing, trust is built, and job satisfaction and retention improve (Sullivan & Decker, 2009; Tomey, 2009). The manager benefits from a better functioning unit and increased time to attend to management tasks like budgeting that cannot be delegated. Lastly, the organization benefits by achieving its goals more efficiently, productivity is increased, and group cohesion results in an increasing commitment to organizational goals (Sullivan & Decker, 2009; Tomey, 2009).

First-line managers may hesitate to relinquish a portion of their authority for a number of reasons (e.g., feeling as though he or she can do the job better or more quickly, staff is inexperienced, workloads will become imbalanced). Consequently, they may underdelegate. Overdelegation occurs when the first-line manager relinquishes inordinate amounts of authority. A number of reasons such as dislike for certain paperwork tasks, feelings

Table 11.7 Effective Meeting Strategies

1. Determine the purpose and participants for the meeting. Managers should first consider the purpose of the meeting and determine if other alternatives like e-mail or conferencing would be more appropriate—perhaps a meeting is not the best way to communicate. If the intent is to relay information, an e-mail or a report would be more effective. Key participants are identified and if they are unable to attend, the meeting is rescheduled. In general, the fewer in attendance, the better. The manager identifies those stakeholders who have the skills and knowledge necessary to deal with the agenda and who represent those impacted by the decisions made during the meeting. The manager may also only need to attend a certain portion of the meeting as identified on the agenda.
2. Develop, finalize, and distribute an agenda. The agenda is the order of business and should have a title for the meeting (Tomey, 2009). When establishing an agenda, the manager needs to include date and time, place, purpose, and items to be discussed. If people have been invited to speak to specific agenda items, their names should be listed next to the agenda item and the time devoted to each agenda item is recorded to the right of the item. Less structure is found with problem solving when attendees are encouraged to brainstorm and express thoughts and feelings important to problem resolution. Organizations may specify the topics and format or follow Robert's Rules of Order when writing an agenda and include general topics such as committee reports, old business, and new business, with specific items listed under each. Regardless of the amount of time assigned to each item, the manager allows 5–10 minutes to orient attendees at the start and another 5–10 minutes to summarize at the conclusion of the meeting.

   It is important that as a manager you prepare your group prior to the meeting, so the agenda should be distributed at least 7 to 10 days prior to the meeting and include any reports or materials that participants should read in advance (Sullivan & Decker, 2009). If it is an ongoing meeting, minutes from the last meeting should be included.
3. Determine when, where, and how long to meet. Time and place are very important to the running of an effective meeting. A manager may have few choices of when and where to meet depending on the schedule of the people needed at the meeting. Accommodations with adequate space, comfort, technology, environmental controls, and proper atmosphere (formal or informal) facilitate productive meetings. Meetings should be limited to no more than 50 to 90 minutes unless the issues are complex and should be scheduled when there is a natural ending time, like before lunch or end of the workday (Sullivan & Decker, 2009). Meetings should start and end on time with the high-priority items on the agenda first followed by those that are not time-sensitive or emotionally laden. If the agenda is completed early, prior to the planned ending time, the manager closes the meeting. Prior to closure, the manager restates conclusions, clearly outlines assignments and deadlines, and identifies any future meeting times and locations. Minutes are sent within 24 hours to the attendees, if possible.
4. Conduct the meeting. As the manager it is up to you to start the meeting on time even if all invited persons have yet to arrive. At the stated time the manager gives a brief overview of the meeting, including the purpose and anticipated outcomes and length of the meeting, background or topics or problems, potential solutions/constraints, the proposed agenda, and any specific rules to be followed. If a person has not been identified to take the minutes, this is the time. Sometimes a meeting before the planned meeting with those key persons or persons with concerns helps the manager anticipate group reactions and hidden agendas that influence attendee behaviors and meeting results.

   The manager adds to meeting effectiveness by guiding discussion adhering to the allotted agenda timeframes. When a topic comes up that takes the group off-topic but is important, the manager advises the group that it will be discussed at another time, possibly at the next meeting, and then returns to the original topic. As the group reaches consensus on a topic, the manager should summarize the position and make sure everyone agrees and then move on to the next topic.

   End the meeting at the agreed-on time. The manager should summarize what has been decided, who is going to do what, and by what time. At this time it may be necessary to ask for volunteers to take responsibility for completing action items agreed to in the meeting. Some people use the technique of "once around the table" as a closure technique; everyone at the table gives his or her interpretation of what was accomplished at the meeting. The next meeting date and time should be set and everyone should be assured that they will be receiving minutes of the meeting within the next few workdays.
5. Follow-up after the meeting. The manager needs to ensure that the minutes are accurate and distributed or posted on the intranet within a couple days of the meeting. Also the manager should make sure that what was agreed on at the meeting is accomplished. Thus the manager may need to call or send out reminder emails to ensure that tasks are accomplished. The manager acknowledges accomplishments and gives credit when credit is due for work performed when the minutes are distributed. The minutes are shared with administrators within the organization to affirm the unit's progress toward organizational goals and with anyone who might be impacted by the meeting outcomes, even if they were not on the attendee list.

of being overworked, awareness that certain employees appear to be interested in specific tasks, and the manager's own inexperience in a management position contribute to overdelegation. The manager needs to affirm the delegate is willing to accept the responsibility and authority and not feel as if work is being dumped on the staff member because it is an undesirable task or as a reward for being a productive staff member (Sullivan & Decker, 2009). Consequently, the manager facilitates delegation by carefully preparing for and assigning tasks. To ensure that a task, function, or decision is properly delegated, the manager takes five steps (Sullivan & Decker, 2009; Tomey, 2009) (refer to Table 11.8).

"No one in health care today can afford not to delegate" (Sullivan & Decker, 2009, p. 143). Delegation is a skill that can be learned yet requires practice. Once developed, the manager and the staff extend their abilities by using each other to help and support common unit and organizational goals.

Learning Outcome
Explain managerial tasks used to negotiate win-win work environments.

Negotiation

Managers communicate through negotiation. *Negotiation* involves two or more persons who have different preferences and must make a joint decision and come to an agreement (Robbins, Decenzo, & Coulter, 2011). Effective negotiation sets up a win-win work environment. An effective negotiator recognizes the needs and objectives of others while expressing in a professional manner points of view that facilitate achievement of unit goals. Negotiation skills are used during performance reviews, employee coaching, conflict resolution, and planning quality and safety-improvement programs. Official negotiations occur with collective bargaining and contract agreements. On a daily basis, the first-line manager negotiates for meeting times, program space or areas, employee benefits, and client contact time. Each of these encounters involves distribution of resources among work units to accomplish outcomes. Thus the manager negotiates with unit staff, other organizational units, and professionals and vendors external to the unit to gain necessary resources like reimbursements or coverage by private insurance companies or fair employee contracts or staff schedules.

A problem-solving approach creates win-win situations (i.e., mutually define the problem, look for alternatives, select and implement the most feasible option, and evaluate and plan for follow-up). When the manager views differences to be resolved as joint efforts, the probability of creating win-win relationships between the manager and staff is likely. The manager uses a problem-solving process to negotiate a positive work environment (refer to Table 11.9) (Sullivan & Decker, 2009; Tomey, 2009).

Learning Outcome
Explain the manager's responsibilities in creating a collaborative environment.

Collaboration

Collaboration is the outcome of win-win situations and one of the more desirable approaches to resolve conflicts. With collaboration, both manager and staff cooperate in order to satisfy each other's expectations. Team building

Table 11.8 Delegation Process

1. The task is clearly defined and within the person's scope of practice and job description.
2. The selected employee has the competence, authority, and resources to accomplish the task and other employees are informed of the delegation.
3. Expectations are defined; the activities to perform, timelines, results, and follow-up communication are outlined.
4. The employee accepts the authority and responsibility, and the employee is expected to respond to problems that arise as the task is carried out.
5. The manager monitors, intervenes if necessary, and provides feedback to ensure that the task will be completed on time and to the desired specification.

Table 11.9 Negotiation Process

1. Clarify the common goal.
2. Concentrate on the facts.
3. Consider trade-offs with potential options.
4. Listen using active listening skills and feedback.
5. Look for options that satisfy staff interests.
6. Establish a climate of cooperation and collaboration.
7. Ask "what if" questions to consider alternatives.
8. Restate the desire to satisfy everyone's needs.
9. Prepare a follow-up document specifying agreed-upon outcomes.

and networking are collaborative. These efforts have become more critical in health and human services as a result of reduced resources, briefer intervention periods, increased accountability demands and attention to measuring outcomes, and the ongoing impact of change on service quality and improvements.

Managers empower staff by creating collaborative environments in which staff have the support and resources to react to and to change events. This occurs through communication that fosters feelings of trust, risk taking, openness, equity, and opportunity finding. Successful collaboration depends on cohesion and dedication to a service mission that reflects common values. Managers create linkages among their staff that promote cooperation, respect, and integration of individual talents so that collective achievement of goals enables unit growth and change.

Learning Outcome

Explain communication modeled by the manager with criticism, complaints, and confrontation.

Criticism, Complaints, and Confrontation

A first-line therapeutic recreation manager is in the middle of the communication loop between upper-level managers, who have the resources or authority, and staff, who use these resources to achieve organizational goals. This position requires interpreting communiqués from two viewpoints, which may or may not be congruent. Also, our profession is naturally vulnerable to the fears, frustrations, and anxiety experienced with health issues, which can result in critical or confrontational communication with clients and caregivers. A therapeutic recreation manager, therefore, is the potential recipient of criticism, complaints, and confrontation for a number of reasons and from a variety of sources.

A first-line manager must model ways to give and receive criticism, complaints, and confrontation to promote constructive outcomes. Complaints arise for a number of reasons: Clients and staff may need information, they may be uncomfortable with decisions or practices, or they may desire more control. Criticism is a negative evaluation of our actions and is considered unpleasant. Confrontation results from discrepancies between performance and expectation. The manager may elect to receive and respond in a number of ways to promote positive outcomes from criticism, complaints, and confrontational situations (refer to Table 11.10). A prudent manager accepts complaints, criticism, and confrontation as an inevitable part of first-line supervisory duties. By modeling constructive ways to receive and respond to these situations, the first-line manager helps staff to gain insight into their own behaviors.

The first-line manager assumes a key role in organizational communication that usually implies a position somewhere between upward (administrative levels) and downward channels (direct-service staff). Strategies appropriate to interpersonal/professional communication introduced in the first section of this chapter also are relevant to organizational communiqués between the

Table 11.10 Managing Criticism, Complaints, Confrontation

- Maintaining confidentiality promotes an atmosphere conducive to disclosing feelings.
- Active listening enables the manager to listen to the verbal and nonverbal message and respond to the whole. A response like "I agree with you, as do other staff" may be enough to enable the manager and staff member to cope with the situation.
- Credibility of the involved parties can be maintained by investigating, determining the real problem, and deliberating alternatives.
- When intervention does occur, the problem behavior and the desired behavior are identified so that the employee is able to regain control and to feel positive about self and work.
- When employees participate in actions that affect their responsibilities, job satisfaction tends to increase and negative input decreases. Employee confidence and cooperation is gained by explaining why and what for.
- Responses are presented in a manner of "kind firmness" and expectations are stated concretely with specific examples of acceptable and unacceptable responses.
- Even when formal grievances have been filed, the manager should respond with consistency and respect. Responses are nonthreatening and save face for the manager and employee. An apology or a request for feedback help the manager to gain additional evaluative information and to handle feelings of inadequacy that may have been projected onto staff.
- Therapeutic recreation managers work in stressful environments. Humor is a constructive mechanism that promotes communication.
- Practitioners tend to respond to fair challenges. The key to change is moving from small points of consensus toward overall agreement. The competent manager agrees with valid complaints, criticism, and confrontation and sets the expectations so that each change or accomplishment is acknowledged and rewarded. Sometimes public reward is all that is needed to gain positive momentum.

manager and unit stakeholders. Communication involves more individuals and authority levels resulting in increased potential for distorted interactions. The manager spends an inordinate amount of the workday in formal and informal meetings; consequently, effective meeting management is important to time management and unit productivity. Through delegation, negotiation, and collaboration, the manager empowers staff to carry out department goals. A positive response to criticism, complaints, and confrontations facilitates the risk taking necessary to change and improve.

Learning Outcome
Describe the advocacy role of the manager during professional communication.

The Manager—A Professional Advocate

The first-line manager is a central figure who represents therapeutic recreation within the organization and to the public and professional stakeholders and audiences external to the organization. In their positions, first-line therapeutic recreation managers inform and educate department staff, organization employees, clients, caregivers, and colleagues about the mission of unit services and scope of our professional practice. The manager conveys the essence of our profession at the work site, within the community, and to the profession at large. This advocacy role is evident during organization meetings, at community-wide events, and during professional gatherings.

The manner in which communication is shared within and outside the organization leaves an impression about therapeutic recreation. Through a number of communication modes (e.g., in-services, presentations, reports, efficacy studies, evidence-based practice articles, and voluntary contributions) the first-line manager is a role model for staff, a representative for the organization, and an advocate of the profession.

First-line managers represent their departments and the organization as they network and collaborate in the agency, community, and profession. Their poise, appearance, mannerisms, promptness, and timeliness are qualities reflective of personal-professional standards of excellence. The manager's written and oral accuracy, follow-through, receptivity, and quality of delivered materials project an image. Real and perceived impressions of the manager affect others' thoughts and feelings about the manager, organization, and profession.

Managers are also judged by the "company they keep." Power associated with positions and roles is communicated through associations. Responsiveness to a manager occurs in a political context. Judgments affect what and how others share information. Before a manager communicates externally, organizational protocol requires that proper internal personnel have been informed and that information to be disseminated has received clearance.

When a therapeutic recreation manager disseminates publications, efficacy findings, and results of evidence-based practices, information representative of the profession is being conveyed to clients, caregivers, and colleagues. The manager's advocacy role is evident during program tours, advisory board meetings, grand rounds, volunteerism, co-sponsorships, and student-intern training.

Professional communication is unique because of the distance communication travels and the impact it makes on audiences wider than those within the organization. E-mail, formal letters, committee reports, and conference calls are impersonal and do not permit the message to project feelings or subjective interpretations. Each professional reads and hears the message from his or her own perspective. Because this frame of reference is unique, the sender and receiver ascribe different meanings to the message. Therefore, to ensure congruence, the first-line manager carefully constructs the message, seeks review prior to transmission, and solicits feedback from the receiver(s) to gauge accuracy of understandings. The manager retains a correspondence file to revisit previous communications to verify information transmitted. Additionally, the manager devotes certain daily time periods to prioritized communications. Busy work times (e.g., Monday mornings, grand rounds or budget hearings) are avoided.

Professional communication is multidirectional and multifaceted. Internal and external professional exchanges leave long-lasting impressions and are primary tools through which the professional and profession mature. How, what, and when messages are conveyed influence perceptions others have of recreation therapy.

Summary

Most of the manager's time is spent in speaking and listening; therefore the manager must have effective interpersonal/professional communication skills.

1. The manager selects appropriate formal communication modes to transfer thoughts and meanings among organization professionals.
2. The manager is aware that the grapevine or informal communication influences organization communiqués.
3. Technology is increasing communication options and access to information while creating access among working professionals "24-7."
4. A number of workplace variables influence communication; these range from physical, emotional, and semantic differences to variations in roles, gender, generations, culture, information overload, and the organizational culture.
5. Feedback and active listening are two tools that enhance communication accuracy and understanding.
6. The manager is central to organizational communication. As a supervisor, the first-line manager ensures that those within the unit and those that support unit activities have timely, factual, accurate information.
7. Through meetings, delegation, negotiation, and collaborative processes, the manager communicates so that win-win situations accomplish unit and organizational goals.
8. When criticism, complaints, and confrontation do arise, the manager separates the significant from the not-so-critical to discern real needs and action steps. In doing so, the manager serves as a model for staff and other professionals who find themselves in challenging situations.
9. Professional communications extend the first-line manager's network beyond the unit. These exchanges inform and educate others about recreation therapy while advocating for the contributions made by our profession.

Critical Thinking Activities

1. Complete an Internet search using keywords like "managerial communication" and "workplace communication." From the resources gathered, identify (1) managerial communication skills that enhance employee productivity and (2) workplace communication skills of employees that are significant to employee retention and delivery of quality services.
2. Attend a formal meeting in an agency. Critique the effectiveness of the meeting using the steps presented in this chapter.
3. What steps can a manager take to improve the processes of delegation, negotiation, and collaboration?
4. How are criticism, complaints, and confrontation managed so win-win work situations result?

References

Guffey, M. E. (2004). *Essentials of business communication* (6th ed.). Mason, OH: Thomson.

Marquis, B. L., & Huston, C. J. (2009). *Leadership roles and management functions in nursing: Theory & application* (4th ed.). Philadelphia: Lippincott Williams & Wilkins.

Robbins, S. P., Decenzo, D. A., & Coulter, M. (2011). *Fundamentals of management essential concepts and application* (7th ed.). Upper Saddle River, NJ: Prentice-Hall.

Sullivan E. J., & Decker, P. J. (2009). *Effective leadership & management in nursing* (7th ed.). Upper Saddle River, NJ: Pearson/Prentice-Hall.

Tomey, A. M. (2009). *Guide to nursing management and leadership* (8th ed.). St. Louis, MO: Mosby Elsevier.

Whitehead, D. K., Weiss, S. A., & Tappen, R. M. (2010). *Essentials of nursing leadership and management* (5th ed.). Philadelphia: F. A. Davis.

Chapter 12
Creating a Motivating Work Environment

Keywords

- Argyris's Maturity-Immaturity Continuum
- Clayton Alderfer's Modified Need Hierarchy (ERG)
- Equity Theory
- Extrinsic motivational factors
- Goal-Setting Theory
- Herzberg's Two-Factor Theory
- Intrinsic motivational factors
- Maslow's Hierarchy of Needs Theory
- McClelland's Three Needs Theory
- McGregor's Theory X and Theory Y
- Motivation
- Skinner's Positive Reinforcement Theory
- Theory Z
- Vroom's Expectancy Theory

Learning Outcomes

After reading this chapter, students will be able to:

1. Describe how each motivational theory explains worker desires and needs.
2. Summarize intrinsic and extrinsic motivators that contribute to job satisfaction.
3. Outline how the work culture and climate, managerial supervisory responsibilities, and the manager's interpersonal behaviors create a supportive environment.
4. Identify strategies first-line managers use to create positive work environments.
5. Explain trends and issues challenging the manager's attempts to positively influence motivation.

Overview

The amount and quality of work accomplished through a first-line manager is a direct reflection of their motivation and that of their subordinates (Marquis & Huston, 2009). Since motivation comes from within the person, managers cannot directly motivate subordinates. However, they can create an environment that promotes job satisfaction while achieving unit goals and enabling professionals to meet their needs (Marquis & Huston, 2009). Motivation is the result of the interaction between the employee and the work situation. Productivity and job satisfaction result when practitioners are "turned on" to their responsibilities. To motivate effectively, a manager must be in tune to each practitioner's personal needs and the interchange between the work environment and employee needs and abilities.

The intent of this chapter is to explore the relationship between motivation and the manager's responsibility to create a productive work environment that sustains job satisfaction within the unit. The first-line manager is responsible for meeting unit and organizational goals. As a consequence, the manager must create an environment "in which both organizational and individual needs are met" (Marquis & Huston, 2009, p. 422). Each staff member is unique. What is significant to one person is not necessarily important to another. Likewise, what motivates a practitioner at one particular time may not be something that fulfills a personal need in the future. Thus, while reaching acceptable levels of productivity and quality, the manager creates a work environment in which both the manager and unit staff and volunteers satisfy their needs and are also satisfied with their work responsibilities.

A number of theories explain motivation. The principles derived from these theories are universal. Successful managers focus on factors that stimulate worker satisfaction and productivity. The first section of this chapter reviews the theories that explain a manager's choice of motivational strategies. A positive supportive environment is created by effective application of motivational concepts. This chapter's second section presents strategies a manager uses to create a supportive environment that promotes managerial and staff performance. A supportive work environment deters factors like burnout that negatively impact morale, job satisfaction, and productivity. The closing section of this chapter highlights a few of the challenges likely to influence the manager's ability to create a motivating environment supportive of employee effectiveness and satisfaction and their own morale and capacity to serve as a role model in the unit.

Motivational Theories

What is motivation? *Motivation* is a degree of readiness or the desire or willingness within an individual to pursue a goal. Why is motivation significant to the first-line therapeutic recreation manager? The most important resource in any organization is human capabilities and competencies. A manager assumes responsibility to maintain productivity, accountability, and quality while encouraging employee job satisfaction. Because intrinsic motivation comes from within, to be intrinsically motivated, an employee must value job performance and productivity (Marquis & Huston, 2009).

The job environment enhances extrinsic motivation. Motivated employees try hard, yet managers cannot assume that employee efforts will be channeled in the direction that benefits the unit nor that they have adequate levels of intrinsic motivation to achieve organizational goals (Marquis & Huston, 2009). As a consequence, the manager must create a climate that stimulates employees' intrinsic and extrinsic drives to use their skills and competencies to achieve unit and organizational goals while satisfying their own needs. Thus, the goal of a first-line manager is to accomplish unit and organizational goals while giving practitioners the opportunity to meet their needs. A number of theories have attempted to explain the role of both intrinsic and extrinsic motivators in high productivity and worker satisfaction. While these theories change with time and tend to reflect the views prevalent during particular time periods, principles derived from these theories are evident in effective staff motivation today. A brief review of these views reveals shifting explanations for employee motivation.

LEARNING OUTCOME
Describe how each motivational theory explains worker desires and needs.

Maslow's Hierarchy of Needs

One of the best known motivational theories is *Maslow's hierarchy of needs theory*. Maslow believed people are motivated to satisfy needs ranging from basic survival to complex needs; and, when the lower-level needs are satisfied, people seek to meet higher-level needs. Also, once the lower-level needs are met, they no longer motivate us (Arnold, Glover, & Beeler, 2012; Marquis & Huston, 2009). The five basic needs ranked in hierarchical order from lowest to highest are physiological, safety, social, esteem, and self-actualization. Maslow separated lower-level needs (physiological and safety) from higher-level needs (social, esteem, and self-actualization), suggesting lower needs are primarily satisfied externally while higher-order level needs are satisfied internally (Robbins, Decenzo, & Coulter, 2011).

As a result of Maslow's work, managers realized employees may have many needs motivating them at any one time yet the key to motivation is to determine where along the developmental continuum an employee is functioning and focus motivational efforts at this level (Marquis & Huston, 2009). For example, money is essential to satisfy physiological needs—an adequate paycheck becomes a desirable goal when securing a position. The need to fulfill one's potential is at the highest level of the continuum. Consequently, employees strive for self-fulfillment, growth, and to better themselves through professional training, job advancement, and humanitarian opportunities (Sadri & Bowen, 2011). While the theory has limitations, not all of us are motivated by the same things and in the same order and there is limited empirical evidence to support the theory; it is clear that motivation is internalized and to increase productivity, managers must help employees meet lower-level needs (Arnold, Glover, & Beeler, 2012; Marquis & Huston, 2009; Robbins, Decenzo, & Coulter, 2011).

Clayton Alderfer's Modified Need Hierarchy (ERG)

Clayton Alderfer proposed a three-level need hierarchy that collapsed Maslow's five levels and suggested that frustrated higher-level needs cause regression to next lower-level needs in the hierarchy (Tomey, 2009). Alderfer also suggested that more than one of the three needs—existence (i.e., physiological and safety), relatedness (i.e., belongingness or social), and growth (i.e., self-esteem and self-actualization)—may be operative at any one point in time. Satisfaction of lower-level needs like affiliation, resulting from participation on a team, activates a need at the highest level. Participation in staff-development activities and continuous quality improvement projects are built on recognition and growth needs of employees in a knowledge-based work environment.

Herzberg's Two-Factor Theory

Frederick Herzberg's concept of motivators parallels concepts of need levels and satisfaction seen in Maslow's and Alderfer's hierarchies. Herzberg investigated what people wanted from their jobs (Robbins, Decenzo, & Coulter, 2011). He believed, on one hand, that *motivators* or job satisfiers are present in work itself and that they give people the desire to work and work well, and on the other hand, there are elements in the environment like working conditions and the need to meet organizational goals, *hygiene* or *maintenance* factors, that act to satisfy but not to motivate employees (Marquis & Huston, 2009). Factors that lead to job satisfaction are separate and distinct from those that lead to dissatisfaction (Robbins, Decenzo, & Coulter, 2011). As a consequence, when managers eliminate factors that create job dissatisfaction (i.e., low salary), they may only be assuring satisfied employees rather than actually motivating their employees.

Intrinsic motivators like achievement, recognition, responsibility, and the potential for growth and work itself lead to job satisfaction. Extrinsic factors, (maintenance and hygiene), like relationships with supervisors and peers; salary; job security; an employee's personal life; and unit policies when perceived as unfair, lacking, or inadequate can lead to employee dissatisfaction. However, if paired with motivators like advancement, an extrinsic factor like salary can be a powerful motivator. For instance, an effective reward system is created when the manager gives employees greater responsibilities, recognition, and commensurate forms of compensation as benchmarks of quality are achieved. Glenn (2010) suggests that Herzberg's two-factor theory explains the success of participatory management practices like those evident with shared management work teams as highly motivated employees increase productivity, client satisfaction, and staff morale while lowering costs. Further, due to the increasing demands and decreasing resources in health care, providers "need recognition, responsibility and professional advancement to fire the 'generator' of employee motivation" (Dalton, 2010, p. 143).

Skinner's Positive Reinforcement Theory

Skinner, like Maslow, Alderfer, and Herzberg, contributed to the understanding of motivation, job satisfaction, and productivity during the 1950s. Skinner's work on operant conditioning and behavior modification demonstrated that people may be conditioned to behave in certain ways (Marquis & Huston, 2009). Rewarded behaviors are repeated, and with plenty of positive praise and reinforcement, these behaviors increase in frequency. When desired behaviors are not present, the first-line manager first considers environmental factors like the adequacy of time or resources; if the environmental scan does not reveal the reason for the absence of the desired behavior (i.e., data entry for treatment or program plans), the manager considers if staff have the abilities or can acquire the abilities or be assigned other duties (i.e., compatible technology skills) (Tomey, 2009).

Argyris's Maturity-Immaturity Continuum

The Argyris maturity-immaturity continuum is grounded on a continuum approach. Individuals vary in their level of maturity along a relative continuum from total immaturity to total maturity. Argyris believed that people "will exert more energy to meet their own needs than those of the organization" (Tomey, 2009, p. 163). Thus, the manager's challenge is to view each employee from his or her respective maturity level and to create a work environment in which each employee's talents and interests are recognized. Consequently a manager creates satisfaction by taking advantage of employee interests and helping personnel meet their needs for self-actualization because employees tend to exert more energy to meet their needs than those of the organization.

McClelland's Three Needs Theory

David McClelland identified three acquired needs that motivate people to work: achievement, affiliation, and power (Marquis & Huston, 2009; Robbins, Decenzo, & Coulter, 2011; Tomey, 2009). McClelland believed the manager can identify these three needs in their employees and design motivational strategies to meet these needs. Further, these needs may compete with each other, as more than one need may be operational at one time (Arnold, Glover, & Beeler, 2012). Some practitioners strive for personal *achievement* by seeing their work through to successful completion. The drive to succeed and improve what is, rather than rewards of success, compels these individuals. An employee operating with this motif is intrinsically motivated, displays a high degree of self-control, and desires to perform more efficiently. High achievers avoid what they perceive as easy or difficult tasks (Robbins, Decenzo, & Coulter, 2011). The manager's task becomes assigning responsibilities of moderate challenge while delegating enough authority so the employee is self-regulating and receives appropriate recognition.

Staff with high *affiliation* needs seek out social networks and meaningful relationships; they are more interested in high morale than overt productivity. Managers who support cooperative team interactions are creating satisfying work environments among affiliation-oriented employees. Finally, people who are *power-oriented* need to be in control and influence others. They are motivated by the power rather than effective performance. Thus, a manager might assign a power-oriented person to a supervisory task like chairing the quality improvement committee or coordinating the annual volunteer recognition event.

McGregor's Theory X and Theory Y

McGregor examined how managers handle people based on their assumptions about workers (Arnold, Glover, & Beeler, 2012). He observed from studying traditional organizational structures that some workers dislike their work, avoid responsibility, lack initiative, and prefer strong direction (i.e., Theory X). Motivation is derived from satisfaction of lower-level needs (e.g., salaries, fringe benefits). This theory assumes the lowest levels of need satisfaction, as detailed by Maslow's and Argyris's theories, motivate behaviors. A manager with this theory would supervise closely and delegate little responsibility (Tomey, 2009).

McGregor proposed an alternative theory, Theory Y, based on higher levels of need satisfaction. Motivators create opportunities for self-control, self-direction, and self-esteem building. Theory Y managers assume people like to work and seek independence. The manager is challenged to create an environment in which Maslow's higher-order social and self-esteem needs are achieved. A manager uses positive incentives like recognition, opportunities for individual growth, and participation on self-regulating teams to realize staff needs and to achieve department goals.

Vroom's Expectancy Theory

In the mid-1960s, a number of theories purported that behavior is not merely motivated by need satisfaction alone—employees' perceptions and expectations of the work environment influence outcomes of work behaviors. Vroom's expectancy theory suggests that an employee is "motivated by expectations (beliefs) about future outcomes (consequences of behavior) and by the value . . . place[d] on those outcomes" (Sullivan & Decker, 2009, p. 227). There are three factors that interact to form the expectations: (1) expectancy or effort-performance linkage—the employee's perception that effort will lead to a certain level of performance; (2) instrumentality or performance-reward linkage—the employee's perception that certain performance levels result in desired outcomes; and (3) valence or attractiveness of reward—the importance or value placed on the potential outcome or reward (Arnold, Glover, & Beeler, 2012; Robbins, Decenzo, & Coulter, 2011; Sullivan & Decker, 2009). The net effect of these three factors determines an employee's effort. Thus, if staff perceive the task is too challenging, or the reward is unlikely, or the value placed on the outcome is low, motivation is reduced. An employee is motivated when effort leads to positive performance appraisal and proper recognition that attain desired outcomes (i.e., tuition reimbursement, conference attendance) valued by the employee.

Vroom's theory suggests the manager should be aware of the unique needs and values of his or her staff. Each staff member places different value on work motivators such as security, financial reward, and recognition. Likewise, the needs fulfilled by work vary. Some therapeutic recreation specialists need "to give or help" while others need to be a part of a "medical team." Also evident from this theory is the significance of a manager's explanation of the reward structure and performance expectations. Consequently, to motivate, first-line managers must clearly articulate the relationship between performance and unit goals and the significance of the unit's reward structure to each member's individual goals (Robbins, Decenzo, & Coulter, 2011).

Equity Theory

Similar to the expectancy theory, equity theory describes the relationship between individual effort and reward and employees' perceptions of the effort and reward received by others. Equity exists when an employee subjectively determines that the ratio of his or her input to reward or outcomes is comparable to that of other employees. When an imbalance exists, the tension that is created causes the employee to be motivated to reduce the inequity and to achieve fairness (Tomey, 2009). When staff "feel over worked and underpaid, they are likely to decrease their productivity" (Tomey, 2009, p. 106).

Employee input includes a number of factors, such as effort, experience, education, and competence. Reward is also broadly defined to include salary level, fringe benefits, recognition, working conditions, and department rewards. Tension is created when, for example, two employees of the same age and years of accumulated work experience are rewarded differently. Inequitable rewards lead to lower job satisfaction and poor job performance (Sullivan & Decker, 2009). In an economically unstable environment, when organizations are being redesigned and positions reduced, problems with employees' perceptions of equity can be anticipated (Sullivan & Decker, 2009).

Goal-Setting Theory

Like expectancy and equity theories, goal-setting theory is a contemporary theory grounded on research, yet unlike the expectancy and equity theories, goal-setting theory suggests a person's efforts are expended because the focus is on the goal itself rather than the expected reward or equity of the outcomes (Robbins, Decenzo, & Coulter, 2011; Sullivan & Decker, 2009). Goal-setting theory says: (1) specific goals lead to higher performance more so than general goals, (2) specific difficult goals, when accepted, lead to higher performance more so than do easy goals, and (3) incentives and rewards help individuals accept a goal or set a more specific, difficult goal (Sullivan & Decker, 2009).

Several factors influence the goal-performance relationship. First, specific challenging goals like "document specific client improvements attributed to your intervention" are preferable motivators to vague imperatives like "do your best to impact client functioning." Second, self-generated feedback rather than feedback from the supervisor is a stronger motivator as the employee monitors his or her own progress. Third, the theory assumes an individual is committed to the goal, which is more likely when the goal is made public, the individual has an internal locus of control, and when the goal is self-set instead of assigned (Robbins, Decenzo, & Coulter, 2011). Fourth, persons with high self-efficacy believe they have the ability to perform, and even with negative feedback are likely to remain motivated and put forth increased effort. Lastly, like expectancy theory, goal-setting theory suggests "staff should know exactly what they should be doing . . . [and] should perceive rewards [are] contingent on performance of assigned tasks" (Sullivan & Decker, 2009, p. 228).

Theory Z

William Ouchi described a contemporary motivational approach that focuses on increasing productivity through participatory management. Theory Z evolved from the Japanese culture. It assumes that increased satisfaction and productivity and reduced turnover result from using collective decision making, with long-term employment, slower rate of promotions, and an emphasis on the development of all aspects of the employees (Tomey, 2009).

Each staff member's efforts are significant to the unit and work of the team. Quality circles work on solving job-related quality problems, such as client scheduling and/or transportation. As a result of feeling a sense of commitment from the unit, employees tend to plan a lifelong career with the organization. Close working relationships develop within the team and each member's contributions are thoroughly evaluated. Supervision is subtle, as workers become a part of the culture and peer approval supports group behavior. Relationships forged by group efforts support each employee's individual needs and job satisfaction.

To summarize this section, each theory offers alternatives to creating motivating environments that contribute to employee satisfaction and productivity. It is apparent that there is no one single approach that drives employee motivation—some methods work better than others with different people or settings (Sullivan & Decker, 2009). Earlier theories tended to limit motivation to behaviors that satisfy needs. More recent theories attribute motivation to broader concepts of need satisfaction. These theories suggest employee behaviors tend to be affected by perceptions and judgments of relationships among a number of factors, including how employees compare and relate to one another. Management practices drawn from the most recent theories acknowledge the influence of the total work environment on the achievement of personal needs and on the inherent relationship between satisfaction of personal needs and unit goals. Effective managers draw from the various theories to create an environment in which unit staff achieve need satisfaction from the work itself.

Need Fulfillment and a Motivating Work Environment

"Getting people to do their best work . . . is one of managers' most enduring . . . challenges . . . What motivates us as human beings is a centuries-old puzzle" (Nohria, Groysberg, & Lee, 2008, p. 78). Accepting and understanding individual uniqueness helps the manager plan alternative motivational strategies for staff. The unique demands of the human-service work environment have lead researchers to consider "a motivating work environment as one in which staff members are effectively supported to work diligently as well as to enjoy their day-to-day employment" (Parsons, Reid, & Crow, 2003, p. 96). Managers realize "employees need a range of motivators in order to remain engaged in their work" (Sadri & Bowen, 2011, p. 45).

A manager's challenge is twofold: (a) to engage staff in experiences that result in need fulfillment and (b) to create a work environment supportive of personal satisfaction, development, and achievement of unit goals. Therefore, the manager is aware of personal drives and work-environment factors that promote productivity, job satisfaction, quality, client satisfaction, organizational citizenship, and employee retention. To create a mutually supportive work experience, managers consider both extrinsic motivators like salary and work schedule and intrinsic motivators like perceptions of staff competence felt from meeting complex client needs or the richness experienced as a team member (Bogo, Paterson, Tufford, & King, 2011). This section overviews both the personal drives or intrinsic motivators and the work-environment strategies or extrinsic motivators that contribute to morale and motivation for the manager and unit staff.

Learning Outcome

Summarize intrinsic and extrinsic motivators that contribute to job satisfaction.

Need Fulfillment through Intrinsic and Extrinsic Motivators

When managers and staff act because something inherent in the job feels good and provides internal satisfaction, *intrinsic motivators* associated directly with job tasks and responsibilities are creating personal drive. Research in therapeutic recreation as well as related health and education professions suggests therapists are driven by motivators associated with their job duties (Riley & Connolly, 2007; Stone, Kline, & Hammond, 2009; Witman & Rakos, 2008). Survey respondents in both a national and state survey noted therapists are satisfied and value their jobs and the contributions they make in the workplace (Riley & Connolly, 2007; Stone, Kline, & Hammond, 2009). Additionally, assuming "'other'" duties like activities of daily living, special events, and management tasks like budgeting and quality improvement also make a positive impact on recreation therapists' job experiences (Witman & Rakos, 2008).

Like research in recreation therapy, studies of social workers, teachers, nurses, and mental health professionals report intrinsic motivators contribute to job satisfaction. Compassion satisfaction or satisfaction derived from caregiving and social interaction opportunities influence performance and job satisfaction among nurses and mental health workers (Bogo, Paterson, Tufford, & King, 2011; Burtson & Stichler, 2010). Another intrinsic motivator among mental health workers, social workers, and teachers is a perception of confidence in meeting client needs and feeling comfortable with one's own identity (self-awareness) in performing work tasks (Bogo, Paterson, Tufford, & King, 2011; Wendt, Tuckey, & Prosser, 2011). Professionals feel positive about working together in teams to plan interventions and learn from each other. Setting boundaries and maintaining balanced personal-professional lives helps therapists accept when the limit of their professional role or impact on clients is reached: This also creates an image of professionalism which helps to separate work from personal lives (Wendt, Tuckey, & Prosser, 2011). Significant motivating factors that explain why these professionals entered their chosen fields and continue to sustain their desire include enjoyment in feeling challenged, diversity of their work, making a difference in people's lives, connecting day-to-day work to a bigger cause—contributing to society, and reflections on themselves as positive professional role models (Wendt, Tuckey, & Prosser, 2011). Do any of these personal drives explain why you selected your major? Intrinsic motivators, while very influential, do not alone fully explain the reason therapists are motivated to be productive, satisfied workers.

First-line managers also consider *extrinsic motivational* factors as they plan strategies to satisfy staff needs, since motivated employees work harder to meet unit goals and are less likely to leave the organization in search of more fulfilling opportunities. Extrinsic rewards are tied to employee behaviors, skills, and roles in the organization. Money, praise, awards, and incentives support employee performance, yet they may be valued differently by each employee. To illustrate, a staff member with a heavy caseload or extra programming responsibilities may value "'time away'" more than receiving extra "'kudos'" from a supervisor. Thus, the manager must first identify what staff members value and desire or what internal motivators drive their behaviors and pair these needs with external motivators. For example, staff members are motivated by social interaction resulting from opportunities to function as team members; therefore, managers foster collaboration and friendships among coworkers in various fields by creating a work culture that rewards team productivity.

Several studies have noted that salary and monetary benefits have only 20% impact on job satisfaction (Sadri & Bowen, 2011). Studies in our field report a "direct positive correlation between high levels of job satisfaction and increased salary levels" (Riley & Connolly, 2007, p. 43) yet TRSs "report being somewhat dissatisfied with pay, as well as opportunities for pay increases and promotion" (Stone, Kline, & Hammond, 2009, p. 55). Results of these studies suggest that with more years of practice, opportunities for professional development, as well as pay appear to have an effect on satisfaction. As a consequence, there is concern about professional attrition, particularly among early career professionals. No single monetary or non-monetary incentive addresses the complexity of human needs. As noted by one author, even money is not enough: "doctors need recognition, responsibility, and professional advancement to fire the 'generator' of employee motivation" (Dalton, 2010, p. 143).

Learning Outcome

Outline how the work culture and climate, managerial supervisory responsibilities, and the manager's interpersonal behaviors create a supportive environment.

Manager's Role in Creating a Motivating Work Environment

The first- line manager recognizes the needs and values of individual employees and the organization's needs and values and uses motivational strategies appropriate for each person and the situation to bring them together to accomplish individual and unit goals. Through a number of interpersonal and professional supervisory processes and roles, the manager creates a supportive work environment within the prevailing work climate and culture. Three areas are reviewed to identify factors that create a motivating work environment: the culture and climate of the organization, the manager's supervisory responsibilities, and the interpersonal aspects of the work environment.

Because the organization impacts the extrinsic motivation of managers and staff, it is important to examine the organizational climate and culture that affect motivation (Marquis & Huston, 2009). A number of variables within the work climate directly influence motivational levels of managers and staff. First-line managers have the opportunity to affect change in some of these variables, whereas other variables remain outside their realm of influence. With an awareness of these variables, managers create opportunities that promote satisfaction, productivity, and retention while reducing conditions that lead to dissatisfied clients and stress and burnout for themselves and their employees.

One variable over which a first-line manager has minimal influence is the complexity of the unit and/or relationship of the unit to the organization. Communication flows through more channels in larger organizations. Structure of the unit and its relationship to other units and/or the organization also is a function of size. Formal policies and procedures codify behavior or work culture in larger complex environments. Where size and complexity are factors, managers organize tasks so that professionals perceive fairness, acceptance, and support within the unit for their needs.

A variable over which the manager does have some influence is the climate within the unit. Within the unit, a manager structures the physical environment to support interpersonal relationships and plans, leads, and communicates so individual and unit goals are realized through team efforts and participatory management. Also, amenities like educational opportunities and comfortable work space boost morale. The degree of control a first-line manager has within the unit is relational to organizational variables; to illustrate, the recognition system, including monetary and nonmonetary rewards, may be overseen by the agency's HR department, leaving only the opportunity to nominate staff to receive awards at the unit level. Consequently, the climate set at the macro level permeates managerial actions within the service unit.

Besides the culture and climate created by the organization's beliefs and protocols, the unit manager also has a tremendous impact in the unit (Marquis & Huston, 2009). Employees want interesting jobs, clinical supervision, feedback, and recognition—managers have a great deal of control over these need-fulfilling activities. Thus, a second way a motivating environment is created is through managerial responsibilities like employee job design, advancement, feedback, recognition, and development. Because the manager's personal motivation is an important factor affecting staff commitment to duties, the manager's outlook and behaviors affect the climate in the unit. As a result, the manager is a role model among staff, clients, and agency personnel.

Through the job-design process, managers enrich employees' jobs and increase their motivation. One approach suggests every job has five key dimensions, and when each is present to a high degree, the job is potentially motivating (Robbins, Decenzo, & Coulter, 2011), (refer to Table 12.1).

Managers must structure work so it is meaningful, satisfying, and productive and so that employees have opportunities to achieve and grow. When the first three variables (skill variety, task identity, significance) are present, a therapist will view the job as important and meaningful. Internal rewards are realized when the therapist learns from feedback that he or she has personally performed (autonomy) well (Robbins, Decenzo, & Coulter, 2011). The more these conditions are present, the greater the satisfaction and productivity.

Table 12.1 Job Dimensions

1. Skill variety (i.e., routine or multifaceted)
2. Task identity (i.e., whole or partial completion)
3. Significance (i.e., minimal to substantial impact on others)
4. Autonomy (i.e., discretion to independently select interventions)
5. Feedback (i.e., degree to which carrying out job duties results in the employee obtaining direct and clear information about effectiveness of therapeutic recreation services)

Advancement usually occurs with promotions to new positions; yet, in practice, the career ladder may be limited to direct care and unit manager. As a consequence, manager's create opportunities 'to advance' through job enhancement, empowerment, and career development (Curtis & O'Connell, 2011; Sadri & Bowen, 2011). These strategies bring new challenges and responsibilities, which meet growth and self-esteem needs and foster retention.

We all desire feedback. We expect feedback to be fair, transparent, trustworthy, and proportional to our effort and performance. Managers are ethically obligated to administer evaluations under these conditions. The use of mentors and teams enhances the opportunities for constructive, relevant feedback. A sense of accomplishment and security comes with knowing our work is significant to achieving unit goals.

One of the main reasons individuals leave their jobs is a lack of recognition from their direct supervisor (Sadri & Bowen, 2011). Self-confidence is increased with recognition, and motivation to work harder is created. The reward system must clearly differentiate between performers and nonperformers and tie directly to achieving our assigned tasks or achieving individual and unit goals. Tangible rewards are motivational, yet positive supervisory feedback may be as effective in motivating staff to carry out their day-to-day responsibilities (Parsons, Reid, & Crow, 2003).

Enhancing staff performance comes through development. Education helps employees keep pace with a changing environment and use relevant evidence-based practices. Growth and self-actualization result from bringing new skills to our responsibilities as we add value to programs and services.

Employees expect managers to do their best in meeting their needs (Nohria, Groysberg, & Lee, 2008). Role models who are optimistic and enthusiastic have positive motivating effects on their employees and the work climate (Curtis & O'Connell, 2011). Unhappy managers contribute to low morale (Marquis & Huston,

2009). A supportive, encouraging work environment comes from energetic happy managers who desire to do the best job possible.

The organizational culture and climate, the manager's formal supervisory responsibilities, and interpersonal factors in the work setting and life collectively create opportunities to meet individual needs and enable job satisfaction. As just mentioned, the manager's demeanor contributes to or detracts from the pleasure of working. Also, as discussed under intrinsic motivation, interrelationships and communication among team members in and outside of work contribute to maintaining a work-life balance and continued personal and professional growth. Managers need to know what each employee values and needs. Each employee values various intrinsic and extrinsic motivators differently. Also, work satisfies different needs—for some, the security of a paycheck is more important than the opportunity to gain a new skill. Values and needs at work are impacted by life. A manager with an awareness of the big picture is likely to better understand challenges employee's face day-to-day. Lastly, managers who listen to and accept their employees are empathetic helpers and are able to respond fairly and with acceptance and respect. As a consequence, employees "feel positive toward their supervisors [and] are more likely to be honest, contribute new ideas, and speak up" (Arnold, Glover, & Beeler, 2012, p. 116).

Learning Outcome

Identify strategies first-line managers use to create positive work environments.

Specifically, what can the manager do to blend individual need fulfillment with opportunities in the work environment to create a positive motivational setting? There are many actions a manager can take to promote worker desire to achieve personal and unit goals. A number of authors (Arnold, Glover, & Beeler, 2012; Marquis & Huston, 2009; Tager, 2002) have identified guidelines managers consider as they organize the work setting to promote worker satisfaction and quality, (refer to Table 12.2).

Managerial actions that promote motivational environments are interrelated. Also, when one element (e.g., individualized recognition) is in place, another is likely to be positively impacted (e.g., performance reviews). The autonomy of the therapeutic recreation unit

Table 12.2 Managerial Guidelines to Promote Satisfaction and Quality

- Know and understand each employee's uniquenesses.
- Communicate candidly so that each staff member and volunteer feels informed and significant to unit outcomes.
- Increase practitioner ability to achieve personal and professional goals through training and opportunities for growth.
- Provide verbal kudos, praise doesn't cost a penny; making sure the praise is deserved and the recipient understands why the praise is being given.
- Adopt meaningful incentives making sure employees see and hear the benefits of their work.
- Introduce challenges so that expectancy is increased, performance is improved, and workers experience a higher level of productivity.
- Be a firm decision maker and encourage commitment to the course of action by involving staff and volunteers in decision-making processes, making sure employees understand the reason behind decisions and actions.
- Promote the concept of teamwork, because teams promote social engagement and professional growth.
- Structure the work environment so that practitioners have the freedom to accomplish clearly delineated tasks, and then reinforce productivity with positive feedback.
- Encourage cooperation and respect for each person's unique contributions by individualized reinforcement and recognition.
- Epitomize ethical behaviors, such as being consistent, objective, equitable, and reliable.
- Maintain a positive, enthusiastic image as a role model.
- Maintain a healthy balanced lifestyle on and off the job and work toward goals.
- Assign work duties commensurate with employee abilities, and whenever possible, credit employees for their achievements.
- Mentor and coach practitioner actions and review progress by setting up observable, measurable goals and planned formal and informal supervisory sessions.
- Create a trustful and helping relationship, giving employees and volunteers control and the opportunity to exercise individual judgment.
- Be consistent in rewarding desirable behavior and managing undesirable behavior.
- Communicate expectations to employees clearly.
- Change the routine, constantly innovate, and stretch staff to promote self-growth and self-actualization.
- Keep humor in the workplace and keeping the work environment fun and comfortable—these are self-motivating and great antidotes to burnout and low morale.

may determine the manager's relative control over motivational strategies. Management views tend to promote work environments that facilitate satisfaction of higher-level needs (e.g., self-esteem, self-fulfillment) through staff and volunteer involvement in day-to-day decisions and planning. This stimulates cohesiveness and unity between personal and unit goals.

Learning Outcome

Explain trends and issues challenging the manager's attempts to positively influence motivation.

Trends and Issues Challenging Motivational Work Environments

A number of management trends, health- care initiatives, and social demographics influence the creation of a supportive work environment. Health and human service work settings will experience increasing rates of change and accountability concerns with a reduced work force and resource base. Cultivating a work environment supportive of staff needs will become increasingly challenging. Traditional motivators, such as promotional opportunities, blanket health-care coverage, and wage increases, will become less significant in the employee- recognition process.

Participatory management, accountability, and quality monitoring are trends impacting employee motivational strategies. Self-regulating teams, supervisor/employee design of development plans, and management/staff operational planning exemplify participatory functions likely to influence practitioner motivation. Managers empower staff to become intimately involved in these activities to encourage self-efficacy and unit advocacy and growth. Decision-making opportunities promote perceptions of value, worth, and control—qualities necessary for one's self-fulfillment.

A focus on accountability and quality through evidence-based practices and outcomes requires each practitioner to assume responsibility. Feedback affirms staff efforts to document best practices. Positive feedback validates accountability actions and fosters motivation. First-line managers transfer to practitioners an increased degree of authority to ensure responsible use of limited resources. Formal and informal acknowledgments reward contributions.

Health and human service professionals are experiencing decreased direct client contact, blending of professional roles, and relocation of services. These trends either motivate or demotivate. Managers will facilitate personnel transformations and assist during periods of role ambiguity, offering training and development opportunities. Without adequate managerial support, employees are likely to perceive job insecurities, feelings of incompetence, and professional abandonment. Mentoring programs that facilitate job satisfaction and advancement are especially important to women and minorities in therapeutic recreation (Bedini & Anderson, 2003).

Just as the work setting and the way that work is managed are changing, so is the nature of the work force. The work force will be more globally and generationally diverse. A diverse workforce brings to the work setting an array of needs. Men place more importance on autonomy in their jobs than women do. Convenient work hours and good social relations are more important to women than men (Bedini & Anderson, 2003; Tomey, 2009). "Younger people tend to be more interested in income, whereas older people are interested in security" (Tomey, 2009, p. 115). Many of the motivational theories were developed and validated on American workers (Robbins, Decenzo, & Coulter 2011). Priorities like individual recognition and achievement are less evident in cultures that value team-based efforts and collectivism, like Hispanic and Latino cultures. Employees, therefore, have different personal needs they are hoping to satisfy on the job. Many of the motivation theories recognize that employees are not homogeneous. As a consequence, managers must vary their motivational techniques with the situation and employee involved.

To motivate, managers will focus on intangibles as well as tangibles in the work setting. Factors like autonomy, variety, group cohesiveness, peer recognition, personal development options like mentoring, and self-determined work schedules will become commonplace in the work environment. Amenities like on-site childcare and access to alternative program resources through telecommunications will accompany the coffee pot, company wellness programs, and flexible and reduced workweeks as standard employment benefits. Staff and volunteers will more readily achieve productivity in a work culture supportive of flexibility, professional growth, and self-management. The manager's challenge becomes communicating options through strategies like delegation of responsibility and adopting alternative incentives. Traditional management preparation tends to focus on day-to-day tasks like budgeting, marketing, and supervision. Future processes will emphasize concepts found in clinical supervision, self-efficacy, and human resource development.

Summary

1. The future will see an increased focus on the first-line manager's ability to motivate staff and volunteers. This is due to the changing nature of the work environment, work force, and health and human services dynamics. As traditional motivators like money and advancements become less available, the manager's ability to manipulate areas that influence the work environment become more critical to effective unit operations.
2. A number of theories have explained motivation. Each purports concepts applicable to manager-practitioner motivational variables. One of the more elementary but significant theories is Maslow's hierarchy of needs. Managers realize employees may have many needs motivating their behaviors at any given time and these vary with their degree of development.
3. Several behaviorists—Alderfer, Herzberg, Argyris, and McClelland—employed the concept of need satisfaction along a continuum from lower- to higher-order needs to describe the significance of need satisfaction to personal development and achievement in the work setting.
4. Skinner believed positive reinforcement improved desired work behaviors.
5. McGregor's now infamous Theory X and Theory Y also applied similar concepts to explain the difference between workers who require a carrot-and-stick approach and those who are motivated by self-growth opportunities.
6. Theories proposed since the 1960s (e.g., expectancy, equity, goal-setting) suggest that behavior alone does not motivate action. Workers are also motivated by perceptions of others, comparisons between their efforts and rewards and that of other employees, and the achievement of realistic goals.
7. The more recent Theory Z contends that participatory management strategies enhance workplace motivation.
8. Recreation therapists tend to be satisfied with their jobs and the contributions they make in the work place (intrinsic motivation) yet are challenged by opportunities for advancement and pay increases (extrinsic motivation).
9. The organizational culture and climate, the manager's formal supervisory responsibilities, and interpersonal behaviors and relationships impact the managers' and employees' motivational levels and desires.
10. As a role model, the manager ensures the use of self and consistent application of specific motivational techniques to create a positive work environment.
11. Management trends, health-care initiatives, and social demographics are causing dynamic work settings, diverse work forces, and adjustments to the way therapeutic recreation is practiced. In the future, managers will focus on tangibles and intangibles to create motivating workplaces.
12. Traditionally assumed motivators like financial reward will be supplemented by creative job design, access to educational opportunities, mentor relations, and management of the social fabric of one's work culture. Managers will craft flexible, supportive networks where interpersonal and professional development support achievement of personal needs and productivity.

Critical Thinking Activities

1. Which behavior theories explain your behavior in the classroom and when you are away from your college or work responsibilities?
2. What are the intrinsic and extrinsic motivators that have influenced your choice of a major/career?
3. For most people, a job is central to their livelihood. So why do first-line managers need to be

concerned about creating a supportive work environment?

4. Conduct an Internet search using "motivation theory" as key words. From this search, select Youtube.com videos that describe the motivational theories presented in this chapter. Review two of these videos and describe how these theories apply to today's work environment.

References

Arnold, M., Glover, R., & Beeler, C. (2012). *Human resource management in recreation, sport, and leisure services.* State College, PA: Venture Publishing, Inc.

Bedini, L. A., & Anderson, D. M. (2003). The benefits of formal mentoring for practitioners in therapeutic recreation. *Therapeutic Recreation Journal, 37*(3), 240–255.

Bogo, M., Paterson, J., Tufford, L., & King, R. (2011). Supporting front-line practitioners' professional development and job satisfaction in mental health and addiction. *Journal of Interprofessional Care, 25,* 209–214. doi:10.3109/13561820.2011.554240

Burtson, P. L., & Stichler, J. F. (2010). Nursing work environment and nursing caring: Relationship among motivation factors. *Journal of Advanced Nursing, 66*(8), 1819–1831.

Curtis, E., & O'Connell, R. (2011). Essential leadership skills for motivating and developing staff. *Nursing Management, 18*(5), 32–35.

Dalton, S. (2010). Motivating medicine: Why money is not enough. *Journal of Paediatrics and Child Health, 46*(4), 142–143.

Glenn, D. W., (2010). How to develop and sustain high performance teams in your laboratory. *Clinical Leadership & Management Review, 24*(4), 1–5.

Marquis B. L., & Huston, C. J., (2009). *Leadership roles and management functions in nursing: Theory & application* (6th ed.). Philadelphia, PA: Lippincott Williams & Wilkins.

Nohria, N., Groysberg, B., & Lee, L. E., (2008). Employee motivation: A powerful new model. *Harvard Business Review, 86* (7/8), 78–84.

Parsons, M. B., Reid, D. H., & Crow, R. E. (2003). Best and worst ways to motivate staff in community agencies: A brief survey of supervisors. *Mental Retardation, 41*(2), 96–102.

Riley, B., & Connolly, P. (2007). A profile of Certified Therapeutic Recreation Specialist practitioners, *Therapeutic Recreation Journal, 41*(1), 29–46.

Robbins, S. P., Decenzo, D. A., & Coulter, M. (2011). *Fundamentals of management essential concepts and applications* (6th ed.). Boston, MA: Prentice-Hall.

Sadri, G., & Bowen, C. (2011). Meeting employee requirements Maslow's hierarchy of needs is still a reliable guide to motivating staff. *Industrial Engineer, 43*(10), 44–48.

Stone, C. F., Kline, S. M., & Hammond, A. (2009). Job satisfaction levels of therapeutic recreation specialists in North Carolina. *Annual in Therapeutic Recreation, 17,* 46–60.

Sullivan, E. J., & Decker, P. J. (2009). *Effective leadership and management in nursing* (7th ed.). Upper Saddle River, NJ: Pearson/ Prentice-Hall.

Tager, S. (2002). Motivating staff. *Camping Magazine, 75*(6), 50–53.

Tomey, A. M. (2009). *Guide to nursing management and leadership* (8th ed.). St. Louis, MO: Mosby Elsevier.

Wendt, S., Tuckey, M. R., & Prosser, B. (2011). Thriving, not just surviving, in emotionally demanding fields of practice. *Health and Social Care in the Community, 19*(3), 317–325. doi: 10.1111/j.1365-2524.2010.00983.x

Witman, J. P., & Rakos, K. S. (2008). Determining the "other related duties" of therapeutic recreation and activity professionals: A pilot study. *American Journal of Recreation Therapy, 7*(2), 29–33.

Section 4

MANAGING SERVICE DELIVERY

Chapter 13
Managing for Service Accountability

Keywords

- Accountability
- APIE
- Coaching
- Consultant educator
- Consultant facilitator
- Consultant practitioner
- Critical pathways
- Electronic health records (EHR)
- Protocol
- Scheduling
- Staffing

Learning Outcomes

After reading this chapter, students will be able to:

1. Identify client, staff, and environmental variables affecting staffing and scheduling options.
2. Explain challenges inherent with staffing and employee scheduling.
3. Describe the manager's accountability functions in each APIE step.
4. Explain the benefits of using protocols and critical pathways in service delivery.
5. Interpret the importance of documentation to the APIE process.
6. Outline the manager's coaching and consulting roles as practitioner performance is monitored.

Overview

Worldwide every day, health-care professionals are being organized to meet the needs of clients. This staffing process is the responsibility of the manager. Managers must ascertain that an adequate number of professionals with the right skills are available daily to meet client needs and organizational goals (Marquis & Huston, 2009). Staffing is a highly dynamic process linked to key measures of health care, including financial performance, efficiency of care delivery, quality, safety, client outcomes, and the strength and safety of the workforce (Douglas & Kerfoot, 2011). The initial section of the chapter outlines influences and challenges faced by the manager as staffing patterns and scheduling policies are administered fairly and economically.

The therapeutic recreation process of assessment, planning, implementation, and evaluation (APIE) is a systematic process used by all professionals regardless of practice setting to achieve desired client outcomes. Adherence to the process promotes accountability, quality, and consistency in the delivery of evidence-based practices. This process is codified in our professional standards of practice (ATRA, 2013; CTRA, 2006), our credentialing standards (NCTRC, 2012), and in competencies for recreation therapy professionals (CTRA, 2006; West, Kinney, & Witman, 2008). Managers need to be acutely aware of and monitor the knowledge and skills of practitioners to carry out this process. The second section of this chapter reviews the accountability features of APIE. Also considered are documentation and the use of protocols and critical pathways to evaluate and standardize services. Managers supervise these activities to ensure data are maintained to verify outcomes of the therapeutic recreation process.

Evidence-based staffing affirms the right person with the right resources is matched with the right client at the right time and place for the right reason to meet client safety and quality outcomes (O'Rourke & White, 2011). Creating the right staffing mix is the manager's responsibility. The manager is accountable for creating and sustaining a work environment that supports and facilities quality service efforts of staff. The right environment encourages staff to actualize their knowledge and skills to achieve the best possible outcomes for clients, caregivers, the team, and the organization. Managers draw upon coaching, supervisory, and consulting techniques to monitor practitioner performance. The chapter closes with a discussion of these workforce-management responsibilities.

Staffing and Scheduling Options

The goal of staffing is to provide the appropriate numbers and mix of staff to match the actual or projected client service needs (Sullivan & Decker, 2009). *Scheduling* is developing a plan for where and when professionals are to work within the parameters dictated by the organization. The therapeutic recreation manager is usually responsible for developing the schedule because he or she is aware of client needs as well as the expertise and personal needs of the staff. *Staffing* goes beyond filling a hole in a schedule—it is an evidence-based process that links client safety, quality outcomes, and caregiver engagement to efficient and effective use of qualified staff and stewardship of the unit's resources (Anderson & Kerfoot, 2012; O'Rourke & White, 2011). Thus the manager considers a number of variables as staffing policies and schedules are designed and implemented. Consequently, the manager is challenged to remain fiscally and ethically accountable, for effective staffing is central to the organization's success and the profession's ability to produce quality results.

Staffing Variables

Creating effective staffing plans and then adjusting them to meet daily client needs is complex. There is no one formula or model to follow. While remaining cognizant of personnel costs, the manager continually processes information on staff work-schedule preferences, schedule equity, regulatory requirements, and balancing staffing competencies with real-time client needs to make the best staffing decisions (Crist-Grundman & Mulrooney, 2011).The manager's staffing goals are presented in Table 13.1.

Table 13.1 Staffing Goals

1. Achievement of department objectives and productivity measures, especially those related to client service.
2. Accurate match of department needs with staff and volunteer abilities and numbers.
3. Maximum use of personnel resources.
4. Equity of treatment to all employees (or equal treatment for all employees within a similar job classification) and volunteers.
5. Optimal use of professional expertise.
6. Satisfaction of practitioners (both as to hours worked and as to perceived sense of scheduling equity) and volunteers.
7. Consideration of unique needs of staff, volunteers, and clients.

A number of client, staff, and environmental factors guide staffing decisions. Client factors include client types, census, and acuity. Staffing factors that guide decisions include staff cultural, linguistic and generational diversity; staff skill mix; job descriptions; mix of work titles or personnel classifications; educational and experience levels of staff; hour and rotational policies; and, the competitive market. Environmental factors like adequacy of the budget; personnel policies; legislation concerning work time and mandatory staffing rates; regulatory criteria from bodies like the Joint Commission that require care based on specific client needs and severity level; supplies, equipment, and resources available; productivity measures; and organizational structure also influence staffing and scheduling options (Marquis & Huston, 2009; Tomey, 2009).

Client types, census, and acuity are primary staffing considerations. Managers assign a certain number of staff with specific educational and experiential backgrounds to programs so clients achieve their treatment or program outcomes. Managers consider staff skill mix when they assign, for example, intervention specialists or inclusion coaches to support CTRSs. Staff skill mix influences the number of staff scheduled to cover specific programs. Managers consider the ethnic and cultural needs of clients and are sensitive to providing culturally and linguistically appropriate services by staff with relevant awareness and competence.

The intergenerational workforce calls upon the manager to assess staff that represents different generations with different values which may impact staffing. For example, Boomers may wish to work longer hours to satisfy their materialistic interests, while Generation Xers and Generation Yers (Millennials) may prefer flexible hours and part-time work to accommodate their volunteer interests and social engagements (Marquis & Huston, 2009). Additionally, because the health-care workforce is predominately female, the manager introduces scheduling flexibility to minimize family and work conflicts ("Want to keep," 2011).

Environmental factors intertwine with staff and client considerations. For example, managers consider direct service versus nonproductive time of staff. In-service programs, staff meetings, documentation, attending conferences, and gathering supplies and equipment are all necessary, yet they take time away from the client and meeting productivity expectations. Nonproductive time includes paid time off for funerals, vacation, holidays, education, and sick leave. Managers assign PRN staff (staff scheduled on an as-needed basis) to cover programs if full-time staff are not present to ensure delivery of services that meet standards, address client needs, and are worthy of reimbursement.

Therapeutic recreation managers have the dual responsibility of planning for sufficient staff numbers to meet client needs while remaining within the unit staffing budget (Marquis & Huston, 2009). Staffing budgets may be based on prior year productivity and budget figures. Growing federal and state/provincial budget deficits have resulted in increased pressure to reduce costs in health-care agencies (Marquis & Huston, 2009). Consequently, managers explore ways to improve productivity (obtaining more work for less overall cost) while holding or decreasing staff hours. Outputs are measured by the number of interventions performed, programs conducted, and clients treated. Thus, the manager constantly compares staff capacity and competence to client results to ensure productivity measures are satisfied.

In devising schedules, the manager is aware of laws concerning work time and ratios. As noted in Chapter 8, there are federal, state/provincial, and even local laws and regulations which deal with wages and hours that must be followed. In most health and human service organizations, the organization's personnel policies or human resources (HR) department can inform the manager of the legal regulations impacting staffing. If employees are unionized, it is important that the manager review any labor contracts for their impact on his or her staffing and scheduling.

Agency personnel policies influence the manager's staffing assignments and may result from legislative and regulatory criteria. Policies "represent the standard of action that is communicated in advance so that employees are not caught unaware regarding personnel matters" (Marquis & Huston, 2009, pp. 413–414). When developed in collaboration with human resource departments, the first-line manager is assured of expertise, for example, pertaining to union contracts, state/provincial labor laws, and organizational-level protocols. With periodic staff input, managers bring flexibility to policy design and implementation. Policies and procedures related to staffing that might be cooperatively designed and implemented include rotation or shift policies; time for online schedule distribution; weekend and holiday policy; tardiness policy; low census procedures; procedures for requesting time off; absenteeism policies; procedures for funerals, vacations, and holiday time requests; emergency request policies; procedures for resolving conflicts regarding days off; education and training request procedures; and procedures for monitoring computerized time reports (Marquis & Huston, 2009).

Learning Outcome
Identify client, staff, and environmental variables affecting staffing and scheduling options.

Scheduling Options and Challenges

Scheduling significantly impacts job satisfaction, productivity, and retention. As there is no one model to follow, patterns of peer professionals, especially in health-care settings, are considered as their schedules impact those of the therapeutic recreation unit. Similarly, within community services, the schedules of feeder agencies like schools influence seasonal plans. Examples of staffing and scheduling options include self-scheduling, flextime, alternating or rotating work shifts, permanent shifts, block or cyclical scheduling, shift bidding, and computerized scheduling.

With self-scheduling, staff assume responsibility to develop their schedules following guidelines agreed on for the department. Flextime allows staff to select time schedules that best meet their personal needs while still meeting their work responsibilities. With alternating work shifts, staff rotate among shifts, whereas with permanent shifts, staff select a preferred shift. In block or cyclical scheduling, the same schedule is used repeatedly. Shift bidding allows staff to bid if desired to work a particular shift with the unit setting the price for the shift. Computerized schedules may be generated with centralized management of scheduling through human resources to ensure agency-wide adherence to various standards. Because all scheduling and staffing patterns impact employees' personal lives, productivity, and budgets, periodically, the manager assesses staffing and scheduling changes to gauge financial costs, retention, productivity, risk and safety management, and employee and client satisfaction (Marquis & Huston, 2009).

Scheduling challenges arise from the client, staff, and environmental factors impacting the manager's decisions. To illustrate, to accommodate the cost of services today, many health and human service organizations combine full-time and part-time practitioners in a therapeutic recreation department. While part-time practitioners may be qualified, there are disadvantages in hiring them. Use of part-time practitioners may pose a threat to continuity of service. In addition, part-time employees are usually involved in in-service training or ongoing education programs and while the cost to orient and train part- and full-time staff is similar, the cost per hour worked by the part-time staff is higher (Tomey, 2009).

Abuse of sick time is another factor that can ruin a well-planned schedule. Some practitioners perceive sick time as time that is owed to them. They use sick days whether or not they are ill. Such practices can be curtailed by good personnel policies concerning chronic absences. Some organizations give back a proportion of unused sick days as extra days off. Other organizations allow the accrual of unlimited sick leave.

These scheduling matters are not the only concerns of the therapeutic recreation manager. Other matters associated with the manager's role in scheduling may or may not result in challenges and include verifying to the fiscal office services provided to clients for billing purposes or collecting fees, monitoring supplies and equipment used, approving department staff payroll, monitoring personnel schedules (e.g., sick time, volunteers), and monitoring productivity (e.g., cost of Program A relative to Program B, effectiveness relative to efficiency in the economic sense).

Regardless of the challenges inherent in scheduling, a management function is accountability for a prenegotiated budget. Because personnel budgets are a major portion of health and human service organizations' budgets, "a small percentage cut in personnel may result in large savings" (Marquis & Huston, 2009, pp. 412–413). It is just as important for the manager to use staff to provide safe and effective care economically as it is to be ethical to clients and staff. Staff have the right to expect reasonable workloads. So as managers address the challenges and take into consideration a number of variables that affect scheduling, they "must ensure that adequate staffing exists to meet the needs of staff and patients" (Marquis & Huston, 2009, p. 413).

Learning Outcome
Explain challenges inherent with staffing and employee scheduling.

Therapeutic Recreation Process

A process is a series of planned actions or operations directed toward a particular result. The therapeutic recreation process of assessment, planning, implementation, and evaluation *(APIE)* is a systematic, rational method of planning and providing therapeutic recreation to the client (O'Morrow & Reynolds, 1989). This process identifies an agreed-upon set of responsibilities practiced by all professionals regardless of population or setting (Mobily & Ostiguy, 2004). Researchers investigating professional responsibilities (LeBlanc & Singleton, 2008) and quality indicators in recreation therapy (Hoss & McCormick, 2007) identify each component of APIE and documentation as essential to practice and to evaluate practice quality. The majority of our work time is spent on implementation and TR treatment. The use of protocols remains limited and as a consequence presents "a barrier to more consistent, standardized and evidence-based practice" (Witman & Ligon, 2011, pp. 3–4).

The APIE or TR process and its documentation present a framework for *accountability*. These processes outline and record the steps taken to achieve and measure client goals through service delivery. Managers integrate protocols into APIE to improve care quality. While service delivery is a central responsibility of therapists, the manager is ultimately accountable for measuring and reporting outcomes resulting from APIE. This section reviews practitioner responsibilities during APIE and the manager's oversight role as it relates to ensuring quality through APIE, protocols, and documentation.

Accountability in the Therapeutic Recreation Process

"Accountability means being held responsible for the production and delivery of therapeutic recreation services that best meet client needs and move clients toward predetermined outcomes in the most timely, efficient, and effective manner possible" (Stumbo & Peterson, 2009, p. 73). The therapeutic recreation process provides a framework for accountability and responsibility in therapeutic recreation and maximizes accountability and responsibility for standards of service (e.g., the Joint Commission, CARF, continuous quality improvement [CQI], ATRA, and CTRA). Therapists are responsible for helping clients achieve predetermined changes through design and consistent delivery of programs, outlined as follows.

Assessing

The therapeutic recreation practitioner is accountable for collecting information, encouraging consumer participation, and judging the validity of the collected data. When assessing, the practitioner is accountable for gaps in data and conflicting data, inaccurate data, and biased data. In addition, the practitioner is accountable for the judgments made about the client problem. For example, is the problem recognized by the client? Did the practitioner consider the client's values, beliefs, and cultural practices when determining the problem? Because assessment is the beginning point for therapy, all decisions and subsequent actions of therapists "should be grounded in some form of assessment" (Long, 2008, p. 80). The manager is responsible for having an assessment process in place and ensuring that staff address the above questions.

Planning

Accountability at the planning stage involves determining priorities, establishing client goals, predicting outcomes, and planning evidence-based practices. They are all incorporated into a written plan and shared with a team. Since planning occurs at multiple levels in therapeutic recreation, therapists are accountable to design and implement individual intervention plans, specific programs, and comprehensive services (Long, 2008; Stumbo & Peterson, 2009). Therapists are responsible to ensure that client needs remain at the heart of programs and that the selected interventions facilitate desired changes defined in each plan's goal statements. Managers oversee staff completion of planning documents and the incorporation of research and evidence in their design.

Implementation

Therapeutic recreation practitioners are responsible for all their actions in delivering services. Although the manager has delegated or assigned practitioners to client interventions, the practitioner is still accountable for the assigned action. During this phase, therapists rely on their facilitation skills to lead a variety of modalities and techniques to achieve mutually agreed-upon outcomes (Shank & Coyle, 2002; Witman & Ligon, 2011). Thus, accountability focuses on the therapist's use of interpersonal skills, leadership skills, and oral and written communication skills to ensure implemented plans realize targeted goals. Processing or debriefing ensures protocols or written program descriptions are consistently implemented and progress toward goals is evident. Lastly, therapists are responsible to document evidence of client reactions to the program. Continued data collection is essential to track changes in the client's functioning, health, and quality of life and also to obtain evidence of goal achievement during the next phase. Managers supervise staff program delivery to ensure consistency and optimal staff performance.

Evaluation

By establishing the degree to which the goals and objectives have been attained, the practitioner is accountable for the success or failure of therapeutic recreation actions. The practitioner must be able to explain why a client goal was not met and what phase or phases of APIE may require change and why. Documentation of program outcomes is expected by insurance companies, federal funders, accreditation agencies, professional organizations, and agency administrators who expect effective, cost-efficient service quality (Long, 2008). The therapist is accountable for meeting predetermined goals through a predetermined course of action (Stumbo & Peterson, 2009). Evaluation holds professionals responsible for their efforts. Decision making is important in every phase of APIE, especially evaluation (O'Morrow, 1986; Stumbo & Peterson, 2009). Through informed decision-making, the therapist and manager determine what data to collect, when and how to collect the information, and why the results document evidence of accountable, cost-effective programs.

The therapeutic recreation manager is ultimately responsible for practitioner activity relating to evaluation of the therapeutic recreation process. The role of the manager relative to this process also incorporates a number to tasks (refer to Table 13.2, p. 210).

Learning Outcome

Describe the manager's accountability functions in each APIE step.

Table 13.2 Manager's Evaluation Tasks

- Update assessment tools.
- Review protocols and program plans to ensure that interventions match individual and group needs and objectives.
- Collect data and audit evaluations to ensure achievement of individual, group, and department outcomes that validate evidence-based practices.
- Facilitate documentation process via monitoring routine maintenance records.
- Communicate to practitioner organizational changes that impact department services and the TR process.
- Ensure training on new interventions and documentation techniques.

Accountability Tools, Protocols, and Critical Pathways

For therapeutic recreation, standardized and evidence-based care are imperative (Stumbo & Peterson, 2009). Protocols and critical pathways are tools that increase the quality of services while holding therapists accountable for achieving predetermined outcomes through deliberately planned interventions. The therapist purposefully selects a specific intervention to use with a particular client or client need because evidence from research, literature, or practice suggests the intervention results in predictable outcomes. When the APIE process incorporates protocols and best-practice guidelines, consistency, cost-effectiveness, and accountability are brought to service delivery.

Protocol

A *protocol* is a series of actions required to manage a specific problem or issue. These problems are associated with the physical, psychological, social, and cognitive functioning of the individual. "Protocols describe the collective and proven strategies of specific interventions to bring about targeted behavioral change in clients" (Stumbo & Peterson, 2009, p. 231). A protocol is a document describing interventions designed and delivered to be repeatable and to attain predetermined outcomes. A protocol may address a specific therapeutic recreation department program or service or a client's therapeutic recreation comprehensive plan from admission to discharge, including assessment, intervention, and outcome. Therefore, there are two kinds of protocols. Treatment or program protocols provide the framework to assess, plan, implement, and evaluate programs based on one profession (i.e., RT/TR, PT, and OT) and outline the way specific services are delivered to clients. Diagnostic or problem-based protocols provide the framework for how a specific group of clients with a common "diagnosis" or "problem" is served in a program (Stumbo & Peterson, 2009). A diagnostic protocol may focus on either a specific diagnosis like Alzheimer's (AD) or on a cluster of problems like depression or disorientation. Since diagnostic protocols focus on client deficits, staff may develop several to address the needs of clients served by the department.

Illustrations of protocols are found through literature and research presented in professional journals (Bonadies, 2010; Lynch, 2006) and publications of ATRA (Buettner, 2001). Additionally, textbooks present samples (Stumbo & Peterson, 2009) and describe recreational therapy practice by specific diagnoses with recommended interventions (Porter & burlingame, 2006). Although there is not one common format to use with either type of protocol, common features include purpose or problem, intended outcomes, descriptive explanation of clientele, specific interventions to be used, procedures to implement the interventions, and evaluation criteria (Shank & Coyle, 2002). The professional who elects to use these publications will note the protocols are presented by describing the APIE process, including a sample protocol and research that documents the effectiveness of the particular intervention. When the therapist incorporates these tools into day-to-day practice, this is a form of evidence-based practice that promotes consistent intervention and accountable program quality.

LEARNING OUTCOME
Explain the benefits of using protocols in service delivery.

Critical Pathway

Critical pathways, care maps, or clinical paths are protocols involving all disciplines; they "are one method of planning, assessing, implementing, and evaluating the cost-effectiveness of patient care" (Marquis & Huston, 2009, p. 221). They are standardized best practices for managing patient care during a specified time period (Sullivan & Decker, 2009). Each pathway identifies an average length of stay with certain interventions prescribed at certain time intervals along the path. This flow chart/

grid format orients staff to the client's needs and the outcomes to be achieved within the desired timeframe. They may replace individual client treatment plans because they include each therapy with expected interventions and outcomes over the length of stay according to a particular diagnostic group (DRG), and they are easily maintained in electronic health records. A pathway quantifies time, money, and staff effort, so the manager is able to evaluate variances from the proposed length of stay to determine financial outcomes.

With the use of protocols and pathways, the therapeutic recreation manager has three responsibilities: (a) overseeing the development and revision of protocols and pathways, (b) advocating the role of therapeutic recreation throughout the organization with protocols and pathways as an illustration of the contribution of therapeutic recreation to outcomes, and (c) conducting efficacy research with protocol/pathway implementation and data collection to verify outcomes of intervention application and advance evidence-based practices.

Learning Outcome
Explain the benefits of using critical pathways in service delivery.

Documenting APIE

Professional responsibility and accountability in therapeutic recreation are among the most important reasons for documentation. Documentation is part of the practitioner's total responsibility in providing service, and it is the manager's responsibility to note its appropriateness and correctness through coaching, training, and auditing. With the therapeutic recreation process as a framework for practice, documentation has evolved as an essential link between the provision of service and evaluation of service. Documentation is the primary method to record service outcomes and is the official and legal record of service (Shank & Coyle, 2002; Stumbo & Peterson, 2009). Accreditation bodies like the Joint Commission and CARF require documentation of services rendered while federal and state/provincial entities require service records to qualify for reimbursement. It is vital for team communication and informing the team of the client's response to interventions. Further documentation is used to improve care quality and identify researchable problems (Austin, 2009). Basically, evaluation of documentation ensures quality management.

Learning Outcome
Interpret the importance of documentation to the APIE process.

While the therapeutic recreation practitioner will document the assessment, planning, and implementation phase of the therapeutic recreation process, documentation of the evaluation phase is an important and ongoing part of the process. Evaluation of the client's status, progress, or achievement of outcomes is provided through a progress or service note. Progress notes are not only vital for evaluation purposes but also used for protection from liability and for reimbursement in health-care facilities.

Progress/service notes document the client's status in relation to the desired outcomes (Shank & Coyle, 2002). The client's responses are compared with the outcomes defined in the treatment or program plan. The frequency with which to document progress depends on organization policy. Within a community-based service organization it may be on a weekly, monthly, or seasonal basis. In health-care facilities, the type of charting system used in the organization may define how often one should document an evaluation. Therapeutic recreation protocols may specify frequency. Last, the therapeutic recreation department, or its intervention procedures, may specify frequency.

One last point on documentation evaluation specifically related to health-care facilities is the transfer and discharge information. Transfer forms are used to communicate important information about the client's status when the client is moved within the health-care facility, between two facilities, or between home and an agency. The client's most significant therapeutic recreation information should be discussed to provide a clear picture of the client's participation in therapeutic recreation service and the needs of the client for follow-up. Depending on the setting, therapeutic recreation discharge information would describe the client's involvement in the program, how well the client achieved the planned outcomes, condition of the client at discharge, and any specific instructions/information/referrals given to the client and/or caregiver (Shank & Coyle, 2002).

Regardless of setting, legible, accurate documentation is imperative. Records communicate important information about the client to a variety of professionals. In the event of a lawsuit, the record may form the basis for the plaintiff's case or the therapeutic recreation practitioner's or manager's defense. Best practice techniques and strategies for quality documentation are summarized in Table 13.3 (Austin, 2009; Shank & Coyle, 2002; Stumbo & Peterson, 2009).

Computers and *electronic health records (EHR)* are impacting documentation protocols and charting systems in health-care and human-service agencies. Health information from all sources is accessed by any authorized health-care provider from multiple locations on computers linked to a secure system. These systems, once integrated, permit access across settings, disciplines, and among clients while standardizing documentation and charting systems, resulting in fewer errors due to illegible handwriting (Stumbo & Peterson, 2009). Additionally, point-of-care systems and handheld devices speed accurate record keeping (Sullivan & Decker, 2009). Redundancies are reduced, medical errors are decreased, and costs are lowered with online records. Refer to Chapter 6 for discussion of technology and health-care records.

Students may find a variety of charting systems in health-care settings. Each may require online data entry. Some of the more popular methods include:

- Source-oriented or narrative charting describes the client's status, any interventions, treatment, and client response to the interventions in a narrative format that focuses on the source of the information;
- SOAP (subjective data, objective data, assessment, and plan) or SOAPIER (same as SOAP but I for interventions, E for evaluation, and R for revision) is a problem-focused method that organizes data around a client problem;
- PIE (problems, interventions, and evaluation) is a method of identifying client concerns and organizing the narrative documentation to include data (D), action (A), and response (R) for each identified concern which is labeled and organized on a flow sheet by number with corresponding numbers assigned to the intervention and evaluation of the concern;
- CBE (charting by exception) records only significant or abnormal occurrences that deviate from professional standards or protocols;
- FACT closely resembles CBE and is named for its four key elements: flow sheets (F), assessment (A), (C)oncise integrated flow sheets and progress notes, and (T)imely entries; and
- Outcomes, which focuses on care processes, especially the client's behaviors and reactions to interventions; documentation includes descriptions of behaviors, standards for measuring behaviors, conditions under which behaviors occurred, and target date or time by which the behaviors should occur (Austin, 2009; Shank & Coyle, 2002; Stumbo & Peterson, 2009).

Depending on the type of computer and health-care record in use, the practitioner may enter data into the system by filling in blanks, entering words or phrases to construct sentences, using blank text or free-form data entry, or selecting from a menu to highlight critical pieces of data such as changes in client responses (Lansky, 1989).

Regardless of what form and system is used, all documentation incorporates assessment, planning, care or program plans, progress or service notes, and a discharge or transition summary. Effective documentation assures clients receive quality services. It facilitates coordination among service providers and is the primary means of accountability among professionals. First-line managers are responsible for ensuring that their unit's

Table 13.3 Documentation Best Practices

1. Write neatly and legibly.
2. Use proper spelling, grammar, and present tense.
3. Document in blue or black ink (examine agency protocol).
4. Use authorized abbreviations.
5. Never leave blank space.
6. Chart promptly (if possible).
7. Chart after the delivery of service, rather than before.
8. Identify late entries correctly.
9. Correct errors.
10. Do not use ditto marks.
11. Chart chronologically on consecutive lines.
12. Do not mention incident reports.
13. Document unusual events and pertinent observations.
14. Document accurately, objectively, and use behavioral language.
15. Document potentially contributing client behaviors.
16. Date, time, and sign each entry.

documentation identifies and evaluates client outcomes and measures evidence of intervention using the therapeutic recreation process.

Monitoring and Consulting Practitioner Performance

Monitoring and consulting new and experienced practitioner performance represents one of the more challenging responsibilities of a first-line manager. The responsibility is a difficult one because of the complexity of making judgments about the very people managers rely on and the colleagues with whom they have developed close working relationships. Nevertheless, the manager is a supervisor whose task is to create and sustain within the department a work environment that supports and facilitates quality service delivery efforts of staff and encourages them to actualize their knowledge and skills as services are delivered. Monitoring or coaching is initially considered, because the day-to-day staff activities determine service delivery quality. A second section outlines the manager's role as a consultant. In this role, the manager works with unit staff as well as others in the agency to improve and advance practitioner performance and competence.

Learning Outcome
Outline the manager's coaching roles as practitioner performance is monitored.

Monitoring/Coaching and Practitioner Performance

Monitoring may be broadly defined as that managerial task concerned with checking and reviewing the day-to-day work activity of the practitioner. *Coaching* is a contemporary term used to convey the day-to-day feedback that managers use to improve work performance and build teams (Marquis & Huston, 2009). Coaching is used to intervene immediately in performance problems before they become subject to discussion during performance appraisal interviews, and coaching also occurs when performance meets the standard but improvement is still possible (Sullivan & Decker, 2009). Coaching guides staff to increased competence, commitment, and confidence while helping them anticipate options for connecting present and future plans (Marquis & Huston, 2009).

Monitoring/coaching may be an on-the-spot forum to collect and to analyze information from the practitioner about work activity and outcomes while ascertaining whether steps should be taken to alter the activity of the practitioner or mode of operation. It may also be an individual conference as a result of reading or hearing case records/presentations or treatment plans. Previewing case records allows the manager to identify problem areas as practitioners pursue their responsibilities. Coaching is undertaken for a number of reasons (refer to Table 13.4).

Routine monitoring is most critical for inexperienced, new practitioners. At the same time, professional development continues throughout one's practice, and practitioners who have had experience also need assistance at times. However, the manager must be sensitive to the types of supervision experienced by practitioners who have accumulated experience. Practitioners who have been monitored previously in their place of work may have positive or negative expectations about upcoming supervision. If the previous experience was negative, the present manager must overcome this mindset, as performance is one of the strongest predictors of an individual's satisfaction with his or her position (Feldman, 1980).

Table 13.4 Coaching Objectives

1. To assess practitioner's attitudes about the job, responsibilities, organization, and the supervision.
2. To further the manager's understanding of the practitioner.
3. To obtain feedback on practitioner's work activity (e.g., complying with regulations, protocols, standards of practice and procedures, achieving desired results).
4. To assist the manager in becoming more aware of differences among practitioners for better practitioner deployment.
5. To assist in clarifying activities associated with annual performance reviews.
6. To assist the manager in making decisions about in-service training needs.
7. To assist the practitioner in his or her self-evaluation.
8. To assist in clarifying activities associated with annual performance reviews.
9. To enable the manager to represent the accomplishments of the program to the organization and to the larger community—a process crucial for building support, correcting misinformation, and relationship and social marketing.

Table 13.5 Manager's Coaching Practices

1. Be specific rather than general.
2. Be descriptive rather than evaluative.
3. Direct the feedback toward the behavior to be changed.
4. Use sensitivity to time the feedback.
5. Be sure the employee has understood the feedback and the manager hears the employee's communication.

The responsibility for monitoring is shared by the manager and practitioner through the joint process of building a relationship, which encourages free discussion of job-related responsibilities. Thus, coaching requires strong communication skills, an ability to reflect back, and to serve as a "mirror" for those being coached (Marquis & Huston, 2009). To become more effective as coaches, managers develop specific communication practices (refer to Table 13.5) (Marquis & Huston, 2009).

Effective coaching nurtures growth and development of employees through learning. While coaching takes time, it will save time, money, and errors by practitioners, which in the long run will benefit all—the manager, the practitioners, the organization, and the clients.

Learning Outcome

Outline the manager's consulting roles as practitioner performance is monitored.

Consultant and Practitioner Performance

Many managers view the term "consultant" as something reserved only for the expert or the outsider. While this view may be correct in some instances, its use here is viewed as a process whereby the manager, as a supervisor, provides assistance to others on the basis of a request for assistance or on the basis of developing an atmosphere for requesting assistance. From another perspective, consulting may be considered a method which gives service indirectly by assisting the practitioner in handling problems associated with the client. Regardless of the method, the ultimate goal of consulting is to increase the competence of the practitioner. In some respects, the manager may serve as a kind of senior practitioner and role model, demonstrating valued behavior, attitudes, and/or skills that aid the practitioner in achieving competence, confidence, and a clear professional identity.

While the manager may be involved in consulting relative to giving colleagues insight into what is going on around them, within them, among them and other people, or in program consulting wherein the manager is invited by top management to assist in organizational planning and program development, the focus here is on therapeutic recreation process consulting. The consulting process begins with the recognition by the practitioner that his or her program responsibility could be enhanced by consulting with the manager. The manager assists practitioners in resolving particular problems related to a client or group for which the practitioner is responsible. The manager may engage in consulting related to helping the practitioner develop a more comprehensive diagnosis of the client's problems, expanding the practitioner's options regarding alternative methods of interventions that might be used to bring about change, or assisting the practitioner in recognizing the relationship of the practitioner's personal feelings and anxieties to the client's needs.

The manager's method of intervention will vary according to his or her personality and professional background as an experienced *practitioner*, *facilitator*, and *educator*. These roles may be conceptualized along a continuum from most directive to least directive, most authoritative to least authoritative. As an *experienced practitioner*, the manager may be viewed as an expert and therefore authoritative and directive, one who imparts special knowledge or skill and who may be expected to have information to resolve all service-delivery concerns. A common occurrence is the desire of the practitioner to be as competent as his or her manager. While such aspirations of this type are a positive motivation for the practitioner to learn the knowledge and skills of the therapeutic recreation profession, it is wise for the manager to disclose his or her own errors, doubts, and disappointments. Good consulting requires that the manager admits fallibility and devotes energy to furthering growth and building strength in the practitioner.

On the other hand, the manager as a consultant may assume a *facilitator* role. This involves the manager in a communication process which utilizes the collective resources of both the manager and the practitioner in problem solving. By skillfully using questions to help define and explore problems, the manager tries to generate alternative solutions from the worker and then discusses the pros and cons of each alternative. The manager might add alternatives not mentioned by the practitioner. Next, the manager helps the practitioner choose the approach that seems most likely to be successful and, equally important, one consistent with practice service delivery. By helping the practitioner to evaluate and choose an approach, the manager is not only assisting the practitioner with the development of professional competency but also is communicating confidence in the practitioner's practice ability, thus encouraging the practitioner to take a major role in the learning process.

The role of the manager as *consultant-educator* to the practitioner is one of the most widely recognized roles. The educator role may involve anything from on-the-spot teaching (e.g., giving evaluative reactions to a specific service delivery approach to the client, offering suggestions of what to do differently to be more effective) to citing specific articles or websites relevant to the problem faced by the practitioner. The manager might also demonstrate a particular technique or approach by role playing with the practitioner. Then, too, the manager may offer strategies or techniques for the practitioner to implement during service delivery.

The practitioner is an active participant in the learning process. The consultant's job is to present ideas and to monitor the way in which the practitioner relates to the ideas. This may range from simply watching the practitioner's eyes to make sure he or she understands the directions for documentation to having regard for the practitioner's feelings while trying to help him or her tackle a difficult treatment plan. It can also mean being sensitive to the subtle interplay taking place between the consultant and the practitioner that has been described as the authority item. The effect resulting from this relationship can enhance the learning or can generate obstacles to the integration of new ideas. Of course, some anxiety will be created by any supervisory technique or discussion, but most managers would agree that some techniques produce more anxiety than others (e.g., a one-on-one in the manager's office may produce more anxiety than a brief hallway conversation between the manager and employee). The authors view supervision here as the management of changes in the practitioner toward ideal professional behavior.

The eventual goal of the consulting role is the engagement of the manager and practitioner in a mutually responsible collegial relationship that values the participation of the practitioner equally with that of the manager. The result of this engagement should assist the practitioner in being able to integrate and apply basic practice skills in the delivery of therapeutic recreation service with consistency. Competency gives a practitioner credibility so that others will tend to seek out and respond to his or her suggestions. As long as both the new and old practitioner and the manager communicate openly and recognize and respond to each other's needs and expectations, mutual development will continue and the satisfaction of all will be enhanced.

Summary

1. Staffing and scheduling ensure that the right staff is in place at the proper time so clients' outcomes are achieved and the associated measures of a unit's performance, such as client safety and cost-effectiveness are also realized. The manager is responsible for staffing patterns and scheduling options in the unit in collaboration with other organizational units.
2. A number of client, staff, and environmental variables influence the manager's staffing decisions and schedule preparation.
3. Challenges arise with developing a staffing schedule that best uses staff and unit resources while achieving client outcomes and agency goals.
4. The APIE process and documentation are best practices and the framework for accountability. The manager uses these accountability tools to ensure that programs achieve desired client, unit, and organizational outcomes.
5. Practitioners tend to spend the majority of their work time on implementation and treatment yet during each phase of the process, they are responsible for specific activities which are overseen by the manager.
6. Protocols and critical pathways offer consistency in program delivery and are elements therapists need to incorporate into the APIE process. Managers oversee development and coordination of these accountability tools.
7. Documentation is critical to accountability as it provides the evidence that links our practice to client outcomes and as such serves to evaluate service-delivery effectiveness.

8. Documentation is essential to reimbursement and may become a legal explanation of the TR process. Managers guide staff and maintain records required by oversight agencies like CARF International.
9. There are various charting systems in use in health-care facilities, yet many health-care facilities have shifted to computerized information systems and electronic health records.
10. The manager monitors staff through coaching that focuses on the day-to-day performance of the practitioner, while managerial consultation addresses activities important to continuing professional development.

Critical Thinking Activities

1. No one is ever completely satisfied with the schedule. How would you handle a staff person who constantly asks to have his/her schedule changed? How would you handle the staff person that continually comes to work late? What unit/agency policies exist to manage these employee behaviors?
2. Using a software program, complete a weekly schedule for four staff and one manager. Develop coverage for 6 days, first with the four staff working 8-hour shifts; second with the staff working 10-hour shifts. Each staff member is to work 40 hours in the 6 days but does not have to work each day, while the manager is to work a total of 40 hours over the 6 days. RT is provided daily from 10:00 am to 8:00 pm.
3. With a classmate, role play a coaching scenario. One is the manager (coach). The other is a staff member who is using the agency's computerized documentation system for the first time. The staff member is only familiar with the computer hardware/software used in college and on a personal laptop, so he or she is challenged to enter the client and program information. Incorporate the 5 monitoring suggestions found in the chapter (p. 214) in your conversation.

References

American Therapeutic Recreation Association (ATRA). (2013). *Standards for the practice of therapeutic recreation, and self-assessment guide.* Hattiesburg, MS: Author.

Anderson, R., & Kerfoot, K. (2012). The time has come for evidence-based staffing and scheduling. *Nursing Economic$, 27*(5), 277–279.

Austin, D. R. (2009). *Therapeutic recreation processes and techniques* (6th ed.). Champaign, IL: Sagamore.

Bonadies, V. (2010). Guided imagery as a therapeutic recreation modality to reduce pain. *Annual in Therapeutic Recreation, 18*, 164–174.

Buettner, L. L. (2001). *A research monograph: Efficacy of prescribed therapeutic recreation protocols on falls and injuries in nursing home residents with dementia.* Alexandria, VA: ATRA.

Canadian Therapeutic Recreation Association (CTRA). (2006). *Standards of practice for recreation therapists & therapeutic recreation assistants.* Calgary, Alberta, Canada: Author.

Crist-Grundman, D., & Mulrooney, G. (2011). Effective workforce management starts with leveraging technology, while staffing optimization requires true collaboration. *Nursing Economic$, 29*(4), 195–200.

Douglas, K., & Kerfoot, K. (2011). Forging the future of staffing based on evidence. *Nursing Economic$, 29*(4), 161, 167.

Feldman, D. A. (1980). A socialization process that helps new recruits succeed. *Personnel, 57*, 163–174.

Hoss, M. A., & McCormick, B. (2007). Survey to identify quality indicators for recreational therapy practice. *Annual in Therapeutic Recreation, 15*, 35–44.

Lansky, D. (1989). Hospital-based outcomes management: Enhancing quality of care with coordinated data systems. In L. M. Kingland (Ed.), *Proceedings of the thirteenth annual symposium on computer applications in medical care: Enhancing quality of care with coordinated data systems* (pp. 732–736). Washington, DC: IEEE Computer Society.

LeBlanc, A., & Singleton, J. F. (2008). Juggling the diverse responsibilities of therapeutic recreation. *Annual in Therapeutic Recreation, 16*, 182–192.

Long, T. (2008). The therapeutic recreation process. In T. Robertson & T. Long (Eds.). *Foundations of therapeutic recreation* (pp. 79–99). Champaign, IL: Human Kinetics.

Lynch, C. J. (2006). Exercise: A treatment intervention for dysthymia in the geriatric population. *American Journal of Recreation Therapy, 5*(2), 27–36.

Marquis, B. L., & Huston, C. J. (2009). *Leadership roles and management functions in nursing: Theory and application* (6th ed.). Philadelphia: Lippincott Williams & Wilkins.

Mobily, K. E., & Ostiguy, L. J. (2004). *Introduction to therapeutic recreation: U.S. and Canadian perspectives.* State College, PA: Venture Publishing, Inc.

National Council for Therapeutic Recreation Certification (NCTRC). (2012). *Certification Standards Part II. NCTRC Exam Information.* New City, NY: NCTRC.

O'Morrow, G. S. (1986). *Therapeutic recreation: A helping profession* (2nd ed.). Englewood Cliffs, NJ: Prentice-Hall.

O'Morrow, G. S., & Reynolds, R. (1989). *Therapeutic recreation: A helping profession* (3rd ed.). Englewood Cliffs, NJ: Prentice-Hall.

O'Rourke, M. W., & White, A. (2011). Professional role clarity and competency in health care staffing—The missing pieces. *Nursing Economic$, 29*(4), 183–188.

Porter, H. R., & burlingame, J. (2006). *Recreational therapy handbook of practice ICF-based diagnosis and treatment.* Enumclaw, WA: Idyll Arbor.

Shank, J., & Coyle C. (2002). *Therapeutic recreation in health promotion and rehabilitation.* State College, PA: Venture Publishing, Inc.

Stumbo, N. J., & Peterson, C. A. (2009). *Therapeutic recreation program design: Principles and procedures* (5th ed.). San Francisco: Pearson Benjamin Cummings.

Sullivan E. J., & Decker, P. J. (2009). *Effective leadership and management in nursing* (7th ed.). Upper Saddle River, NJ: Pearson/Prentice-Hall.

Tomey, A.M. (2009). *Guide to nursing management and leadership* (8th ed.). St. Louis, MO; Mosby Inc.

Want to keep employees happy? Offer flexible schedules, concierges to run errands. *Supplement to Same-Day Surgery, 35*(2), 1–4.

West, R. E., Kinney, T., & Witman, J. (Eds.). (2008). *Guidelines for competency assessment and curriculum planning for recreational therapy practice.* Hattiesburg, MS: ATRA.

Witman, J., & Ligon, M. (2011, summer). Planning and implementation. *American Therapeutic Recreation Association newsletter, 27*(2), 1–4.

Chapter 14
Managing Risk, Safety, Security, and Legal Aspects

Keywords

- Accident
- Adverse event
- Avoidance
- Error
- Informed consent
- Near miss
- Negligence
- Professional malpractice
- Reduction
- Reportable incident
- Retention
- Risk evaluation
- Risk identification
- Risk implementation and reporting
- Risk management program
- Risk management strategies
- Root-cause analysis
- Safety and security plans
- Sentinel event
- Standard of care
- Tort law
- Transference
- Unpreventable adverse event

Learning Outcomes

After reading this chapter, students will be able to:

1. Describe the manager's responsibilities in each step of a risk management program: risk identification, risk evaluation, risk management strategies, and risk implementation and reporting.
2. Identify recommended contents of incident-reporting forms.
3. Define the four risk management strategies managers may use in their programs.
4. Identify the documents and practices outlined in risk management plans.
5. List the content to include in unit safety and security plans.
6. Identify the types of security devices found in health-care and human-service settings.
7. Describe the legislation and laws, organizations, and professional resources that support security and safety in the United States and Canada.
8. Explain the difference between negligence and professional malpractice.
9. Summarize the legal concerns managers face as programs and services are delivered.

Overview

Initially, the focus of risk management was on managing monetary losses from plaintiff's judgments. More recently, concern for patient safety and the security of all stakeholders has changed the focus of risk management from a retroactive approach (e.g., locating the root cause and blaming the guilty party) to a proactive approach (e.g., creating a fault-tolerant system that increases safety through prevention, disclosure, education, and decreased exposure to liability) by aligning risk management and quality improvement initiatives. A concern for security and safety of clients, caregivers, and professionals shifts the focus from individuals and errors to systemic organizational changes that support quality. Chapter 15 provides a more in-depth discussion of quality issues in health care.

The watershed reports from the Institute of Medicine, *To Err is Human: Building a Safer Health System* (1999) and *Crossing the Quality Chasm: A New Health System for the 21st Century* (2001), provided evidence that the right processes were used at the right time with the right client in only one half of the cases examined in the United States (Liang & Mackey, 2011).

These reports proposed strategies that create a culture of safety and align with CQI by focusing on agency leadership, respecting human limits, promoting team functioning, anticipating the unexpected, and creating learning environments (Anderson, 2010). A number of entities in the United States, including the Veterans Health Administration and the Joint Commission on Accreditation of Healthcare Organizations (JCAHO, the Joint Commission), are using root-cause analysis, a continuous quality improvement (CQI) approach to improve care (Vincent, 2003). The Joint Commission published national patient-safety goals requiring collaborative efforts among organizations and professionals to identify barriers to and strategies for improving patient safety. Further, the National Patient Safety Foundation (NPSF) of the AMA was developed to serve as the catalyst through research and education for transitioning from a culture of blame to one of safety (Hemman, 2002). Federal legislation and the law will affect health-care delivery in the future, as evidenced by the Patient Safety and Quality Improvement Act (2005) and the Patient Protection and Affordable Care Act (ACA) (2010), which focus on quality and transparency and respond to consumerism in health care.

The Royal College of Physicians and Surgeons of Canada, in response to the need to create a culture of safety, hosted a one-day forum on patient safety during their 2001 annual conference. A National Steering Committee representing government and non-government health-care associations prepared a report, Building a Safer System, A National Integrated Strategy for Improving Patient Safety (2002, September), that recommended the creation of a Canadian Patient Safety Institute (CPSI) to facilitate a national strategy to improve patient safety. CPSI was established in 2003 by Health Canada to improve patient safety and quality. As in the United States, a number of national initiatives and organizations address patient safety in Canada. Likewise, Canadian federal laws (Privacy Act of 1983, Personal Information Protection and Electronic Documents Act of 2000) and provincial and territorial laws identify how organizations may collect, use, and disclose personal information.

Risk managers will experience new tasks as the paradigm shifts from reactive reporting of incidents that cause financial losses to a culture of security and safety. Within a CQI environment, loss control encompasses not only clients but also the safety and security of employees, volunteers, and guests. This chapter first considers responsibilities of managers to design risk management plans in order to create a culture of safety and prevention of future errors. Second, security and safety responsibilities of the manager are introduced. Managers' duties now address threats to security and personal safety triggered by natural causes (e.g., weather, plants, and animals) and actions attributed to crime and terrorism. Lastly, laws and legislation are introduced with a discussion of legal concerns the manager may experience as the unit conducts its routine responsibilities.

Risk Management

Risk management is a component of quality management that identifies, analyzes, and evaluates risk, then develops a plan to reduce the frequency and severity of accidents and injuries (Sullivan & Decker, 2009). Thus, the risk management process includes risk identification, analysis, treatment, evaluation, and follow-up (Tomey, 2009). It is a continuous agency-wide program of detection, education, and prevention (Sullivan & Decker, 2009) that varies from agency to agency and within facilities and programs in the same agency due to the unique clientele, staff, and resources within each setting.

Risk has been described as the probability or predictability that something will happen. A negative connotation is associated with risk. A client incident or a family's expression of dissatisfaction regarding service not only indicates some slippage in quality of service but it also indicates potential liability. A distraught, dissatisfied, complaining client is a high risk; a satisfied client is a low risk. Risk management, on the other hand, usually refers to positive results achieved through some form of activity. Thus, a *risk management program* is a planned approach to deliver safe, quality services (Carter & Van Andel, 2011): "The intent of risk and safety management, like quality improvement programs, is to develop, monitor, and evaluate procedures so both providers and participants avoid harm while operations are continuously improved" (p. 177). Specific goals of risk management are: (1) to provide client, staff, caregiver, and guest safety and prevent injury or harm to them; (2) to avoid liability exposure by evaluating services, practices, and procedures; (3) to maintain incident-reporting systems to track patterns of practices that could become adverse occurrences so measures are implemented to prevent these events; and (4) to maintain a quality improvement program that identifies risk and reduces its impact on clients (Tomey, 2009).

A risk management program consists of policies and tasks that must be in place and performed on a daily basis. In large organizations and governmental units, the program is formal—a risk management department and a full-time risk manager are in place. In smaller organizations, the direction of the program is usually the responsibility of a manager who has other assigned duties. In some health-care facilities, the risk management manager and quality improvement manager may be the same. As a consequence, the degree of involvement of therapeutic recreation managers in the development of risk management and safety programs will vary from setting to setting. Some will be directly involved as a result of being a manager of a therapeutic recreation department within an organization. Others will collaborate with the agency risk and or quality improvement manager to ensure that staff-reporting practices adhere to agency protocol. In either situation, the first-line manager carries out several risk management responsibilities (refer to Table 14.1, p. 222).

Components of a Risk Management Program

Risk and safety management programs include writing and disseminating philosophical/policy statements; identifying, analyzing, and evaluating risks and threats; and selecting, implementing, and monitoring the plan (these components are identified in Figure 14.1). The key to an effective risk management program is the development of a culture of safety throughout the organization. A culture of safety promotes trust and

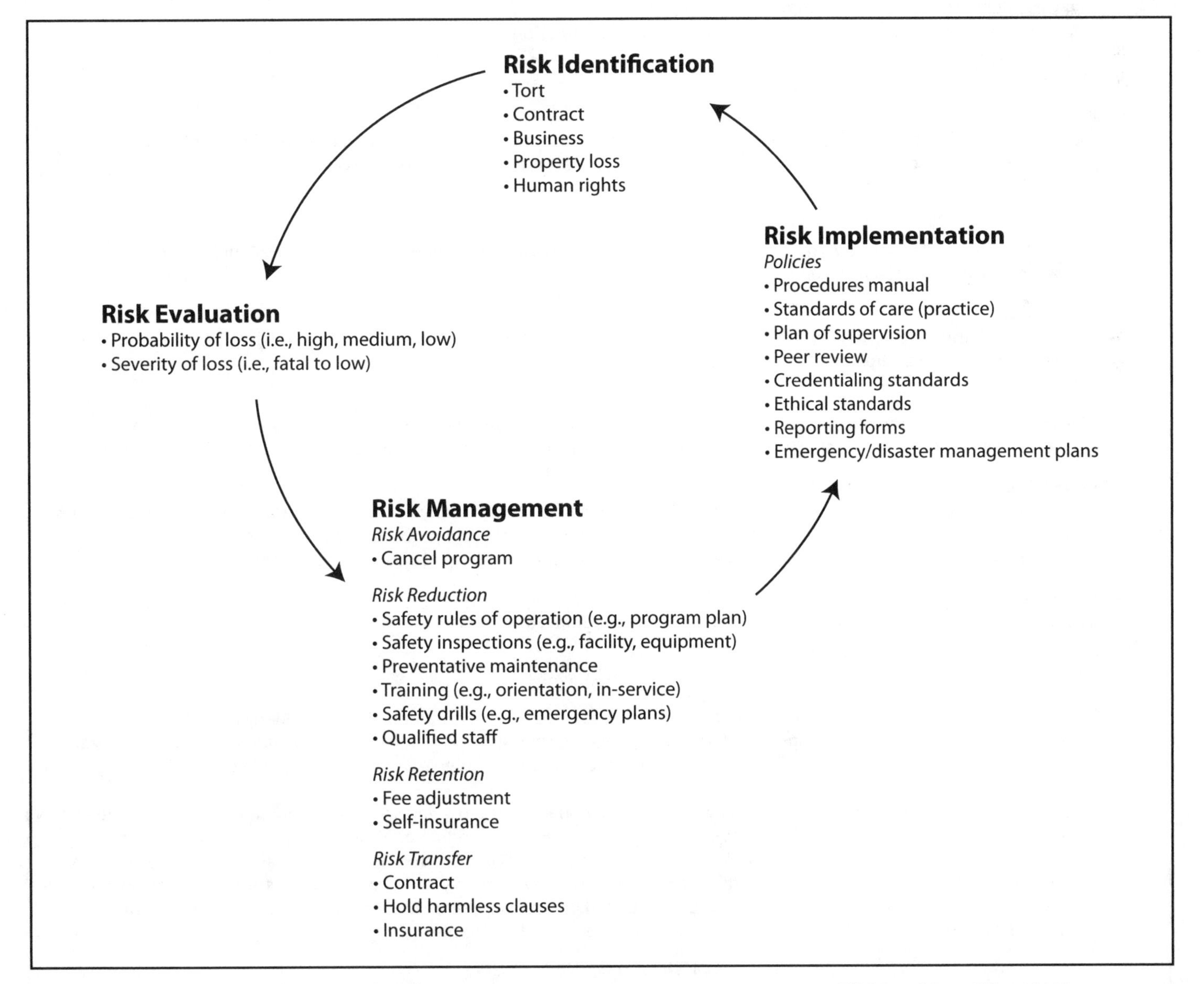

Figure 14.1 Risk Management Decision-Making Process in Therapeutic Recreation (Adapted from Rios, 1992)

Table 14.1 Risk Management Responsibilities of Manager

1. Identification of potential risks for accident, injury, or financial loss.
2. Oversee monitoring systems like incident reports to provide factual data for risk control.
3. Analyze frequency, severity, and causes of incident types to estimate outcomes of these events.
4. Review safety and risk of procedures and programs.
5. Monitor laws, legislation, and codes on health-care issues.
6. Eliminate or reduce risks.
7. Identify educational needs of staff, clients, and caregivers implementing appropriate programs.
8. Evaluate and report the results of risk management programs.

Table 14.2 Risk Management Policy Statement

Departmental Policy, Genesis Medical Center, Davenport, Iowa
Subject: SAFETY, Genesis Physical Medicine and Rehabilitation Programs
Effective Date:
Primary Responsibility Medical Director/Administrative Director
Cross Reference: Genesis Safety Policies; Genesis Infection Prevention and Control Policies
Review Cycle: Annual
Approved by:

I. POLICY:

Genesis Physical Medicine and Rehabilitation Programs will promote and maintain a safe and clean environment in which rehabilitative services are provided, taking into account special patient needs related to physical, sensory, perceptual, emotional, and cognitive deficits.

II. PURPOSE:

To promote independence within the health-care environment and at the same time decrease the risk of injury and illness to patients, visitors, and staff.

III. DEFINITIONS:

Rehab Safety Committee: A subcommittee of the Physical Medicine and Rehabilitation Performance Improvement Committee with management and/or direct-care staff representation from each discipline.

IV. PRACTICE:

All staff will attend the mandatory safety instruction programs during orientation and periodically thereafter as determined by the Genesis Medical Center Safety Committee and Physical Medicine & Rehabilitation Service Line Operations Committee.

VI. RESPONSIBILITY:

All staff are responsible to be familiar with their role as described in the hospital safety and infection prevention and control policies, to report unsafe work areas or conditions and all injuries, to observe rules and procedures when exposed to contagious and infectious diseases or hazardous chemicals, to use correct body mechanics, and to handle sharp instruments with care.

VII. PROCEDURE:

A. All new employees will attend the required orientation programs. Information reviewed:
   1. General
   2. Direct patient care
   3. Department specific

B. All employees will complete annual mandatory safety-related education as required by Genesis Medical Center.

C. All rehabilitation: At least one program staff member providing services to patients outside of the medical center facilities will have knowledge of first aid care. All staff are required to have first aid training, as well as be certified in basic cardiopulmonary resuscitation.

D. Safety inspections will be conducted semiannually, in each department providing services to Genesis Physical Medicine and Rehabilitation Program patients. Findings will be documented on the Accreditation Readiness Checklist. A report outlining the findings will be submitted to the Administrative Director, Medical Director, and Genesis Medical Center Safety Specialist. The Rehab Safety Committee will review the findings and develop an action plan to correct deficits as deemed necessary.

E. Equipment maintenance and calibrations will be completed in accordance with the manufacturer's recommendations through Engineering and Maintenance or an outside contractor, if deemed necessary.

(CONTINUED ON NEXT PAGE)

(CONTINUED FROM PREVIOUS PAGE)

F. Rehab departments will have a designated person to provide necessary and regular maintenance on the vehicles as dictated by the owner's manuals in the vehicles. Examples of such vehicles would be the Occupational Therapy car, Therapeutic Recreation car, or Rehab van used to transport patients. Vehicles used to transport patients will be serviced and inspected according to the pre-determined schedule developed by Engineering and Maintenance.

G. Emergency Plans will be tested annually on each shift. This will include actual occurrences, simulated drills, or unannounced quizzes.

1. Fire—Code Red
2. Bomb Threat—Code Black
3. Natural Disasters—Tornado Watch/Tornado Warning
4. Power Failures
5. Medical Emergencies—Code Blue/Code Pink
6. Violent Situations
    a. Non-Violent Crisis Management—Code Green
    b. Armed Intruder—Code Strong
7. Child Abduction—Code Angel
8. Elopement—Code Walker
9. Hazardous Material Spill
10. Disaster Plan
11. Evacuation Plan
    a. These may include actual patients being served or evacuees simulating persons with disabilities depending on the type of drill.
    b. The type of evacuees will be determined by the Rehabilitation Safety Committee.
    c. A report outlining the findings will be submitted to the Administrative Director, Medical Director, and Genesis Medical Center Safety Specialist.

H. Each patient-care area will have immediate access to basic first aid equipment and expertise.

I. An off-campus location will be utilized for services only if it is deemed necessary, it does not pose a threat to staff or patient safety and security, adequate communication capabilities can be maintained, and there are no known weather forecasts that could put patients or staff at unnecessary risk. If the weather should change suddenly, staff and patients are to return to the campus. If time does not permit, they are to take cover in a safe area and report to the department by cell phone.

J. The Rehab Safety Committee will critique drills and safety inspections and identify needs for additional staff training, environmental changes, or changes in practice on a regular basis to be not less than quarterly. The Genesis Medical Center Safety Specialist will serve as a consultant to the committee.

VIII. REFERENCES:

CARF The Rehabilitation Accreditation Commission (2009). Medical Rehabilitation Standards Manual. Section 1. H: Health and Safety Pages 58–66.

IX. ENDORSEMENTS:

Physical Medicine and Rehabilitation Service Line Operations Committee

Safety, Rehabilitation Safety Committee

Reviewed 6/97; 3/00, 2/02, 3/05

Reviewed/Revised 6/96; 3/98; 3/99; 3/01, 3/02, 3/03, 3/04; 3/06; 3/07; 3/08; 3/09; 3/10; 5/11

transparency (Whitehead, Weiss, & Tappen, 2010). In this environment, staff report errors so data and information are available to understand why an error occurred, and to improve services and proactively prevent negative outcomes and liability concerns. Philosophical/policy statements found on websites set forth the scope and nature of risk and safety activities in each unit (refer to the statement from the physical medicine and rehabilitation department of a health-care system, Table 14.2). These statements are regularly reviewed and updated to account for unavoidable, unpredictable, and unintentional human error. Additionally, philosophical/policy statements serve as guides to education that is key to implementing proactive risk and safety plans.

Step 1: Risk Identification

The therapeutic recreation manager, like other managers, first identifies potential and actual risks and safety concerns for accidents, injury, or financial losses (Tomey, 2009). Several terms are used in health and human service settings to identify and explain risk and safety concerns (Rapala, 2011; Sherwin, 2011; Tomey, 2009; Whitehead, Weiss, & Tappen, 2010). See Table 14.3.

Table 14.3 Risk Management Concerns in Health-Care Agencies

- *Accident* involves damage to a system that disrupts the output of the system and is usually unplanned or unforeseen.
- *Adverse event* is an injury caused by medical management rather than the client's health status.
- *Error* is failure of a planned action to be completed or use of the wrong plan to achieve a goal.
- *Near miss* is an event that could have resulted in accident, injury, or illness but results in no or minimal harm due to chance or timely intervention.
- *Root-cause analysis* (RCA) is a prevention tool used to discover causes in performance associated with adverse events or close calls.
- *Sentinel event* is an unexpected occurrence unrelated to the client's health status that involves risk, death, or serious physical or psychological injury and is attributable to a preventable adverse event.
- *Unpreventable adverse event* is an adverse event that resulted from complications that could not be prevented given the available information.

Table 14.4 Illustrations of Potential Errors in Recreation Therapy

APIE

Failure to identify a client need from review of assessment results

Failure to achieve a client outcome with selected intervention

Inadequate follow-up plans reported in discharge or transition plan

Resources and environmental features

Hazards from weather to mechanical failure (transporting)

Psychological or physical issues like stress or violence

Chemical and biological situations like allergies or medication issues

Professional interactions

Communication errors in documentation

Noncompliance with protocols and standards

Failure to prevent or foresee or anticipate client or caregiver behavior

One way to identify errors is to use terms found in Table 14.3 to describe events that may occur (1) during the APIE process, (2) as resources are used and operated during programs and interventions, and (3) as staff and constituents interact with professionals during and following interventions. Examples of actions or events that might lead to errors in recreation therapy are found in Table 14.4.

A second way to identify risk and safety concerns is to consider hazards encountered by agencies (Kaiser & Robinson, 2005). Hazards are associated with a number of service features (refer to Table 14.5).

Learning Outcome

Describe the manager's responsibilities in risk identification.

Table 14.5 Hazards in Recreation Therapy Services

Environment: slippery surfaces, holes, weather conditions

Infrastructure: uneven surfaces, protruding objects

Program: proper supervision, safety rule enforcement, appropriate interventions

Emergency care: proper transport and care

Crisis management: weather, violence, chemicals

Transportation: properly maintained vehicles and trained drivers

Several high-risk areas in health care include medications, treatment complications, falls, client and caregiver dissatisfaction, and refusal to sign treatment consent or refusal of the treatment (Sullivan & Decker, 2009). Identification of these concerns occurs in a number of ways, including incident reports; quality reviews or audits; professional, regulatory, or state reviews or inspections; evaluation of client satisfaction surveys or grievances; litigation; retrospective document reviews; and education and training simulations. The manager completes a unit-wide analysis of policies, procedures, and activities to identify potential and actual risks and safety issues and to recommend changes that will prevent errors or threats and reduce potential losses.

Step 2: Risk Evaluation

After the identification of risks, the manager will analyze and evaluate the frequency and severity of problems that might impact constituents and the organization. Because no two risks, errors, or threats are alike, each is analyzed and evaluated. The manager considers the "severity or consequence of a failure, the occurrence or frequency of the problem, and the detection or the probability of detecting the problem before the impact of the effect is realized" (Tomey, 2009, p. 483). Data are categorized with rating scales applied to represent the probability—high, medium, or low—of the risk occurring. Severity of injury and organizational impact is also placed on scales (e.g., fatal to low and catastrophic to minimal financial losses). The team then can prioritize the identified risks and safety issues and design a strategy to manage future incidents. This assessment relies on data from incident reports, client charts and reports, staff documentation, and data from other units in the organization. Some managers will find that sufficient historical data are not available for reliable objective analysis. In such cases, the manager can compare data to that of a similar department within the same organization (e.g., occupational therapy) or to a like therapeutic recreation department in another organization.

A *reportable incident* is any unexpected or unplanned occurrence that affects or could affect a client, staff member, caregiver, or constituent (Marquis & Huston, 2009; Sullivan & Decker, 2009). The report is only as effective as the form used, so attention to the adequacy of the form and required data is critical. Although all organizations will develop their own incident report form and provide instruction for completion, van der Smissen (1990, pp. 54–56) and Sullivan (2003) suggested several items to be included in the report information (see Table 14.6).

Learning Outcome
Identify recommended contents of incident-reporting forms.

These reports need to be completed with extreme care because they can be used as evidence if a lawsuit is brought against the organization or any person involved. Because incident reports are used to defend an agency, they are considered confidential, yet if reports are disclosed to the plaintiff they are no longer considered confidential and can be subpoenaed in court (Marquis & Huston, 2009). Consequently, no entry is placed in clients' records indicating incident reports have been written; only enough information about the occurrence is reported so proper care is given. Depending on the state/province/territory, lawsuits can be filed until the statute of limitations runs out; thus, reports are maintained in agency files for a number of years.

Table 14.6 Content of Incident Reports

1. Identification information
2. Date, time, and exact location of occurrence, or if unknown, date and time of discovery
3. Action of injured
4. Sequence of activity
5. Preventive measures by injured (e.g., What could or should have been done to have prevented the accident?)
6. Procedures followed in rendering aid, including notification of caregivers
7. Disposition, including securing report in a locked file

Learning Outcome
Describe the manager's responsibilities in risk evaluation.

Step 3: Risk Management Strategies

Learning Outcome
Define the four risk management strategies managers may use in their programs.

Once errors and threats are identified and evaluated, the manager and staff consider selection of risk management strategies to control and finance the consequences of risk and safety issues. Managers may select one or a combination of four options: avoidance, reduction, retention, and transference (refer to Figure 14.1, p. 221). *Avoidance* is simply doing away with the service or activity because its risk is too great. *Reduction* considers minimizing the frequency and severity of incidents through planning, staff training, information management, and better procedures. The keeping of risk is *retention* (e.g., fee adjustments, self-insurance). There will always be risk, and the organization accepts a certain level of loss. *Transference* is having the responsibility of risk carried by an individual, contract, lease, bond, or harmless clauses. Financing strategies occur through retention, self-insurance, or through transfer, hold-harmless clauses, or commercial insurance.

After strategies are selected, policies and practices are prepared in a risk and safety plan codified in agency protocols and presented on websites and in manuals. Responsibility is assigned for data input, changes to documents and procedures, review of laws and regulations, and corresponding with government and private organizations that advocate for quality and safety in health care. In order to implement a proactive approach that creates a culture of safety, managers and staff unit-wide focus on customer satisfaction, safety and security, continuous quality improvement, and liability control (Tomey, 2009).

Managers create a safety culture by setting expectations, providing education and training, and building accountability through measurement, feedback, and coaching ("Creating cultures of safety," 2011; Stewart, 2011).

Learning Outcome
Describe the manager's responsibilities in selecting risk management strategies.

Step 4: Risk Management Implementation and Reporting

The next step in the risk management process is implementation, monitoring, and reporting. This step includes (1) ensuring that all aspects of the plan and its administrative procedures are incorporated in the organization's and unit's policy-and-procedures documents and websites, (2) observing practices while continually providing education and training, and (3) evaluating the plan's goals and reporting outcomes. These steps involve the organization of several documents and practices (Rios, 1992, p. 172). See Table 14.7.

Learning Outcome
Identify the documents and practices outlined in risk management plans.

The therapeutic recreation manager monitors the unit's risk and safety program, recommending, if need be, preventive or corrective action and achievement of the plan's goals. On an ongoing basis, the manager evaluates the effectiveness of the program and reports to the administration or risk management manager for the agency. The therapeutic recreation manager will gather information from staff and regularly inspect and observe current practices. The manager involves the staff in determining desirable practices and establishing safety rules, regulations, and procedures. This involvement fosters a safety awareness attitude and makes routine safety inspections more palatable. Additionally, the upkeep and maintenance of information documentation systems becomes a shared and significant responsibility of everyone.

Education about risk, safety, and security is another major element. For a program to be effective, every employee must be involved, including staff, volunteers, and interns. Staff and volunteers must understand the significance of hazards and associated liabilities. Merely knowing what to do and the liabilities associated with incidents is not enough. There must be an emotional acceptance of risk and safety management by the manager and professionals of the unit.

Everyone is a safety officer. Staff are empowered to take immediate action, make recommendations, and report the status of the plan's goals (Hronek, Spengler, & Baker III, 2007). After each incident is identified and evaluated and strategies are planned, staff and management must act to change the situation. Reasonable strategies are implemented as soon as possible, with documentation and reporting of all incidents and steps taken to minimize risk and enhance safety. Information

Table 14.7 Risk Management Plan Documents and Practices

1. A plan for supervision for all interventions and staff
2. Standards of practice referencing accreditation and professional standards
3. Ethical standards of conduct
4. Credentialing standards and clinical privileging
5. Process for reporting and investigating accidents and incidents
6. Process for safety inspections
7. Procedures for preventative maintenance
8. Procedures for routine maintenance
9. Emergency plans (e.g., search and rescue, fire evacuation, power outage, weather-related)
10. Procedures for managing behavior (e.g., unauthorized leave, aggression, violence)
11. Safety guidelines for all interventions
12. Specific program guidelines for any individual program or intervention of moderate frequency or severity of risk (moderate risk includes any injury, such as minor fractures, strains, sprains, or infected lacerations, and can be contrasted with inconsequential injuries, such as minor lacerations, contusions, or abrasions)
13. Job specifications that include duties and responsibilities; reportability; minimum knowledge, skills, and abilities to provide service; and level of supervision
14. Internal peer review system

gathered is integrated into the unit's risk and safety management data analysis system. When the plan's goals are achieved, they are adjusted upward to continue improvement and liability control.

LEARNING OUTCOME
Describe the manager's responsibilities in risk implementation and reporting.

Security and Personal Safety

A contemporary social issue is security and a sense of personal safety in the workplace (Tomey, 2009; Whitehead, Weiss, & Tappen, 2010). The health-care work environment is unique. Globally, health-care personnel are more likely to be assaulted than prison guards or police officers (Barnes, 2011). Professionals, as well as clients and caregivers, are exposed not only to infections, hazards, and products that trigger allergic reactions and hypersensitivity, such as latex, but also violence-prone individuals, substance misuse, and dissatisfied customers (Whitehead, Weiss, & Tappen, 2010). Additional threats to the personal safety of staff, clients, and caregivers come from unsafe equipment, unsafe or unsecured facilities (e.g., slippery floors, unsecured, continuous-access health-care facilities), weather and natural disasters, fire, electric shock, power loss, bioterrorism, technological emergencies, and those caused by actions of others (e.g., crime, harassment, violence, impaired workers, bullying, terrorism) (Peterson & Hronek, 2011; Tomey, 2009; Whitehead, Weiss, & Tappen, 2009).

Threats to safety in the workplace vary from one setting to another and one individual to another. A pregnant person is more vulnerable in the presence of a physically violent person than is another adult; staff in locked units are more at risk than those in other behavioral health areas; and staff in physical medicine and rehabilitation and geriatrics are more vulnerable to ergonomic injuries due to added transport responsibilities. Likewise, staff involved in outdoor settings experience different threats than do staff working inside health-care settings during inclement weather, while staff and constituents in urban areas experience different challenges than do staff and participants in rural areas during emergencies and disasters. The manager's challenge is to create a sense of trust and personal safety in the environment through a reliable team that relies on education, training, and effective communication systems (Tomey, 2009).

While identified as part of the unit's ongoing risk analysis, security and safety issues are managed through *safety and security plans* for specific settings and programs. So in addition to identifying the situational security risks, written plans detail personnel (chain of command, responsibilities, coordination, training), equipment and supplies, and communication processes (signage, emergency responses, codes, attire, command location) (Nelson & Colley, 2005). A culture of safety is achieved through a team effort among management, staff, and constituents as errors are realized and documented, responses to emergencies are rehearsed, and collaboration with security and law enforcement result in protective measures. In addition to preparing written plans, security present in service areas may include several protective devices (Nelson & Colley, 2005; Peterson & Hronek, 2011; Whitehead, Weiss, & Tappen, 2009). See Table 14.8.

The manager also monitors the unit's quality improvement initiatives to assure compliance with safety regulations of governing organizations and

LEARNING OUTCOME
List the content to include in unit safety and security plans.

Table 14.8 Security Devices

- Controlled entry with proper identification
- Electronic surveillance (TV, cameras, sound sensing, motion detection)
- Recorded license plate numbers
- Uniformed and non-uniformed security officers and escorts
- Alarm systems and metal detectors
- Identification of potential or illegal acts with immediate law enforcement follow-up
- Color coding and alert response levels
- Panic buttons
- Locked or key-coded access doors
- Handheld noise devices
- Enforced wearing of photo ID badges

LEARNING OUTCOME
Identify the types of security devices found in health-care and human-service settings.

congruence with legislation and laws. Online training programs contribute to staff awareness of, for example, harassment, bullying, crisis intervention, and potentially violent behaviors. Lastly, the manager reaches out to a number of organizations and agencies that provide tools and resources for improving quality and safety.

Legislation and Laws, United States and Canada

In 1999 the Institute of Medicine (IOM) of the National Academy of Sciences released a report, *To Err Is Human: Building a Safer Health System*. This report became the catalyst for a patient safety agenda in the United States and the instigator to shift the role of risk management from a reactive case-by-case identification of error to a proactive focus on providing quality experiences in a safe surrounding (Hemman, 2002; Liang & Mackey, 2011). This report summarized the human cost of medical errors and found that most medical errors result from flaws in the system rather than individual recklessness (Anderson, 2010). The report concluded that with adequate leadership, awareness, and resources, errors may be reduced by half within five years (Hemman, 2002). A subsequent IOM report, *Crossing the Quality Chasm: A New Health System for the 21st Century*, suggested the risk management focus must become more strategic and systems-based in order to create safer health-care environments (Kuhn & Youngberg, 2002). These reports shifted the focus from blaming individuals for past errors to preventing future errors by building safety into health-care systems and following the CQI principles of providing leadership, promoting team functioning, creating a learning environment, anticipating the unexpected, and respecting human limits (Anderson, 2010). The call for more effective improvement in quality and safety of health-care delivery has resulted in legislation and increasing policy influences affecting care provision (Liang & Mackey, 2011).

The Occupational Safety and Health Act of 1970 established safety guidelines and standards for healthful working conditions for the first time (Tomey, 2009). This act created OSHA (Occupational Safety and Health Administration) and NIOSH (National Institute of Occupational Safety and Health). OSHA is responsible for developing and enforcing workplace safety and health regulations, while NIOSH provides research, information, education, and training (Whitehead, Weiss, & Tappen, 2010). In 1980 OSHA introduced new guidelines to identify risk factors and recommend policies to mitigate workplace violence in health-care and social-service agencies (Henry & Ginn, 2002).

Since this first initiative, a number of federal laws have been enacted to protect a diverse workforce in the United States, including the following: Equal Pay Act of 1963; Title VII of the Civil Rights Act of 1964, Age Discrimination Act of 1968, Pregnancy Discrimination Act of 1968, Fair Credit Reporting Act of 1970, Vocational Rehabilitation Act of 1973, Family Education Rights and Privacy Act-Buckley Amendment of 1974, Immigration Reform and Control Act of 1986, Americans with Disabilities Act of 1990, Family Medical Leave Act of 1993, and the Needlestick Safety and Prevention Act of 2001 (Whitehead, Weiss, & Tappen, 2010).

Several pieces of legislation have considered the cost of care and the quality of the client's experience. Public Law 92-603 in 1972 created PSROs (Professional Standards Review Organizations) to review quality and costs in Medicaid and Medicare. In 1986, the Health Care Quality Improvement Act created a federal data bank to identify incompetent professionals. The Health Insurance Portability and Accountability Act (HIPAA) of 1996 provided clients portability of their health-care coverage and control over how protected health information is used and disclosed with organizations receiving personal information accountable for its protection (Tomey, 2009). The Uniform Health Care Information Act of 1997 allows clients access to health-care information to make informed decisions and provide informed consent (Tomey, 2009). The 2009 Health Information Technology for Economic and Clinical Health (HITECH) Act broadened the scope of HIPAA by applying security and privacy rules to business associates (persons who use client data) and electronic health record disclosures (Nicholls, 2010).

The Patient Safety and Quality Improvement Act of 2005 authorizes the creation of a client safety database network to serve as a resource to health-care organizations (McBride, Greening, & Redmond, 2006). A PSO or Patient Safety Network allows health-care providers to share data on errors including causes and solutions creating an evidence-based approach to client safety by making this data available to other health-care settings. One piece of legislation, resulting from the health-care reform initiatives, the Patient Protection and Affordable Care Act (ACA) signed into law in 2010, extends client safety through quality improvement plans that outline person-centeredness and family engagement relative to all individuals and links reimbursement to quality and safety performances of systems- and team-based approaches (Liang & Mackey, 2011).

The blueprint for patient safety and quality initiatives in Canada, *Building a Safer System* (National Steering Committee on Patient Safety, 2002), called for the integration of strategies to improve patient safety among provinces and territories that implement the national health insurance system created by the Canada Health Act (1984). In 2003, Health Canada created CPSI to facilitate collaborative efforts among governments, organizations, and providers to improve safety and quality. To develop, maintain, and nurture a culture of safety, the document recommended a focus on evidence-based practices, audits, and a team approach to reduce human error. Also recommended was standardization in legislation on privacy and confidentiality to increase access to patient-safety data and enhanced research and funding to improve evaluation processes, professional development, and communication. All facts related to adverse events recorded on health records accessible to patients are to be protected from disclosure in legal proceedings; as a consequence, privacy legislation including the Evidence Act, Privacy Act, and PIPEDA (Personal Information Protection and Electronic Documents Act-2000, updated 2011) were to be reviewed and revised if necessary to ensure proper collection, use, and disclosure of personal information (Office of the Privacy Commissioner of Canada, 2009).

Organizations in United States and Canada

The ongoing movement to improve safety and quality and control costs has led to the creation of organizations and agencies as well as legislation that will affect the provision of care and delivery of services. These initiatives are occurring worldwide, as evidenced by the WHO's efforts during World Health Day and their launching of the World Alliance for Patient Safety. In the United States and Canada, a number of government agencies, private companies, and nonprofit organizations are responsible for oversight and assessment of safety and quality in health care (National Steering Committee on Patient Safety, 2009; Tomey, 2009; Whitehead, Weiss, & Tappen, 2010). See Table 14.9. Information in this section also applies to the discussion in the next chapter (15) on quality.

Table 14.9 Safety and Quality related Organizations in US and Canada

Government Agencies

- Centers for Disease Control and Prevention (cdc.gov)
- U.S. Department of Health and Human Services (hhs.gov)
- Center for Medicare and Medicaid Services (CMS) (cms.hhs.gov)
- Agency for Healthcare Research and Quality (AHRQ) (ahrq.gov)
- VA National Center for Patient Safety (va.gov/ncps/)
- Occupational Safety and Health Administration (osha.gov)
- National Institute of Occupational Safety and Health (cdc.gov/niosh/about)
- Health Canada (hc-sc.gc.ca)
- The Canadian Institutes of Health Research (cihr-irsc.gc.ca)
- The Canadian Institute for Health Information (cihi.ca)
- Canadian Coalition on Medication Incident Reporting and Prevention (CCMIRP) (ismp-canada.org)

Private and Non-Profit Organizations

- Institute of Medicine (iom.edu)
- The Leapfrog Group (leapfroggroup.org)
- Kaiser Family Foundation (kff.org)
- Robert Wood Johnson Foundation—Quality/Equality in Healthcare (rwjf.org/qualityequality/index.jsp)
- National Patient Safety Foundation (npsf.org)
- Canadian Patient Safety Institute (CPSI) (patientsafetyinstitute.ca)
- The Institute for Safe Medication Practices (ISMP Canada) (ismp.org)

Quality Organizations

- Institute for Healthcare Improvement (IHI) (ihi.org)
- The Joint Commission (jointcommission.org)
- National Committee for Quality Assurance (NCQA) (ncqa.org)
- Canadian Council on Health Services Accreditation (CCHSA) (accreditation.ca)
- Canadian Healthcare Association (CHA) (cha.ca)

Managers also rely on standards evident in professional credentialing bodies and those put forth by membership associations. Thus, the job tasks of the CTRS (http://www.nctrc.org/documents/5JobAnalysis.pdf), the ATRA Code of Ethics and the standards for the practice of therapeutic recreation (http://www.atra-online.com/), and the CTRA Code of Ethics and standards of practice (http://www.canadian-tr.org) provide risk management and quality guidelines governing program delivery and professional practices. Each setting in which programs are offered may, in addition to posted policies and operating documents, have Patient Bill of Rights statements and satisfaction surveys that the manager shares with clients in order to collect safety/quality data on a regular basis. Thus, while risk concerns have shifted from a focus on managing monetary losses from plaintiff's judgments to a culture of safety and security for all clients, professionals, and stakeholders in health-care settings, the manager remains responsible for compliance with regulations, laws, and guidelines governing quality, security and personal safety of the unit's constituents.

Learning Outcome
Describe the legislation and laws, organizations, and professional resources that support security and safety in the United States and Canada.

Legal Issues and Concerns

Therapeutic recreation managers and professionals have a responsibility to ensure that certain service expectations are met. When client expectations are not met, liability and the potential for litigation are possible. Recently the public's trust in health-care professionals has declined (Whitehead, Weiss, & Tappen, 2010). Clients and caregivers are better informed and more assertive regarding their health-care needs. As a result, they demand quality responsible intervention and are more likely to sue for what they view as errors if the behavior and communication of professionals appears uncaring or impersonal, regardless of professionals' technical competence (Marquis & Huston, 2009; Whitehead, Weiss, & Tappen, 2010).

Negligence and malpractice fall under civil law (violation of one person's rights by another person) as opposed to criminal law (offense against society). A *tort law* is a legal or civil wrong committed against a person or property of another that renders the person who commits the wrong liable for damage in civil action (Marquis & Huston, 2009; Whitehead, Weiss, & Tappen, 2010). Tort laws recognize that persons in their relationships with others have a duty not to harm one another. Consequently, professionals have duties to intervene in a manner that does not harm clients; however, these legal duties may be violated intentionally or unintentionally.

Negligence is an unintentional tort that involves "the omission to do something that a reasonable person, guided by the considerations that ordinarily regulate human affairs, would do—or doing something that a reasonable and prudent person would not do" (Marquis & Huston, 2009, p. 98): Further, reasonable and prudent is defined as the "average judgment, foresight, intelligence, and skill that would be expected of a person with similar training and experience" (p. 98). Likewise, *professional malpractice* is also an unintentional tort described as "the failure of a person with professional training to act in a reasonable and prudent manner" (Marquis & Huston, 2009, p. 98). This definition holds professionals to higher expectations resulting from the fulfillment of their duties that require specialized education and training (Tomey, 2009; Whitehead, Weiss, & Tappen, 2010). Examples of intentional torts are assault and battery while examples of a quasi-intentional torts are libel or slander (Peterson & Hronek, 2011; Whitehead, Weiss, & Tappen, 2010).

Learning Outcome
Explain the difference between negligence and professional malpractice.

A *standard of care* is the duty of care owed to a client that a reasonable, prudent practitioner with similar education and experience would do or not do in similar circumstances; the standard usually represents the skills defined by a profession as the minimal level of acceptable care (Marquis & Huston, 2009; Whitehead, Weiss, & Tappen, 2010). Thus, professionals in recreation therapy have academic and experiential training, professional certification/licensure, continuing education, and Ethics Codes that imply the level of competency and care owed to clients (Taniguchi, Widmer, & Taniguchi, 2008). In addition to the level or degree of quality considered adequate in the practice of recreation therapy, four elements must be present for an act to be considered tort or for

Table 14.10 Criteria for Tort

- Duty: A legal duty to not injure and protect the client from being injured
- Breach: A breach of duty that requires the professional to conform to the standard
- Causation: A direct connection or cause between the professional's behavior or legal duty and the injury
- Injury: The client sustained provable damages or loss

which a professional can be held liable for damages (Peterson & Hronek, 2011; Taniguchi, Widmer, & Taniguchi, 2008), which are listed in Table 14.10.

The first and last items in the above list are usually more easily proven than the breach and the causation (Taniguchi, Widmer, & Taniguchi, 2008). Common acts of negligence associated with therapeutic recreation, regardless of setting, would include high-risk activities, falls, property loss, poor safety directions or measures, failure to communicate inappropriate activities, defects in equipment, and a variety of other activities or circumstances wherein the participant feels the agency or organization failed in its responsibility to prevent the incident or injury. There are a number of recognized legal protections that influence the viability of a claim against a professional and the employing agency (Hronek, Spengler, & Baker III, 2007; Peterson & Hronek, 2011), several of which are listed in Table 14.11.

All professionals are accountable for their actions and adhering to accepted standards of practice—most negligence and malpractice cases arise from violation of accepted practice standards and employing agency policies (Whitehead, Weiss, & Tappen, 2010). Therefore, in addition to maintaining an adequate standard of care and putting forth the effort to meet client expectations and communicate in a caring manner, professionals can reduce the risk of malpractice claims by taking several actions (Marquis & Huston, 2009). Refer to Table 14.12.

Any professional person may be called on to testify in court regarding standards of quality in his or her own agency or in some other agency or organization if there is a lawsuit. The expertise of a witness in a trial or hearing largely depends on education, experience, and recognition by colleagues in the field. Such testimony may have a profound influence on litigation involving therapeutic recreation services or the quality of service provided by an agency or organization.

Many health-care facilities cover employees in the event of a lawsuit. On the other hand, some agencies require their employees to purchase professional liability insurance. Some agencies require students to show proof

Table 14.12 Professional Behavior Important to Minimizing Litigation

- Practice within the scope of care defined by our standards of practice and state practice acts
- Adhere to agency policies and procedures
- Use evidence-based practices to guide programs and services
- First consider client rights
- Adhere to laws, executive orders, legal doctrines, and protocols
- Practice within the limits of individual competence
- Continue to maintain and upgrade skills through professional development and continuing education programs

Table 14.11 Legal Considerations for Professional Liability

- Act of God: the direct cause of the accident was the result of an unusual situation or circumstance (e.g., flood, tornado)
- Assumption of risk: plaintiffs who voluntarily subject themselves to a known and appreciated danger may not recover damages and therefore assume part of the responsibility that harm may happen
- Comparative negligence: the amount of contribution to the accident it is assessed that each party made, with damages assessed accordingly; laws may allow some form of recovery when part of the fault lies with a plaintiff
- Contributory negligence: conduct on the part of the injured party that helped to cause his or her own damage or injury
- Failure of proof: the injured party is unable to prove all four elements of negligence
- Governmental immunity: the government in some instances may be immune from suits or may limit the amount of the claims or eliminate claims in certain categories of administration like personnel actions, budget distribution, and decisions involving planning and policy
- Notice of claim: governments may require an injured or damaged person to file a claim in 30 to 120 days. This allows time for proper investigation and payment of legitimate claims. Failure to provide notice negates proceedings
- Statute of limitations: governments have varying time periods between the accident and when the suit can be filed, one to three years for injury or property loss and up to five for wrongful death
- Waivers, releases, agreements to participate: these documents are normally not considered part of tort doctrine but may assist in a defense when (a) they involve adults and target specific dangers in an experience, (b) minors and their parents have read the specific dangers and rules of conduct required for safety of a particular experience, and (c) the parents have allowed their minor children to participate and agree to inform them of the rules and safety aspects of the program

of personal liability before beginning an internship or fieldwork experience.

Legal Responsibilities of the Manager

Managers have legal responsibility for quality control in their unit. This includes such duties as checking staff credentials and qualifications, carrying out appropriate discipline, checking equipment conditions, and ensuring that written protocols, policies, and procedures are followed. This section highlights a number of additional responsibilities, including patient rights, medical charts, invasion of privacy, confidential communication, research, informed consent, and diversity in the workplace.

Some of the *rights of consumers* (i.e., patients) are spelled out in legal statutes or have been tested in court; others are not found in law books and might simply be considered the patient's human rights. Legal rights may vary from one locale to another; therapeutic recreation managers should be aware of what laws require of them. Conversely, human rights are felt to exist by the very nature of the relationship between client and health-care provider. A bill of rights that has become a regulation has the most legal recourse; those developed by organizations and associations, although not legally binding, may influence "funding and certainly should be considered professionally binding" (Marquis & Huston, 2009, p. 123). Today's clients are more involved and informed about their health. Their participation has led to conflicts in the areas of access to medical charts and informed consent. Depending on the setting, therapeutic recreation managers need to be aware of client rights and adhere to them.

The *medical record* is a primary source of information that helps clients as they make decisions regarding their health care. Therefore, professionals are responsible for legally credible documentation that accurately accounts for care received by the client (Whitehead, Weiss, & Tappen, 2010). Also, clear, concise, and accurate documentation reflects the professional's competence. The court assumes that if one did not write something down, it did not happen. While clients own the information in the medical record, the actual record belongs to the host agency. It is the responsibility of the professional to create a collaborative helping relationship. This promotes trust and helps clients access their medical information useful to their education and health-care decision making.

Therapeutic recreation managers and their staff may become liable for *invasion of privacy* if they divulge information from a client's medical record to improper sources or if they commit unwarranted intrusions into the client's personal affairs. However, there are occasions when one has a legal obligation or duty to disclose information.

Confidential communication is also a concern as related to treatment, observation, or conversation. It is associated with invasion of privacy. One has a professional obligation to keep secret information relating to a client's illness or treatment which is learned during the course of professional duties. It is a tenet of the therapeutic recreation ethics codes. There are federal statutes that address this matter and health-care organizations have their own regulations.

Since the final regulations were published August 14, 2002, for HIPAA, managers have been required to review their policies and procedures in view of a national health privacy framework in the United States (Yang & Kombarakaran, 2006). The intent of the HIPAA regulations is to clarify and limit situations in which a client's personal health information (PHI) can be used by health-care providers, care plans, and health-care clearinghouses (Marquis & Huston, 2009; Yang & Kombarakaran, 2006). PHI is any demographic information that identifies the client, such as Social Security number. This law continues to be modified as it is being implemented, so managers remain vigilant in review of newer versions of the act. Several key components of the privacy act guide the manager's actions (Marquis & Huston, 2009; Yang & Kombarakaran, 2006), refer to Table 14.13. In Canada, PIPEDA defines personal health information with jurisdiction by the Department of Justice (Department of Justice, updated 2011). Refer to Table 14.13.

Research on humans requires consent to be obtained in writing from clients or their representatives. In all health-care organizations, there is a committee responsible for reviewing human research proposals. As therapeutic recreation research becomes more prevalent outside university centers, therapeutic recreation managers will find more requests for access to clients to investigate evidence-based practices. While research provides the opportunity to validate the theoretical or conceptual basis for practice, it must be proposed and conducted in a professional manner. Further, HIPAA requires health-care providers to obtain client authorization to

Table 14.13 HIPAA and PIPEDA Regulations

HIPAA

- Direct-care providers must make a good faith effort to obtain written acknowledgement of the notice of privacy rights and practices from clients prior to services.
- Health-care providers must disclose protected health information to clients upon request and to oversight agencies who request data.
- Reasonable efforts must be taken to limit disclosure of PHI to the minimum necessary to complete the transaction.
- The use of client information is limited for marketing purposes.
- Providers must notify clients in writing regarding their policies on release and transmittal of PHI.
- Professionals are responsible for protecting confidentiality by establishing their policies, protocols, and procedures in accordance with their business needs.

PIPEDA

- Personal health information with respect to an individual means
  - Information concerning physical or mental health;
  - Information concerning any health service provided to the individual;
  - Information concerning the donation by the individual of any body part or any bodily substance of the individual or information derived from the testing or examination of a body part or bodily substance of the individual;
  - Information that is collected in the course of providing health services to the individual; or
  - Information that is collected incidentally to the provision of health services to the individual.

use or disclose protected health information for research purposes. For example, only professionals directly involved with clients can access information, so researchers who are not involved in direct care cannot contact or recruit a client directly (Wilson, 2006). Likewise, PIPEDA requires research information is used in a manner that respects individual confidentiality.

Informed consent is obtained when a person is undergoing a procedure, surgery, or treatment. "It involves legal individual capacity to consent, voluntary freedom of choice, and access to understandable information" (Tomey, 2009). When the client is not a competent adult, others may give consent like legal guardians, parent of child, married minor, or through a court order. The person giving consent must understand the intervention, risks, outcomes, side effects, and alternatives (Marquis & Huston, 2009). Additionally, the client can withdraw consent at any time and should have the opportunity to ask questions. In an emergency, to save a person's life, consent is not legally required from either the client or authorized individual. Each therapist delivering a service is responsible to provide informed-consent information. In intervention plans, department protocols specify informed-consent statements.

An increasingly diverse workforce calls upon the manager to be a role model of cultural and generational sensitivity as well as to comply with Title VII (Civil Rights Act of 1964) in the United States. Managers must be fair and just as they consider promotions and assignments. Language, personal space, our sense of time or timing, concepts of individual vs. group (family) performance, and variation in generational values impact performance and safety of the unit team. A manager's interactions, if viewed as discriminatory, may contribute to a complaint being filed with civil rights or equal opportunity agents. A manager's decisions and actions greatly influence the social climate, which in turn affects employee performance and well-being.

LEARNING OUTCOME

Summarize the legal concerns managers face as programs and services are delivered.

Summary

1. A climate of transparency, consumerism, and continuing concern for quality health care has shifted the focus of risk management from a focus on error reporting to client and constituent health, security, and safety.
2. The components of a risk management program include identification and evaluation of risks, selecting management strategies, and implementing and reporting on the plan.
3. Risk management concerns in health-care settings include accidents, adverse events, errors, near misses, sentinel events, and unpreventable adverse events.

4. Errors in recreation therapy occur during the APIE process, professional interactions, and as resources and environments are used to deliver services.
5. Recommended contents of incident reports were summarized.
6. The four risk management strategies are avoidance, reduction, retention, and transference.
7. The documents and practices contained in a risk management plan were presented.
8. The contents of a unit safety and security plan were outlined.
9. Settings incorporate a number of security devices to protect their constituents; a list provided examples.
10. In both Canada and the United States, a number of laws, organizations, and professional regulations govern and provide resources to ensure safety, quality, and privacy of health information. Several websites are available to locate these resources.
11. Therapeutic recreation managers are responsible for ensuring that neither negligence nor professional malpractice result from the operation of their unit.
12. Professionals are held to a standard of care defined by four criteria: duty, breach, causation, and injury.
13. A number of considerations were listed that may deter the filing of a complaint against a professional or the employing agency; included was a list of professional behavior that might minimize litigation.
14. Several legal concerns associated with consumer rights, medical records, invasion of privacy, confidential communication, research, informed consent, and a diverse workplace were considered as the manager is responsible for ensuring proper use and disclosure of client, staff, and stakeholder information.

Critical Thinking Activities

1. Have you, a friend, relative, or someone you have met had a serious problem in a health-care organization that resulted in health concerns? What was the outcome? How was the problem handled?
2. Observe the security and safety measures taken on your college campus with those you find in a health-care setting. What precautions and practices are in place in each setting? Describe similarities and differences.
3. Review the websites of the Joint Commission (www.jointcommission.org), the Department of Health and Human Services (hhs.gov/ocr/hipaa), and Health Canada (hc-sc.gc.ca) to identify their recommendations for client safety and the privacy and confidentiality of PHI.

References

American Therapeutic Recreation Association (ATRA). (2013). *Standards for the practice of therapeutic recreation and self-assessment guide.* Hattiesburg, MS: Author.

American Therapeutic Recreation Association (ATRA). (2009, July). *ATRA code of ethics.* Hattiesburg, MS: Author.

Anderson, J. A. (2010). Evolution of the health care quality journey from cost reduction to facilitating patient safety. *Journal of Legal Medicine, 31*(1), 59–72.

Barnes, I. (2011). Violence in long-term care. *Canadian Nursing Home, 22*(3), 15–19.

Carter, M. J., & Van Andel, G. E. (2011). *Therapeutic recreation: A practical approach* (4th ed.). Prospect Heights, IL: Waveland Press.

Creating cultures of safety. (Fall, 2011). *Washington Nurse, 41*(3), 27–29.

Department of Justice, Canada. (2011). Personal information protection and electronic documents act. S.C. 2000. c.5 (section 2). Retrieved from http://laws-lois.justice.gc.ca/Search/Search.aspx?txtS3archA11=personal+health+information&txtT1tl3=%22Personal+Information+Protection+and+Electronic+Documents+Act%22&h1ts0n1y=0&ddC0nt3ntTyp3=Acts

Hemman, E. A. (2002). Creating healthcare cultures of patient safety. *Journal of Nursing Administration, 32*(7/8), 419–427.

Henry, J., & Ginn, G. O. (2002). Violence prevention in health-care organizations within a total quality management framework. *Journal of Nursing Administration, 32*(9), 479–486.

Hronek, B. B., Spengler, J. O., & Baker III, T. A. (2007). *Legal liability in recreation, sports, and tourism* (3rd ed.). Champaign, IL: Sagamore.

Institute of Medicine (IOM). (1999). *To err is human: Building a safer health system.* Washington, DC: Author.

Institute of Medicine (IOM). (2001). *Crossing the quality care chasm: A new health system for the 21st century.* Washington, DC: Author.

Kaiser, R., & Robinson, K. (2005). Risk management. In B. van der Smissen, M. Moiseichik, & V. J. Hartenburg (Eds.), *Management of park and recreation agencies* (2nd ed., pp. 593–615). Ashburn, VA: National Recreation and Park Association.

Kuhn, A. M., & Youngberg, B. J. (2002). The need for risk management to evolve to assure a culture of safety. *Quality and Safety in Health Care, 11*(2), 158–163.

Liang, B. A., & Mackey, T. (2011). Quality and safety in medical care: What does the future hold? *Archives of pathology & laboratory medicine, 135*(11), 1425–1431. doi 10.5858/arpa 2011_0154_OA

Marquis, B. L., & Huston, C. J. (2009). *Leadership roles and management functions in nursing: Theory & application* (6th ed.). Philadelphia: Lippincott Williams & Wilkins.

McBride, D., Greening, A., & Redmond, D. (2006). Path to safety benefits of the 2005 Patient Safety and Quality Improvement Act. *Healthcare Financial Management: Journal of the Healthcare Financial Management Association, 60*(6), 84–88.

National Council for Therapeutic Recreation Certification. (January, 2011). *Certification standards part V: NCTRC national job analysis.* New City, NY: Author.

National Steering Committee on Patient Safety. (2009). *Building a safer system a national integrated strategy for improving patient safety in Canadian health care.* Ottawa, ON: Author.

Nelson, C. M., & Colley, J. A. (2005). Law enforcement and security. In B. van der Smissen, M. Moiseichik, & V. J. Hartenburg (Eds.), *Management of park and recreation agencies* (2nd ed., pp. 617–654). Ashburn, VA: National Recreation and Park Association.

Nicholls, S. (2010). HITECH highlights: A new law refines HIPAA privacy and security provisions, with implications for physical therapists. *PT in Motion, 2*(6), 40–43.

Office of the Privacy Commissioner of Canada. (2009). *Fact sheet: Privacy legislation in Canada.* Retrieved from http://www.priv.gc.ca/resource/fs-fi/02_05_d_15_e.asp.

Peterson, J. A., & Hronek, B. B. (2011). *Risk management for park, recreation, and leisure services* (6th ed.). Champaign, IL: Sagamore.

Rapala, K. G. (2011). Staffing excellence: Moving from retrospective to prospective management of risk. *Nursing Economic$, 29*(4), 211–214.

Rios, D. (1992). Risk management. In R. M. Winslow & K. J. Halberg (Eds.), *Management of therapeutic recreation services* (pp. 163–176). Arlington, VA: National Recreation and Park Association.

Sherwin, J. (2011). Contemporary topics in health care: Root cause analysis. *PT in motion, 3*(4), 26–31.

Stewart, A. (2011). Risk management: The reactive versus proactive struggle. *Journal of Nursing Law, 14*(3 & 4), 91–95. doi 10.1891/1073-7472.14.3.4.91

Sullivan, G. H. (2003). Incident reports are a must. Legally speaking. *RN, 66*(11), 71–74.

Sullivan, E. J., & Decker, P. J. (2009). *Effective leadership and management in nursing* (7th ed.). Upper Saddle River, NJ: Prentice-Hall.

Taniguchi, S. T., Widmer, M. A., & Taniguchi, A. M. (2008). Tort liability considerations for therapeutic recreation professionals. *Therapeutic Recreation Journal, 42*(3), 161–169.

Tomey, A. M. (2009). *Guide to nursing management and leadership* (8th ed.). St. Louis: Mosby Elsevier.

van der Smissen, B. (1990). *Legal liability and risk management for public and private entities* (Vol. 2). Cincinnati, OH: Anderson.

Vincent, C. (2003). Understanding and responding to adverse events. *New England Journal of Medicine, 348*(11), 1051–1056.

Whitehead, D. K., Weiss, S. A., & Tappen, R. M. (2010). *Essentials of nursing leadership and management* (5th ed.). Philadelphia: F. A. Davis.

Wilson, J. F. (2006). Health Insurance Portability and Accountability Act privacy rule causes ongoing concerns among clinicians and researchers. *Annals of Internal Medicine, 145*(4), 313–316.

Yang, J. A., & Kombarakaran, F. A. (2006). A practitioner's response to the new health privacy regulations. *Health & Social Work, 31*(2), 129–136.

Chapter 15
Managing Service Quality in Health Care

Keywords

- Benchmarking
- Consumer or customer
- Continuous Quality Improvement
- Deming cycle
- Evidence-based practice (EBP)
- Indicator
- Outcome
- Process
- Quality assurance
- Quality of care
- Quality improvement
- Structure
- Threshold
- Total Quality Management

Learning Outcomes

After reading this chapter, students will be able to:

1. Outline the evolution of quality concerns in health care.
2. Summarize the dimensions that define quality.
3. Explain the consumer's role in defining quality care.
4. Define the basic tenets of total quality management or TQM.
5. Describe the process of continuous quality improvement or CQI.
6. Explain the components of comprehensive quality assurance.
7. Identify structure, process, and outcome indicators.
8. Explain the intent of quality improvement.
9. Outline the role of evidence-based practice to improve quality.

Overview

It is evident that in the coming years, health-care consumers and funders alike will continue to demand more information, transparency, and value. Throughout the world, major structural reform to the ways in which health care is funded, managed, and evaluated is occurring. These reforms are at least partially due to the wider efforts by governmental and private funders to streamline services and increase the efficiency and effectiveness of services performed. Not only have these reforms brought about significant changes in the working relationship between health specialists and administrators, but they have also brought greater focus to the critical role that consumers themselves play in the exchange process (Sullivan & Decker, 2009). Whether these reforms will universally deliver the results expected—in terms of reduced cost, higher quality, and better access (Stumbo & Keogh Hoss, 2009)—remains very much an issue of open and vigorous debate, both within and outside the health-care sector.

Interestingly enough, reduced costs, higher quality, and improved access in health care are sometimes at direct odds against each other. Higher quality of and improved access to health-care services are often at odds with cost reduction. Better technology and more highly specialized staff who are assumed to provide higher-quality care come at a steep cost to the health-care consumer and third-party payers, such as insurance companies (Stumbo & Keogh Hoss, 2009). These three intersecting yet competing concerns will continue to be the focus of health-care discussions and debate for decades to come. Figure 15.1 (p. 238) shows this triad of health-care concerns.

In the present climate of change, it is clear that the focus will remain on managing the quality of services provided to clients. As such, the focus of the therapeutic recreation manager in today's modern health-care setting is on ensuring the provision of safe and high-quality

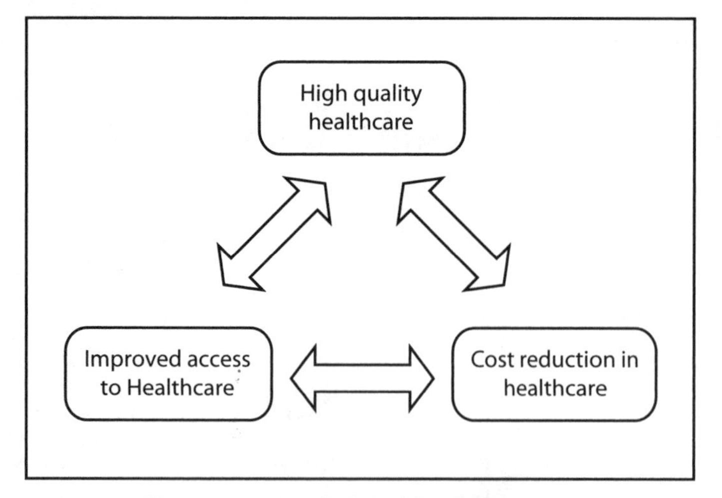

Figure 15.1 Triad of Health Care Concerns

services to consumers. The first section of this chapter provides a brief overview of the history of quality concerns in health care. The second section describes how various entities define quality in health care. At the heart of the interpretation of quality is the consumer. Thus in the third section, the integral role of the consumer in defining quality of care is explored.

A number of quality initiatives have been applied to health care. The next section addresses four of the prominent quality initiatives that emerged from manufacturing, engineering, and business and have been applied to health care. Even though each initiative may seem unique, however, they all address the notion that quality is measurable and is a never-ending quest of improvement. These four quality initiatives—Total Quality Management (TQM), Continuous Quality Improvement (CQI), Quality Assurance (QA), and Quality Improvement (QI)—guide the manager and teams as they manage change to improve each service component. Each APIE component is measured with structure, process, and outcome indicators, as outlined in this section.

A concluding section of the chapter addresses how outcome measures found with evidence-based practices are used to improve service quality. This is deemed important because, as noted previously by McCormick (2003), "the future is likely to only intensify the emphasis on data-driven decision-making. Health and human service professions that are able to employ basic quantitative methodologies will be well-equipped to participate in their own destinies" (p. 224). Discussion in Chapter 6 suggests the importance of applying technology to research that supports evidence-based practices.

Brief Evolution of Quality Concerns in Health Care

The first recorded instance of institutionalized concern for quality of care in hospitals comes from the National Convention of the French Revolution, in 1793. The measure decreed that there should be only one patient in a bed, as opposed to the usual two to eight, and that beds should be at least 3 feet apart (Rosenberg, 1987). In the United States, the oldest recognized quality control is that of hospital accreditation, which began in 1918 when the American College of Surgeons (1946) drew up a one-page list of basic criteria and standards for hospital facilities. In 1951 the Joint Commission on Accreditation of Hospitals (JCAH; now JCAHO or Joint Commission), which included the Canadian Medical Association, was formed. Standards developed by the American College of Surgeons over a period of some 35 years were adopted by the Joint Commission. They officially began to survey hospitals in 1952 using 11 standards (Scalenghe, 1994). In 1966, the Commission on Accreditation of Rehabilitation Facilities (CARF) was established and entered into an administration relationship with the Joint Commission for accreditation purposes. It became an independent organization in 1971 (Toppel, Beach, & Hutchinson-Troyer, 1991).

The Joint Commission's initial efforts to provide standards to accredit hospitals brought to the attention of the public and other professional bodies the importance of adequate care. Public Health Law 92-603 in 1972 created the establishment of Professional Standards Review Organizations (PSROs) to review quality and cost of care in federally supported programs like Medicaid and Medicare. Quality assurance programs became a focus of review processes. This concept gave way to TQM. The focus on improvement and customer satisfaction was described as "the right thing to do the first time, on time, all the time" (Tomey, 2009, p. 457). Legislation like the Health Care Quality Improvement Act (P.L. 99-660), which was enacted in 1986, created a federal data bank to identify incompetent practitioners. The Health Insurance Portability and Accountability Act (HIPAA) of 1996 created the Healthcare Integrity and Protection Data Bank (HIPDB) to combat fraud and abuse in both health-care insurance and health-care delivery. In 2013, as a result of the Affordable Care

Act, this database was merged with the National Practitioner Data Bank (NPDB) into one database with the intent of protecting consumers from unfit health-care practitioners.

The Joint Commission standards in the early 1990s emphasized quality monitoring and evaluating important aspects of care (McCormick, 2003). The objective was to provide quality health care in the appropriate setting at the most economical cost (Tomey, 2009). CQI thus became the evaluative tool chosen by many in the field to ensure quality and service delivery success. In the late 1990s, the Joint Commission instituted its "Agenda for Change" that shifted the focus of accreditation from organizational structure and process to performance or outcomes (Marquis & Huston, 2009; McCormick, 2003). A major thrust of the Joint Commission came in 1997 when they launched the ORYX initiative, a process that aimed to incorporate outcomes and other performance data into the hospital-accreditation process. Hospitals seeking accreditation collected data on standardized performance measures in order to track and benchmark their performance and identify areas of needed improvement (AHA, 2012).

In 2000, the Institute of Medicine, an independent, nonprofit organization that informs the U.S. government of health issues, issued a sentinel report, *To Err is Human: Building a Safer Health System*, that highlighted patient safety being a serious issue affecting health care. The report made four crucial recommendations to improve health-care quality: (a) improve leadership and knowledge, (b) identify and learn from errors, (c) set performance standards and expectations for safety, and (d) implement safety systems in health-care organizations. The IOM then followed with *Crossing the Quality Chasm* (2001), a report that proposed a shared health-care agenda, guided by a set of principles and priorities aimed at higher quality services, greater institutional support for quality changes, and better support and recognition by the U.S. Department of Health and Human Services (Buttell, Hendler, & Daley, 2006). Soon after, the Joint Com-mission (2004) published *Shared Visions—New Pathways*, in which the dimension of safety was included under the broader concept of quality, emphasizing a greater recognition that service providers must be fully cognizant of ensuring workplace safety and security early in the new millennium.

Learning Outcome
Outline the evolution of quality concerns in health care.

As a consequence, federal agencies, regulatory bodies, and professional organizations started to emphasize health and safety at all times for all constituents in practice standards. Some of these entities in the United States include the Joint Commission, the Rehabilitation Accreditation Commission (CARF), the National Committee for Quality Assurance (NCQA), and Centers for Medicare and Medicaid Services (CMS). An expanded list of agencies concerned with quality in the United States and Canada is presented in Chapter 14. In addition, third-party payers (such as insurance companies) and global organizations [such as the World Health Organization (WHO)] have also focused on and provided parameters of what they consider to be quality health-care services. While these examples are just a tip of the iceberg in terms of defining and regulating quality in health care, they exemplify some of the most prominent efforts in the health-care arena.

How is Quality Defined in Health Care?

From the outset it must be noted that quality is recognized as being an abstract and somewhat elusive construct to be measured (Hariharan & Dey, 2010; Lee, Delene, Bunda, & Kim, 2000). Kumar (2004, p. 45) noted that a lack of "consensus on a definition of quality, agreement on how to measure it, and how to evaluate the quality of health-care delivery systems has been an ongoing challenge" for many in the industry, both nationally and internationally.

However, some effort needs be made to seek to better understand what the concept is, the variables associated with it, and why the issue of quality of care is critically important to what those working in therapeutic recreation service delivery do on a day-to-day basis. This is because how the concept is defined is central to the identification of service quality determinants that, in turn, are a base requirement for specifying, measuring, controlling, and ultimately enhancing the services being delivered (Nwabueze & Mileski, 2008).

Mainz (2003, p. 523) argued that *quality of care* is "the degree to which health services for individuals and populations increase the likelihood of desired health outcomes and are consistent with current professional knowledge." Buttell et al. (2006, p. 62) defined quality as

> the degree to which health services for individual and populations increase the likelihood of desired health outcomes (quality principles), are consistent with current professional knowledge (professional practitioner skills), and meet the expectations of health-care users (the marketplace).

Quality is a somewhat abstract but a crucial concept in health care. The definitional difficulty is grounded somewhat in the reality that the term "quality" actually possesses several distinct dimensions. Thus, when people disagree about what quality is, they are often simply demonstrating their own preference for differing functional and technical dimensions of quality. However, the concept of quality refers to the achievement of some pre-established standard or a desired level of service. What then needs to happen is to choose the "indicators" that can be measured to indicate that quality services are provided. The Institute of Medicine and the World Health Organization provide two excellent examples of "indicators" that can be examined and measured with regard to quality.

In 2001, in the *Crossing the Quality Chasm* report, the IOM noted that quality healthcare should be:

- **Safe**: Avoiding injuries to patients from the care that is intended to help them;
- **Effective**: Providing services based on scientific knowledge to all who could benefit and refraining from providing services to those not likely to benefit (avoiding underuse and overuse, respectively);
- **Patient-centered**: Providing care that is respectful of and responsive to individual patient preferences, needs, and values and ensuring that patient values guide all clinical decisions;
- **Timely**: Reducing wait times and sometimes harmful delays for both those who receive and those who give care;
- **Efficient**: Avoiding waste, including waste of equipment, supplies, ideas, and energy; and
- **Equitable**: Providing care that does not vary in quality due to demographic characteristics such as gender, geographic location, and socioeconomic status.

In a largely parallel effort 5 years later, the World Health Organization (2006) defined six areas or dimensions of quality in health care:

- **Effectiveness**: Health care that adheres to an evidence base and results in improved health-care outcomes for individuals and communities, based on need;
- **Efficiency**: Health care delivered in a manner which maximizes resource use and avoids waste;
- **Accessibility**: Health care that is timely, geographically reasonable, and provided in settings in which skills and resources are appropriate to medical needs;
- **Acceptability/Patient-Centeredness**: Health care that takes into account the preferences and aspiration of clients and the cultures of their communities;
- **Equity**: Health care that does not vary in quality due to personal demographics such as gender, race, ethnicity, geographic location, or socio-economic status;
- **Safety**: Health care that minimizes risks and harm to clients.

The IOM and WHO components, while not providing a precise definition of quality, do provide nearly identical frameworks from which to base quality-improvement initiatives. Similarly, other organizations such as the Joint Commission, CARF, the National Committee for Quality Assurance (NCQA), and Centers for Medicare and Medicaid Services (CMS) have set expectations about quality that must be met. Third-party payers have specific perceptions of quality—ones that can be described by cost per case, length of stay, and other measurable criteria. Quality is also found in statutes that have been enacted over

Learning Outcome

Summarize the dimensions that define quality.

the years at all levels of government to protect the public.

Client Perceptions of Quality in Health Care

Yet, for all this effort to date, no universally accepted definition of the term quality currently exists. An interesting conundrum, given that one is very often immediately aware of it when it is lacking in some manner or other. Quality it seems, like beauty, truly lies in the eye of the beholder. What the professional considers to be a substantial achievement, the consumer may consider to be less than satisfactory. The problem is grounded somewhat in the reality that the term "quality" actually possesses several distinct dimensions. Thus, when people disagree about what quality is, they are often simply demonstrating their own preference for differing functional and technical dimensions of quality. As O'Leary (1993, p. 219) observed: "Quality of care is a judgment shaped by the interests of the individual or group making the judgment." As noted by Rashid and Jusoff (2009, p. 473), "the health consumer's perception of quality is nowadays heavily influenced by variations or gaps in provision which impede the delivery of services that the consumers themselves perceive to be of high quality." These failures on the part of the service provider tend to be expressed in terms of differences between:

- Patient expectations and management perceptions of patient expectations;
- Management perceptions of patient expectations and service-quality specifications;
- Service-quality specifications and service actually delivered;
- Service delivery and what is communicated about the service to patients; and
- Consumer expectations and perceptions, which in turn depends on the size and direction of the gaps associated with the delivery of service quality on the service provider's side (Rashid & Jusoff, 2009, pp. 473–474).

The provider should also be highly interested in the quality of the review being conducted by the consumer. According to Peterson (cited in Rhodes, 1991, p. 84) "between 54 and 78 percent of consumers feel that they can tell which hospitals provide quality care." That is a statistic not lost on those working in the health-care system, who nowadays openly acknowledge that service quality can greatly influence the consumers' choice of current (and future) service providers. As a consequence, the end game for many health-service providers is now cased firmly in terms of service excellence and achieving, as best possible, zero defections to other competitors in the health-care marketplace (Chahal, 2010; Lim & Tang, 2000).

Learning Outcome
Explain the consumer's role in defining quality care.

The consumer as the customer in the exchange process today effectively determines the relative importance of quality (Bell, 2004; Crosby, 1986; Juran, 1989). As Kaluzny and McLaughlin (1994, p. 202) noted, "[It] is a shift from a technical definition of quality to a recognition that effective care requires a subjective as well as technical evaluation. Specifically, a definition of health-care quality is inadequate if it does not include the customer." This is a notion supported more recently by Ristea, Stegaroiu, and Dinu (2009), who contended that the performance of a health system needs to be assessed from the perspective of an integrated system, in which responsiveness to patients' expectations of how they wish to be treated by health-care providers is a central concern. In general, consumers (i.e., patients) in health-care facilities tend to judge quality of care by the interpersonal aspects of the clinical process, because these aspects are the most obvious to them. Consumer-defined quality, regardless of setting, represents a way of achieving the health and human service goal of putting the needs of consumers first. Quality is determined, or defined, very much today by the consumer (Martin, 1993; Rashid & Jusoff, 2009).

Quality Initiatives Applied to Health Care

In the early 1960s, health and human service organizations were viewed generally by society as providing low-quality, highly variable, and largely ineffective services. Over time, the price consumers paid for these services increased rapidly due to budget deficits as well as the high cost of emerging medical technologies and health-care specialization. Rising health-care costs were then pitted against consumer groups who wanted to hold health-related professionals, agencies, and organizations more accountable for the provision of safe, high-quality, and evidence-based care. In this initial period, hospitals were allowed to create their own measures and initiatives for service quality and the resulting variation created an even greater confusion and inconsistencies. In addition, many health-care workers felt that quality initiatives were an unnecessary and unwanted burden on their jobs as care providers and became somewhat resentful of these efforts (Stumbo & Keogh Hoss, 2009).

Each successive decade has seen these growing pains diminish as accountability and quality care become the cornerstones of service provision. One of the ways that health care has addressed quality issues is to borrow theories, concepts, and methods from the business and industry sectors. Below are some of the more popular quality-improvement initiatives that have been embraced by health care throughout the decades:

- 1960s
  - Program Planning and Budgeting System (PPBS; Mosher, 1969)
  - Zero-Based Budgeting (ZBB; Wildavsky & Hammond, 1965)
- 1970s
  - Management by Objectives (MBO; Drucker, 1976)
  - Quality Circles (QC; cf. Macdonald, 1998).
- 1980s
  - Quality Assurance (Albrecht, 1992)
  - Total Quality Management
  - Continuous Quality Improvement (Deming, 1986)
    - Deming's Plan, Do, Check, Act cycle

While the current terminology preference is "quality improvement" (QI) (American Hospital Association, 2012), a brief review of TQM and CQI presents concepts that underpin much of what is practiced today in health-care settings. After this review, a discussion of quality assurance and quality improvement outlines practices and foci that define quality. Figure 15.2 provides a summary of the most popular quality initiatives that were often started in manufacturing, engineering, and business, before they were adopted by health-care agencies and institutions.

TQM as a Broad Philosophy of Quality Improvement

TQM is a philosophy of management that differs markedly from previous managerial efforts at enhancing

Continuous Quality Improvement (CQI): Focuses on "process" rather than the individual, recognizes both internal and external "customers," and promotes the need for objective data to analyze and improve processes. This approach to quality management builds upon traditional quality-assurance methods by emphasizing organization and systems (Health Resources and Services Administration, n.d.).

Total Quality Management (TQM): Set of management practices throughout the total organization geared to ensure the organization consistently meets or exceeds the expectations of customers (HRSA, n.d.).

Lean: Based on Toyota Production System, process-improvement methodology to increase efficiency and productivity while reducing costs. In health care, staff would collaborate to determine inefficiencies in care processes and to boost productivity. Hopefully, this process leads to reductions in care errors, and improvement in physician, employee, and patient satisfaction (AHA, 2012).

Six Sigma (DMAIC): Developed by Motorola, this process uses statistics to identify defects and then uses variety of techniques to identify sources of defects and changes that may eliminate or reduce them. The five steps are: (a) Define, (b) Measure, (c), Analyze, (d) Improve, and (e) Control. Approach requires total organizational commitment to error-free delivery of health care (AHA, 2012; HRSA, n.d.).

Plan-Do-Study-Act (PDSA): Deming's four-step cycle includes: (a) develop plan to test a change, (b) execute the test, (c) observe and learn from results, and (d) determine potential modifications (AHA, 2012).

FADE: Four broad steps include: (a) Focus—define and verify the process to be improved; (b) Analyze—collect and analyze data to establish baselines, identify root causes, and point toward possible solutions; (c) Develop— based on data, develop action plans for improvement, including implementation, communication, and measuring/monitoring; and (d) Execute and Ensure—implement the action plans on a pilot basis, and provide ongoing measuring/monitoring to ensure success (HRSA, n.d.).

Figure 15.2 Quality Initiatives

productivity and benchmarking quality. Past managerial reforms, in the form of PPBS, MBO, and ZBB, were essentially tool-based efforts that could be adopted by a health and human service organization without a requirement for any significant change being made to the basic approach to management that historically had been utilized. Although TQM has morphed since the 1980s in many ways, it remains essentially grounded in a very different and broader philosophical approach than previous initiatives (Yong & Wilkinson, 2001).

Broadly speaking, TQM is a proactive, innovative management philosophy applied to all individuals, departments, and units within an organization. It is an approach based "on a quest for progress and continual improvement in the areas of cost, reliability, quality, innovative efficiency, and business effectiveness" (Lakhe & Mohanty, 1994, p. 10). There are six commonly accepted elements of TQM in terms of it being a philosophy of management (Carr & Littman, 1990; Milakovich, 1990). See Figure 15.3.

TQM is based on the premise that the client is the focal point on which all services depend and that the quest for quality is an ongoing and desired process (Marquis & Huston, 2009). Thus, TQM is both process-driven and consumer-oriented. As a result, focusing on quality requires continuous improvements in all organizational activities or processes, including agency-wide procedures, client admissions, and program registration; management functions, risk, and safety; and clinical interventions, protocols, and programs (Sullivan & Decker, 2009). The TQM culture requires a high level of intensive and systematic communication between the various stakeholders, whether they are directly or indirectly involved in the delivery of services, in the provision of the highest quality of care (Mosadeghrad, 2005).

- Quality is a primary organizational goal.
- Customers determine what quality is.
- Customer satisfaction drives the organization.
- Variation in processes must be understood and reduced.
- Change is continuous and is accomplished by teams and teamwork.
- Top management commitment promotes a culture of quality, employee improvement, and a long-term perspective.

Source: Martin, L. L. (1993). Total quality management in human services organization (p. 24). Newbury Park, CA: Sage. Reproduced with permission.

Figure 15.3 Elements of TQM as a Philosophy of Management

One of the key goals of quality management nowadays is to empower employees to make a real difference in the services they provide to the full range of customers, both internal and external to the organization (Sullivan & Decker, 2009; Yong & Wilkinson, 2001). This requires strong leadership and management commitment to support employees (Levis, Brady, & Helfert, 2008). TQM is grounded in the notion that management trusts employees to be knowledgeable and accountable, and employee training is plentiful at all levels (Marquis & Huston, 2009).

Learning Outcome

Define the basic tenets of total quality management or TQM.

However, the behavior of the employees is an often-overlooked dimension of TQM that frequently leads to service and quality failures (Mosadeghrad, 2006). For instance, a lack of concurrent management attention towards issues of organizational culture, management practices, and organizational structures and systems has been found to often lead to issues of staff alienation and depersonalization of work, which in turn often led to TQM failures (Candido & Santos, 2011; Hoogervorst, Koopman, & Flier, 2005).

CQI as a Process of Quality Improvement

While TQM is viewed generally as the overall philosophy, continuous quality improvement *(CQI)* is the process by which resources are applied in order to improve the level of quality and the operating performance of the functional unit (Sullivan & Decker, 2009). CQI attempts to improve quality through programs often referred to under the banner of "quality assurance" and "risk management." The process itself involves a systematic monitoring, evaluation, and improvement of the effectiveness and efficiency of work procedures through teamwork. A key characteristic of CQI is that it empowers staff to bring about improvements in service performance. Rohlin et al. (2002, p. 70) argued that in a well-developed CQI process, results and recommendations from internal and external evaluations should be used in an integrated manner in order to achieve improvements, which may lead to adapted, or in some cases new, goals and measures that then form the basis of a new cycle of evaluation.

A basic assumption underpinning CQI is that when problems arise, or when deficiencies in quality in either process or service are identified, they are neither the result of a single person, nor are they only a concern for a single department or unit. They are an issue for the collective in which multidisciplinary teams are used as a proactive means of realizing improvements. A team approach requires cooperation and a willingness to share knowledge and expertise. It serves to reduce or replace competition as the interpersonal value to be maximized. At the same time, such an approach provides the opportunity for individual members to gain a greater understanding of and appreciation for the function of each discipline in the process. It also serves to facilitate for members a greater understanding of the roles and responsibilities of management beyond that of the top-down decision-making process (Triolo, Hansen, Kazzaz, Chung, & Dobbs, 2002).

CQI recognizes two groups of *consumers* as *customers*: those internal and external to the organization (Sullivan & Decker, 2009). Internal customers are the professionals and employees of the organization as well as departments or units that provide services of various kinds to each other and to the consumer. External customers, on the other hand, comprise the patients or clients (i.e., consumers), friends and family members of the consumer, regulatory agents, and third-party payers. The community is also considered an external consumer (or stakeholder in this context) because some of its needs are met by the health-care facility (i.e., suppliers of equipment; Macintyre & Kleman, 1994).

Learning Outcome

Describe the process of continuous quality improvement or CQI.

The Deming Cycle

CQI incorporates what has come to be known as the *Deming cycle*— the Plan-Do-Check-Act (PDCA) cycle. It was adapted by W. Edwards Deming from Walter Shewhart (Deming, 1986). In short, this approach is similar in nature to active problem solving. Figure 15.4 illustrates the Deming cycle.

In brief, the Deming cycle begins with the Plan stage. At the plan stage, a proposal is made to implement a change that hopefully will result in correcting a quality problem. The proposed improvement has not been arrived at by guesswork but rather by the analysis of data to determine the most probable cause of the problem and the most likely solution. One of the CQI tools used to generate as many ideas as possible about the causes of a quality problem is brainstorming. The Do stage is the actual implementation of the proposed change, while holding constant all other aspects of the system or process. At the Check stage, the results of the change are evaluated. Did quality improve? At the Act stage, the change, if successful in improving quality, is made into a standard operating procedure. If the Change does not improve quality, then it is abandoned, and other probable causes of the quality problem are studied. In either case, the Deming cycle is never

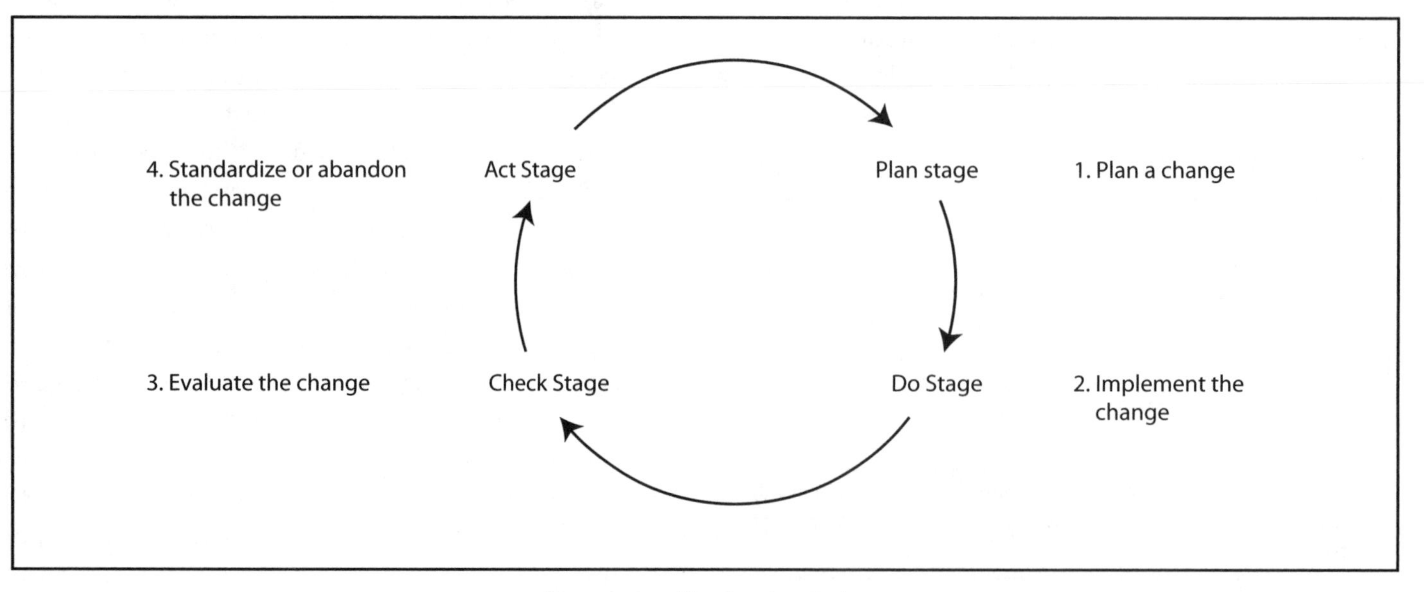

Figure 15.4 The Deming Cycle

completed; there is no end state to the pursuit of quality improvement. It focuses on continuous improvement to increase consumer satisfaction, to enhance productivity, and to lower cost (Deming, 1986; Tindill & Stewart, 1993).

Quality Assurance

Avedis Donabedian's (1969) approach to improving the efficiency and effectiveness of the services rendered has had the widest application and is most commonly associated with QA. *QA* is a process that monitors and evaluates service quality through the ongoing use of standards and mechanisms that evaluate services to ensure standards are met. Donabedian's framework has the advantage of being relatively simple yet comprehensive in nature. Comprehensive QA includes the structure in which service is given, the process of service, and the outcome of that service (Donabedian, 1969).

Structure

Structure not only refers to the setting or location where services are provided but also includes the resources. While the setting is perhaps the easiest of the three aspects to measure, it is many times overlooked in some evaluation procedures. The following offers examples of some of the structural aspects that are monitored:

- facilities: accessibility, adequate space to conduct programs, convenience of areas, safety
- equipment: adequate supplies and equipment, staff ability to use it
- staff: credentials (e.g., state licensure, certification), continuing education and professional development, performance evaluation, absenteeism
- finances: adequate budget, adequate salaries
- management: written statements of vision, mission, and objectives; ethical statement of practice; scope of practice
- organizational arrangement: management structure, organization of practice, styles of supervision
- legal authority: accreditation, licensure
- program or treatment plan: procedures associated with assessment, planning, implementation, evaluation, and documentation of treatment plan appropriateness

None of these structural factors alone can guarantee that good service will be given, but they are factors that make good service more likely to occur (Whitehead, Weiss, & Tappen, 2010). These factors "ensure a safe and effective environment but do not address the actual care provided" (Marquis & Huston, 2009, p. 547). As Riley (1991, p. 57) noted, "structure variables measure the probability or propensity for quality care." Without adequate policies and facilities, for example, the process of delivering service is impeded, and outcomes are adversely affected.

Process

Process refers to the nature and sequence of activities carried out by management and practitioners. It usually involves two aspects: the technical and the interpersonal. Process standards assess the performance of specified and, at times, prescribed activities. Protocols and best-practice guidelines standardize practices and serve as process standards. Examples include:

- Facilitating psychosocial interventions (such as teaching a skill)
- Leading programs
- Formulating an individual treatment plan, progress note and/or discharge referral summary
- Assisting in discharge planning and referral with the larger team of professionals
- Evaluating program outcomes (i.e., formative and summative) and client outcomes
- Documenting intervention results
- Contributing to the advancement of a profession through participating in research projects

It also encompasses what is and what is not done, and what should or should not be done. A critical difference between structural and process standards is that process standards require a professional judgment to determine whether a criterion has been met.

There are several ways to collect process data. The most direct is by observation of practitioner activities. Another is self-reporting done by the practitioner. A third source is a review of the chart or records that are kept, and lastly, various kinds of assessment tools can be used.

Whatever source of data collection is used, some set of objectives (i.e., protocols or best practices) is needed as a standard against which to compare the activities. This set of objectives should be specific and measurable, such as a list of the steps in the development of a treatment plan. The objective is not only to collect valid, appropriate, and comprehensive data but also to collect these data in an efficient, standardized, and error-free manner. It is perhaps at this point timely to point out that while completion of these various process activities may seem relatively straightforward, some caution on the part of the TR specialist, and in some cases additional effort, is justified.

Outcome

An *outcome* is the end result of a process and is the product of actions. It refers to the results of the activities in which the practitioners have been involved. As noted by Stumbo and Pegg (2010, p. 12), outcomes are the differences noted in the client (behaviors, knowledge, skills, attitudes, abilities, preferences, etc.) from entry into the program or service compared to exit from the treatment. Outcome measures evaluate the efficiency and effectiveness of these activities by answering questions such as:

- Was the service to the consumer of an appropriate type and quality?
- Is the consumer more independent (or healthy or able) as a consequence of their exposure to the service or program?
- Were there unexpected or unanticipated consequences during participation?

Whether the questions are general or specific, a major problem in using outcome measures in evaluation is that they are influenced by many factors, not by just one factor or by just one person (e.g., medication, diagnosis, assessments by various staff disciplines, treatment plans, documentation, and age of the consumer). It is important to note that outcomes are particularly sensitive to subjective value judgments. Thus, it is extremely important to determine criteria that indicate if standards are being met and, more particularly, to what degree they are met.

Examples of consumer outcomes (Stumbo, 2003) might include:

- Rehabilitation potential
- Recidivism and health-care utilization
- Functional or health status
- Patient's or client's satisfaction with services
- Costs per service provided
- Resource consumption
- Quality of life, including leisure-related knowledge, skills, and awareness

The focus on safe, high-quality services through continuous systematic performance improvement broadens the realm of relevant outcomes from the client to a number of internal and external audiences; outcomes valued by multiple stakeholders are considered, as are the system-wide influences impacting safety and quality in the environment (McCormick, 2003).

Three forms of outcome measures commonly recognized throughout the allied health field are goals and objectives, standards and criteria, and instruments. Goals and objectives are an important measurement device in any health-care organization but are often poorly used or worse, not used at all (Grol, 2001). Departments use goal and objective statements to provide direction and to identify the degree to which a program achieves its intended goals and objectives. Practitioners incorporate goals and objectives into the design of comprehensive and specific programs (Stumbo & Peterson, 2009). Measurable improvements evaluate change in clients as a result of their program participation (Carruthers, 2003). "Effectiveness evaluation determines the extent to which a program meets its intended goals and objectives" (Carruthers, 2003, p. 187).

The basic principles of outcome measurement rely on well-defined standards. Standards are criteria for judging the work of a practitioner, team, or organization, and they vary in their specificity. They supply a basis for comparison. Within an organization, they form a consensus of professional thinking. In addition, standards are established and derived from a variety of sources. Managers must determine what standards will be used to measure the quality of service, then develop and implement a quality-improvement program that can measure end results against the developed standards. Thereafter, managers have the responsibility to monitor the quality of the care or service to the consumer.

The major reason for setting standards is to increase objectivity by defining as clearly as possible what is acceptable and what is not acceptable. In addition, they must be achievable, measurable, and objective (Marquis & Huston, 2009). Realistic standards that are achievable lessen the likelihood of frustration, increase the motivation to perform well, and are more acceptable to staff. Without this approach, the judgments that take place in the evaluation process can be variable, subjective, and susceptible to the biases of the evaluator.

A second function of standards is to communicate clearly to everyone involved (i.e., staff, administrators, consumers, accreditors, and regulators) what level of service is expected in the department. This can be done only if the standards are available to everyone. The implementation of standards and their measurements for evaluating performance may vary from organization to organization, the purpose of the evaluation, and the evaluator.

Outcome measures also may be instruments. Examples may include the World Health Organization's WHO Quality of Life-BREF (WHOQOL-BREF) instrument and the Minimum Data System (MDS, Centers for Medicare and Medicaid, 2013). Instruments such as these may be used to measure client outcomes when and if the instrument's results produce valid and reliable results for those interventions.

Learning Outcome
Explain the components of comprehensive quality assurance.

Indicators

Indicators are also an important piece in the quality puzzle. An *indicator* is a predetermined (i.e., written), measurable, well-defined component of an aspect of care or service such as elements in the APIE process. Indicators may evaluate the structure or process of service, although they are more often associated with outcome. Once these indicators are identified, *benchmarking* or comparing performance using these quality indicators across settings is the key to quality improvement. When one indicator is measured and no longer a concern, another indicator is considered.

Structural indicators may include staffing, correct use of equipment, and adherence to policies. Processes consist of appropriate assessment of the consumer on admission and documentation of therapeutic recreation service given. The actual results of consumer service are the outcomes that show or reflect achievement or non-achievement of goals. In developing indicators, the following guidelines need to be kept in mind:

- Decide whether the indicators should evaluate compliance, appropriateness, or outcome. Compliance refers to procedures found within policies, while appropriateness is concerned with the adequacy of service, and outcome is the result of the performance (or nonperformance) of a process.
- Indicators should be limited to a few important or critical indicators based on standards.
- Indicators should be stated in positive terms.
- Indicators should ask for one piece of information. Each point to be addressed should be the subject of a separate indicator.
- Indicators should be reliable, valid, and tested. Indicators are usually selected from practice standards, policies, protocols, and guidelines. After they are developed, others should review them for clarity. The reliability and validity of the indicators should be evaluated.
- Determine if exceptions to the indicators will be allowed. While there should be no exceptions, there may be situations that do develop.
- Establish the *threshold* for evaluation. The threshold for evaluation of an indicator is established before the monitoring process begins. When the results are less than hoped for, some type of problem solving is required. The projected threshold is the number or percentage established when the monitoring activity is developed or planned. Thresholds are usually expressed as a number or percentage. It is unrealistic to set thresholds for evaluation at 100%, although the percentage may change after testing.

Examples of types of indicators might include the following:

- Assessment—Complete an assessment of patient functional and leisure abilities within 72 hours after admission to the unit 95% of the time.
- Program—Patient is seen by the therapeutic recreation specialist a minimum of three times during hospitalization 95% of the time.
- Discharge plan—Complete a discharge plan with patient involvement no later than 24 hours prior to discharge 90% of the time.

Learning Outcome

Identify structure, process, and outcome indicators.

Quality Improvement

In essence, the concept of quality is often considered in relation to the achievement of some pre-established standard or a desired level of service. Different stakeholders (e.g., third-party payers, consumers, accreditation agencies) might require different activities or outcomes (e.g., accessibility, cost, efficiency) to be measured and different processes (e.g., TQM or CQI) might be used to get there, but in the end, *quality improvement* is concerned with measurement of some kind as "proof" of quality.

As a road map, three questions become essential to quality improvement in health care. As noted by the HRSA (n.d., p. 2):

> In the process of quality improvement, regardless of which model is chosen, there are three questions that implementers should consider:
>
> - What are we trying to accomplish?
> - How will we know that a change is an improvement?
> - What change can we make that will result in improvement?

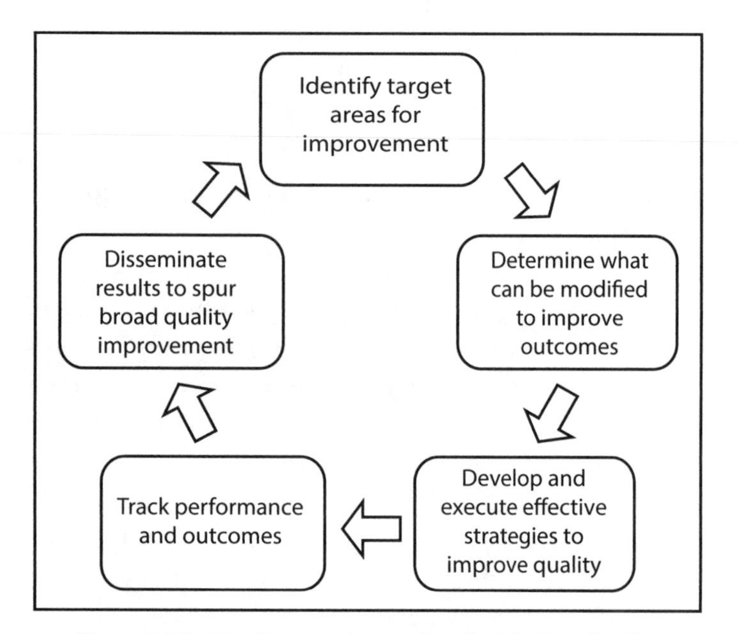

Figure 15.5 Five Steps to Improving Health-Care Quality

HRSA (n.d.) noted that selecting a quality-improvement model (e.g., TQM or CQI) to address these questions is not a strictly defined process. There is not a specific model—one size fits all—that works best in every situation or for every concern. When selecting a model for quality improvement, the health-care organization should choose one that fits best within its existing organizational structure and workflow (HRSA, n.d., pp. 2–3). The AHA (2012) provides a basic quality-improvement model with five steps: (a) identify target areas for improvement, (b) determine what can be modified to improve outcomes, (c) develop and execute effective strategies to improve quality, (d) track performance and outcomes, and (e) disseminate results to spur broad quality improvement. These five, circular steps are shown in Figure 15.5.

One of the most important parts to note is that quality improvement is a never-ending process, with higher goals being continuously established and targeted for improvement (e.g., further reductions in hospital-based infections, fewer readmissions, higher patient satisfaction). As noted by the American Hospital Association (AHA, 2012):

> Hospitals are on a never-ending journey of quality improvement—employing new technologies and techniques and research on what works, as well as continuously training new workers and meeting the needs of sicker patients. While hospitals are at different points on their quality path, all hospitals are committed to quality improvement. This commitment has helped hospitals make great strides in increasing adherence to treatment protocols and improving patient outcomes. (p. 1)

Learning Outcome

Explain the intent of quality improvement.

Quality Improvement through Evidence-Based Practice

What began initially with accreditation efforts to evaluate adequate client care in the 1950s has now evolved to a focus on forward-thinking, evidence-based practices that are outcome-directed (Hoffmann, Bennett, & Del Mar, 2010; Lee & McCormick, 2002). Although the terminology used in the field has changed over time, the core intent of professional and regulatory agencies remains largely unchanged, as the focus remains firmly on documenting quality outcomes through the application of accountability processes that measure ongoing improvements in consumer safety and care.

Assessing the quality of care has become important in recent years, as medical advances have proliferated and consumers have become better informed and developed higher expectations of health-care professionals (Tomey, 2009). "Indicators for performance and outcome measurement allow the quality of care and services to be measured" (Mainz, 2003, p. 523). This occurs by creating quality indicators to describe performance resulting from specific interventions with particular clients, then evaluating whether the intervention outcomes are consistent with indicators based on evidence-based standards of practice. Indicators are based on standards of practice and are derived from literature, experts, and use of effectiveness evidence (often research results) (Mainz, 2003; Stumbo & Wardlaw, 2011). Measurements allow professionals to verify the results of their interactions with clients, and by quantifying the results, the professional and consumer are better able to make decisions about further services and care (Stumbo & Pegg, 2010).

One of the core competencies for health professionals, described by the Institute of Medicine (2003), is the use of *evidence-based practice (EBP)*. This report defines EBP as the integration of the best research with clinical expertise and client values and preferences—thus the therapist applies the best scientific evidence to each consumer's unique situation to make clinical decisions (Sullivan & Decker, 2009). Refer to Chapter 6 for a discussion of research in therapeutic recreation.

This approach provides a scientific basis for making decisions. A systematic approach is used to identify documentable information that demonstrates therapeutic recreation intervention effectiveness (Stumbo, 2003). Outcome measurement quantifies data and compares relative costs of achieving outcomes (Neuman, 2003). Performance measures quantify efficiency and effectiveness of service-delivery methods (Zimmermann, Cooper, & Allen, 2001). Professionals choose performance measures that reflect cost, quality, and time concerns (Leandri, 2001). Cost measures cover economic aspects of performance like cost-benefit analysis. Quality or effectiveness measures address how well services meet client needs, preferences, and satisfaction, and they contribute to behavioral changes and quality-of-life issues like leisure options. Time measures reflect efficiency of using resources to deliver services (e.g., unit cost per participant, performance relative to regulatory or professional practice standards) (Zimmermann, Cooper, & Allen, 2001). Once the manager decides how to measure outcomes, training is planned to ensure staff preparedness to continuously monitor and document relationships among interventions and consumer outcomes.

The last step in a systems approach to evaluating quality is using a feedback loop. The quality-improvement process itself deals with structure and process, while the ultimate improvement is reflected in the outcome. Evaluating quality requires evaluating the outcome of the implemented therapeutic recreation plan. It is essential to monitor structure, process, and outcome indicators to determine if modifications in resources (structure) and service delivery (processes) are necessary to improve (performance). The application of systems like APIE is cyclical: The manager has evidence to make decisions relative to structure and process factors that impact outcomes or benefits. With outcomes measurement, therapeutic recreation practices are based on evidence of practice effectiveness [e.g., Does A program produce B outcomes with C consumers? (Stumbo & Peterson 2009)]. Using evidence-based practices, professionals rely on the best available information gained through scientific processes to improve performance and remain accountable.

Although each term—continuous quality improvement, quality assurance, and quality or performance improvement (PI)—may have a unique meaning created by its sponsoring agency (e.g., the Joint Commission, CARF, NCQA, CMS), the goal of each is essentially similar—that is, to document accountability for improvement of health-care services for all individuals (Stumbo & Peterson, 2009). Accountability is concerned with the extent to which a program's goals are achieved and whether resources are used efficiently. Improvement, on the other hand, refers to changes made to increase or enhance service effectiveness and efficiency to ensure consumers receive the safest, highest quality of care with the available resources (Widmer, Zabriskie, & Wells, 2003). Decision making is a component part of the process of reasoned action and is, in and of itself, the end result of evaluating; evaluation provides information to the manager to make informed decisions for future action (Stumbo & Peterson, 2009; Stumbo & Wardlaw, 2011). When a therapeutic recreation manager uses the APIE process, performance measures identify expected outcomes reached through standardized interventions. Decisions concerning future services are based on knowledge and clinical judgment that guide evidence-based practices.

LEARNING OUTCOME

Outline the role of evidence-based practice to improve quality.

Summary

1. This chapter focused on understanding quality and its characteristics in health and human-service organizations.
2. The Joint Commission's initial efforts in the 1950s to provide standards to accredit hospitals brought to the attention of the public and other professional bodies the importance of adequate care.
3. As a consequence of legislation and governmental and nongovernmental reports, federal agencies, regulatory bodies, and professional organizations started to emphasize health and safety at all times for all constituents in practice standards and also focused on and provided parameters of what they consider to be quality health-care services.
4. Consensus on a definition of quality, agreement on how to measure it, and how to evaluate the quality of health-care delivery systems has been an ongoing challenge both nationally and internationally.
5. "Quality" refers to the achievement of some pre-established standard or a desired level of service.
6. The consumer as the customer in the exchange process today effectively determines the relative importance of quality—the performance of a health system needs to be assessed from the perspective of how the system responds to patients' expectations of how they wish to be treated by health-care providers. In general, consumers (i.e., patients) in health-care facilities tend to judge quality of care by the interpersonal aspects of the clinical process because these aspects are the most obvious to them.
7. Since the 1960s, health care has borrowed a number of theories, concepts, and methods from business and industry to address quality issues and bring accountability to service provision.
8. TQM is a proactive, innovative management philosophy applied to all individuals, departments, and units within an organization. It is an approach based on a quest for progress and continual improvement in the areas of cost, reliability, quality, innovative efficiency, and business effectiveness.
9. CQI is the process by which resources are applied in order to improve the level of quality and the operating performance of the functional unit. The process involves a systematic monitoring, evaluation, and improvement of the effectiveness and efficiency of work procedures through teamwork and is evident in QA and risk management activities.
10. Deming cycle—the Plan-Do-Check-Act (PDCA) cycle—is integral to CQI and is a four-step problem-solving process: (1) plan for change, (2) implement the change, (3) evaluate the change, and (4) standardize or abandon the change.
11. QA is a process that monitors and evaluates service quality through the ongoing use of standards and mechanisms that evaluate services to ensure standards are met.
12. Comprehensive QA includes the structure in which service is given, the process of service, and the outcome of that service.
13. "Structure" refers to the setting or location where services are provided and includes the resources.
14. "Process" refers to the nature and sequence of activities carried out by management and practitioners.
15. Outcome is the end result of a process and is the product of actions. It refers to the results

of the activities in which the practitioners have been involved.

16. Three forms of outcome measurement are commonly recognized throughout health care: goals and objectives, standards and criteria, and instruments.
17. An indicator is a predetermined (i.e., written), measurable, well-defined component of an aspect of care or service, such as elements in the APIE process. Indicators may evaluate the structure, process, or outcome of service, although they are more associated with outcome.
18. Quality improvement is concerned with measurement of some kind as "proof" of quality.
19. Evidence-based practice (EBP) is the integration of the best research with clinical expertise and client values and preferences—the therapist applies the best scientific evidence to each consumer's unique situation to make clinical decisions. Gathering data will document service accountability and measurement of outcomes to show performance improvement and ultimately quality improvement in services.

Critical Thinking Activities

1. Review the websites of the Joint Commission (www.jointcommission.org), the Department of Health and Human Services (hhs.gov), and Health Canada (hc-sc.gc.ca) to identify their indicators for quality and recommendations for evidence-based practices.
2. Review professional literature to locate protocols and guidelines for best practices. For example, locate research articles and studies on the use of specific interventions with defined client populations. Then explain how professionals use this evidence to drive their decision-making.
3. Locate the latest editions of professional practice standards and within the documents (CTRA and ATRA) determine how the standards measure quality of the therapeutic recreation process.

References

Albrecht, K. (1992). *The only thing that matters.* New York: Harper Business.

American College of Surgeons. (1946). 29th annual hospital standardization report. *Bulletin of the American College of Surgeons, 31*(4), 301–308.

American Hospital Association (AHA). (2012, October). Hospitals demonstrate commitment to quality improvement. *Trendwatch.*

Bell, L. (2004). Developing service quality in mental health services. *International Journal of Health Care Quality Assurance, 17*(7), 401–406.

Buttell, P., Hendler, R., & Daley, J. (2006). Quality in healthcare: Concepts and practice. In K. H. Cohn & D. E. Hough (Eds.), *The business of healthcare, Volume 3* (pp. 62–95). Westport, CT: Praeger.

Candido, C. J. F., & Santos, S. P. (2011). Is TQM more difficult to implement than other transformational strategies? *Total Quality Management, 22*(11), 1139–1164.

Carr, D., & Littman, I. (1990). *Excellence in government—Total quality management in the 1990s.* Arlington, VA: Coopers and Lybrand.

Carruthers, C. (2003). Objectives-based approach to evaluating the effectiveness of therapeutic recreation services. In N. J. Stumbo (Ed.), *Client outcomes in therapeutic recreation services* (pp. 185–200). State College, PA: Venture Publishing, Inc.

Centers for Medicare & Medicare. (2013) *Minimum Data Set.* Retrieved from: http://www.cms.gov/Research-Statistics-Data-and-Systems/Files-for-Order/IdentifiableDataFiles/LongTermCareMinimumDataSetMDS.html

Chahal, H. (2010). Two component customer relationship management model for healthcare services. *Managing Service Quality, 20*(4), 343–365.

Crosby, P. B. (1986). *Quality is free: The art of making quality certain.* New York: McGraw-Hill.

Deming, W. E. (1986). *Out of the crisis.* Cambridge, MA: MIT Center for Advanced Engineering Study.

Donabedian, A. A. (1969). *A guide to medical care administration, II: Medical care appraisal—Quality & utilization.* New York: American Public Health Association.

Drucker, P. F. (1976). What results should you expect? A users' guide to MBO. *Public Administration Review, 36*(1), 12–19.

Grol, R. (2001). Successes and failures in the implementation of evidence-based guidelines for clinical practice. *Medical Care, 39*(8), 46–54.

Hariharan, S., & Dey, P. (2010). A comprehensive approach to quality management of intensive care services. *International Journal of Health Care Quality Assurance, 23*(3), 287–300.

Health Resources and Services Administration. (n.d.). *What is quality improvement?* Available at: http://www.hrsa.gov/healthit/toolbox/HealthITAdoptiontoolbox/QualityImprovement/whatisqi.html

Hoffmann, T., Bennett, S., & Del Mar, C. (2010). *Evidence-based practice across the health professions.* Sydney: Elsevier.

Hoogervorst, J., Koopman, P., & Flier, H. (2005). Total quality management: The need for an employee-centred, coherent approach. *TQM Magazine, 17*(1), 92–106.

Institute of Medicine. (2001). *Crossing the quality chasm: A new health system for the 21st century.* Retrieved from: http://www.iom.edu/~/media/Files/Report%20Files/2001/Crossing-the-Quality-Chasm/Quality%20Chasm%202001%20%20report%20brief.pdf

Institute of Medicine. (2003). *Health professions education: A bridge to quality.* Retrieved from: http://www.iom.edu/Reports/2003/Health-Professions-Education-A-Bridge-to-Quality.aspx

Institute of Medicine. (2013). *Definition of quality.* Retrieved from: http://www.iom.edu/Global/News%20Announcements/Crossing-the-Quality-Chasm-The-IOM-Health-Care-Quality-Initiative.aspx

Joint Commission Resources. (January 2004). "The launch of shared visions-new pathways" *Joint Commission Perspectives [Special Issue], 24*(1), p. 1-4.

Juran, J. (1989). *Juran on leadership for quality: An executive handbook.* New York: Free Press.

Kaluzny, A. D., & McLaughlin, C. P. (1994). Managing transitions: Assuring the adoption and impact of TQM. In C. P. McLaughlin & A. D. Kaluzny (Eds.), *Continuous quality improvement in healthcare* (pp. 198–206). Gaithersburg, MD: Aspen.

Kumar, S. (2004). Quality in allied health service delivery: Rhetoric vs. reality? *Australian Epidemiologist, 11*, 45–47.

Lakhe, R., & Mohanty, R. (1994). Total quality management: Concepts, evolution and acceptability in developing countries. *International Journal of Quality & Reliability Management, 11*(9), 9–33.

Leandri, S. J. (2001). Measures that matter: How to fine-tune your performance measures. *Journal for Quality and Participation Profound Change at Work, 24*(1), 39–41.

Lee, H., Delene, L., Bunda, M., & Kim, C. (2000). Methods of measuring health-care service quality. *Journal of Business Research, 48*, 233-246.

Lee, Y., & McCormick, B. P. (2002). Toward evidence-based therapeutic recreation practice. In D. R. Austin, J. Dattilo, & B. P. McCormick (Eds.), *Conceptual foundations for therapeutic recreation* (pp. 165–184). State College, PA: Venture Publishing, Inc.

Levis, M., Brady, M., & Helfert, M. (2008). Total quality management underpins information quality management. *Journal of American Academy of Business, 14*(1), 172–178.

Lim, P., & Tang, N. (2000). A study of patients' expectations and satisfaction in Singapore hospitals. *International Journal of Health and Quality Assurance, 13*(7), 290–299.

Macdonald, J. (1998). The quality revolution—in retrospect. *TQM Magazine, 10*(5), 321–333.

Macintyre, K., & Kleman, C. C. (1994). Measuring customer satisfaction. In C. P. McLaughlin & A. D. Kaluzny (Eds.), *Continuous quality improvement in healthcare* (pp. 102–126). Gaithersburg, MD: Aspen.

Mainz, J. (2003). Defining and classifying clinical indicators for quality improvement. *International Journal for Quality in Health Care, 15*(6), 523–530.

Marquis, B. L., & Huston, C. J. (2009). *Leadership roles and management functions in nursing: Theory & application* (6th ed.). Philadelphia: Lippincott Williams & Wilkins.

Martin, L. L. (1993). *Total quality management in human services organization.* Newbury Park, CA: Sage.

McCormick, B. P. (2003). Outcomes measurement as a tool for performance improvement. In N. J. Stumbo (Ed.), *Client outcomes in therapeutic recreation services* (pp. 221–232). State College, PA: Venture Publishing, Inc.

Milakovich, M. (1990). Total quality management for public sector productivity improvement. *Public Productivity and Management Review, 14*, 19–32.

Mosadeghrad, A. M. (2005). A survey of total quality management in Iran: Barriers to successful implementation in health care organizations. *International Journal of Health Care Quality Assurance, 18*(3), xii–xxxiv.

Mosadeghrad, A. M. (2006). The impact of organizational culture on the successful implementation of total quality management. *TQM Magazine, 18*(6), 606–625.

Mosher, F. C. (1969). Limitations and problems of PPBS in the States. *Public Administration Review, 29*(2), 160–167.

Neuman, K. M. (2003). Developing a comprehensive outcomes management program: A ten-step process. *Administration in Social Work, 27*(1), 5–21.

Nwabueze, U., & Mileski, J. (2008). The three dimensions of quality service: The case of service quality gaps in the U.K. national health service. *International Journal of Public Administration, 31*(10–11), 1328–1353.

O'Leary, T. (1993). Defining performance of organizations. *Journal of Quality Improvement, 19*(7), 218–223.

Rashid, W., & Jusoff, H. (2009). Service quality in health care setting. *International Journal of Health Care Quality Assurance, 22*(5), 471–482.

Rhodes, M. (1991). The use of patient satisfaction data as an outcome monitor in therapeutic recreation quality assurance. In B. Riley (Ed.), *Quality management: Applications for therapeutic recreation* (pp. 83–106). State College, PA: Venture Publishing, Inc.

Riley, B. (Ed.). (1991). *Quality management: Applications for therapeutic recreation.* State College, PA: Venture Publishing, Inc.

Ristea, A., Stegaroiu, V., & Dinu, V. (2009). Responsiveness of health systems: A barometer of the quality of health services. *Quality Management in Services, 11*(26), 277–287.

Rohlin, M., Schaub, R., Holbrook, P., Leibur, E., Levy, G., Roubalikova, L., Nilner, M., Roger-Leroi, V., Danner, G., Iseri, H., & Feldman, C. (2002). Continuous quality improvement. *European Journal of Dental Education, 6*, 67–77.

Rosenberg, C. E. (1987). *The care of strangers.* New York: Basic Books.

Scalenghe, R. (1994, October 13). *In introduction to the JCAHO.* Presentation at the National Therapeutic Recreation Institute, Minneapolis, MN.

Stumbo, N. J. (2003). Outcomes, accountability, and therapeutic recreation. In N. J. Stumbo (Ed.), *Client outcomes in therapeutic recreation services* (pp. 1–24). State College, PA: Venture Publishing, Inc.

Stumbo, N. J., & Keogh Hoss, M. A. (2009). Higher education and healthcare: Parallel issues of quality, cost, and access. In N. J. Stumbo (Ed.), *Professional issues in therapeutic recreation* (2nd ed., pp. 367–388). Champaign, IL: Sagamore.

Stumbo, N. J., & Pegg, S. (2010). Outcomes and evidence-based practice: Moving forward. *Annual in Therapeutic Recreation, 18*, 12–23.

Stumbo, N. J., & Peterson, C. A. (2009). *Therapeutic recreation program design: Principles & procedures* (5th ed.). San Francisco: Pearson/Benjamin Cummings.

Stumbo, N. J., & Wardlaw, B. (Eds.). (2011). *Facilitation of therapeutic recreation services: An evidence-based and best practice approach to techniques and process.* State College, PA: Venture Publishing, Inc.

Sullivan, E. J., & Decker, P. J. (2009). *Effective leadership and management in nursing* (7th ed.). Upper Saddle River, NJ: Pearson/Prentice-Hall.

Tindill, B. S., & Stewart, D. W. (1993). Integration of total quality and quality assurance. In A. F. Al-Assaf and J. A. Schmele (Eds.), *The textbook of total quality in health-care* (pp. 209–220). Delray Beach, FL: Saint Lucie.

Tomey, A. M. (2009). *Guide to nursing management and leadership* (8th ed.). St. Louis, MO: Mosby Elsevier.

Toppel, A. H., Beach, B. A., & Hutchinson-Troyer, L. (1991). Standards: A tool for accountability the CARF process. *Annual in Therapeutic Recreation, 2*, 96–98.

Triolo, P. K., Hansen, P., Kazzaz, Y., Chung, H., & Dobbs, S. (2002). Improving patient satisfaction through multidisciplinary performance improvement teams. *Journal of Nursing Administration, 32*(9), 448–454.

Whitehead, D. K., Weiss, S. A., & Tappen, R. M. (2010). *Essentials of nursing leadership and management* (5th ed.). Philadelphia: F. A. Davis.

Widmer, M. A., Zabriskie, R. B., & Wells, M. S. (2003). Program evaluation: Collecting data to measure outcomes. In N. J. Stumbo (Ed.), *Client outcomes in therapeutic recreation services* (pp. 201–219). State College, PA: Venture Publishing, Inc.

Wildavsky, A., & Hammond, A. (1965). Comprehensive versus incremental budgeting in the Department of Agriculture. *Administrative Science Quarterly, 10*(3), 321–346.

World Health Organization. (2006). *Quality of care: A process for making strategic choices in health systems.* Geneva, Switzerland: Author.

World Health Organization. (2013). WHO Quality of Life-BREF (WHOQOL-BREF). Retrieved from: http://www.who.int/substance_abuse/research_tools/whoqolbref/en/

Yong, J., & Wilkinson, A. (2001). Rethinking total quality management. *Total Quality Management, 12*(2), 247–258.

Zimmermann, J. A., Cooper, N., & Allen, L. R. (2001). Performance measurement: It's a benefit. *Parks & Recreation, 36*(6), 70–78.

Chapter 16
Managing Your Future: Professional Qualities and Career Planning

Keywords

- Accountability
- Autonomy
- Beneficence
- Career planning
- Code of ethics
- Competence
- Confidentiality
- Ethical principles
- Ethics
- Fidelity
- Justice
- Nonmaleficence
- Professional qualities and behaviors
- Respect
- Rights
- SWOT analysis
- Values
- Veracity

Learning Outcomes

After reading this chapter, students will be able to:

1. Identify characteristics of our profession influencing a first-line manager.
2. Define the ethical principles that guide professional practice.
3. Clarify the relationship between values and rights and professional responsibilities.
4. Describe the functions a professional ethics code assumes in the manager's day-to-day responsibilities.
5. Outline strategies found in a career plan and SWOT analysis that help build a successful career.
6. Summarize trends, issues, and challenges impacting your future and our profession.
7. Identify text topics important to the competence of a first-line manager.

Overview

Every day, change occurs in health and human services and the pace seems to get faster and faster. We do not know what the future holds for us. Yet as a change agent, you have the opportunity to shape our profession as you manage your career. While we know the trends and issues introduced in Chapter 1 are changing where and how professionals deliver services and practice APIE and how clients access and pay for their services, the certainty of recreation therapy/therapeutic recreation as a critical member of the care team is unknown. As future first-line managers and professionals, you should recognize that your daily decisions will guide your career and influence the receptivity of our profession as an essential piece of global health care.

The intent of this chapter is to summarize professional expectations of managers and professionals noted throughout the text; present a model to use in ethical and moral decision-making; share a model for your career management and advancement; and summarize through a SWOT analysis the trends, issues, and challenges impacting your future and our professional future while reaffirming text topics important to the success of the first-line manager.

A Professional Career

What are the distinguishing characteristics of professional first-line managers? How do these qualities influence roles and responsibilities of the first-line manager?

Throughout the text, reference is made to standards of practice (for example, CTRS standards), research- and evidence-based practices, professional organization standards, advocacy, and culturally competent professionals. In this closing section, a model is presented for ethical decision-making. These are qualities that distinguish a profession. A *professional* exhibits certain *qualities* and *behaviors* defined by a profession. Thus a profession is defined by standards, credentials, scientific practices, formal education and training, professional organizations, and acceptance as a necessary public service (Carter & Van Andel, 2011). The stature of our profession greatly affects the public's acknowledgment of RT/TR as a necessary public service, which, in turn, influences the first-line manager's acceptance as an essential team member. The decisions you make during your career, such as whether to seek specialty certification or use the ethics codes of our professional organizations (ATRA and CTRA) as you make practical decisions will influence the views of other professionals and the public toward you as an individual and professional and the acceptance of our profession as a contributor to health and client well-being.

Learning Outcome

Identify characteristics of our profession influencing a first-line manager.

Ethical Practices and Principles

In an era of limited resources, decision making by managers involves ethics (Marquis & Huston, 2009). A number of environmental factors ensure that ethics will become an even greater element in management decision making in the future: increasing technology, regulatory pressures, competitiveness among health-care providers, reduced fiscal resources, spiraling health-care costs, and the public's increasing distrust of the health-care system (Marquis & Huston, 2009).

A first-line manager often receives the first level of inquiry from staff, volunteers, and interns as to what is ethical and legal. As a leader the first-line manager is aware of his or her values and beliefs about the rights and duties of others. As an ethical person, therefore, the leader-manager is a role model for his or her subordinates in their decision making. Likewise, the manager is responsible for directing the ongoing professional growth and development of staff and interns. This task involves knowing how to recognize the ethical dimensions of therapeutic recreation and how to make ethical decisions in practice. Because ethical decisions are complex and the cost of poor decision making is high, the manager attempts to make decisions that increase "the chances that the best possible decision will be made at the least possible cost in terms of fiscal and human resources" (Marquis & Huston, 2009, p. 88).

Ethics deals with questions of human conduct, the values and rights that determine human conduct, and how these elements change over time. The ultimate goal of ethics is to be able to determine what is right or good to do in a given situation.

How do managers decide what is right and wrong? Dealing with moral situations is difficult and there may be no clear alternative. The manager uses a professional approach to eliminate trial and error. "Moral reasoning entails identification of relevant theory principles, and rules, as well as pertinent facts and circumstances" (Sylvester, Voelkl, & Ellis, 2001, p. 64). Moral reasoning tends to take place at the level of rules and principles, which become the guidelines for moral or appropriate behavior. Essentially, *ethical principles* become the standard or judge to measure our professional actions. One or more of these principles may be evident with each dilemma, and at times, they may be in conflict. To illustrate, a staff member makes a decision to come in late to work (autonomy) and tells the manager he/she had a flat tire when actually the alarm was not set (veracity). Several of the principles important to moral reasoning in our practice are listed in Table 16.1 with examples of the context in which CTRSs and first-line managers might consider each guideline (Austin, 2009; Marquis & Huston, 2009; Tomey, 2009; Whitehead, Weiss, & Tappen, 2010).These principles are foundational guidelines used by the professional organizations to design our ethics codes (ATRA, 2009; CTRA, 1995).

While the principles identified in Table 16.1 are foundational to ethical decision making, three factors influence each individual's ethical practices. First, ethics are individually defined. How the individual operates in a management role is influenced by his or her beliefs and values. Second, what constitutes ethical behavior can vary from one person to another. The manager is influenced by the experiences that form him or her as an individual and as a leader. Third, ethics are relative, not absolute. Thus, ethical behavior is in the eye of the beholder, but it is usually behavior that conforms to generally accepted social norms, whereas unethical behavior does not.

Table 16.1 Ethical Principles that Guide Practice Behaviors

- **Accountability:** CTRSs and managers are responsible for their actions; managers ensure professional standards of practice are followed by employees.
- **Autonomy:** The right of each individual to make his/her own choices; informed consent recognizes autonomy; managers applying progressive discipline are recognizing the employee's autonomy.
- **Beneficence:** Actions of the CTRS should be done in an effort to promote good; managers promote employees' positive attributes through training and performance reviews.
- **Competence:** Professionals use current practices for which they are trained and/or have experience; managers support professional development and supervise staff to ensure their performance is not impaired.
- **Confidentiality:** Professionals secure private or privileged information through silence; managers are responsible by law to report, for example, staff drug abuse; CTRSs are to report suspected child abuse.
- **Fidelity:** CTRSs are to keep promises to their clients and colleagues as loyal employees; managers honor their commitment to employees' requested days off.
- **Justice:** (Distributive justice) People are to be treated equally and are to receive equitable services; managers make equitable decisions about scarce resources like salaries or access to training opportunities.
- **Nonmaleficence:** CTRSs are obligated to help clients while not doing harm; managers provide direction for improved performance rather than minimize staff competence through inappropriate comments.
- **Respect:** Transcends and incorporates all other principles; managers acknowledge that clients and staff have the right to make and live by their decisions.
- **Veracity:** CTRSs are honest and tell the truth; clients and staff are better able to make informed decisions; managers encourage staff to document accurately and completely.

Learning Outcome

Define the ethical principles that guide professional practice.

Values and Rights

Dilemmas occur when there are good reasons to support a number of alternative decisions. An individual's values and beliefs play a major role in the manager's daily decision making (Marquis & Huston, 2009). The way the manager solves ethical dilemmas is a reflection of values and beliefs about the rights of human beings. Self-awareness is a leadership role in ethical decision making—and the manager is aware that a degree of uncertainty exists with each practice decision.

Values

Values are a set of beliefs and attitudes about the truth, worth, or importance of any thought, objective, or behavior. Values are qualities that are intrinsically desirable to everyone. Every decision made or behavior is based consciously or unconsciously on such values and beliefs. In other words, what is really important, and what are the priorities in life, what is one willing to sacrifice or suffer in order to achieve, obtain, protect, or maintain are basic value issues for everyone. Values become a part of a person's worldview that guide behavior and assist in making choices (Whitehead, Weiss, & Tappen, 2010). Our value systems, beliefs that we prize, are learned and change with experience and maturity (Whitehead, Weiss, & Tappen, 2010). One person may value social aspects like objects and status while another person values concepts like caring and kindness to one another. Because these systems influence our decisions, to illustrate, the first person might make a decision based on cost of the object while the second's decision would be based on the quality the product or experience would bring to the client's well-being. Thus, values may cloud our objectivity by influencing what is right and wrong, implying certain behaviors are preferred over others (Tomey, 2009).

Values are critical to us as they provide a foundation for the way we live, our personality, roles, perceptions, and attitudes (Austin, 2009; Tomey, 2009). Without values, there are no standards and hence no moral code, no right nor wrong, and ultimately chaos results. When a person has at least a tentative idea of what is considered to be truth and right or wrong, he or she is able to act in a manner consistent with those values. Jourard (1964, p. 27) wrote: "That until an individual knows his values he cannot know himself. Until one knows what he values or what lines in life he is going to cross, an individual doesn't know himself very well."

As an individual grows, develops, and matures, values are defined and clarified, tested and revised, and gradually become all-pervasive to the individual's existence. To illustrate, a young child may value objects like a specific toy; youth may value an event or peer rather than parental views; and, young adults may value beauty or certain athletes or artists (Whitehead, Weiss, & Tappen, 2010). Thus an adult through experience, learning, and thought becomes an agent of value or, more commonly, a moral agent. The terms "value" and "moral" frequently are used interchangeably because they both deal with human behavior and values (Uustal, 1977).

When individuals have developed values, generally their decisions are made in terms of those values. Thus, it is easy to understand the magnitude and extent of the effect that values have on lives. Values have significance for people as individuals and collectively as societies. Values are useful because they provide order and predictability. Values can be considered as a means to a good end. Inherently, values can make an individual feel good inside. Finally, values contribute to social order and societal maturation.

As you progress through your major, professional values are identified as being important to practice like caring, playfulness, ethical behavior, creativity, and honesty (Whitehead, Weiss & Tappen, 2010; Witman & Ligon, 2011). Values accepted by our profession, professional values, are evident in practice models that explain the intent of the therapeutic recreation process and in the literature, research, and evidence-based practices that define intervention outcomes. Examples of these values include health, self-determination, well-being, enjoyment, choice, independent leisure functioning, and client-centeredness. The priority given to these professional values by each CTRS and first-line manager help guide their professional behavior and explain why, for example, each therapist and manager may select and financially support different interventions to include in a client's plan to accomplish a particular goal.

Rights

Individuals have the human right to existence and therefore have the right to choose or to make decisions concerning themselves as long as they are willing to accept the consequences. Nevertheless, because individuals exist within societies, the actions associated with these choices cannot infringe on another person's *rights*. Within the concept of human rights is the associated concept of duties and responsibilities. Rights equate with responsibilities. If a client has a right to privacy, other persons and society have a duty or obligation to secure privileged information. Thus, health professionals, because of the roles they assume within society, assume additional responsibilities toward others that other individuals do not assume.

Scholars suggest the existence of six conditions associated with the fundamental rights of individuals. First, there is an accompanying condition of the freedom to exercise the right or not to exercise the right if the individual so chooses. Second, rights are associated with duties for others to facilitate, or at least not to interfere with, the exercise of those rights. Third, rights are usually defined or defended in basic terms that equate with the principles of fairness, equality, or justice. Fourth, a basic fundamental or significant right is considered enforceable by society. Fifth is the right to express oneself without fear of punishment. The final condition is also the result of societal maturation because this condition concerns compensation due an individual whose rights have been violated (Cavanaugh, Moberg, & Velasquez, 1981).

In decision making, the rights of the individuals are respected. The decision maker need only avoid violating the rights of the individual affected by the decision. As an example, firing an employee for wrongdoing without first a verbal warning followed by a written reprimand and suspension would violate that person's right to due process. Of course, there are many situations where the issue is clouded. For instance, to what degree does a therapeutic recreation manager have the right to interfere with a staff member's right to privacy if that member's use of drugs or alcohol appears to be affecting his or her job performance?

We must remember that human beings have rights because they are unique creatures that possess the ability to know, think, and believe. What a person knows about himself or herself, what he or she defines as unique, and what is valued become the source of human right. As a result of the increased attention given to moral and ethical issues, society through professional organizations defines rights and responsibilities. To illustrate, in 1973, the American Hospital Association created a statement called the Patient's Bill of Rights. This statement was replaced in 2003 by the Patient Care Partnership (Whitehead, Weiss, & Tappen, 2010).

Professional organizations develop position statements to identify values and rights of organizational stakeholders. To illustrate, the ATRA statement on diversity reads, in part, "We acknowledge that diversity includes any aspect that makes him or her unique. Our association values and actively promotes diverse and inclusive participation by its leaders, members, and affiliates" (ATRA, 2006). The most basic and universal ethical principle is respect for people (Marquis & Huston, 2009). Thus, the ATRA statement is foundational to rights and responsibilities of CTRSs. One further illustration presents the relationship between ethical principles and rights and responsibilities. A patient rights-and-responsibilities document shared upon admission to one health system includes the following statements: "Patient Right: You have the right to receive care from competent staff in a safe setting, free from environmental hazards; Patient Responsibility: All patients are responsible for following hospital rules and regulations affecting patient care and conduct" (Samaritan Regional Health System, n.d.).

Learning Outcome

Clarify the relationship between values and rights and professional responsibilities.

The Manager and Professional Ethics

How the manager operates in a management role is influenced by the beliefs, values, and experiences (e.g., family, peers, and situations) that inform him or her as an individual and leader. Mark Pastin (1986) describes the individual's values as a set of "ground rules" for making what the individual considers to be a "right" decision. In addition to personal values, the manager is guided by values of the profession. Professional values are found in ethical codes, standards of practice, credentialing expectations, and in agency structures like ethics committees and review boards.

A *code of ethics* is a set of principles, defined by a profession, to guide the behavior expected of its members (Marquis & Huston, 2009; Shank & Coyle, 2002; Whitehead, Weiss, & Tappen, 2010). ATRA published a code of ethics (2009), standards of practice (2013), a position statement on diversity [see illustration in preceding section (2006)], and curriculum guidelines that seek to assist managers and practitioners in making ethical decisions in practice (West, Kinney, & Witman, 2008). Similarly, CTRA presented an ethics code (1995) and standards of practice (2006) to guide professional behaviors of Canadian professionals. Each code of ethics presents a list of principles with a brief description of professional behavior appropriate to each principle. Within each standards of practice document, standards on ethical conduct require professionals to adhere to the code of ethics in providing humane and professional services (ATRA, 2013) and ensure that client safety and rights are promoted to allow service quality (CTRA, 2006). Curriculum guidelines include knowledge of ethical codes and current ethical issues, skill in applying ethical standards to practice, and the ability to manage recreation therapy practice within ethical requirements of health care and human services (West, Kinney, & Witman, 2008). Credentialing expectations are outlined in the 2007 NCTRC job tasks and knowledge areas (NCTRC, 2013). Adherence to professional standards of practice and code of ethics is listed under Job Tasks while standards of practice, ethics code, professional standards, and accepted ethical practices are found under Knowledge Areas.

The manager is also guided by formal agency structures like ethics committees and review boards. Review boards protect the rights of research subjects, while ethics committees deal with questions concerning client policies. Organizations may also have their own list of values and ethics codes. Together, organization structures and codes are intended to be specific enough to guide managers and non-managerial employees "in what they are supposed to do yet . . . allow for freedom of judgment" (Robbins, Decenzo, & Coulter, 2011, p. 41). The challenge experienced by managers is that a number of codes like the provincial code of ethics and the organization's value statements may appear to supersede the professional code; consequently, professionals are not sure which code actually governs their decision making (Lee, Cripps, Malloy, & Cox, 2011). Although there is no simple answer, this practice reality concerns our profession because students and professionals have limited awareness of and training on the use of professional codes in decision making.

Ethics codes are dynamic—"Changes occur as society and technology evolve" (Whitehead, Weiss, & Tappen, 2010, p. 47). Technology has increased our knowledge and skills, yet our ability to make decisions and resolve moral dilemmas about us and our clients is guided by the foundational principles in these codes, which survived the test of time (see Table 16.2, p. 260).

The manager, because of his or her role in the organization, is expected to further the organization's ethics and to assist staff and other practitioners in doing

Table 16.2 ATRA and CTRA Ethical Principles

ATRA Ethics Code	CTRA Ethics Code
Beneficence	Professional virtues
Nonmaleficence	Obligation to the individual and society
Autonomy	Professional practices
Justice	Responsibilities to colleagues and the profession
Fidelity	
Veracity	
Informed Consent	
Confidentiality and privacy	
Competence	
Compliance with laws and regulations	

the same. The manager has a responsibility to create a climate in which ethical behavior is the norm (Marquis & Huston, 2009). Managers have special obligations to exercise their power—derived from their position, responsibility, and relationships—responsibly and ethically (Levy, 1982). What the manager does is far more critical than what is said in creating ethical behaviors among employees (Robbins, Decenzo, & Coulter, 2011). The effectiveness of codes, standards, and guidelines depends heavily on managerial support and their immersion in the organizational culture.

Ethical Decision-Making and Moral-Reasoning Model

To make appropriate decisions, "the manager must use a professional approach that eliminates trial and error and focuses on proven decision-making models" (Marquis & Huston, 2009, p. 70). The quality of ethical problem solving is evaluated in terms of the process used to make a decision. With a structured approach similar to APIE (assessment, planning, implementation, evaluation), data gathering is adequate and multiple alternatives are analyzed: "The best possible decisions stem from structured problem solving, adequate data collection, and examination of multiple alternatives—even if outcomes are poor" (Marquis & Huston, 2009, p. 78). The manager is often the decision maker in ethical issues and accepts that some of the outcomes of his/her actions may be undesirable or unavoidable. The manager realizes evaluation of the problem-solving process used to resolve a dilemma determines the quality of his/her actions (Marquis & Huston, 2009).

A dilemma exists when the problem forces a choice between two or more ethical principles (Whitehead, Weiss & Tappen, 2010), as illustrated above when the autonomy and veracity of the manager and employee conflicted; deciding in favor of one principle violates the other and either choice has "goodness" and "badness" (Whitehead, Weiss, & Tappen, 2010). In other words, two or more values that would usually lead to consistent behavior are conflicted and this causes the CTRS and first-line manager to question or examine practices like informed consent and self-determination. The reasoning process concludes when a decision of a morally acceptable action to be taken in a given situation is reached. Knowledge of ethical perspectives and principles helps a manager to identify the ethical dimensions of the situation while providing the moral justification for the final selection of action to take.

The authors have developed a ten-step model for ethical decision making based on moral reasoning, (refer to Table 16.3). Like the APIE process, the nature of this model allows for feedback at each step and for the process to be repeated until adequate information and alternatives exist to make the decision. This approach also clarifies the values and beliefs of the people involved.

One of the major responsibilities of the therapeutic recreation manager is to encourage and to guide ethical decision-making efforts. Ethical dilemmas arise as a result of conflict in values. Difficult ethical dilemmas (e.g., consumer abuse, practitioner substance abuse, coworker incompetence) that go unnoticed and/or unresolved may lead to unethical (i.e., unprofessional) service as well as job dissatisfaction and apathy on the part of staff. All daily decisions have an ethical dimension that requires ethical decision making. Many of these are relatively minor; some are major. One of the greatest challenges of management is making right, good decisions.

Learning Outcome

Describe the functions a professional ethics code assumes in the manager's day-to-day responsibilities.

Table 16.3 Ethical Decision-Making/Moral-Reasoning Model

1. Identify the problem, including decisions needed and key individuals.
2. Gather additional information to clarify the situation.
3. Identify the ethical principles involved in the situation.
4. Define personal and professional moral positions of the problem.
5. Identify moral positions of key individuals involved in the situation.
6. Identify value conflicts.
7. Determine who should make the decision.
8. Identify the alternative actions with anticipated outcomes.
9. Decide on a course of action and carry it out.
10. Evaluate and review the results of the decision or action, including monitoring the situation over time.

Managing and Advancing Your Career

"To be a fully engaged professional requires commitment to career development" (Marquis & Huston, 2009, p. 239). In other words, being aware of and displaying the professional behaviors just described is only one key element in managing and advancing your career. A second significant responsibility is intentional planning to advance your career. This involves managers and their staff in helping you to create choices to better satisfy your professional goals. "The working world has shifted from long-term environments to strategic, competitive, global environments . . . quick to respond to changing conditions" (Gower & Mulvaney, 2012, p. 180). In this new environment, managers and employees realize success results when each professional has relevant knowledge, skills, and abilities (KSAs) and the flexibility to adapt to change. Career planning is a process similar to APIE (refer to Chapter 13) that results in a master plan outlining short- and long-term goals with various strategies to manage and advance your career.

Another tool, mentioned in the chapter on marketing and advocacy (Chapter 7), a SWOT analysis, guides you through the assessment of your own strengths and weaknesses and helps you evaluate the trends, issues, and challenges (opportunities and threats) affecting your career. These two models are shared so you can explore your future and our professional future by thinking about your performance and those influences shaping the nature of our profession. Also, a first-line manager may use these tools with employees to support their career development and to create a more satisfying work environment responsive to political, social, economic, and scientific advances influencing unit outcomes and professional expectations.

Career Planning

Where am I . . . and what is my preferred future?

Career planning provides you with choices rather than leaving your future to chance. Like APIE, it is ongoing and involves assessing your assets and preferences (A); setting goals, exploring opportunities, and preparing for these potential experiences (P); using appropriate developmental activities to attain your potential options (I); and evaluating and revising your future plans (E). The professionals who engage in career planning invest themselves in their agency and professions beyond their job descriptions, and as a result, they have a clearer picture of their goals and future professional options (Gower & Mulvaney, 2012). This model is immediately applicable to where you are in your professional development (i.e., student, intern, first position), and, as your career advances, this process fosters staff development and advances the profession (Robertson, 2008). See Table 16.4 (p. 262) for the career planning model.

Assessment

Assessment considers your performance, experiences, KSAs, and personal factors like personality patterns. Also assessed is your agency, including but not limited to opportunities, culture, expectations, and standards. Third, the environment surrounding you and your school or worksite is considered (e.g., what opportunities exist? what global trends, issues, and challenges impact the future?). Lastly, your relationship to our profession is assessed—do you satisfy or plan to meet professional expectations like credentials, ethical behavior, and practice using theory and evidence?

Planning

Goal setting considers each of the four assessed areas. Personal goals relate to competency and performance measures; types of experiences that address practice diversity and job tasks beyond customary duties like attending to ADLs or coordinating special events; and knowledge and personal capabilities like cultural competence, adaptability to change, team qualities, judgment, willingness to learn, and respect for expertise of experienced professionals (Whitehead, Weiss, & Tappen, 2010). Goals resulting from assessment of your current position

Table 16.4 Career Planning Model

Assessment: Where am I?

1. Personal assessment
    a. What are my experiences, KSAs, and personal characteristics?
2. Agency assessment
    a. What are the agency opportunities, culture, expectations, and standards?
3. Environmental (worldview) assessment
    a. What global opportunities, trends, issues, and challenges are influencing my future?
4. Professional assessment
    a. What is my status related to professional expectations like credentials and ethical practices?

Planning: What are my goals?

1. Do my personal goals consider . . .
    a. The diverse responsibilities of therapeutic recreation
    b. Cultural competence
    c. Ability to adapt to change
    d. Collaboration and team qualities
    e. Clinical and moral decision making and judgment
    f. Ability to learn and develop
2. Do my current work goals consider . . .
    a. Advancement or transfer options within the agency
    b. Ability to become organizationally savvy
    c. Mastery of changing responsibilities resulting from technology impacts
    d. Relationships with my supervisor and mentor
3. Do my goals represent a worldview . . .
    a. Consideration of opportunities in other settings
    b. Consideration of trends (health promotion and chronic disease management, use of the ICF), issues (care-access among those with cultural and demographic disparities), and challenges (fiscal limitations)
4. Do my goals include professional competencies . . .
    a. Use of standards of practice and ethics codes to guide practice decisions
    b. Advocacy for public acceptance of our profession
    c. Acquisition of professional credentials and active engagement in professional association
    d. Advancement of professional recognition through theory- and evidence-based practices

Implementation: What strategies best accomplish my goals?

1. Personal
    a. Do I have an up-to-date portfolio? Am I assessing continuously my professional competence?
2. Agency
    a. Are available agency in-services attended? Am I using a mentor or career coach?
3. Worldview
    a. Which provincial or international conferences best address trends, issues, and challenges?
4. Professional
    a. Do I participate as a professional team member advocating for holistic client-centered health?

Evaluation: What is the status of my preferred future?

- Do outcomes of formal and informal reviews suggest mutual growth and support of my goals and the unit's goals or is now the time to explore new relationships to advance my goals and the unit's success?

include identifying advancement options within the agency; becoming organizationally savvy (i.e., knowing what is important to your supervisor); mastering changing position expectations attributed to technology; and establishing mentor relationships to guide you in satisfying agency standards. Setting goals after reviewing global dynamics helps you discover future opportunities in other settings, prepares you to develop competencies relevant to future options like medical homes with aging and at-risk clients, and makes you aware of challenges like continuing reductions in resources. Lastly, setting professional goals will benefit you, for example, by creating options to advance your career with specialty certification through NCTRC or participating in efficacy research that contributes to evidence-based practices that advance our profession.

Implementation

A variety of strategies are available to manage and advance your career plan so you achieve your career goals. These development activities may include building a portfolio; competency assessment using professional association resources (West, Kinney, & Witman, 2008) or recertification and specialty certification through a credentialing body such as NCTRC (http://www.nctrc.org) or a local licensure board; agency in-services and training or career coaching; attendance at professional workshops at the provincial or international level (CTRA, ATRA); engaging in advocacy like public forums on alternative and complementary interventions; contributing to a professional newsletter or journal; and acting as a mentor or coach with interns or entry-level professionals. Documentation, reflection, and feedback are vital to your development and our professional growth. Thus with each strategy, evidence and a record of outcomes are maintained.

Evaluation

Periodic formal and informal evaluations gauge our progress and help update our personal and professional goals. Formal experiences occur with agency performance reviews or professional credential assessments. Informal appraisals take place as you revisit career goals and ensure progress is properly documented and statements are updated to reflect changing agency, global, and professional needs. Each opportunity is a relationship, and with each, we ask, "how does this job, mentor, supervisor, credential, or conference help me achieve my goals?" Likewise, a manager assesses if the employee's and organization's goals are mutual and supportive. The time to think about the next goal or job is the moment you commit to the first—asking "how much can I learn and how well can I adapt or respond to change?" Likewise, the manager considers the organization's needs and when an employee has "outlived" a position to ensure timely employee transitions while maintaining a workforce that is comfortable and suited to achieving unit outcomes.

Advancing Your Professional Future

On any given workday, professionals juggle diverse and varied responsibilities yet are primarily responsible for the delivery of client-centered programs (LeBlanc & Singleton, 2008; Witman & Rakos, 2008). While your preparation and professional assessments (like certification and licensure examinations) will remain focused on the delivery, documentation, and management of client services through APIE, professionals are experiencing more increasingly complicated jobs. Responsibilities consist not only of your performance related to the TR process but also helper qualities and "other related duties" like balancing self-care with service obstacles that arise (e.g., the necessity of providing regular in-services to articulate the benefits of therapeutic recreation to new colleagues or becoming involved in managerial tasks like customer services and events). Each workday we experience unplanned events. While our futures will continue to see diversity we can plan for contingencies and obstacles through our career plan and by conducting a SWOT analysis. These tools require us to be creative and visionary to design a flexible path to a preferred future.

A *SWOT analysis* identifies our personal and professional strengths and weaknesses and the opportunities and threats shaping our future. The opportunities and threats summarize some of the trends, issues, and challenges shaping our professional world and disclose several of the professional expectations and competencies of first-line managers as presented in this text. You have the ability to influence the changes affecting your career and our profession if you take advantage of the opportunities and manage the threats (Robertson, 2008). These tools bring clarity to your vision and leadership to our profession. The SWOT analysis in Table 16.5 (p. 264) is a template for your self-assessment. Content for the example is drawn from topics presented in the text and documented in our professional literature (Finegan, 2006; Hoss, Powell, & Sable, 2006; Whitehead, Weiss, & Tappen, 2010).

Learning Outcome

Summarize trends, issues, and challenges impacting your future and our profession. Identify text topics important to the competence of a first-line manager.

Summary

1. A profession is defined by several qualities: standards, credentials, scientific practices, formal education and training, professional organizations, ethical conduct, and acceptance as a necessary public service.
2. Ethics deals with questions of human conduct, the values and rights that determine human conduct, and how these elements change over

time. The ultimate goal of ethics is to be able to determine what is right or good to do in a given situation.

3. Ethical principles become the standard or judge to measure our professional actions. These principles include autonomy, beneficence, nonmaleficence, competence, justice, veracity, fidelity, accountability, confidentiality, and respect.
4. Values are a set of beliefs and attitudes about the truth, worth, or importance of any thought, objective, or behavior. Every decision made or behavior is based consciously or unconsciously on our values and beliefs, which are learned as we grow and mature.

Learning Outcome
Outline strategies found in a career plan and SWOT analysis that help build a successful career.

Table 16.5 SWOT Analysis to Manage and Advance Your Career

Personal and Professional Strengths	Chapter Topics
Ability to manage time	2
Ability to write goals and objectives	3
Communication skills fundamental to helping relationships	11
Computer competence and comfort with alternative web-based training	6
Documentation of the APIE process	13
Motivation to succeed in our profession	12
Protocol design to inform consistency in practice	13
Personal and Professional Weaknesses	
Lack of awareness of health care as a business	8
Lack of experience in ethical and moral decision-making and problem-solving	5, 16
Lack of interdisciplinary practice or holistic person-centered care	4
Limited experience with clinical supervision and staff training	9
Limited exposure to organizational behavior and politics	4
Limited outcomes and evidence-based care resources	6, 15
Limited supervisory experiences with interns and volunteers	10
Minimal exposure to professional and regulatory standards and review processes	8, 13, 15
Global and Professional Opportunities	
Continue involvement with standard organizations (e.g., CARF International)	15
Continue public policy representation at state/provincial/national levels	7
Expanding care continuum	7
Expanding financial options like value-driven payment models	8
Expanding markets and advocacy roles	7, 11
Expanding technology applications	6
Strengthen applications of the ICF	7
Global and Professional Threats	
Address global health-care concerns like poverty, terrorism, pandemics	1
Affordable accessible health care	8
Demand for accountable quality care	15
Equal support for prevention, health promotion, mental health care	8
Gain recognition as critical public service and care-team participant	7, 8
Increased stakeholder concerns for risk, safety, security	14, 15
Need for efficacy research	6, 15

5. Individuals have the human right to existence and therefore have the right to choose or to make decisions concerning themselves as long as they are willing to accept the consequences. And, because individuals exist within societies, the actions associated with these choices cannot infringe on another person's rights.
6. Professional organizations develop position statements to identify values and rights of organizational stakeholders. Also, professions define a code of ethics, which is a set of principles that guides the behavior expected of its members.
7. A dilemma exists when a problem forces a choice between two or more ethical principles; in other words two or more values that would usually lead to consistent behavior are conflicted and this causes the CTRS and first-line manager to question deciding in favor of one or the other principle because either choice has "goodness" and "badness" consequences.
8. The manager, because of his or her role in the organization, is expected to further the organization's ethics and to assist staff and other practitioners in doing the same. The manager has a responsibility to create a climate in which ethical behavior is the norm.
9. Career planning is a process similar to APIE that results in a master plan outlining short- and long-term goals with various strategies to manage and advance your career.
10. A SWOT analysis identifies our personal and professional strengths and weaknesses and the opportunities and threats shaping our future.
11. Together these tools identify the changes you encounter during your career and the text topics critical to your development as a professional and first-line manager.
12. When you choose to use these tools, you can plan for contingencies and obstacles and design a flexible path to a preferred future. Likewise, you will have the ability to influence the changes affecting your career and our profession, bringing clarity to your vision and leadership to our profession.

Critical Thinking Activities

1. Using the ethical decision-making and moral-reasoning model presented in the chapter, consider the ethical dilemma found in each scenario and write a response to each step in the model:

   Scenario 1: I am a CTRS on an inpatient physical rehabilitation unit. A male patient, 15 CA, as a result of a car accident, has a T-6 spinal cord injury, complete paralysis. The team's goal is wheelchair ambulation and return to his home community. During a care meeting attended by family, his parents state their hope is for their son to ambulate without any assistive devices. Should I share with the family that due to the level of the injury, the patient will not likely be able to achieve their desired goal?

   Scenario 2: I am a CTRS coordinating the outpatient rehabilitation program with clients having neurological injuries including strokes and head injuries. Each week at a golf program, clients develop with a therapist a weekly exercise goal. The goal is recorded on a log sent home with the client to document daily exercise. At the next golf program the weekly log information is recorded by the therapist in the client's file to document compliance with the selected exercise goal. One client forgets his log each week and when asked by the therapist states "it's probably still in the car or at home" but he assures the therapist he exercised daily to accomplish his goal. Should this response be permitted by the therapist as evidence of compliance with the weekly goal?

2. What are your career plan goals? What are your strengths, weaknesses, opportunities, and threats influencing your future directions? Which strategies will best advance your career and contribute to the growth of our profession?

3. Review websites like http://www.cdc.gov/nchs/data/misc/healthcare.pdf or http://www.hc-sc.gc.ca to explore trends in healthcare. From your review, what appear to be opportunities and threats to our profession?

References

American Therapeutic Recreation Association (ATRA). (2013). *Standards for the practice of therapeutic recreation: A self-assessment guide* (Rev. ed.). Hattiesburg, MS: Author.

American Therapeutic Recreation Association (ATRA). (2006). *Statement on diversity*. Retrieved from http://www.atra-online.com/

American Therapeutic Recreation Association (ATRA). (2009). *ATRA code of ethics, revised 2009*. Retrieved from http://www.atra-online.com/

Austin, D. R. (2009). *Therapeutic recreation processes and techniques* (6th ed.). Champaign, IL: Sagamore.

Canadian Therapeutic Recreation Association (CTRA). (1995). *CTRA code of ethics.* Retrieved from http://canadian-tr.org/Code-of-Ethics

Canadian Therapeutic Recreation Association (CTRA). (2006). *Standards of practice for recreation therapists & therapeutic recreation assistants.* Calgary, Alberta, Canada: Author.

Carter, M. J., & Van Andel, G. E. (2011). *Therapeutic recreation a practical approach* (4th ed.). Long Grove, IL: Waveland Press.

Cavanagh, G. F., Moberg, D. J., & Velasquez, M. (1981, July). The ethics of organizational politics. *Academy of Management Review, 6*(3), 363–374.

Finegan, J. (2006). A response to health care trends: Implications for therapeutic recreation. In M. J. Carter & J. E. Folkerth (Eds.), *Therapeutic recreation education: Challenges and changes* (pp. 123–128). Ashburn, VA: NTRS/NRPA.

Gower, R. K., & Mulvaney, M. A. (2012). *Making the most of your internship: A strategic approach.* Champaign, IL; Sagamore.

Hoss, M. A. K., Powell, L., & Sable, J. (2006). Healthcare trends: Implications for therapeutic recreation. In M. J. Carter & J. E. Folkerth (Eds.), *Therapeutic recreation education: Challenges and changes* (pp. 107–122). Ashburn, VA: NTRS/NRPA.

Jourard, S. (1964). *The transparent self: Self-disclosure and well-being*. New York: Van Nostrand Reinhold.

LeBlanc, A., & Singleton, J. F. (2008). Juggling the diverse responsibilities of therapeutic recreation. *Annual in Therapeutic Recreation, 16*, 182–192.

Lee, Y., Cripps, D., Malloy, D. C., & Cox, S. (2011). Code of ethics: Is it time to reconsider? *Annual in Therapeutic Recreation, 19*, 140–149.

Levy, C. S. (1982). *Guide to ethical decisions and actions for social service administration: A handbook for managerial personnel.* New York: Haworth.

Marquis, B. L., & Huston, C. J. (2009). *Leadership roles and management functions in nursing theory and application* (6th ed.). Philadelphia: Wolters Kluwer/Lippincott Williams & Wilkins.

National Council for Therapeutic Recreation Certification (NCTRC). (2013). *Part V: NCTRC national job analysis.* New City, NY. Retrieved from http://www.nctrc.org/documents/5JobAnalysis.pdf

Pastin, M. (1986). *The hard problem of management: Gaining the ethics edge.* San Francisco: Jossey-Bass.

Robbins, S. P., Decenzo, D. A., & Coulter, M. (2011). *Fundamentals of management essential concepts and applications* (7th ed.). Upper Saddle River, NJ: Prentice-Hall.

Robertson, T. (2008). Envisioning the future: Therapeutic recreation as a profession. In T. Robertson & T. Long (Eds.), *Foundations of therapeutic recreation* (pp. 267–277). Champaign, IL: Human Kinetics.

Samaritan Regional Health System. (n.d.). *Patient rights and responsibilities* [Brochure]. Ashland, OH: Author.

Shank, J., & Coyle, C. (2002). *Therapeutic recreation in health promotion and rehabilitation.* State College, PA: Venture Publishing, Inc.

Sylvester, C., Voelkl, J. E., & Ellis, G. D. (2001). *Therapeutic recreation programming: Theory and practice.* State College, PA: Venture Publishing, Inc.

Tomey, A. M. (2009). *Guide to nursing management and leadership* (8th ed.). St Louis, MO: Mosby Elsevier.

Uustal, D. B. (1977). Searching for values. *Image, 9*(1), 15–17.

West, R. E., Kinney, T, & Witman, J. (2008). *Guidelines for competency assessment and curriculum planning for recreational therapy practice (rev.).* Hattiesburg, MS: ATRA.

Whitehead, D. K., Weiss, S. A., & Tappen, R. M. (2010). *Essentials of nursing leadership and management* (5th ed.). Philadelphia: F. A. Davis Company.

Witman, J., & Ligon, M. (2011, summer). Planning and implementation. *American Therapeutic Recreation Association newsletter, 27*(2), 1–4.

Witman, J. P., & Rakos, K. S. (2008). Determining the "other related duties" of therapeutic recreation and activity professionals: A pilot study. *American Journal of Recreation Therapy, 7*(2), 29–33.

Index

D

E

F

N

O

P

Q

R

S

T

Other Books by Venture Publishing, Inc.

21st Century Leisure: Current Issues, Second Edition
by Valeria J. Freysinger and John R. Kelly
Active Living in Older Adulthood: Principles and Practices of Activity Programs
by Barbara A. Hawkins
Adventure Programming
edited by John C. Miles and Simon Priest
Adventure Programming and Travel for the 21st Century
by Rosemary Black and Kelly Bricker
Boredom Busters: Themed Special Events to Dazzle and Delight Your Group
by Annette C. Moore
Brain Fitness
by Suzanne Fitzsimmons
Client Assessment in Therapeutic Recreation Services
by Norma J. Stumbo
Client Outcomes in Therapeutic Recreation Services
by Norma J. Stumbo
Conceptual Foundations for Therapeutic Recreation
edited by David R. Austin, John Dattilo, and Bryan P. McCormick
Dementia Care Programming: An Identity-Focused Approach
by Rosemary Dunne
Dimensions of Choice: Qualitative Approaches to Parks, Recreation, Tourism, Sport, and Leisure Research, Second Edition
by Karla A. Henderson
Diversity and the Recreation Profession: Organizational Perspectives (Revised Edition)
edited by Maria T. Allison and Ingrid E. Schneider
Effective Management in Therapeutic Recreation Service, Second Edition
by Marcia Jean Carter and Gerald S. O'Morrow
Evaluating Leisure Services: Making Enlightened Decisions, Third Edition
by Karla A. Henderson and M. Deborah Bialeschki
Facilitation of Therapeutic Recreation Services: An Evidence-Based and Best Practice Approach to Techniques and Processes
edited by Norma J. Stumbo and Brad Wardlaw
Facilitation Techniques in Therapeutic Recreation, Second Edition
by John Dattilo and Alexis McKenney
File o' Fun: A Recreation Planner for Games & Activities, Third Edition
by Jane Harris Ericson and Diane Ruth Albright
The Game Finder: A Leader's Guide to Great Activities
by Annette C. Moore
Health Promotion for Mind, Body, and Spirit
by Suzanne Fitzsimmons and Linda L. Buettner
Human Resource Management in Recreation, Sport, and Leisure Services
by Margaret Arnold, Regina Glover, and Cheryl Beeler
Inclusion: Including People With Disabilities in Parks and Recreation Opportunities
by Lynn Anderson and Carla Brown Kress
Inclusive Leisure Services, Third Edition
by John Dattilo
Internships in Recreation and Leisure Services: A Practical Guide for Students, Fifth Edition
by Edward E. Seagle, Jr., Tammy B. Smith, and Ralph W. Smith
Internships in Sport Management
by Robin Ammon, Jr., Matthew Walker, Edward E. Seagle, and Ralph W. Smith
Interpretation of Cultural and Natural Resources, Second Edition
by Douglas M. Knudson, Ted T. Cable, and Larry Beck
Intervention Activities for At-Risk Youth
by Norma J. Stumbo
Introduction to Outdoor Recreation: Providing and Managing Resource Based Opportunities
by Roger L. Moore and B. L. Driver

Introduction to Recreation Services: Sustainability for a Changing World
By Karla A. Henderson
Introduction to Therapeutic Recreation: U.S. and Canadian Perspectives
by Kenneth Mobily and Lisa Ostiguy
An Introduction to Tourism
by Robert W. Wyllie
Introduction to Writing Goals and Objectives: A Manual for Recreation Therapy Students and Entry-Level Professionals
by Suzanne Melcher
The Leader's Handbook: Learning Leadership Skills by Facilitating Fun, Games, Play, and Positive Interaction, Second Edition
by Bill Michaelis and John M. O'Connell
Leadership and Administration of Outdoor Pursuits, Third Edition
by James Blanchard, Michael Strong, and Phyllis Ford
Leadership in Leisure Services: Making a Difference, Third Edition
by Debra J. Jordan
Leisure and Leisure Services in the 21st Century: Toward Mid Century
by Geoffrey Godbey
Leisure Education I: A Manual of Activities and Resources, Second Edition
by Norma J. Stumbo
Leisure Education II: More Activities and Resources, Second Edition
by Norma J. Stumbo
Leisure Education III: More Goal-Oriented Activities
by Norma J. Stumbo
Leisure Education IV: Activities for Individuals with Substance Addictions
by Norma J. Stumbo
Leisure Education Program Planning: A Systematic Approach, Third Edition
by John Dattilo
Leisure for Canadians, Second Edition
by Ron McCarville and Kelly MacKay
Leisure, Health, and Wellness: Making the Connections
by Laura Payne, Barbara Ainsworth, and Geoffrey Godbey
Leisure in Your Life: New Perspectives
by Geoffrey Godbey
Leisure Studies: Prospects for the Twenty-First Century
edited by Edgar L. Jackson and Thomas L. Burton
Leisure, Women, and Gender
edited by Valeria J. Freysinger, Susan M. Shaw, Karla A. Henderson, and M. Deborah Bialeschki
Making a Difference in Academic Life: A Handbook for Park, Recreation, and Tourism Educators and Graduate Students
edited by Dan Dustin and Tom Goodale
Managing to Optimize the Beneficial Outcomes of Leisure
edited by B. L. Driver
Marketing in Leisure and Tourism: Reaching New Heights
by Patricia Click Janes
More Than a Game: A New Focus on Senior Activity Services
by Brenda Corbett
N.E.S.T. Approach: Dementia Practice Guidelines for Disturbing Behaviors
by Linda L. Buettner and Suzanne Fitzsimmons
Parks for Life: Moving the Goal Posts, Changing the Rules, and Expanding the Field
by Will LaPage
Planning and Organizing Group Activities in Social Recreation
by John V. Valentine
Planning for Recreation and Parks Facilities: Predesign Process, Principles, and Strategies
by Jack Harper
Programming for Parks, Recreation, and Leisure Services: A Servant Leadership Approach, Third Edition
by Donald G. DeGraaf, Debra J. Jordan, and Kathy H. DeGraaf
Recreation and Youth Development
by Peter A. Witt and Linda L. Caldwell
Recreation for Older Adults: Individual and Group Activities
by Judith A. Elliott and Jerold E. Elliott

Recreation Program Planning Manual for Older Adults
by Karen Kindrachuk
Reference Manual for Writing Rehabilitation Therapy Treatment Plans
by Penny Hogberg and Mary Johnson
Service Living: Building Community through Public Parks and Recreation
by Doug Wellman, Dan Dustin, Karla Henderson, and Roger Moore
A Social Psychology of Leisure, Second Edition
by Douglas A. Kleiber, Gordon J. Walker, and Roger C. Mannell
Special Events and Festivals: How to Organize, Plan, and Implement
by Angie Prosser and Ashli Rutledge
The Sportsman's Voice: Hunting and Fishing in America
by Mark Damian Duda, Martin F. Jones, and Andrea Criscione
Survey Research and Analysis: Applications in Parks, Recreation, and Human Dimensions
by Jerry Vaske
Taking the Initiative: Activities to Enhance Effectiveness and Promote Fun
by J. P. Witman
Therapeutic Recreation and the Nature of Disabilities
by Kenneth E. Mobily and Richard D. MacNeil
Therapeutic Recreation: Cases and Exercises, Second Edition
by Barbara C. Wilhite and M. Jean Keller
Therapeutic Recreation in Health Promotion and Rehabilitation
by John Shank and Catherine Coyle
Therapeutic Recreation Practice: A Strengths Approach
by Lynn Anderson and Linda Heyne

NOVA SCOTIA COMMUNITY COLLEGE
3 1998 03693768 6

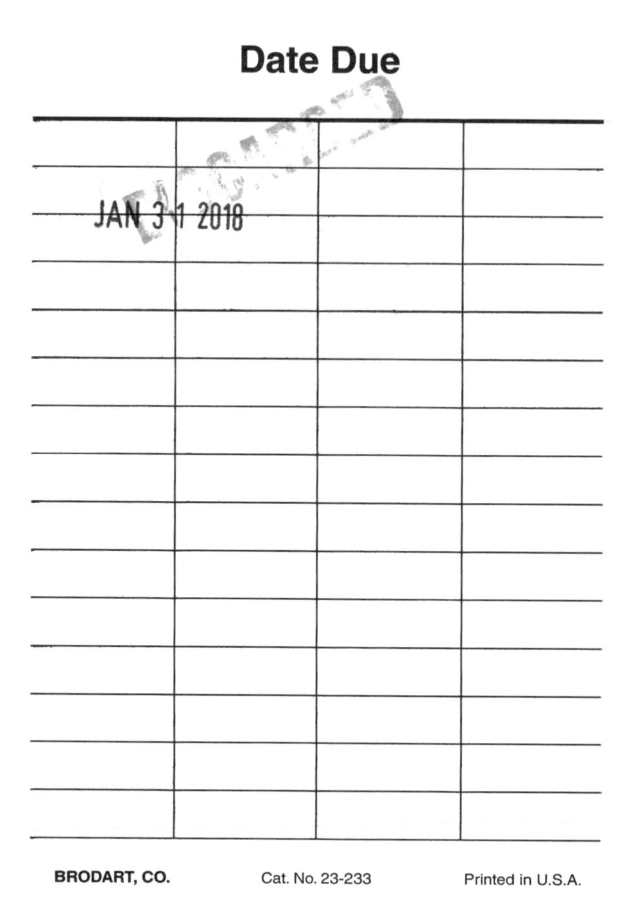
Date Due
JAN 31 2018
BRODART, CO.
Cat. No. 23-233
Printed in U.S.A.